Lecture Notes in Computer Science   9846

Commenced Publication in 1973
Founding and Former Series Editors:
Gerhard Goos, Juris Hartmanis, and Jan van Leeuwen

More information about this series at http://www.springer.com/series/7408

Marco Aiello · Einar Broch Johnsen
Schahram Dustdar · Ilche Georgievski (Eds.)

Service-Oriented
and Cloud Computing

5th IFIP WG 2.14 European Conference, ESOCC 2016
Vienna, Austria, September 5–7, 2016
Proceedings

Springer

Editors
Marco Aiello
University of Groningen
Groningen
The Netherlands

Schahram Dustdar
Vienna University of Technology
Vienna
Austria

Einar Broch Johnsen
University of Oslo
Oslo
Norway

Ilche Georgievski
University of Groningen
Groningen
The Netherlands

ISSN 0302-9743 ISSN 1611-3349 (electronic)
Lecture Notes in Computer Science
ISBN 978-3-319-44481-9 ISBN 978-3-319-44482-6 (eBook)
DOI 10.1007/978-3-319-44482-6

Library of Congress Control Number: 2016947513

LNCS Sublibrary: SL2 – Programming and Software Engineering

Printed on acid-free paper

This Springer imprint is published by Springer Nature
The registered company is Springer International Publishing AG Switzerland

Preface

It is an interesting time to be a researcher in the field of service-oriented and cloud computing. While the former has been one of the most important paradigms for the development of distributed software applications for a number of years now, the use of services in cloud infrastructures is increasing constantly and rapidly. The European Conference on Service-Oriented and Cloud Computing (ESOCC) is the premier conference on advances in the state of the art and practice of service-oriented computing and cloud computing in Europe. ESOCC evolved from the ECOWS (European Conference on Web Services) conference series. The first edition of the new series, ESSOC 2012, was successfully held in Bertinoro, Italy, the second edition, ESOCC 2013, was held in Malaga, Spain, the third edition, ESOCC 2014, was held in Manchester, UK, and the fourth edition, ESOCC 2015, in Taormina (Messina), Italy. ESOCC 2016 was the fifth edition and was held in Vienna, Austria, during September 5–7, 2016.

ESOCC 2016 featured a research track dedicated to technical explorations and findings in service-oriented computing and cloud computing. After thorough reviewing, 16 papers were accepted for presentation at the research track of ESOCC 2016. These contributions are included as full-length papers in these proceedings. The Program Committee (PC) did a thorough review of the submitted papers. While each paper received at least two reviews, the majority received three. The reviews were provided by the members of the PC, sometimes with the help of additional reviewers. The program chairs initiated discussions and worked closely together to make the final decisions.

As part of the main technical program, we had two excellent keynote talks given by Frank Leymann (Professor of Computer Science at the University of Stuttgart, Germany) and David Costa (CTO and Head of R&D at Fredhopper, The Netherlands). Their talks represent explorations and success stories on topics such as formal methods, loose coupling, architectures, software as a service, and distributive laws.

Along with the main conference program, ESOCC 2016 featured five workshops: the 4th International Workshop on CLoud for IoT (CLIoT 2016), the Second International Workshop on Cloud Adoption and Migration (CloudWays 2016), the First International Workshop on Patterns and Pattern Languages for SOCC: Discovery and Use (PATTWORLD), the First International Workshop on Performance and Conformance of Workflow Engines (PEaCE), and the IFIP WG SOS Workshop 2016 Rethinking Services ResearCH (ReSeRCH). The program of ESOCC 2016 also included a PhD symposium and an EU-projects track.

The end result was a successful ESOCC 2016 program. We express our deep appreciation to the track chairs for the organization of the review process. We also thank all 53 PC members and additional reviewers for taking part in the reviewing and selection process. Our gratitude extends to the chairs and organizers of the EU-project track, workshops, and PhD symposium. We thank the invited speakers for their valuable contribution to the program. We are grateful to the local Organizing Committee for their support, organization, and hospitality.

Finally, we thank all the authors of technical papers and those who presented their research for contributing to this successful conference. With their work and dedication, ESOCC continues its tradition in advancing the field of service-oriented computing and cloud computing.

September 2016

Marco Aiello
Einar Broch Johnsen
Schahram Dustdar
Ilche Georgievski

Organization

ESOCC 2016 was organized by the Distributed Systems Group of the TU Wien.

Organizing Committee

General Chair

Schahram Dustdar   TU Wien, Austria

Program Chairs

Marco Aiello   University of Groningen, The Netherlands
Einar Broch Johnsen   University of Oslo, Norway

Industry Track Chairs

Matteo Melideo   Engineering Ingegneria Informatica SPA, Italy
Audris Mockus   University of Tennessee, USA

Workshop Chairs

Stefan Schulte   TU Wien, Austria
Alexander Lazovik   University of Groningen, The Netherlands

IFIP WG Chairs

Luciano Baresi   Politecnico di Milano, Italy
Winfried Lamersdorf   Hamburg University, Germany

EU Projects Chair

Antonio Brogi   University of Pisa, Italy

Publicity Chair

Daniel Moldovan   TU Wien, Austria

Publication Chair

Ilche Georgievski   University of Groningen, The Netherlands

Local Chair

Stefan Schulte   TU Wien, Austria

Website Chairs

Philipp Hoenisch   TU Wien, Austria
Philipp Waibel   TU Wien, Austria

Steering Committee

Antonio Brogi	University of Pisa, Italy
Schahram Dustdar	TU Wien, Austria
Paul Grefen	Eindhoven University of Technology, The Netherlands
Kung Kiu Lau	University of Manchester, UK
Winfried Lamersdorf	University of Hamburg, Germany
Frank Leymann	University of Stuttgart, Germany
Flavio de Paoli	University of Milano-Bicocca, Italy
Cesare Pautasso	University of Lugano, Switzerland
Ernesto Pimentel	University of Malaga, Spain
Ulf Schreier	Hochschule Furtwangen University, Germany
Massimo Villari	University of Messina, Italy
John Erik Wittern	IBM T.J. Watson Research Center, USA
Gianluigi Zavattaro	University of Bologna, Italy
Olaf Zimmermann	HSR FHO Rapperswil, Switzerland
Wolf Zimmermann	Martin Luther University, Germany

Program Committee

Marco Aiello	University of Groningen, The Netherlands
Vasilios Andrikopoulos	University of Stuttgart, Germany
Farhad Arbab	CWI, The Netherlands
Marcello Bonsangue	University of Leiden, The Netherlands
Mario Bravetti	University of Bologna, Italy
Antonio Brogi	University of Pisa, Italy
Christoph Bussler	Xtime, Inc., USA
Giacomo Cabri	University of Modena and Reggio Emilia, Italy
Javier Cubo	University of Malaga, Spain
Frank de Boer	CWI, The Netherlands
Roberto di Cosmo	Université Paris Diderot, France
Juergen Dunkel	FH Hannover, Germany
Schahram Dustdar	TU Wien, Austria
Rik Eshuis	Eindhoven University of Technology, The Netherlands
David Eyers	University of Otago, New Zealand
George Feuerlicht	Prague University of Economics, Czech Republic
Marisol García-Valls	Universidad Carlos III de Madrid, Spain
Claude Godart	University of Lorraine, France
Paul Grefen	Eindhoven University of Technology, The Netherlands
Heerko Groefsema	University of Groningen, The Netherlands
Michael Goedicke	University of Duisburg-Essen, Germany
Thomas Gschwind	IBM Zurich Research Lab, Switzerland
Reiner Haehnle	TU Darmstadt, Germany
Martin Henkel	Stockholm University, Sweden
Philipp Hoenisch	TU Wien, Austria
Einar Broch Johnsen	University of Oslo, Norway

Kung Kiu Lau   University of Manchester, UK
Birgitta Koenig-Ries   Universität Jena, Germany
Ernoe Kovacs   NEC Europe Network Labs, Germany
Peep Kungas   University of Tartu, Estonia
Patricia Lago   VU University Amsterdam, The Netherlands
Winfried Lamersdorf   University of Hamburg, Germany
Frank Leymann   University of Stuttgart, Germany
Welf Loewe   Linnaeus University, Sweden
Ingo Melzer   DaimlerChrysler Research, Germany
Roy Oberhauser   Aalen University, Germany
Guadalupe Ortiz   University of Cádiz, Spain
Claus Pahl   Dublin City University, Ireland
Cesare Pautasso   University of Lugano, Switzerland
Ernesto Pimentel   University of Malaga, Spain
Alessandro Rossini   Sintef ICT, Norway
Ulf Schreier   Furtwangen University, Germany
Stefan Schulte   TU Wien, Austria
Rainer Unland   University of Duisburg-Essen, Germany
Maarten van Steen   University of Twente, The Netherlands
Massimo Villari   University of Messina, Italy
Erik Wilde   UC Berkeley, USA
Martin Wirsing   Ludwig Maximilians University of Munich, Germany
Lai Xu   Bournemouth University, UK
Gianluigi Zavattaro   University of Bologna, Italy
Olaf Zimmermann   HSR FHO Rapperswil, Switzerland
Wolf Zimmermann   Martin Luther University, Germany
Christian Zirpins   KIT/Seeburger AG, Karlsruhe, Germany

Additional Reviewers

Arshad, Rehman   Kaat, Marijke   Rutle, Adrian
Bezirgiannis, Nikolaos   Ibrahim, Ahmad   Serbanescu, Vlad Nicolae
Vukojevic-Haupt,   Qian, Chen   Kalinowski, Julian
  Karolina   Orsini, Gabriel   Skouradaki, Marigianna
Boubeta-Puig, Juan   Jamshidi, Pooyan

Contents

Compositionality

Fault Tolerance

Policies and Performance

Updating Policies in CP-ABE-Based Access Control: An Optimized and Secure Service

Somchart Fugkeaw[✉] and Hiroyuki Sato

Department of Electrical Engineering and Information Systems,
The University of Tokyo, Tokyo, Japan
{somchart, schuko}@satolab.itc.u-tokyo.ac.jp

Abstract. Policy update management is one of the key problems in the ciphertext policy-attribute-based encryption (CP-ABE) supporting access control in data outsourcing scenario. The problem is that the policy is tightly coupled with the encryption itself. Hence, if the policy is updated, the data owner needs to re-encrypt files and sends them back to the cloud. This incurs overheads including computation, communication, and maintenance cost at data owner side. The computation and communication overheads are even more costly if there are frequent changes of access control elements such as users, attributes and access rules. In this paper, we extend the capability of our access control scheme: C-CP-ARBE to be capable to support secure and flexible policy updating in data outsourcing environment. We propose a policy updating method and exploit a very lightweight proxy re-encryption (VL-PRE) technique to enable policies to be dynamically and effectively updated in the cloud. Finally, we demonstrate the efficiency and performance of our proposed scheme through our evaluation and implementation.

1 Introduction

To consider adopting a cloud solution for storing large scales of highly value data, security and privacy are of paramount importance. Existing research works and cloud applications generally deploy encryption techniques and applicable access control model to satisfy the security requirement.

Access Control is among the most effective solutions for full-fledged network security control. Data access control for outsourced data should not only support the security but it should also provide a flexible and efficient management of the policy enforced over a large number of users as well as the optimized cost for handling the change of access control elements such as users, attributes, access policies. Importantly, the access control policy must be up-to-date to support the right and effective control and enforcement. In addition, access control supporting collaborative accesses across the data sources outsourced at the cloud servers is very important.

Attribute-based encryption (ABE) [6] is regarded as an effective solution for formulating a lightweight access control to outsourced data and unknown decrypting parties. To date, several works apply ciphertext attribute-based encryption (CP-ABE) [2–5, 8] for the access control solutions and generally concentrate on minimizing key management cost, reducing computing cost of interaction between data owner and

© IFIP International Federation for Information Processing 2016
Published by Springer International Publishing Switzerland 2016. All Rights Reserved
M. Aiello et al. (Eds.): ESOCC 2016, LNCS 9846, pp. 3–17, 2016.
DOI: 10.1007/978-3-319-44482-6_1

outsourced data storage, improving scalability and efficient revocation. However, these works have not addressed the policy evolution or policy updating problem in their proposed models.

In fact, policy updating is one of the critical administrative tasks to control the most up-to-date access policy enforcement. The policy update in CP-ABE renders the cost of policy update operation, cost of file re-encryption and communication cost for loading the file back to the cloud. All of these costs are usually occurred at data owner's side.

Therefore, in addition to the fine-grained and scalable access control model supporting data outsourced in the cloud, optimizing the policy update is also another grand challenge. For the operational point of view, the issues including correctness, security, and accountability of the subsequent update of policy are the requirements to be provided by CP-ABE policy updating scheme. These requirements are described as follows.

- Correctness: An updated policy must be syntactically correct and the policy updating must support any types of CP-ABE policy boolean. In addition, users who hold the keys containing a set of attributes satisfying the policy are able to decrypt the data encrypted by an updated policy.
- Security: A policy must be updated by the data owner or authorized administrator only in the secure manner and a new policy should not introduce problems for the existing access control.
- Accountability: All policy updating events must be traceable for auditing.

The remainder of the paper is organized as follows. Section 2 discusses related works. Section 3 presents detail of our proposed approach. Section 4 describes the policy updating method and presents concept of our proxy re-encryption scheme. Section 5 gives the evaluation and implementation detail. Finally, the conclusion and future work are depicted in Sect. 6.

2 Related Work

Ciphertext Policy Attribute Based Encryption (CP-ABE) was originally proposed in [7]. In CP-ABE, each user is given a set of attributes, which is embedded into the user's secret key, and a public key is defined for each user attribute. The ciphertext is associated with the access policy structure in which the encryptor can define the access policy by her own control. Users are able to decrypt a ciphertext if their attributes satisfy the ciphertext access structure.

However, policy update in ABE scheme has attracted less attention by existing research works. In [13], the authors introduced a ciphertext delegation method to update the policy of ciphertext in attribute-based access control. Their method aimed at solving user revocation based on a re-encryption delegation technique to protect newly encrypted data. Nevertheless, the performance on updating the ciphertext over the complex access policy was not examined by the authors.

Recently, Yang et al. [3, 9] proposed a method to outsource a policy updating to the cloud server. They proposed policy updating algorithms for adding and removing attributes in the AND, OR, and threshold gate of LSSS policy. The proposed scheme is to update ciphertext in order to avoid file re-encryption. Cost for ciphertext update is also linear to the number of attributes updated over the access structure. Besides, the authors have not discussed how updated polices are maintained and how the security and accountability are supported when there is the policy update.

Proxy-based Re-encryption (PRE) was initially introduced by Mambo and Oka-moto [11]. They proposed a technique that uses a concept of delegator to perform re-encryption of the ciphertext sent by the originator. In this scheme, the delegator learns neither the decryption keys nor original plaintext. Later, Ateniese et al. [12] introduced a proxy re-encryption scheme that improves security in preventing collusion attack over the bilinear map. They implemented the PRE to show its efficiency in a few PRE scenarios. This approach becomes adopted by several PRE-based scheme.

In 2014, Liang et al. [15] proposed a cloud-based revocable identity-based proxy re-encryption (CB-IB-PRE) scheme to support user revocation in the cloud data sharing systems. Hereafter, several works [e.g., 10, 14, 17, 19] have adopted PRE to optimize the revocation overhead, specifically the re-encryption cost in attribute-based access control.

In [16], the authors introduced adaptable CP-ABE scheme to handle policy changes in CP-ABE encryption for data outsourced in cloud computing. In this scheme, a trapdoor is generated from the central authority and it is used to transform a ciphertext under one access policy into ciphertexts under any other access policies. With this scheme, a data owner outsources ciphertext re-encryption task to the proxy and the proxy can not learn the content from the plaintext encrypted. However, the trapdoor generation is still the computation burden that the authority has to compute every time of all policy update events.

In [17], Yukata Kawai proposed a flexible CP-ABE proxy re-encryption scheme by combining key randomized and encrypted methodology and adaptive CP-ABE. The proposed scheme focuses on reducing the computation cost at client side by out-sourcing the re-encryption key generation to cloud server. The universal re-encryption key (urk) is proposed to be used together with the decryption key (Sk_s) for generating the re-encryption key. The decryption key is concealed by randomized parameters and sent to the cloud for computing the re-encryption key. Importantly, Kawai's approach is the first attempt dealing with the outsourcing concept of re-encryption key generation in PRE setting. However, the author does not provide the performance evaluation to demonstrate the efficiency of the proposed scheme.

However, the proposed schemes [16, 17] only provide the security function while the implementation result and performance have not been provided. Hence, the efficiency of the proposed CP-ABE proxy re-encryption in handling the policy changes cannot be inferred.

In [19], Fugkeaw and Sato proposed PRE scheme that fully outsources re-encryption key generation to the proxy; the computation cost at data owner is minimized. However, if there are frequent revocation or policy update cases, the re-encryption key needs to be re-generated in every cases and data owners require to prepare and submit data package to the proxy for computing the re-encryption key

To the best of our knowledge, existing normal PRE schemes are not practical for policy updating in large-scale data outsourcing environment where the access control elements are changed frequently. This is because cost for re-encryption key generation is unpredictable at the data owner side. However, offloading too much computation cost to a proxy may introduce the delay for re-encryption task and thus cause efficiency problem. Besides, this strategy is also not advisable for the cloud model that the cloud provider charges the fee based on CPU usage. Thus optimizing both setup cost at data owner side and re-encryption cost at cloud side is a real challenge. Unfortunately, this computation optimization aspect has not been addressed by the existing PRE schemes. In this paper, we entail the practical solutions for handling policy evolution in the evolvable cloud environment with the consideration on computation and communication cost reduction in both data owner and cloud side.

3 Background

3.1 C-CP-ARBE Model

In this section, we give basic system definitions of our proposed access control called Collaborative-Ciphertext Policy-Attribute Role-based Encryption (C-CP-ARBE). The proposed access control model integrates role-based access control (RBAC) model into the CP-ABE. The model thus accommodates the benefits of RBAC feature with the attribute–based attribute encryption. RBAC provides more scalable management over a number of attributes [15]. Here, a set of attributes in CP-ABE is assigned to the specific roles and the privileges are included to compliment the expressiveness of access control mechanism. Definitions 1 and 2 show the complete set of our access control elements and access control policy (ACP).

Definition 1: User (U), Role (R), Attributes (attr), and Permission (P)

- User (U) is a subject who requests to access (read or write) the data outsourced by the data owner in the cloud. Each user is assigned the set of attributes with respect to his/her role by the attribute authority.
- Attributes (Attr) are a set of attributes used to characterize the user and associated to the particular attribute "role". A set of attributes is issued by attribute authority (AA).
- Role (R) is a super set of attribute where users and respective attributes are assigned to.
- Permission (P) is an action or privilege having value read (r) and write (w).

Definition 2: Access Control Policy (ACP)

ACP is a tree-based structure. Let ACP T is a tree represent the access structure in C-CP-ARBE. Each non-leaf node of the ACP tree represents the Role node and threshold gate where the Role node is a parent of threshold gate node. The threshold gate rule is the same as access tree of CP-ABE. We denote the parent of the children node x in the tree by parent(x). Thus, the parent of leaf node x is the pair of {Role node, threshold gate}. The function attr(x) is defined only x is in a leaf node of the tree.

To provide a fine-grained access control, we introduce special attribute "privilege" as an extended leaf (EL) node of the ACP T in order to identify the read or write privilege of the role. Figure 1 illustrates a sample access control policy used to enforce access rules to hospital staffs and patients in accessing disease diagnostic data.

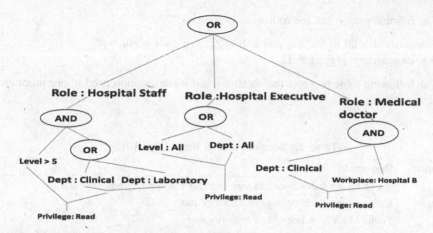

Fig. 1. Access control policy of disease diagnosis file

Figure 1 illustrates a sample access control policy used to enforce access rules to restrict the access of hospital staff and patients to the healthcare data. As seen from the figure, hospital staffs, hospital executives, and a specific group of medical doctor from another hospital is allowed to access the disease diagnostic data.

The policy is administered by the host hospital and it is able to be updated by authorized administrator. In reality, such a policy can be changed anytime. For example, the senior nurse may be allowed to access the diagnosis file for preparing the summarized report. In this case, the data owner needs to update the above policy tree by adding role "nurse" and its attributes with the logical rules specifying the authorized access to the diagnosis file. In addition to updating the policy, the file encrypted by the before-updated policy needs to be retrieved from the cloud and it will be decrypted and re-encrypted with a new policy. Then, it will be uploaded back to the cloud. This is a cumbersome task especially when there is a large amount of data as well as the high chance of policy changes. We will discuss how the policy change is securely and efficiently managed in Sect. 4.

3.2 C-CP-ARBE Constructs

Our proposed cryptographic process of C-CP-ARBE scheme [1] is a kind of Multi-Authority CP-ABE (MA-CP-ABE). We use attribute authority identification (a_{id}) to identify the authority who issues the attributes to users. Each user who is issued the attributes by the attribute authority is identified with uid.aid. Basically, bilinear map is a major construct in our user key generation protocol.

Definition 3: Bilinear Map [7]

Let G_1 and G_2 be two multiplicative cyclic groups of prime order p and e be a bilinear map, $e: G_1 \times G_1 \rightarrow G_2$. Let g be a generator of G_1. Let H: $\{0,1\}^* \rightarrow G_1$ be a hash function that is modeled in a random oracle.

The bilinear map e has the following properties:

1. Bilinearity: for all u, v $\in G_1$ and a, b $\in Z_p$, $e(u^a, v^b) = e(u, v)^{ab}$
2. Non-degeneracy: $e(g, g) \neq 1$.

The following table presents the notations and its description used in our proposed algorithms (Table 1).

Table 1. Notations used in the C-CP-ARBE

Notation	Description
$S_{uid.aid}$	Set of all attributes issued to user *uid* and managed by authority *aid*
SK_{aid}	a secret key which belongs to authority *aid*
PK_{aid}	Public key which belongs to authority *aid*
GSK_{uid}	A global secret key of a user *uid*. GSK is a private key issued by the certification authority CA
$Cert_{uid}$	A public key certificate containing user's public key issued by a certification authority CA
$UDK_{uid.aid}$	User Decryption key issued by authority *aid*
$EDK_{uid.aid}$	EDK is an encrypted form of a UDK which is encrypted by a user public key
GRP	Group role parameter is a seed numbers computed from a set of user members of the roles
SS	Secret seal is a symmetric key created from the AES algorithm together with the GRP
ACP	An access control policy used to encrypt the data files
SCT	A sealed ciphertext is a ciphertext encrypted with the SS

Here, we present our four major cryptographic algorithms including AA setup, user key generation, encryption, and decryption.

1. **AuthoritySetUp**

   Attribute Authority Setup (AA_k where each AA is identified with a_{id})
   Each AA_k ($k \in$ set of all authority S_A).
   Let S (a_K) be a set of attributes issued and managed by the authority AA_k.
   The AA setup (AA_k) chooses two random numbers $\alpha, \beta \in Z_p$.
   Then the Public Key AA_k(or PK_{aid}) = G_1, g, $h = g\beta_k$, $f = g^{1/}\beta_k$,
   $e(g, g)^{\alpha_k}$; and the Secret Key AA_k (or SK_{aid}) is (β_k, g^{α_k}).

2. **UserKeyGen**($S_{uid,aid}$, SK_{aid}, $Cert_{uid}$) $\rightarrow EDK_{uid,aid}$, RDK_{aid}. The KeyGen algorithm takes continuous two steps as follows:
   (1) The algorithm takes input as set of attributes $S_{uid,aid}$, attribute authority's secret key SK_{aid}, then it returns the set of user decryption keys UDK.
   (2) A UDK is encrypted with the global public key of the user $Cert_{uid}$ and outputs an encrypted decryption key $EDK_{uid,aid}$. In addition to the UDK generated, the

system will also produce the root decryption key RDK_{aid} for further use in re-encryption key generation. It contains the data owner's ID attribute and digital signature attribute of the data owner. Thus, the RDK_{aid} is very small and it can be used to decrypt the files they created because these two attributes are bounded in the ACP as default attributes. RDK_{aid} is also encrypted by the data owner's public key.

3. **Enc**(PK_{aid}, [SS, GRP], M, ACP, $Cert_{uid}$) $\rightarrow$ SCT. The encryption algorithm performs two continuous steps as follows:
   (1) *Inner Layer:* the algorithm takes as inputs authority public key PK_{aid}, access control policy ACP, and data M. Then it returns a ciphertext CT.
   (2) *Outer Layer:* the algorithm takes group role parameter GRP which is randomly generated from a set of user members (i.e. Users' IDs) of all roles. GRP is used as a key together with AES algorithm to generate the session key referred as a secret seal SS. The SS is used to encrypt the ciphertext CT. Then, the algorithm returns sealed ciphertext SCT. Finally, a SS is encrypted with user's public key $Cert_{uid}$, and stored in the cloud server.

4. **Decrypt**(PK_{aid}, SCT, GSK_{uid}, EDK_{uid},) $\rightarrow$ M. The decryption algorithm performs two continuous steps as follows:
   (1) Decrypt the secret seal SS. The algorithm takes user's global secret key GSK_{uid} and then obtains the session key to decrypt the SCT and gets the CT.
   (2) Decrypt the encrypted decryption key (EDK_{uid}). The algorithm takes user's global secret key GSK_{uid} and then obtains the user decryption key UDK. Then, if the set of attribute S satisfies the ACP structure, the algorithm returns the original M.

4　Policy Updating Method

To complete the policy updating process, two tasks including policy updating and file re-encryption are required. To this end, we propose a policy updating algorithm and a proxy re-encryption technique called a very lightweight PRE (VL-PRE) to efficiently support the required tasks respectively.

4.1　Flexible and Secure Policy Update Management

Outsourcing policy update to the cloud enhances the service availability and reduces computing costs at data owner side.

In typical cloud-based access control systems, if there is a change to the policy, data owners apply a new policy to re-encrypt the files at their local side and send them back to the cloud server. Accordingly, policy update introduces the communication, computation, and maintenance cost at data owners.

Therefore, a flexible and secure policy update should be provided to allow data owners or administrators to manage the attributes (add, update, delete) in polices stored in a cloud server in a practical manner. We develop policy updating algorithm to support access policy updating in the cloud. This reduces computation and communication cost and allows the data owners to update the policy anytime and anywhere.

```
Input newleafnode (Y')
Input currentleafnode (Y)
Input typeupdate
Input policyid_input
Set ACP = get policy where policyid = policyid_input
if (typeupdate  == delete)
        Set newpolicy ACP' = ACP.replace((Y), "")
else if (typeupdate  == edit)
        Set  ACP' = ACP.replace ((Y ), (Y'))
else if (typeupdate  == add)
        Set ACP' = ACP.insert (Y')
policy = ACP'
files_set = get fileid where policyid = policyid_input
        foreach (files_set as id)
                        id.reencrypt(ACP')
        end foreach
If(Verify_Policy_Syntax (ACP'))
        output ACP'
else
        output "policy syntax error"
```

Fig. 2. Policy updating algorithm

```
Input policy ACP
   If (policy.contain(comparison between an attribute name and
a negative integer))
        return false
   else If (policy.contain(comparison between an attribute
name and an attribute name))
        return false
   else if (policy.contain(attribute name start with integer))
        return false
   else if (policy.contain ("and" | "or" using in attribute))
        return false
   else if(!policy.contain(operator is 'and' , 'or' , 'of' ,
'>' , '<' , '>=' , '<=' , '=' only))
        return false
   else if(policy.contain(threshold gate operator as 'K of
(P1, P2, ... PN)' && K is negative integer))
        return false
   else
   return true
```

Fig. 3. Policy update syntax validation

Figures 2 and 3 illustrate the policy updating process and policy updating syntax validation. The policy updating undertakes the updating operations including add, update, and delete of the attributes contained in the policy together the syntax checking. For the syntax checking, the algorithm checks the possible operands taken on the attribute type and attribute value. This guarantees that the updated policy is syntactically correct. In our scheme, after the policy updating is done, the proxy will automatically take the updated policy to re-encrypt all files encrypted by the before-updated policy.

4.2   Very Lightweight Proxy Re-Encryption (VL-PRE)

VL-PRE is an extended PRE model that is specifically designed to deliver a very lightweight PRE operation in supporting attribute revocation or policy update in CP-ABE based access control. The process of VL-PRE is divided into three phases: Generate re-encryption key, Update re-encryption key, and Renew re-encryption key. Generally, the proposed three-phase PRE is triggered when there is a case of attribute revocation or policy update. Basically, the proxy transforms ciphertext CT_{k1} to CT_{k2} with a re-encryption key $RK(rk_{s1 \rightarrow s2})$ where RK is generated by a proxy server.

Phase 1: Generate Re-encryption Key:

For the initial phase, it consists of Pre-process, ReKeyGen and ReEnc algorithms which are described as follows.

1. **Pre-process:** Data owner (1) chooses random seeds and generates secure random number R and applies random number R_{vn} (tagged with the current version number vn) to encrypt the root decryption key RDK_{aid} generated since the key generation phase. (2) applies R_{vn} to append the attributes in the leaf node of the updated version of access control policy ACP_{vn}, and gets the $ACP_{vn}^{R_{vn}}$. Then, data owner submits encrypted RDK_{aid} and $ACP_{v_n}^{R_{vn}}$ as parts of re-encryption key to the cloud proxy.

2. **ReKeyGen** (param; SS, $R_{vn}(RDK_{aid})$, $(ACP_{v_n}^{R_{vn}})$, ExpireTime) $\rightarrow rk_{s2 \rightarrow (M', ACP')}$. The algorithm takes input param, secret seal SS, root decryption key encrypted by the Random R_{vn}, $R_{vn}(RDK_{aid})$, a new access policy embedded with Random R_{vn}, $ACP_{v_n}^{R_{vn}}$, and Expire_time. First, the SS is used to decrypt the sealed ciphertext (SCT) and the original ciphertext (CT) is derived. The Expire_time is used to indicate the validity of re-encryption key rk_{s2}. Hence, if the key expires, the owner needs to initiate re-key generation with a new random R_{vn}.

   Then, the algorithm outputs a re-encryption key $rk_{s2 \rightarrow (M', ACP')}$ that can be used to transform a ciphertext under (M, ACP) to another ciphertext under (M', ACP').

- **ReEnc**(param; $rk_{s2 \rightarrow (M', ACP')}$, CMR function, CT(M, ACP)) $\rightarrow CT_{k2}$: The algorithm takes input param, a re-encryption key $rk_{s2 \rightarrow (M', ACP')}$, CombineMatchRemove function CMR, and an original CT(M, ACP). It outputs a re-encrypted ciphertext $CT'(M', ACP')$.

According to the element of rk_{s2}, we embed the CombineMatchRemove (CMR) function to support the re-encryption process as follows:

(1) Combine pieces of R applied in leaf nodes of a new $ACP_{v_n}^{R_{vn}}$.
(2) Match R between R_{vn} (RDK_{aid}) and $ACP_{v_n}^{R_{vn}}$.
(3) Remove R from $R_{vn}(RDK_{aid})$.

Then, the RDK_{aid} is automatically used to decrypt the old ciphertext and the algorithm applies a new ACP' to re-encrypt the data. Finally, the proxy takes SS to encrypt a new Ciphertext (CT_{k2}).

Phase 2: Update Re-encryption Key:

There are two algorithms for updating re-encryption key.

1. **UpdateACP(R_{vn},ACP$_{vn+1}$)** $\rightarrow ACP^{R_{vn}}_{v_{n+1}}$

Data owner applies current random number R_{vn} to encrypt the updated ACP, and the $ACP^{R_{vn}}_{v_{n+1}}$ is obtained and sent to the proxy.

2. **UpdateReEncKey(rk$_{s2,vn}$, $ACP^{R_{vn}}_{v_{n+1}}$)** $\rightarrow$ rk$_{s2,vn+1}$

The proxy runs the algorithm by taking the updated ACP,$ACP^{R_{vn}}_{v_{n+1}}$ to update the current version of re-encryption key, rk$_{s2,vn}$. The new rk$_{s2,vn+1}$ is used to re-encrypt the existing ciphertext.

The algorithms help to reduce both computation and communication overhead at both data owner side and proxy since the RDK needs not to be encrypted every time and the information (only the updated ACP) sent out to the proxy is small. Besides, the proxy does not need to fully compute a new re-encryption key upon policy update, it only updates the key instead.

Phase 3: Renew Re-encryption Key

In this phase, if the current re-encryption key rk$_{s2,vn}$ expires, the algorithms in phase 1 will be run.

Here, the owner needs to initiate re-key generation with a new set of random seeds R_{vn+1} and updated ACP. Then, re-encryption key generation and ciphertext re-encryption are performed by the proxy.

However, re-encryption key renewal is not required to perform instantly when the key expires, it will be executed when there is the next policy update.

4.3   Security Model

Our C-CP-ARBE is secure under the random oracle model in the following security game.

1. **Initialization.** Adversary A outputs a challenge access policy ACP^C to Challenger C.
2. **Setup.** C runs CreateAttributeAuthority algorithm and gives a public keys PK to the adversary A. For corrupted authorities S'_A, the challenger sends both the public keys and secret keys to adversary.
3. **Query Phase1:**
   (a) Private key extraction: C runs UserKeyGen on the attribute set S ($S_{uid,aid}$) of the corrupted AA and returns UDK to A.
   (b) Re-encryption key extraction oracle O_{rk} (S, ACP^C): With attribute set S, and an access control policy ACP^C, C returns reKeyGen(param; SS, R_{vn}(RDK$_{aid}$), (ACP$^{CR_{vn}}$)) $\rightarrow$ rk$_{s2,vn}$ $\rightarrow$ (M′, ACP′) to A, where rk$_{s2,vn}$ is a generated re-encryption key and (S, SK$_{aid}$) $\rightarrow$ UDK.

(c) RE-encryption oracle O_{rk} (S, ACP^C, $CT_{(M, ACP)}$): With the input an attribute set S, an access control policy ACP^C, and an original ciphertext $CT_{(M, ACP)}$, C returns $rk_{s2 \rightarrow (M', ACP')}, CT_{(M, ACP)}) \rightarrow CT^R_{(M', ACP')}$, where reKeyGen(param, SS, $R_{vn}(RDK_{aid})$, $(ACP'^R)) \rightarrow rk_{s2 \rightarrow (M', ACP')}$, $(S, SK_{aid}) \rightarrow$ UDK and S| = ACP.

(d) Original ciphertext decryption oracle $O_{d2}(S, CT_{(M, ACP)})$. With the input an attribute set S and an original ciphertext $CT_{(M, ACP)}$, C returns Decrypt(S, UDK, $CT_{(M, ACP)}) \rightarrow$ M to A, where $(S, SK_{aid}) \rightarrow$ UDK and S| = ACP.

(e) Re-encrypted ciphertext decryption oracle $O_{d2}(S', CT^R_{(M', ACP')})$. With the input an attribute set S' and a re-encrypted ciphertext $CT^R_{(M', ACP')}$, C returns Decrypt $(S', UDK', CT^R_{(M', ACP')}) \rightarrow$ M, where $(S', SK_{aid}) \rightarrow$ UDK' and S'| = ACP'.

Note that if the ciphertexts queried to oracles O_{re}, O_{d2}, and O_{d1} are invalid, C simply outputs a ⊥.

1. **Challenge.** A outputs two equal length messages M_0 and M_1 to C. C returns $CT^*(M^*, ACP^*)$ = Enc(ACP^*, M_b) to A, where b ∈ {0,1}.
2. **Query Phase II:** A performs as it did in Phase 1.

Guess. A submits a guess bit b' ∈ {0,1}. If b' = b, A wins. The advantage of A in this game is defined as $\Pr[b' = b | \mu = 0] = \frac{1}{2}$. ☐

In the security point of view of VL-PRE, we use random encryption to secure re-encryption key component while our core access control enforcement is based on CP-ABE. The detailed security proof is as presented in the original CP-ABE [7].

4.4 Policy Update Evaluation

We analyze and evaluate our policy update scheme based on the correctness, accountability, and security requirement.

Correctness: An updated policy must be syntactically correct and users who hold the keys containing a set of attributes satisfying the policy are able to decrypt the data encrypted by an updated policy.

Proof: The syntax of the updating is validated through the CP-ABE tree structure. Hence, attributes updated to AND, OR, K *out of* N is done at the policy structure. The policy checking for the update is controlled by our policy updating algorithm. The algorithm verifies the syntax of the threshold gates to ensure the correctness of grammar of tree-based model. Also, if the policy is updated with valid attributes (issued trusted AA with $PK_{x.aid}$) the users who hold sufficient attributes satisfying a new policy are able to decrypt the file encrypted by a new policy. This correctness is guaranteed by CP-ABE model.

Security: A policy must be updated by the data owner or authorized administrator only in the secure manner and a new policy should not introduce problems for the existing access control.

Proof: To enable the policies to be securely stored and managed in cloud, we make use a simple CP-ABE tree policy to encrypt the ACP. The policy encryption is simply formed by a set of identity attributes of the data owners and authorized users. Hence, only data owners and authorized users are allowed to access the policy and can use the policy to encrypt the data. Here, the data owner can selectively delegate the policy update function to the users. In addition, our scheme requires data owner's digital signature for executing and committing the update.

Accountability: All policy updating events must be traceable.

Proof: When the policy is updated, event log keeps the details of update including login users, update time, and update operations. In addition, the system requires digital signing of the authorized data owner or administrator to commit the update.

5   Evaluation

5.1   Comparison of Policy Update Cost

We analytically compare policy update features and update cost between the C-CP-ARBE, Yang et al. scheme [3], and Lai et al. scheme [16].

Table 2. Comparison of policy update feature and cost

Operation	Yang et al. [3]	Lai et al. [16]	Our C-CP-ARBE
Update key generation	At owner side	At owner/authority side	At cloud server
Policy storage outsourcing	No	No	Yes
Policy update method	Ciphertext update	PRE	VL-PRE
Computation	$O(t_c)$	$O(1)$	$O(1)$

t_c = the total number of attributes in the updated ciphertext

From Table 2, according to Yang et al. scheme, data owner has to update key generation and to update the ciphertext to complete the policy updating process. For the ciphertext update, the data owner needs to compute ciphertext components for new attributes. The entire computation cost is subject to the number of attributes and the type of update operations (i.e. OR, AND) over the access structure. In Lai et al. scheme, PRE concept is used to convert the existing ciphertext according to the updated policy. In this scheme, the trapdoor or re-encryption key is generated at key generation authority or at data owner side. This limits the operation with the dependability on the availability of the authority or data owner. In contrast, we delegate the major cost of re-encryption key generation and file re-encryption to the delegated proxy in the cloud.

Our scheme has no limitation for update operations and number attributes involving in the policy. The computation cost for re-encryption is $O(1)$ as the re-encryption is performed once to complete the policy update. In addition, our scheme allows policies to be securely stored in the cloud. This enables flexible and efficient policy management in data outsourcing scenario.

5.2 Performance Evaluation

In our experiments, we implement the application service using PHP and Java language which are run on the Apache Sever. The service is run on Intel Xeon, E562 processor 240 GHz. with Ubuntu Linux. We use the Pairing-Based Cryptography library version 0.5.12 to simulate the cryptographic constructs of those two compared schemes. Our core cryptographic library is extended and developed from the CP-ABE programming library provided in [18]. On the client (data owner) end, a simulation was run on MacBook Pro Intel Core i5 Dual-core, 2.7 GHz.

In the experiment setting, we simulate KeyUpdate and CiphertextUpdate algorithms for Yang et al. scheme, while Trapdoor generation and policy update based on PRE are simulated for Lai et al. scheme. For our C-CP-ARBE scheme, the time used for executing policy updating algorithm and processing the VL-PRE are used to measure the total cost of policy update.

To demonstrate the performance improvement, we compare total time used for policy updating and re-encryption between these three approaches. We simulate the policy updating protocols of Yang et al. scheme by simulating the key update generation and ciphertext update while Lai et al. scheme and our C-CP-ARBE use the PRE strategy. To measure the performance, we vary the number of attributes updated in the given access policy. The access policy contains up to 120 attributes and it is used to encrypt 2-MB file. Then, we measure the total time for the policy update and file re-encryption or ciphertext update used by these three schemes.

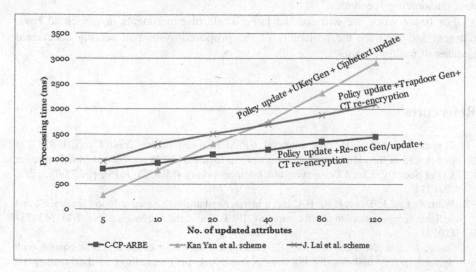

Fig. 4. Comparison of policy update cost

As of the Fig. 4, compared with Yang et al. scheme and Lai et al. scheme, our C-CP-ARBE fully outsources the PRE process to the proxy. Thus, the computation at data owner side is significantly reduced. With our scheme, the data owner only updates at her own machine, while the policy and the subsequent costs (re-encryption key generation and ciphertext re-encryption) are fully outsourced to the delegated proxy. With a small re-encryption key size and key update strategy of VL-PRE, the processing workload performed by the proxy at cloud is also optimized. In Lai et al. scheme, even though the PRE is used to transform the ciphertext, the data owner still needs to compute the trapdoor and update the policy before the proxy performs the re-encryption task. Obviously, both C-CP-ARBE and Lai et al. scheme do not get significant impact from the number of attributes changed or the operations used in the policy. In contrast, with the ciphertext update strategy of Yang et al. scheme, it is very practical to support a small number of updated attributes. However, when the number of updated attributes increases, the processing time sharply increases.

6 Conclusion

In this paper, we have presented a privacy-preserving CP-ABE based access control model with the capability of policy change management in the data outsourcing scenario. Our core access control policy contains roles, attributes, and privileges logically modeled in a tree-based structure. We introduce our proposed policy updating algorithm and VL-PRE to securely and economically support policy evolution in cloud data access control. VL-PRE uses a small package of re-encryption key generation and relies on key updates strategy instead of key generations. Therefore, it outperforms existing PRE schemes. Finally, we conduct the experiments to evaluate the performance of our proposed policy update scheme. The results reveal that our proposed scheme is efficient and promising for real deployment in supporting policy update for data outsourcing scenario.

For future work, we will conduct larger scale of experiments in real cloud environment and measure the scalability of the proposed system in serving concurrent updates of multiple policies.

References

1. Fugkeaw, S., Sato, H.: An extended CP-ABE based access control model for data outsourced in the cloud. In: Proceedings of the International Workshop on Middleware for Cyber Security, Cloud Computing and Internetworking (MidCCI 2015), pp. 73–78. IEEE (2015)
2. Wan, Z., Liu, J., Deng, H.R.: HASBE: a hierarchical attribute-based solution for flexible and scalable access control in cloud computing. IEEE Trans. Inf. Forensics Secur. 7(2), 743–754 (2012)
3. Yang, K., Jia, X., Ren, K., Xie, R., Huang, L.: Enabling efficient access control with dynamic policy updating for big data in the cloud. In: Proceedings of the International Conference on Computer Communications (INFOCOM 2014), pp. 2013–2021. IEEE (2014)

 4. Li, M., Yu, S., Zheng, Y., Ren, K., Lou, W.: Scalable and secure sharing of personal health records in cloud computing using attribute-based encryption. IEEE Trans. Parallel Distrib. Syst. **24**(1), 131–143 (2013)
 5. Yang, K., Jia, X., Ren, K., Zhang, B., Xie, R.: Expressive, efficient, and revocable data access control for multi-authority cloud storage. IEEE Trans. Parallel Distrib. Syst. **25**(7), 1735–1744 (2014)
 6. Goyal, V., Pandey, O., Sahai, A., Waters, B.: Attribute-based encryption for fine-grained access control of encrypted data. In: Proceedings of the International Conference on Computer and Communications Security (CCS 2006), pp. 89–98. ACM (2006)
 7. Bethencourt, J., Sahai, A., Waters, B.: Ciphertext-policy attribute-based encryption. In: Proceedings of IEEE Symposium of Security and Privacy, pp. 321–334. IEEE (2007)
 8. Fugkeaw, S.: Achieving privacy and security in multi-owner data outsourcing. In: Proceedings of the International Conference on Digital and Information Management (ICDIM 2012), pp. 239–244. IEEE (2012)
 9. Yang, K., Jia, X., Ren, K.: Secure and verifiable policy update outsourcing for big data access control in the cloud. IEEE Trans. Parallel Distrib. Syst. (TPDS) **26**(12), 3461–3470 (2015). IEEE
10. Tysowski, P.K., Hasan, M.A.: Hybrid attribute- and re-encryption-based key management for secure and scalable mobile applications in clouds. IEEE Trans. Cloud Comput. **1**(2), 172–186 (2013). IEEE
11. Mambo, M., Okamoto, E.: Proxy cryptosystems: delegation of the power to decrypt ciphertexts. IEICE Trans. **E80-A**(1), 54–63 (1997)
12. Ateniese, G., Fu, K., Green, M., Hohenberger, S.: Improved proxy re-encryption schemes with applications to secure distributed storage. ACM Trans. Inf. Syst. Secur. **9**, 1–30 (2006). ACM
13. Sahai, A., Seyalioglu, H., Waters, B.: Dynamic credentials and ciphertext delegation for attribute-based encryption. In: Safavi-Naini, R., Canetti, R. (eds.) CRYPTO 2012. LNCS, vol. 7417, pp. 199–217. Springer, Heidelberg (2012)
14. Liang, X., Cao, Z., Lin, H., Shao, J.: Attribute based proxy re-encryption with delegating capabilities. In: Li, W., Susilo, W., Tupakula, K.U., Safavi-Naini, R., Varadharajan, V. (eds.) ASIACCS, pp. 276–286. ACM, New York (2009)
15. Liang, K., Liu, J.K., Wong, D.S., Susilo, W.: An efficient cloud-based revocable identity-based proxy re-encryption scheme for public clouds data sharing. In: Kutyłowski, M., Vaidya, J. (eds.) ICAIS 2014, Part I. LNCS, vol. 8712, pp. 257–272. Springer, Heidelberg (2014)
16. Lai, J., Deng, R.H., Yang, Y., Weng, J.: Adaptable ciphertext-policy attribute-based encryption. In: Cao, Z., Zhang, F. (eds.) Pairing 2013. LNCS, vol. 8365, pp. 199–214. Springer, Heidelberg (2014)
17. Kawai, Y.: Outsourcing the re-encryption key generation: flexible ciphertext-policy attribute-based proxy re-encryption. In: Lopez, J., Wu, Y. (eds.) ISPEC 2015. LNCS, vol. 9065, pp. 301–315. Springer, Heidelberg (2015)
18. CP-ABE Library. http://acsc.cs.utexas.edu/cpabe/
19. Fugkeaw, S., Sato, H.: Embeding lightweight proxy re-encryption for efficient attribute revocation in cloud computing. Int. J. High Perform. Comput. Netw. (in press)

vmBBThrPred: A Black-Box Throughput Predictor for Virtual Machines in Cloud Environments

Javid Taheri[1(✉)], Albert Y. Zomaya[2], and Andreas Kassler[1]

[1] Department of Computer Science, Karlstad University, Karlstad, Sweden
{javid.taheri,andreas.kassler}@kau.se
[2] School of Information Technologies, University of Sydney, Sydney, Australia
albert.zomaya@sydney.edu.au

Abstract. In today's ever computerized society, Cloud Data Centers are packed with numerous online services to promptly respond to users and provide services on demand. In such complex environments, guaranteeing throughput of Virtual Machines (VMs) is crucial to minimize performance degradation for all applications. vmBBThrPred, our novel approach in this work, is an application-oblivious approach to predict performance of virtualized applications based on only basic Hypervisor level metrics. vmBBThrPred is different from other approaches in the literature that usually either inject monitoring codes to VMs or use peripheral devices to directly report their actual throughput. vmBBThrPred, instead, uses sensitivity values of VMs to cloud resources (CPU, Mem, and Disk) to predict their throughput under various working scenarios (free or under contention); sensitivity values are calculated by vmBBProfiler that also uses only Hypervisor level metrics. We used a variety of resource intensive benchmarks to gauge efficiency of our approach in our VMware-vSphere based private cloud. Results proved accuracy of 95 % (on average) for predicting throughput of 12 benchmarks over 1200 h of operation.

Keywords: Performance prediction and modeling · Throughput degradation · Cloud infrastructure

1 Introduction

The demand for cloud computing has been constantly increasing during recent years. Nowadays, Virtualized Data Centers (vDCs) accommodate thousands of Physical Machines (PMs) to host millions of Virtual Machines (VMs) and fulfill today's large-scale web applications and cloud services. Many organizations even deploy their own private clouds to better manage their computing infrastructure [7]. In fact, it is shown that more than 75 % of current enterprise workloads

© IFIP International Federation for Information Processing 2016
Published by Springer International Publishing Switzerland 2016. All Rights Reserved
M. Aiello et al. (Eds.): ESOCC 2016, LNCS 9846, pp. 18–33, 2016.
DOI: 10.1007/978-3-319-44482-6_2

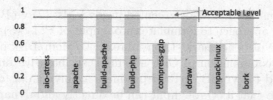

Fig. 1. Relative performance of eight applications when co-located with a Mem+Disk (unzipping large files) intensive application

are currently running on virtualized environments [11]. Despite massive capital investments (tens to hundreds of millions of dollars) however, their resource utilization rarely exceeds 20 % of their full capacity [11,14]. This is because, alongside its many benefits, sharing PMs also leads to performance degradation of sensitive co-located VMs and could undesirably reduce their quality of service (QoS) [13]. Figure 1 shows relative throughput (with regard to their isolated run) of eight high resource demanding VMs when co-located with a background VM running a high Memory+Disk intensive application (unzipping large files). All VMs had 2vCPU, 2 GB of RAM, and 20 GB of Disk. For each test, VMs were pinned on the same set of CPUs/Cores and placed on the same disk to compete for CPU cycles, conflict on L1/L2/L3 memory caches, and interfere with each others' disk access. As it can be inferred from Fig. 1, despite being classified as resource demanding, five of these applications (e.g., apache) could be safely co-located with the background resource intensive application (Mem+Disk) – assuming that performance degradation of up to 10 % is allowed. Nevertheless, a conservative view would separate/isolate all VMs to allocate them on separate PMs. This simple example shows/motivates that understanding, measuring, and predicting performance degradation is essential to identify VMs that can be safely co-located with minimum interference to each other. It also motivates the importance of designing effective affinity rules to guarantee optimal placement of VMs, and consequently maximize the overall performance of vDCs.

This work is a major step to predict throughput, and consequently performance degradation of general purpose applications/VMs through profiling a variety of benchmarks under different working scenarios and resource limitations. Such profiles are then used to predict throughput of a VM only based on the amount of resources (CPU, Mem, and Disk) it is consuming as seen by the Hypervisor. We used 12 well-known benchmarks with different resource usage signatures (CPU/Mem/Disk intensive and various combinations of them) to run on three different PMs. Results were collected and used to model throughput, and consequently performance degradation. We finally aligned our results with actual throughput of these benchmarks to show the accuracy of our approach: VM Black-Box Throughput Predictor (vmBBThrPred).

Our contribution in this work can be highlighted as: unlike all available similar approaches, (1) vmBBThrPred uses only Hypervisor level metrics to predict throughput and performance degradation of a VM. No code/agent is required to be developed, installed, and/or executed inside VMs; (2) vmBBThrPred provides a systematic approach to formulate throughput of VMs; (3) vmBBThrPred uses a wider range of benchmarks (from pure CPU/Mem/Disk intensive benchmarks to various combination of CPU+Mem+Disk intensive ones) to produce such formulas; and (4) vmBBThrPred produces a polynomial formula for each application/VM so that its throughput can be directly and dynamically (online) calculated according to its current CPU, Mem, and Disk utilization.

The remainder of this paper is structured as follows. Section 2 reviews the related work. Section 3 explains the architecture of vmBBThrPred and elaborates on its components. Section 4 demonstrates vmBBThrPred's step-by-step procedures. Section 5 lays out our experimental setup. Results are discussed and analyzed in Sect. 6, followed by Conclusion in Sect. 7.

2   Related Work

The ever increasing popularity of virtualization [12] in vDCs is probably one of the most significant paradigm shifts in the IT industry. Through virtualization, PM resources are partitioned for VMs to run services. Running a highly efficient vDC is however not a trivial task. Firstly, vDCs are envisaged to run several VMs on each PM assuming proper partitioning of its resources. Although resources like CPU and Network seem to be fairly partition-able, Mem and Disk are proven to be much more cumbersome. Secondly, vDCs need to provide accurate/online operational information to both administrators and users so that functionality of deployed services can be monitored, controlled, and ensured at all times. This requires identifying under-performing VMs – those who suffer the most because of co-location – immediately, effectively, and dynamically. This also demands the ability of vDC management systems to accurately – at least within acceptable margins – predict the performance of different VMs in various working scenarios; i.e., isolated or co-located as well as under or free of resource contentions. This concern, in particular, seems to be more important than the other two because it could directly lead to further optimizations of the whole system as well as significant increase of the productivity of vDCs.

To date, many approaches are proposed to measure throughput, and consequently performance degradation of VMs in vDCs; they can be categorized into the following two main themes.

High-Level (SLA) Based Measurements: Approaches in this group use high-level metrics to measure actual throughout of an application/VM (e.g., the number of transactions a SQL server responds to per second) in its current situation. They all rely on developing tailor-made foreign agents/codes for each application, installing them in VMs, and giving them enough system privileges to collect and send out performance data.

Xu et al. [19] proposed two Fuzzy based systems (global and local) to monitor resource utilization of workloads in VMs. The local system is an SLA sensor that is injected into a VM to directly compare its performance with the desired SLA, and request or relinquish resources (e.g., CPU share) if required.

The global controller receives all local requests and decides what VM should get more resources in cases of contention. Tested for CPU-intensive workloads, their self-learning fuzzy systems could efficiently tune itself to demand for "just right" amount of resources. Their approach however assumed that high-level SLAs (e.g., http requests per second) can be accurately defined and measured per application/VM. Rao et al. [16] proposed VCONF, an auto-configuration RL-based agent, to automatically adjust CPU and Memory shares of VMs to avoid performance degradation. They, too, used direct application measurements to generate efficient polices for their Xen based environment. Watson et al. [18] used probabilistic performance modeling to control system utilization and response time of 3-tier applications such as RUBiS. They showed that CPU allocation of VMs are enough to control high level SLAs such as response time of applications. Caglar et al. [9] proposed hALT, an online algorithm that uses Artificial Neural Networks (ANNs) to link CPU and Memory utilization of CPU intensive applications/tasks in Google trace data to performance degradation of VMs. They used another ANN to recommend migration of VMs to assure QoS for Google services. For real deployments, they still need an agent to report "performance" of an application/VM to feed and train their ANNs. Bartolini et al. [8] proposed AutoPro to take a user-defined metric and adjust VMs' resources to close the gap between their desired performances and their current ones. AutoPro uses a PI controller to asymptotically close this gap and can work with any metric – such as frame/s, MB/s, etc. – as long as developers can provide it.

Approaches in this group are generally more accurate than others because they use direct measurements/feedback from applications inside VMs. Their usage however could be very limited, because (1) they all rely on an inside tailor-made agent to report the exact throughput of an application/VM, and (2) their focus is mostly to improve performance of VMs rather than modeling throughput of applications/VMs according to their resource utilization.

Low-Level (Resource) Measurements: Approaches in this group use low-level metrics (e.g., CPU utilization) to predict throughput (e.g., the response time of a web-server) of an application/VM in its current situation. They too rely on developing tailor-made foreign agents/codes for each application/VM, installing them in the VM, and giving them enough system privileges to collect and send out performance data.

Q-cloud [15] uses a feedback-agent inside each VM to report its CPU utilization. They used five CPU intensive application from SPECjbb [1] and showed that there are direct relations between the amount of CPU a VM uses with its actual throughput. Using a MIMO linear model, authors then model interference of CPU intensive applications and feedback "root" in Hyper-V to adjust CPU allocations of VMs to improve their performances. Du et al. [10] proposed two profiling agents to collect guest-wide and system-wide performance metrics for developers so that they can accurately collect information about their products in KVM-based virtualized environments. They did not use any specific benchmark, but simple programs to engage different parts of a system.

Approaches in this group generally predict throughput of an application/VM in relation to its resource utilization, although mostly to avoid performance degradations rather than modeling and predicting throughput. Also, although these approaches can be easily modified to use Hypervisor level metrics – instead of reports from their inside agents – to predict applications' throughout, their focus on only CPU or Disk intensive applications makes them non-generalizable.

After close examination of many techniques presented to date, we have noticed the following shortcomings. Firstly, many techniques require an agent/code to be injected to a VM to report either its throughput or its performance data. The need to have access to VMs and permission to run tailor-made foreign codes is neither acceptable not practical in most general cases. Secondly, many techniques aim to predict throughput of an application only to avoid contention by using/controlling one resource type (CPU, Mem, or Disk). Finally, most approaches target known applications that do not have multidimensional resource demands: they are pure CPU, Mem, or Disk intensive.

To address these shortcomings, we designed vmBBThrPred to directly model and formulate throughput of an unknown application/VM according to its resource usages. vmBBThrPred is an application-agnostic non-intrusive approach that does not require access to the VM to run foreign agents/codes: it only uses Hypervisor level metrics to systematically relate multidimensional resource usage of a VM to its actual throughput, and consequently performance degradation for various working scenarios (free or under resource contention).

3   Architecture of vmBBThrPred

The key idea of vmBBThrPred is to use the sensitivity values of an application to model/formulate its throughout. vmBBProfiler, our systematic sensitivity analysis approach in [17], was designed to pressure an unknown VM to work under different working scenarios and reveal its sensitivity to each resource type. vmBBProfiler calculates three sensitivity values ($\in [0, 1]$) upon profiling a VM: Sen^c, Sen^m, and Sen^d to respectively reflect sensitivity of a VM to its CPU, Mem, and Disk. For example, $Sen^c = 1$ implies that the profiled VM significantly changes its behavior, and consequently its throughput when it suffers to access CPU. $Sen^c = 0$ implies that throughput of the profiled VM is insensitive to its CPU share; e.g., when the VM is running a Disk intensive application. Other values of $Sec^{c/m/d}$ reflect other levels of sensitivity: the larger the $Sec^{c/m/d}$ the more sensitivity to a resource type. vmBBProfiler is also application-oblivious and uses no internal information about the nature of the applications running inside the VM when profiling it; Fig. 2 shows the architecture of both vmBBProfiler and vmBBThrPred and how they are related to each other. All components of vmBBProfiler and vmBBThrPred are totally separate and performing non-redundant procedures; both are run outside the VM and are currently implemented using PowerShell [2] and PowerCLI [4] scripts for Windows-7 and above.

vmBBProfiler: The key idea in vmBBProfiler is to identify how a VM behaves under resource contention. Its architecture relies on two components (Fig. 2):

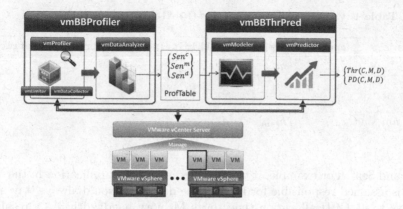

Fig. 2. Architecture of vmBBProfiler and vmBBThrPred

vmProfiler and vmDataAnalyser. The vmProfiler, in turn, consists of two parts: vmLimiter and vmDataCollector to respectively command a Hypervisor, through VMware-vCenter [5] in our case, to impose resource limits to a VM, and collect/record its behavior under the imposed limits.

vmProfiler aims to emulate contention through limitation. That is, instead of challenging a VM to compete with other co-located VMs to access/use resources (CPU, Mem, and/or Disk), the vmLimiter limits resource usage of the VM so that it reveals its behavior under hypothetical contentions. We showed in [17] that although resource starvation under "contention" and "limitation" are different, they always lead to very similar performance degradation (less than 5 % different on average). `cpu/mem/diskLimit` $\in [0,1]$ sets the percentage of CPU/Mem/Disk that the VM can use. For example, if a VM has two 2.4 GHz vCPUs, `cpuLimit = 0.25` would limit CPU usage of this VM to $0.25 \times 2 \times 2.4 = 1.2$ GHz. After imposing a set of limits to resources, vmDataCollector is then launched to collect/record performance of the VM through polling several Hypervisor level metrics; it only polls VM metrics (e.g., CPU utilization) that are already collected by the Hypervisor: it neither demands nor needs any specific metric from the VM itself.

Table 1 shows a sample profiling table upon completion of vmBBProfiler; this table will be refereed to as "ProfTable" for the rest of this article. In this table, `cpuLimit` $\in \{c_1, c_2, \ldots, c_{nc}\}$, `memLimit` $\in \{m_1, m_2, \ldots, m_{nm}\}$, and `diskLimit` $\in \{d_1, d_2, \ldots, d_{nd}\}$ produce a total number of $nc \times nm \times nd$ profiling scenarios. `metricX` is the average of the X-th Hypervisor metrics (e.g., disk.read.average (KBps)) during the imposed limitation scenario. It is worth noting that each metric is a series of values during the profiling phase (e.g., 15 values for 5 min of profiling in [17]), however because they showed to have negligible standard deviation, their average values proved to be accurate enough to be used in vmBBThrPred.

Upon profiling behavior of a VM under several limitation profiles, vmData-Analyser is invoked to analyze the profiled data and calculate sensitivity of the VM to its CPU, Memory, and Disk allowances; they are respectively named Sen^c,

Table 1. vmBBProfiler output table (ProfTable) after profiling a VM

Scenario #	cpuLimit	memLimit	diskLimit	(metric1, metric2, ..., metricK)
1	c_1	m_1	d_1	$\cdots$
2	c_1	m_1	d_2	$\cdots$
$\cdots$	$\cdots$	$\cdots$	$\cdots$	$\cdots$
$nc \times nm \times nd$	c_{nc}	m_{nm}	d_{nd}	$\cdots$

Sen^m, and Sen^d. For example, it would suggest that the application in the VM, which is assumed responsible for its resource demands, would always stay more sensitive to its CPU allocation than to its Memory bandwidth. As a result, it speculates that performance of this VM, for example, would be degraded more if its CPU-share – as opposed to its Memory share – is halved.

vmBBThrPred: After profiling a VM using vmBBProfiler, vmBBThrPred is launched to use its sensitivity values and predict its throughput under any working scenario, even those that have not been observed in Table 1. vmBBThrPred consists of two parts: vmModeler and vmPredictor. vmModeler uses $\text{Sen}^{c/m/d}$ values and the ProfTable (both calculated and provided by vmBBProfiler) to produce a polynomial model to relate resource utilization of a VM to its throughput; vmPredictor connects directly to VMware-vCenter [5], dynamically (online) polls CPU, Mem, and Disk utilization of a VM, and uses the produced formula to predict throughout (Thr) and performance degradation (PD = 1 − Thr) of the VM at its current working condition.

4   Procedures of vmBBThrPred

The first step before delving into the procedures of vmBBThrPred is to select several Hypervisor metrics that can directly or indirectly relate to the actual throughout of an application/VM. Here, because vmBBThrPred is designed to be application-oblivious, we define the term "throughput" as a normalized value ($\in [0, 1]$) where Thr = 1 always reflect the maximum performance of a VM. Similarly, "performance degradation" (PD) is defined as (1−Thr) to reflect the amount of degradation a VM encounters in its current working situation. For the apache server (2vCPUs, 2 GB of RAM, and 20 GB) in our experimental setup (Sect. 5) for example, we observed the maximum response rate of 10900 'requests per second', when the VM hosting the apache server was run in an isolated environment. After migrating the VM to a contention environment, its respond rate was reduced to 4045. In this case, the respond rate of 10900 and 4045 would map to Thr = 1.00 (PD = 0.00) and Thr = 4045/10900 = 0.37 (PD = 0.63), respectively.

4.1   Identify Relevant Hypervisor Metrics

We performed a series of engineered experiments to find Hypervisor metrics that have significant correlations with the actual throughput of different applications. Note that the actual throughput of applications/VMs is not accessible/measurable for general purpose VMs – because of the need to install/inject monitoring codes. However, we could have access to these values because the Phoronix Test Suits [3] that we used in this article actually provides such detailed values at the end of its runs. It is worth noting that we used such detailed values only to identify (reverse-engineer) relative Hypervisor metrics; general use cases of vmBBThrPred does not require actual throughput measurements.

To this end, we used four benchmarks (out of the total 12 for this article) with different resource utilization behavior from the Phoronix Test Suite [3] to identify correlated metrics. They were 'apache' to represent CPU intensive (H/–/–), 'blogbench' to represent Memory intensive (–/H/L), 'aio-stress' to represent Disk intensive (–/–/H), and 'unpack-linux' to represent CPU+Mem+Disk intensive (L/L/L) applications/VMs. We tested each benchmark on three different PMs (Table 2) for 64 different contention scenarios (Table 1). Actual throughput values of these runs (provided by the Phoronix at the end of each run) are statistically correlated with 134 metrics provided by our VMware-vSphere [6] private cloud to identify the most significant/influential ones. Table 3 lists five metrics with the highest correlation to the actual throughput for each benchmark.

Table 2. Characteristics of used physical machines

PM name	CPU family	# Cores (speed)	Memory	Cache (L1/L2/L3)
AMD	AMD Opteron 6282 SE	64 (2.599 GHz)	256 GB	(768 KB/16 MB/16 MB)
DELL	Intel i7-3770	8 (3.40 GHz)	16 GB	(256 KB/1 MB/8 MB)
SGI	Intel Xeon(R) E5420	8 (2.493 GHz)	32 GB	(256 KB/12 MB/–)

As it can be seen, for one-resource-intensive benchmarks (Table 3a–c), throughput of apache, blogbench, and aio-stress is highly correlated with CPU, Mem, and Disk, respectively. For the unpack-linux with multi-resource-intensive nature however, metrics for all three resource types are listed. To compile a list of metrics to cover all cases, we averaged correlation values for all four benchmarks and build Table 4. Based on this table, we chose the cpu.usage.average (%), mem.usage.average (%), and disk.usage.average (KBps) as the three most correlated metrics to actual throughput of general purpose/unknown applications/VMs. In Sect. 5, we will show that throughout, and consequently performance degradation of all sorts of applications with various utilization patterns can be accurately (≈90–95 %) predicted using these selected metrics.

4.2   Blind Prediction

After selecting three of the most correlated Hypervisor metrics to actual throughput of applications/VMs, we performed another set of statistical analysis to dis-

Table 3. Five most correlated Hypervisor metrics for the selected benchmarks

(a) apache

Metric Name	Correlation
cpu.run.summation(millisecond)	0.99
cpu.usage.average(%)	0.99
cpu.ready.summation(millisecond)	0.99
cpu.demand.average(MHz)	0.99
cpu.overlap.summation(millisecond)	0.98

(b) blogbench

Metric Name	Correlation
mem.active.average(KB)	0.69
mem.usage.average(%)	0.69
mem.granted.average(KB)	0.68
mem.activewrite.average(KB)	0.67
mem.entitlement.average(KB)	0.65

(c) aio-stress

Metric Name	Correlation
virtualdisk.write.average(KBps)	0.99
datastore.write.average(KBps)	0.98
disk.usage.average(KBps)	0.98
virtualdisk.mediumseeks.latest(number)	0.98
disk.numberwrite.summation(number)	0.97

(d) unpack-linux

Metric Name	Correlation
disk.usage.average(KBps)	0.94
virtualdisk.mediumseeks.latest(number)	0.90
cpu.used.summation(millisecond)	0.89
cpu.usage.average(%)	0.88
mem.usage.average(%)	0.79

Table 4. Six most correlated Hypervisor metrics for all benchmarks

Metric name	Correlation
disk.numberwrite.summation (number)	0.87
disk.usage.average (KBps)	0.85
cpu.usage.average (%)	0.77
cpu.used.summation (millisecond)	0.77
mem.usage.average (%)	0.61
mem.latency.average (%)	0.55

cover the actual relation (formula) between the selected metrics and throughput values. To this end, we observed that there is a significant alignment between sensitivity values computed by vmBBProfiler and calculated correlation values. Figure 3 aligns "Correlation to Throughput" with "Sensitivity" values calculated by vmBBProfiler for all benchmarks in Table 5 on all PMs in Table 2. Comparing such alignments with the "ideal" line, which represent a perfect alignment, in these sub-figures motivates us to believe/hypothesize that the actual throughput of applications/VMs can be accurately predicted using their sensitivity values instead of their correlation values. To mathematically formulate this, we designed the following formula to predict "throughput" of a VM using only its current normalized CPU, Mem, and Disk utilization values.

$$\text{Thr(C,M,D)} = \frac{C \times \text{Sen}^c + M \times \text{Sen}^m + D \times \text{Sen}^d}{\text{Sen}^c + \text{Sen}^m + \text{Sen}^d} \tag{1}$$

In this formula, C, M, and D are respectively the proportional of CPU, Mem, and Disk utilization of a VM with respect to their counterpart values in an isolated run. For example, assume a VM with sensitivity values of $\text{Sen}^c = 1.00$, $\text{Sen}^m = 0.05$, and $\text{Sen}^d = 0.03$ uses 80 % of its CPU, occupies 22 % of its Mem, performs 25 KBps of Disk activity, and responds to 200 requests per second when it is run in a contention free environment (isolated run). Also assume its hosting

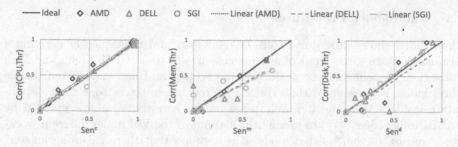

Fig. 3. Point-by-point alignment of "Correlation to Throughout" with "Sensitivity" values

VM is migrated to a PM where utilization of its resources are reduced to 45 % of CPU, 10 % of Mem, and 8 KBps of Disk because of contention. According to Eq. 1, its throughout, in this case, is predicted to be 55 % of its maximum throughout (200) in the isolated run; i.e.:

$$\text{Thr} = \left(\frac{\frac{45\%}{80\%} \times 1.00 + \frac{10\%}{22\%} \times 0.05 + \frac{8\text{KBps}}{25\text{KBps}} \times 0.03}{1.00 + 0.05 + 0.03} \right) \times 200 = 0.55 \times 200$$

The rationale behind this formula is based on our direct observations across months of profiling. To explain it, assume CPU-usage of a CPU intensive application (such as an apache server) is 90 % and it responds to 10000 requests per seconds. Now assume that its CPU-usage is reduce to 30 % because of contention. The general sense, also confirmed by direct measurements, dictates that the VM should respond to one-third of 10000; i.e. $30/90 \times 10000 = 3333$. For more complicated cases where a VM is sensitive to more than one resource, assume a Mem+Disk application (such as blogbench) is using 10 % of CPU, 70 % of Mem, and perform 17,000 KBps on Disk to conduct 100,000 blog activities in a contention free environment. Now assume this VM is migrated to another PM and its resource usages are reduced to 9 % of CPU, 63 % of Mem, and 8500 KBps because of contention. In this case, although its Mem- and disk-usage are respectively reduce by 10 % and 50 %, its final throughput will not reduce by $\max(10\%, 50\%) = 50\%$. This is because a VM's throughput is actually reduced based on its nature and in proportion to how sensitive it is to each of its resources. For blogbench in this example with $\text{Sen}^c = 0.00$, $\text{Sen}^m = 0.75$, and $\text{Sen}^d = 0.20$, we observed (measured) the final throughput of 83,460 that is very close to 82,000 that Eq. 1 predicts as:

$$\text{Thr} = \left(\frac{\frac{9}{10} \times 0.00 + \frac{63}{70} \times 0.75 + \frac{8500}{17000} \times 0.20}{0.00 + 0.75 + 0.20} \right) \times 100000 = 0.82 \times 100000$$

In Sect. 5 we will show that using sensitivity values to weight average usage proportion of resources leads to accurate blind prediction of throughput for all benchmarks we used in this work.

4.3   VmModeler Procedures

Algorithm 1 shows procedural steps of modeling, and consequently deriving a formula to relate throughput of an application/VM to its CPU, Mem, and Disk utilization. Modeling can be performed in two modes: Blind or Assisted. In the Blind mode, it is assumed that vmBBThrPred has no knowledge of the application inside a VM, and it purely relies on the sensitivity values reported by vmBBProfiler ($Sen^{c/m/d}$) to predict throughput of the VM under different working scenarios. In the Assisted mode, it is assumes that there exists a "known" measurement/metric that could directly or indirectly reflect the actual performance of a VM. For example, the amount of network traffic for an apache server or the amount of IOPs (i/o operation per second) for an ftp server can both indirectly reflect performance of these servers. The Assisted mode is to address the current theme of using internal and/or external measurements to predict throughput, and consequently performance degradation of a VM in its current working condition. We included this mode only to show that not only vmBBThrPred can be easily adopted/employed by current systems, but also its bundling with vmBBProfiler yields more than 95 % accuracy in predicting throughout of any application with any resource sensitivity. Similar to vmBBProfiler [17], vmModeler also uses the normalized values of C, M, and D to propose a polynomial function with prototype

$$\text{Thr}(C,M,D) = x_1 C + x_2 M + x_3 D + x_4 CM + x_5 CD + x_6 MD + x_7 CMD + x_8 \quad (2)$$

where C, M, and D are the current values of cpu.usage.average (%) divided by 100, mem.usage.average (%) divided by 100, and disk.usage.average (KBps) divided by 50000 (the maximum read/write speed for our testing environment), respectively.

To calculate $x_1 \ldots x_8$, we use ProfTable (Table 1) generated during calculation of $Sen^{c/m/d}$ by vmBBProfiler. In this table, for $nc = nm = nd = 4$ (where $c_x = m_x = d_x = x \times 0.25$, ProfTable would have 64 rows. Using these 64 runs, we define:

$$A = \begin{bmatrix} C_1 & M_1 & D_1 & (C_1 M_1) & (C_1 D_1) & (M_1 D_1) & (C_1 M_1 D_1) & 1 \\ \vdots & \vdots & \vdots & \vdots & \vdots & \vdots & \vdots & \vdots \\ C_{64} & M_{64} & D_{64} & (C_{64} M_{64}) & (C_{64} D_{64}) & (M_{64} D_{64}) & (C_{64} M_{64} D_{64}) & 1 \end{bmatrix} \quad (3)$$

$$X = \begin{bmatrix} x_1 \\ \vdots \\ x_8 \end{bmatrix} \quad Y1 = \begin{bmatrix} \frac{\frac{C_1}{C_{64}} Sen^c + \frac{M_1}{M_{64}} Sen^m + \frac{D_1}{D_{64}} Sen^d}{Sen^c + Sen^m + Sen^d} \\ \vdots \\ \frac{\frac{C_{64}}{C_{64}} Sen^c + \frac{M_{64}}{M_{64}} Sen^m + \frac{D_{64}}{D_{64}} Sen^d}{Sen^c + Sen^m + Sen^d} \end{bmatrix} \quad Y2 = \begin{bmatrix} \frac{T_1}{T_{64}} \\ \vdots \\ \frac{T_{64}}{T_{64}} \end{bmatrix} \quad (4)$$

In Eq. 3, normalized values of C, M, and D for the k-th run in ProfTable are used to fill the k-th row of matrix A. In Eq. 4, each element/row of vector Y1 is the weighted average of relative CPU, Mem, and Disk utilization of the

Algorithm 1. Algorithm for vmModeler in both modes

1: **procedure** vmModeler((Sen$^{c/m/d}$, ProfTable)) **Input** : Sen$^{c/m/d}$ and ProfTable
   $\rightarrow$ calculated and provided by vmBBProfiler
      Output: ThrA(C,M,D) and/or ThrB(C,M,D)
2:     Use ProfTable to Initialize Matrix A   ▷ Eq. 3
3:     Use ProfTable and Sen$^{c/m/d}$ to Initialize Matrixes Y1,Y2   ▷ Eq. 4
4:     Calculate X for Y← Y1 and Build ThrB(C,M,D)   ▷ Eqs. 5, 2
5:     Calculate X for Y← Y2 and Build ThrA(C,M,D)   ▷ Eqs. 5, 2
       return ThrA and/or ThrB
6: **end procedure**

---

k-th run with respect to the 64-th run (the run with no limitation and maximum performance). Vector Y2, only for the assisted mode, records the relative performance value of an indirect-metric that can be used to directly or indirectly reflect the performance of a VM; it is assumed that T64 reflects the maximum throughput/performance. For example, we used disk.usage.average (KBps) (T64 = 46000 KBps) as the indirect-metric for aio-stress in our experimental setup (more information in Sect. 5). Using linear regression, the optimal value of X can be calculated as:

$$A_{64\times8} \times X_{8\times1} = Y_{64\times1} \Longrightarrow X = (A^T A)^{-1} A^T Y \tag{5}$$

For Y←Y1, the X calculated using Eq. 5 yields ThrB (B for Blind) in Eq. 2; Y←Y2 yields ThrA (A for assisted) in Eq. 2.

In Algorithm 1, operations 2–3 initialize three matrices; operation 4 calculates and builds ThrB; operation 5 builds ThrA. Note that computing ThrB and ThrA are independent of each other; therefore if no "indirect-metric" could be identified to calculate ThrA, vmModeler can still build ThrB. In Sect. 5 we will show that ThrA is, as expected, more accurate ($\approx$96 %) than ThrB ($\approx$90 %) for all cases/benchmarks.

5   Experimental Results

To validate our proposed vmBBThrPred, we ran about 1200 h (50 days) of actual running and profiling benchmarks on our private cloud in the School of Information Technologies at the University of Sydney. We used three different PMs (Table 2) and profiled 12 different benchmarks (Table 5), varying from pure CPU/Mem/Disk intensive to various combination of CPU+Mem+Disk ones.

Benchmark Selection: We used the Phoronix Test Suite [3] (one of the most comprehensive testing and benchmarking platform) to evaluate performance and accuracy of vmBBThrPred. Table 5 lists the 12 benchmarks (out of 168 available ones in v5.2.1) we used for our experiments. We deliberately picked benchmarks with different intensities of resource usage profile of CPU, Mem, and Disk to cover realistic applications. In this table 'H', 'L', and '–' respectively mean High,

Low, and Negligible resource utilization. From the 12 benchmarks in Table 5, eight run CPU intensive, four run Memory intensive, and five run Disk intensive processes.

Experimental Results: Table 5 shows experimental results of using our approach (vmBBThrPred) to derive polynomial formulas for the selected 12 benchmarks. There are three rows for each benchmark: one row for each PM in Table 2. As it was explained in Sect. 4, vmBBThrPred can work in two modes: Blind and Assisted. ThrB is built purely based on $Sen^{c/m/d}$ and the ProfTable (Table 1); ThrA additionally uses the mentioned indirect-metric in Table 5.

6 Discussion and Analysis

We highlight the most stimulating conclusions from Table 5 in this section.

6.1 Accuracy of vmBBThrPred

Table 5 shows different prediction accuracy for different benchmarks: ranging from 76 %–99 % for the Blind (ThrB) and 94 %–100 % for the Assisted (ThrA) mode. For CPU intensive applications (marked as (*/−/−)), the accuracy of

Table 5. Results for using vmBBThrPred on the selected benchmarks

Benchmark	PM	Sen^c / Sen^m / Sen^d	ThrB(C,M,D) formula	acc.	ThrA(C,M,D) formula	acc.	indirect-metric
apache (H/−/−)	AMD	0.95 / 0.00 / 0.00	(1.02)C	95%	(1.03)C−0.05	98%	cpu.latency.average(%)
	DELL	0.97 / 0.00 / 0.00	(1.02)C	97%	(0.94)C+0.06	98%	
	SGI	0.97 / 0.03 / 0.00	(0.99)C	96%	(1.00)C+0.04	98%	
john-the-ripper (H/−/−)	AMD	0.93 / 0.00 / 0.00	(1.18)C	95%	(1.14)C+0.04	95%	cpu.latency.average(%)
	DELL	0.96 / 0.00 / 0.00	(1.09)C+0.01	95%	(1.06)C+0.08	97%	
	SGI	0.96 / 0.00 / 0.00	(1.17)C	91%	(1.11)C+0.13	95%	
n-queens (H/−/−)	AMD	0.95 / 0.00 / 0.00	(1.02)C	97%	(1.07)C−0.05	99%	cpu.idle.summation(msec)
	DELL	0.97 / 0.00 / 0.00	(1.01)C	99%	(1.02)C	100%	
	SGI	0.97 / 0.00 / 0.00	(1.02)C	99%	(1.03)C	100%	
build-apache (H/−/−)	AMD	0.94 / 0.00 / 0.00	(1.13)C+0.01	97%	(1.19)C−0.03	97%	cpu.latency.average(%)
	DELL	0.96 / 0.00 / 0.00	(1.05)C	99%	(1.07)C−0.01	99%	
	SGI	0.96 / 0.04 / 0.00	(1.10)C+0.01	98%	(1.16)C−0.01	99%	
build-php (H/−/−)	AMD	0.95 / 0.02 / 0.00	(1.01)C	98%	(1.02)C−0.01	98%	cpu.latency.average(%)
	DELL	0.96 / 0.00 / 0.00	(1.04)C	98%	(1.03)C+0.02	98%	
	SGI	0.97 / 0.07 / 0.00	(0.96)C+0.01	95%	(1.00)C+0.03	98%	
dcraw (L/−/−)	AMD	0.54 / 0.00 / 0.00	(2.10)C	98%	(2.38)C−0.11	99%	cpu.idle.summation(msec)
	DELL	0.55 / 0.00 / 0.00	(2.16)C+0.02	98%	(2.26)C−0.02	98%	
	SGI	0.48 / 0.04 / 0.00	(2.01)C	94%	(2.24)C−0.03	98%	
x264 (L/−/−)	AMD	0.33 / 0.01 / 0.00	(1.28)C	96%	(1.32)C−0.06	97%	cpu.latency.average(%)
	DELL	0.39 / 0.00 / 0.00	(1.27)C	95%	(1.34)C−0.08	98%	
	SGI	0.41 / 0.02 / 0.00	(1.28)C	98%	(1.30)C−0.02	98%	
unpack-linux (L/L/L)	AMD	0.19 / 0.10 / 0.40	(1.59)C+(1.61)D−(1.14)CD−0.07	95%	(1.76)C+(4.91)D−(6.04)CD−0.53	98%	disk.numwrite.summation
	DELL	0.21 / 0.09 / 0.25	(1.36)D+0.01	95%	(1.60)D−0.07	96%	
	SGI	0.18 / 0.09 / 0.35	(0.91)C+(1.09)D−(0.18)CD−0.01	94%	(0.58)C−(0.26)D+(5.04)CD+0.33	95%	
blogbench (−/H/L)	AMD	0.09 / 0.74 / 0.16	(0.93)M	77%	(0.60)M+0.41	90%	mem.latency.average(%)
	DELL	0.00 / 0.75 / 0.20	(0.20)M+(0.64)D+(0.16)MD+0.37	76%	−(0.89)M+(0.40)D+(0.34)MD+0.98	90%	
	SGI	0.11 / 0.81 / 0.18	(0.15)C+(0.93)M−(0.03)CM	84%	(0.46)C+(0.20)M+(0.06)CM+0.28	91%	
bork (−/L/L)	AMD	0.00 / 0.47 / 0.18	(0.75)M+(0.26)D+(0.05)MD+0.02	84%	−(0.03)M+(0.94)D+(0.11)MD	99%	mem.activewrite.average(KB)
	DELL	0.00 / 0.45 / 0.09	(0.80)M+(0.39)D−(0.10)MD	82%	(0.03)M+(1.14)D−(0.03)MD+0.05	98%	
	SGI	0.00 / 0.53 / 0.20	(0.82)M+(0.43)D−(0.15)MD	83%	(0.04)M+(1.24)D−(0.08)MD−0.01	97%	
compress-gzip (−/L/H)	AMD	0.00 / 0.00 / 0.55	(1.37)D+0.07	94%	(0.85)D+0.40	97%	disk.numwrite.summation
	DELL	0.00 / 0.00 / 0.45	(0.48)M+(0.52)D+(0.22)MD+0.11	87%	(0.16)M+(1.01)D+(0.42)MD	94%	
	SGI	0.00 / 0.00 / 0.47	(0.51)M+(0.48)D+(0.25)MD+0.09	83%	(0.10)M+(1.08)D+(0.40)MD	95%	
aio-stress (−/−/H)	AMD	0.00 / 0.31 / 0.84	(0.60)M+(0.68)D−(0.02)MD	90%	(1.10)D+(0.33)MD	99%	disk.maxtotal latency.latest
	DELL	0.00 / 0.32 / 0.91	(0.40)M+(0.95)D−(0.11)MD−0.01	96%	(0.13)M+(1.22)D−(0.06)MD−0.05	98%	
	SGI	0.00 / 0.30 / 0.80	(1.00)M+(0.75)D−(0.19)MD−0.02	86%	−(0.05)M+(2.01)D+(0.75)MD+0.02	99%	

vmBBThrPred were significantly high (>94%). Accuracy of ThrA/B for disk intensive applications ((−/L/L) and (−/*/H)) were also noticeably high with the minimum accuracy of 82% and 94% for ThrB and ThrA, respectively. Memory intensive applications, (−/H/*) and (−/L/*), proved to be much more cumbersome than the other two. In this case, vmBBThrPred accuracy dropped as low as 76% and 90% for the Blind and Assisted modes, respectively. This is well aligned with other experiments in the literature that identify Memory Caches (L1/L2/L3) as one of the most influential components in virtualized environments. It is also well aligned with Table 4 in which Memory bandwidth showed less correlation with throughput as compared with CPU and Disk.

6.2   Transferability of Results

Table 5 shows a variety of formulas for different benchmarks on different PMs. Nevertheless, in most cases the formula was almost identical across PMs. For CPU intensive applications, (*/−/−), ThrA/B are almost identical across PMs. Disk intensive applications, (−/L/L) and (−/*/H), have also led to similar formulas. Throughput of memory intensive applications however, (−/H/*) and (−/L/*), could not be modeled using similar formulas; they also varied across PMs. This could be related to the internal nature of CPU structure and the size of caches in these PMs. As it can be observed in Table 2, these PMs have different cache sizes. The AMD machine for example has the largest cache size; we believe this is why it has the most straight forward formula for all cases. For example, ThrA/B formulas for blogbench with the highest sensitivity to memory is calculated as a function of 'M', while on the other two PMs they are related to 'C' and 'D' too. This also confirms that the cache size/structure is very important for virtualized environments.

6.3   Indirect Metrics

Table 5 also shows the indirect-metric we used for each benchmark to build its ThrA formulas to achieve slightly better (5%–10% more) accuracy than ThrB. This proves that having "known" metrics to directly or indirectly measure performance of applications could in fact lead to more accurate results. Nevertheless, we argue that selecting the right "indirect metric" could not be very easy sometimes because not only we need to know the nature of the application/VM, but we also need to make sure that the chosen metric has a linear relation with the actual throughput of the application/VM. In fact, selecting a wrong metric could lead to meaningless formulas, such as selecting a disk related metric (e.g., disk.usage.average (KBps)) for a CPU-intensive applications (e.g., apache).

7   Conclusion

In this work, we presented vmBBThrPred to predict throughput, and consequently the performance degradation of general purpose applications/VMs based on their CPU, Mem, and Disk utilization as seen by the Hypervisor, and the sensitivity values calculated for them by vmBBProfiler. vmBBThrPred can work in two modes: Blind and Assisted. In the Blind mode, it uses only the Hypervisor level metrics to derive a polynomial formula in which normalized CPU, Mem, and Disk utilization values of working VMs can be dynamically (online) plugged in to predict the immediate throughput of each VM. For the Assisted mode, an indirect-metric could be nominated by the user so that vmBBThrPred can derive more accurate formulas. vmBBThrPred was implemented in our VMware-vSphere based private cloud and proved its efficiency across 1200 h of empirical studies. Using 12 well known benchmarks to cover all sorts of possible applications, it managed to successfully build accurate formulas (90 % for Blind and 95 % for Assisted on average) for a various range of applications with different resource intensity usage profiles. vmBBThrPred is the first Black-Box throughput predictor, to the best of our knowledge, that uses only basic Hypervisor level metrics for its very systematic calculations.

References

1. Specjbb (2016). https://www.spec.org/jbb2015/
2. Microsoft powershell (2016). https://msdn.microsoft.com/en-us/mt173057.aspx
3. Phoronix test suite (2016). www.phoronix-test-suite.com/
4. Vmware-powercli (2016). www.vmware.com/support/developer/powercli/
5. Vmware-vcenter (2016). www.vmware.com/products/vcenter-server
6. Vmware-vsphere (2016). www.vmware.com/products/vsphere/
7. Banga, G., Druschel, P., Mogul, J.C.: Resource containers: a new facility for resource management in server systems (1999)
8. Bartolini, D.B., Sironi, F., Sciuto, D., Santambrogio, M.D.: Automated fine-grained CPU provisioning for virtual machines. ACM Trans. Architect. Code Optim. (TACO) 11(3), 27 (2014)
9. Caglar, F., Shekhar, S., Gokhale, A.: Towards a performance interference-aware virtual machine placement strategy for supporting soft real-time applications in the cloud (2011)
10. Du, J., Sehrawat, N., Zwaenepoel, W.: Performance profiling of virtual machines. SIGPLAN Not. 46(7), 3–14 (2011)
11. Hui, C., Shinan, W., Weisong, S.: Where does the power go in a computer system: experimental analysis and implications. In: 2011 International Green Computing Conference and Workshops (IGCC), pp. 1–6 (2011)
12. Kundu, S., Rangaswami, R., Dutta, K., Ming, Z.: Application performance modeling in a virtualized environment. In: 2010 IEEE 16th International Symposium on High Performance Computer Architecture (HPCA), pp. 1–10 (2010)
13. Lingjia, T., Mars, J., Vachharajani, N., Hundt, R., Soffa, M.L.: The impact of memory subsystem resource sharing on datacenter applications. In: 2011 38th Annual International Symposium on Computer Architecture (ISCA), pp. 283–294 (2011)
14. Mars, J., Tang, L., Hundt, R., Skadron, K., Soffa, M.L.: Bubble-up: increasing utilization in modern warehouse scale computers via sensible co-locations (2011)
15. Nathuji, R., Kansal, A., Ghaffarkhah, A.: Q-clouds: managing performance interference effects for QoS-aware clouds (2010)

16. Rao, J., Bu, X., Xu, C.Z., Wang, L., Yin, G.: VCONF: a reinforcement learning approach to virtual machines auto-configuration (2009)
17. Taheri, J., Zomaya, A.Y., Kassler, A.: vmbbprofiler: A black-box profiling approach to quantify sensitivity of virtual machines to shared cloud resources. ACM Trans. Model. Perform. Eval. Comput. Syst. (March 2016, submitted)
18. Watson, B.J., Marwah, M., Gmach, D., Chen, Y., Arlitt, M., Wang, Z.: Probabilistic performance modeling of virtualized resource allocation (2010)
19. Xu, J., Zhao, M., Fortes, J., Carpenter, R., Yousif, M.: Autonomic resource management in virtualized data centers using fuzzy logic-based approaches. Clust. Comput. 11(3), 213–227 (2008)

Dynamic SLAs for Clouds

Rafael Brundo Uriarte[1(✉)], Francesco Tiezzi[2], and Rocco De Nicola[1]

[1] IMT School for Advanced Studies Lucca, Lucca, Italy
{rafael.uriarte,rocco.denicola}@imtlucca.it
[2] University of Camerino, Camerino, Italy
francesco.tiezzi@unicam.it

Abstract. In the Cloud domain, to guarantee adaptation to the needs of users and providers, Service-Level-Agreements (SLAs) would benefit from mechanisms to capture the dynamism of services. The existing SLA languages attempt to address this challenge by focusing on renegotiation of the agreement terms, which is a heavy-weight process, not really suitable for dealing with cloud dynamism. In this paper, we propose an extension of SLAC, a SLA language for clouds that we have recently defined, with a mechanism that enable dynamic modifications of the service agreement. We formally describe this extension, implement it in the SLAC framework and analyse the impacts of dynamic SLAs in some applications. The advantages of dynamic SLAs are demonstrated by comparing their effect with that of static SLA and of the "renegotiation" approach.

1 Introduction

The cloud paradigm is inherently dynamic from both the consumer and the provider perspectives. From the provider's standpoint, new resources are added and removed on-the-fly, whilst service requests and prices vary over time as the pay-per-use model is employed. From the consumer's perspective, instead, the requirements may vary considerably when, e.g., clouds are used to outsource internal services or to complement the computing capacity through a hybrid cloud. Such dynamism might change providers and consumers requirements during the service provision period. Providers might need to change the agreements, e.g., to avoid the violation of agreements and to maximise revenues by serving consumers willing to pay for immediate use of the service [6]. On the other hand, consumers may modify the service, e.g., to respond to unexpected demands, to extend the expiration date of a contract or to change the amount of resources to be provided.

Clouds commonly use Service-Level-Agreements (SLAs) to regulate the provision of services. A SLA is the formalisation of the service provision characteristics, which are composed of obligations, rights and guarantees for the involved parties. In clouds, where consumers entrust crucial data and processes to other

Published by Springer International Publishing Switzerland 2016. All Rights Reserved
M. Aiello et al. (Eds.): ESOCC 2016, LNCS 9846, pp. 34–49, 2016.
DOI: 10.1007/978-3-319-44482-6_3

parties, SLAs are necessary and reflecting cloud's dynamism in contracts is a crucial open issue. The need for dynamicity can be perceived by considering a situation in which a cloud provider has overbooked its resources and the load unexpectedly raises. In such case, the provider to avoid breaching SLAs, paying fines and violating the consumers' trust, might want to activate a clause in the contract that allows him to reduce the resources provided to some consumers (e.g., number of VMs) offering monetary discounts to compensate this reduction. Unfortunately, none of the existing SLA definition languages offers this possibility. Two solutions are commonly employed to mitigate this problem.

In the first, only a generic specification of the service and its quality is defined. Providers specify generic terms, such as service availability, or even service classes, such as Silver and Gold, under which new instances are created. However, this approach provides only a high-level account of the service, which may be a source of ambiguity for the verification of the service quality. Moreover, the addition of resources or changes in the provided service are subject to the prices and availability at the moment of the request, which may vary considerable since the original agreement does not impose them any restriction.

The second approach to mitigate the dynamicity problem in clouds is the renegotiation of the SLA. However, automatic (re)negotiation of SLAs is complex and time consuming [8,9,14,16]; it entails the costs of formulating, taking decision and analysing the proposed SLA modifications [9]. It does not offer the flexibility of acting/planning without the authorisation of the other parties, and does not guarantee elasticity to the service because requests can always be refused. Furthermore, renegotiation cannot replace contracts specified in natural language because they may include conditional clauses which trigger automatic changes.

To overcome the lack of support for dynamic changes in the SLA definition languages, we introduce a conceptual framework, devised for the cloud domain, that enables the specification of conditions and events in which changes (triggered by, e.g., violations or requests from parties) are explicitly permitted by the SLA. We propose two mechanisms to perform changes in the SLA. The first mechanism allows unilateral changes, where the authorisation by the involved parties is not necessary if the conditions defined in the SLA are satisfied. The second mechanism enables changes only with the explicit authorisation of the involved parties. Differently from the renegotiation approach, in this case, the modifications are defined in the contract, which allows the parties to predict possible changes and speed up the decision-making process. We implement this framework as an extension of SLAC [17], a SLA definition language for clouds which, as the other existing definition languages, did not include mechanisms to support dynamic SLAs.

The main contributions of this paper are: (i) an innovative approach to capture the dynamism of clouds in the SLAs through the definition of cases in which the terms of the SLA can be changed; (ii) a formal extension of the SLAC language to support dynamic SLAs, and (iii) the implementation and comparison of our approach against the traditional SLA renegotiation. Before presenting the extension of SLAC to support dynamism (Sect. 2), some experiments (Sect. 3) and the impact of dynamic SLAs in different fields (Sect. 4), we briefly discuss the related works.

A generic SLA framework that supports the reservation of long term capacity at pre-specified prices is proposed in [7]. The focus is on the service admission control from the provider side and on providing solutions for capacity allocation in scenarios in which consumers reserve resources for fixed prices. This approach is problem specific and the authors clarify that the work is a pragmatic first step towards more dynamic pricing scenarios. Neither the framework, nor the SLA definition language to support this feature, nor the mechanism to reserve the resources are discussed. Similarly, other works provide solutions considering implicit changes in the services quality level, but, to the best of our knowledge, none of them defines a conceptual framework with an actual implementation or studies the contractual nature of such changes and its implications in the SLA.

An interesting discussion on the management perspective of dynamic SLAs is reported in [9] where the authors stress that, due to rapidly changing requirements of consumers and providers, clouds require dynamic SLAs. Also possible design choices for such systems are surveyed and the main phases of SLA management, such as admission control, monitoring, SLA evaluation and enforcement are clearly introduced. The focus, however, is on the discussion of the requirements of management systems, in particular of Openstack, to provide this flexibility in clouds but the issues of creating dynamic SLAs for clouds are not addressed.

The WS agreement language is extended in [3,4] to support modifications at run time using renegotiation; this involves a party requesting the desired modification and the other one accepting it. An on-line renegotiation extension for WS-Agreement is instead proposed in [5]; renegotiation templates are introduced which specify the terms that can be modified during the renegotiation (dynamic or static Service-Level-Objectives). Similarly, many other works propose renegotiation of SLAs (e.g., [6,11,13]). However, they are not suitable for the cloud domain since they do not enable the specification of changes in the agreement without a negotiation process, which involves requests, proposals and decision-making from the involved parties.

2   Supporting Dynamism in SLAC

The requirements of the parties involved in the service provision in clouds change rapidly. This changes are not limited to elasticity but can range from business aspects, e.g., expiration date and payment model, to the quality-of-service, e.g., response time. However, SLAs are commonly non-modifiable documents, unless a renegotiation process is carried out and the involved parties agree on new terms. Aiming to reflect the dynamism of clouds into SLAs without the weight of a renegotiation process, we have developed a mechanism to enable changes in SLAs inspired by contracts specified in natural language. The intuition behind this mechanism is the specification in the contract itself of the conditions and the terms which can be changed.

Table 1. Syntax of the SLAC language (an excerpt from [17]).

$SLA ::=$ id: Id parties: $PartyDef\ PartyDef^+$
          term groups: $Group^*$ terms: $Term^+$ guarantees: $Guarantee^*$

$Group ::= GroupName : Term^+$

$Term ::= Party \rightarrow Party^+ : Metric\ |\ [Expr, Expr]$ of $GroupName$

$Party ::= Role\ |\ PartyName$

$Metric ::= NumericMetric$ not$^?$ in $Interval\ Unit\ |\ \ldots$

$NumericMetric ::=$ cCPU $|$ RT_delay $|$ response_time $|$ RAM $|$ price $|\ \ldots$

$Interval ::=\ ]Expr, Expr[\ |\ ]Expr, Expr]\ |\ [Expr, Expr[\ |\ [Expr, Expr]$

$Unit ::=$ GB $|$ # $|$ ms $|$ EUR/Hour $|\ \ldots$

$Event ::=$ violation

We designed an extension of SLAC [17], named dSLAC, to support this mechanism and enable parties to modify the terms during the service provision. The SLA itself contains the specification of the conditions and terms which can be modified and is divided into two sections: the *Dynamism*, where the triggers for changes, the conditions and the modifications are specified; and the *Invariants*, which defines fixed bounds for the SLA terms.

2.1 Syntax

SLAC is a language for the specification of SLA for clouds, which focusses on: *(i)* formal aspects of SLAs; *(ii)* supporting multi-party agreements; *(iii)* business and utility aspects; and *(iv)* proactive management of the agreement as well as the cloud system. For the sake of readability and self-containedness, we report in Table 1 (an excerpt of) the syntax of the the SLAC core language (the complete syntax of SLAC and its extensions can be found in the project's web page [1]). The syntax is formally defined in the Extended Backus Naur Form (EBNF), in which *italic* denotes non-terminal symbols, while teletype denote terminal ones.

The *description* of a *SLA* comprises a unique identification code (*Id*) and at least two involved parties. The *terms* of the agreement express the characteristics of the service together with their respective expected values. Each SLA requires the definition of at least one term, which can be either a *Metric* or a *Group* of terms (which enables the re-use of the same terms in different contexts). Each term defines the party responsible to fulfil the term (a single party) and the contractors of the service (one or more). SLAC supports different *metrics*, e.g., the *NumericMetric*, which is constrained by open or closed *Intervals* of values and a particular *Unit*. The specification of intervals in numeric metrics relies on the evaluation of expressions (*Expr*). Finally, *Guarantees* ensure that the terms of the agreement will be enforced or, in case of a violation *Event*, define the actions that will be taken.

Table 2. Syntax of the dSLAC language.Syntax of the dSLAC language.

$$SLA \mathrel{+}= \text{Dynamism: } Dynamism^* \text{ Invariants: } Metric^*$$

$$Dynamism \mathrel{+}= \text{on } Event : ConditionModification$$

$$ConditionModification ::= (\text{if } ExprModification \text{ then } Modifications)^+$$
$$(\text{else } Modifications)^? \mid Modifications$$

$$ExprModification ::= Expr \mid Party \text{ authorises}$$

$$Modifications ::= Modification \text{ and } Modifications$$
$$\mid Modification \text{ or } Modifications \mid Modification$$

$$Modification ::= \text{add term } Term \mid \text{delete term } RefTerm$$
$$\mid \text{replace value of } RefTerm \text{ with } MetricValue$$

$$RefTerm ::= (Party \Rightarrow Party^+ :)^? (GroupName:)^* \ ComposedMetric$$

$$ComposedMetric ::= NumericMetric \mid ListMetric \mid BooleanMetric$$
$$\mid GroupName$$

$$MetricValue ::= Interval \ Unit \mid Boolean \mid \{ListElement^+\}$$
$$\text{or } \{ListElement^+\}^*$$

$$Event \mathrel{+}= Party \text{ request} \mid \text{SLA\_expiration} \mid \ldots$$

The syntax of dSLAC is obtained by extending that of *SLA* and is presented in Table 2. The symbol ::= is used when a new rule is added to the syntax, while += is used to extend an existing syntactic rule.

The dynamic changes cover two sections of the SLA: *Dynamism* and *Invariants*. The former specifies events, conditions and changes, whilst the latter provides fixed rules that regulate these changes, i.e. the modification of the agreements specified in the *Dynamism* section are only performed when they are compliant with the conditions defined in the *Invariants* section. Although the invariants could be specified as conditions in the *Dynamism* part of the agreement, we opted to specify them as separated sections to have clearer specification and semantics.

The changes in the *Dynamism* section are based on *Events*, such as requests from parties or SLA violations. Then, one or more conditions can be defined (*ConditionModification*), which can be an expression *Expr*, as defined in the core language, or express the need of the authorisation from one or more parties.

Afterwards, the modification are specified using three actions: *add term*, *delete term* and *replace value*. The *add term* operation inserts a new term, which is not specified in the initial SLA. It requires a *Term*, which includes the involved parties, metric and value. The *delete term* removes a SLA term, which requires only the reference to an existing term (*RefTerm*). The *replace value* operation substitutes the value of an existing term with a new value (*MetricValue*), which can be, according to the metric type, an *Interval* and its *Unit*, a *Boolean* or a set of lists. Replacements can use reserved variable names, which refer to, e.g., the current values of the existing term, of another term or the number of times the

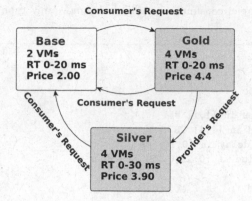

Fig. 1. Automaton of an excerpt of the example in Table 4.

SLA was violated. In case of multiple terms using the same metric (e.g., in different groups) the reference to the metric must be complete, including involved parties and groups, to avoid ambiguity.

Finally, the *Invariants* section defines rules that cannot be changed by dynamic actions, i.e. fix bounds for terms of the contract. They can define, for example, that a user cannot request more than 1000 Virtual Machines (VMs) and never less than 1 or that the provider must always backup the data of the consumer. Events that trigger changes in the contract will not be applied unless they are compliant with the terms defined in this section.

2.2 Semantics

The semantics of a SLA specified via SLAC is formulated as a Constraint Satisfaction Problem (CSP) that verifies: (i) at negotiation-time, whether the terms composing the agreement are consistent; and (ii) at enforcement-time, whether the characteristics of the service are within the specified values.

In the formal SLAC semantics [17] a *SLA* was given by means of a function $[\![SLA]\!]$ that returned a pair composed of a set of group definitions and a constraint representing the semantics of *SLA*'s terms. This pair constituted the CSP associated to the agreement; details can be found in [17].

In dSLAC the possibility of changing the set of valid constraints calls for a different approach. The agreement is represented by an *automaton* in which each state is labelled by a set of constraints and each transition by the event that modifies the constraints. The initial state of the automaton is created using the original semantics of a SLA, which converts the agreement without the *Dynamism* and *Invariants* sections into a CSP. Then, all possible new states are created considering events, conditions and the triggered changes to the SLA constraints specified in the *Dynamism* section, as well as the invariants of the agreement, which are defined as additional conditions to every transition of the automaton.

Table 3. IaaS Example: consumer can add and remove any type of VM up to 200 VMs.

SLA

...
 Term Groups:
 Small_VM:
  Imt → Rafael:cCpu in [1,1] #
  Imt → Rafael:RAM in [4,4] GB
  Imt → Rafael:RT_delay in [0,10] ms
  Imt → Rafael:price in [0.22,0.22] EUR/Hour
 Terms:
  [2,2] of Small_VM
 Dynamism:
 on consumer request:
  replace value of Small_VM with [#1+1, #2+1] *or*
  replace value of Small_VM with [#1-1, #2-1]
 Invariants:
  Small_VM in [0,200]

Figure 1 illustrates this approach based on the second example of dynamic SLA, discussed in the next section and presented in Table 4. For the sake of simplicity, the automaton does not include the dynamic part that requires authorisation from the consumer. In this case, the consumer can request 2 additional VMs when the SLA state is the initial one (corresponding to the service quality level *Base* and passing to state *Gold*) and remove 2 of them when the total number of VMs is 4 (from state *Gold* back to sate *Base*). Also, the provider can request an increase in the Response Time in state *Gold* compensating the consumer with a reduction in the price (passing to the state *Silver*). Even if in the state *Silver*, the consumer can reduce the number of VMs to 2 and return to state *Base*.

2.3   Examples

We illustrate the dynamism of SLAs using two examples. The first is presented in Table 3; it is an instance of an Infrastructure-as-a-Service SLA from a provider named *IMT* which initially delivers 2 VM to consumer *Rafael*. In this scenario, the consumer adds and removes VMs according to his needs, if the number of VMs does not exceed 200. The #1 represents the current value of the lower bound of the interval of the term and #2 the upper bound.

In the second example, presented in Table 4, we use the same scenario and base SLA as the first example, modifying only the *Dynamism* and *Invariant* parts. In this case, the consumer adds and removes VMs for a fixed price but must respect the limits defined in the Invariants, that is, in this case, he can have only 2 or 4 VMs at the same time. The provider may request an increase in the response time if the number of VMs is equal to 4. If so, as a compensation to the consumer, the price is then reduced by 50 cents. Moreover, on provider's request, a consumer may accept an increase in the response time of 5 ms, for a reduction of 10 cents in the price, always considering the ranges defined in the Invariants section that, in this example, limits the response time between 0 and 35 ms.

3   Experiments

To illustrate the SLAC extension and the benefits of dynamic SLAs we present a case study in a cloud testbed for the execution of cloud services and simulates the interaction between a provider and multiple consumers.

For the sake of simplicity, apart from the Dynamism and Invariant sections, the SLAs have only: the definition of the service execution deadline, the price to execute the service and the penalty in case of violation of the deadline. We compare three different approaches: *Static SLAs*, in which SLAs do not change during their lifetime; *Renegotiation*, in which the parties can renegotiate the existing SLA; and our approach, *Dynamic* SLAs, which enables the definition of modifications in the agreements. For this comparison, we analyse the number of violations, penalty and the total revenue of the provider.

The need for dynamism in this use case is demonstrated in three cases:

- Request for modification from the consumers, commonly caused by change of requirements, which we simulated by randomly selecting services in execution;

Table 4. Example of a more complex dynamic SLA.

SLA
...
 Dynamism:
  on consumer request:
   if Small_VM == 2
    replace value of Small_VM with [#1+2,#2+2] *and*
    replace value of Price with [#1+2.4,#2+2.4]
  on consumer request:
    replace value of Small_VM with [#1-2,#2-2] *and*
    replace value of Price with [2.0, 2.0]
  on providers request:
   if Small_VM == 4 and RT_delay == [0,20]:
    replace value of RT_delay with [0,30] *and*
    replace value of Price with [#1-0.5,#2-0.5]
  on providers request:
   if consumer authorises:
    replace value of RT_delay with [0,#2+5] *and*
    replace value of Price with [#1-0.1,#2-0.1]
 Invariants:
  RT_delay in [0,35]
  Small_VM in [2,4]

- High violation risk, which is detected during the service execution to enables the provider to change the agreement and avoid violations;
- Low violation risk, which is also detected during the service execution and enables the provider to increase its revenue, for example increasing the price but reducing the deadline of the service.

The results demonstrate the flexibility dSLAC and its capacity to reduce the number of SLA violations and to improve the revenue of the involved parties.

3.1   Use Case Model

The framework developed for the coordination of the execution of services has several components, as depicted in Fig. 2. The *SLAC Framework* parses and evaluates SLAs, which contain the service specification and requirements, and sends this description to the *Service Execution Framework*. This latter component is specifically designed to guarantee the correct deployment and execution of services and to manage the cloud infrastructure and employes schedules services using the approach presented in [18]. The Panoptes *Monitoring System* [19] provides the status of the system and services to the Violation Risk Analyser and to the SLAC Framework and is directly configured by the Service Execution Framework. The *Violation Risk Analyser* measures the risk of the running services of not meeting the deadline specified in the SLA and updates the Renegotiation Decision System. Finally, the *Renegotiation Decision System* creates proposals of modifications for the SLA and decides, when using the Renegotiation approach, whether to accept changes in the services. The violation risk analysis is performed using Supervised Random Forest [2], a machine learning technique, and is based on the monitoring information of services and the SLA itself.

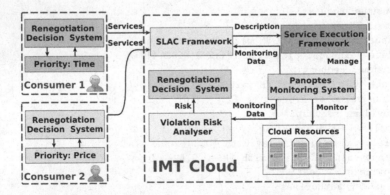

Fig. 2. Components of the use case framework.

The algorithm defined for the experiments is used for each service regardless the evaluated approaches and is depicted in Fig. 3. Each service is evaluated only

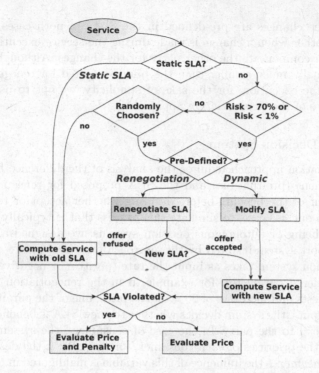

Fig. 3. Flow diagram of the tested approaches: Static, Renegotiation and Dynamic.

once during its execution lifetime, in time t_r, which is a random point between the initial time and the deadline of the service defined in the SLA. In the case of *Static SLAs*, the services are computed employing the SLA defined at design time and, when the service ends or the deadline is achieved, the system verifies whether the SLA was violated and then assesses the price paid and the possible penalties. In the *Renegotiation* approach, first the violation risk is measured. If it is not higher or lower than a specific value, the system verifies whether the service was randomly chosen. If not, the service is computed normally with the SLA defined at design time. Renegotiation take place in case of high violation risk to avoid penalties and customer insatisfaction; in case of the payment of low violation risk, to raise provider revenues by, e.g., shortening the deadline; and to simulate changes of requirements from consumers when the service was randomly chosen. A party sends a SLA proposal to the other party that analyses it according to its priorities using a Fuzzy Decision System, as described in the next section. If the new agreement is accepted, the service continues and is evaluated considering the new SLA, otherwise the initially defined agreement is the valid one till the end of the service.

In this use case, compared to Renegotiation, the only difference of the *Dynamic* approach is that the renegotiation and consentment of the involved parties is not necessary, that is, in case of low violation risk or high violation risk or the service being randomly chosen, the agreement is modified automatically since the changes are pre-defined in the SLA. In both cases a bonus is given to the other when a change is made during the service execution in order to motivate or compensate the other party for the changes. Although the bonus a priori is usually much smaller than the bonus required for renegotiating the SLA during the execution, for the sake of simplicity, we opt to use the same range of values of the *Renegotiation* approach.

3.2 Fuzzy Decision System

The Renegotiation approach requires the analysis of the difference between the initial agreement (pre-runtime) and the SLA proposed for renegotiation, and the assessment of the benefits before deciding whether accept or refuse a new agreement. In our use case, to simulate this process that is typically carried out by a human being or autonomous decision systems, we designed a fuzzy logic decision support system inspired by the approach presented in [5].

Our decision system takes as input the rate (positive or negative) of change for the considered parameter; for example, if in the renegotiation process the provider requests and increases of 20 % on the price, one of the parameters is 20. With these inputs, the system decides whether the new SLA is beneficial, neutral or not beneficial to the party. In the case of consumers, the system also takes into account the priorities of each consumer, for example, if the deadline is the priority of *consumer 1* the influence of this variable is highlighted in the decision.

Fuzzy rules interpret the relationships between the inputs and outputs and are constructed in the logical form. In the use case, the inputs are: the deadline for the service (D), the price to be paid for the service (P_r) and the penalty in case of violation (P_e). Table 5 exemplifies some rules exploited in the use case and applied by the provider's fuzzy decision system. Despite being fixed for the provider, the rules change according to the priorities of each consumer. For a complete account of the fuzzy rules and the framework used in the experiments, we refer to the website of the SLAC project [1].

Table 5. Fuzzy rules of the provider decision system.

Rule	Evaluation
If P_e increases	not beneficial
If P_r or D increases	beneficial
If P_r and D increase	very beneficial
If P_e increase $< 10\%$	neutral

3.3 Evaluation

The experiments were conducted in a cloud with 2 physical machines, providing 12 heterogeneous VMs, in which the agents are employed to execute services.

In the experiments, services are generated based on the distribution of a trace of real-world cloud environment, the Google's cloud dataset [15], and the same services are executed using all three described approaches. Each service has an associated SLAC SLA, which is created along with the service, according to an estimation of the resources necessary to finish the service within the completion time. The features are: CPU, RAM, Requirements, Disk Space, Completion Time and Network Bandwidth. Different types of services are used in the experiments, such as web crawling, word count, machine learning algorithms, number generation and format conversion, which are close to real-world applications [10]. Service's penalty and price are generated along with the SLA and are based on the service execution time and a randomly defined number. Penalties are always higher than the price, since the price is paid even if a service is violated.

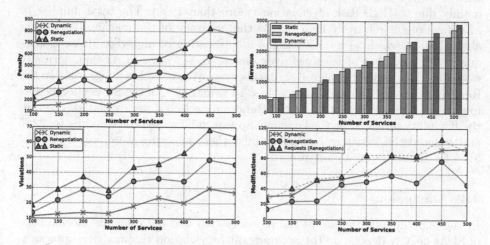

Fig. 4. Performance analysis

The training set for the SLA Risk assessment is built in every round of experiments by executing 1000 services. Then, it is used to train the machine learning algorithm to provide the probability of classifying a new service into the *violated* and *not violated* classes.

In each round of experiments, new services are generated (for creating the training set and for testing the approaches) and the same services are executed for all approaches. The number of services ranges from 100 to 500 (with 50 services interval). We assume that the services' arrival is a Poisson process, i.e. the time between consecutive arrivals has an exponential distribution and, in our case, a service arrives in average every 0.7 s.

The Fuzzy decision system accepts proposals which are beneficial to the requested party. Therefore, the requester and the Renegotiation Decision System usually offer compensations for the requested party that fulfil the need of the requester, e.g., if the violation risk is high, the provider requests more time to finish the service but offers it with a discount on the price and higher penalty. The definition of the exact parameters of the considered metrics of the SLA modification proposal, which are used by Renegotiation and Dynamic approaches (though the latter applies changes without requesting the approval of the other party), are randomly generated in a predefined range.

The results of these experiments are illustrated in Fig. 4 considering different number of services. Table 6 presents the overall results, relative to the Renegotiation and Dynamic approaches, expressed as percentages: in the case of Penalties and Revenue characteristics, the results correspond to a comparison with the Static approach, whilst in the case of the other measured characteristics they result from a comparison with the total number of services. Considering the parameters defined for the Renegotiation approach and the benefit threshold used in the experiments, around 60 % of the Modification Requests were accepted and carried out. Using the Dynamic approach, 21 % of the services were Modified mainly due to High Risk of violation (more than 19 %). The total number of Modifications is relatively high due to the accuracy of the machining learning algorithm, in which we prioritised the identification of high-risk SLAs. Consequently, the number of false positives increased, i.e. some SLAs that normally would not be classified as high-risk, in this case, were considered high-risk. In the Renegotiation and Dynamic approaches, 14 % and 19 % of the SLAs classified as high-risk and more than 10 % of the Randomly selected were violated. Overall, the flexibility provided by the Dynamic approach increased the Revenue by 22 % and reduced the Penalties by 64 %, whilst these measures were only 13 % and 31 % for the Renegotiation approach.

3.4   Discussion

In the experiments, the use of the renegotiation and the dynamic mechanisms of SLAs heavily depend on the accuracy of the violation risk analyses approach. The results show that, although the penalties were reduced by 64 %, the impact

Table 6. Experimental results

	Renegotiation	Dynamic
Modification Requests	24 %	0 %
Modifications	13 %	21 %
High Risk	11 %	19 %
Low Risk	0.1 %	0.2 %
Random	1.8 %	1.1 %
Violated High Risk	19 %	14 %
Violated Low Risk	0 %	3 %
Violated Random	10 %	12 %
Penalties	−31 %	−64 %
Revenue	13 %	22 %

on the total revenue was an increase of around 22 %. The main reasons for this difference are: the limited impact of the penalties on the total revenue due to the average number of violations; the compensation provided to the consumers when a modification is requested, which lowers the price paid for that service and sets higher penalties in case of violation; and the number of modified SLAs which were violated since most of the modification requests increase the penalty as a compensation to increasing the service completion time, which suggests that performing an analysis to define the additional time required to avoid violations instead of generating a random number could improve the total revenue.

The experiments were focused on avoiding SLA violations, and in few opportunities the Dynamic and Renegotiation mechanisms were used to improve the revenue of the parties (only around 1.4 % of the services were considered low-risk or randomly selected). In most scenarios, these mechanisms can be more aggressively employed to improve the revenue, mainly when a better accuracy is reached by the risk analysis.

Also, the parameters defined in the SLA modification proposal may have a considerable impact on the results. We adjusted these parameters to simulate a real-world situation, where every party defends his interest.

Finally, the results demonstrate that dSLAC provides flexibility for the parties and significantly improves the optimisation of the SLA management. Moreover, it can always be used together with the renegotiation approach in case not all relevant modifications are included in the SLA.

4   Conclusions and Future Works

To address the lack of support for the cloud dynamism in the existing SLA definition languages we have introduced a new approach for the specification of dynamic SLAs for clouds. This dynamism is achieved through the specifications, in the SLA itself, of the conditions and of the modifications that will be applied to the SLA once the related conditions are met. We have introduced syntax and semantics of an extension of the SLAC language and described its implementation and possible usage. We have provided evidence of the advantages of our approach in comparison to static SLAs and the use of renegotiation.

Since our approach is devised also for business, it may be used to back-up legal disputes. In fact, in designing dSLAC, we took the legal aspects of contract formation into account. Our approach is compliant with the norms defined in [12], where the authors discuss the provision of services from the legal standpoint using the European Union directives for E-Commerce as reference. Thus, dynamic SLAs, i.e. SLAs with pre-defined changes based on events and conditions, can be used in legally binding contracts.

We conclude by discussing the impact of dynamic SLAs in the cloud domain and the related challenges that we plan to address as future work. Indeed, this approach impacts in areas related to the creation and management of services and poses new important challenges in the field while looking at them from different perspectives.

The *negotiation* process needs considerable changes to support this feature. The first challenge is the matching of offers and requests of services since the possible changes must be considered. This matching mechanism needs to verify whether the requirements of the parties comply with all possible states of the SLA, taking into account the conditions for such changes. Depending on the changes defined on the SLA, a large number of states need to be analysed, which is a computation intensive process, and new techniques are needed to address possible problems, such as explosion of states. Moreover, crisp solutions that simply verify whether there exist a single state that is not compatible with the specification of the parties may imply low matching rates, whilst an algorithm considering the probability of reaching a non-desired state could improve this rate. Considering the complexity of this process, the negotiation can hardly be performed by humans and new algorithms, for example, based on model checking, that take into account the priorities of the involved parties should be develop to define SLA proposals and to assess their benefits.

The *scheduling, service admission* and *resource reservation* areas also need to consider the possible changes in the services. As the modifications in the agreement do not need the authorisation from the provider, the consumer can request changes in unexpected times and the provider must cope with them. Although most of the existing methodologies already employ statistical methods to predict the load of the system, the agreement with pre-defined changes is valuable source of knowledge as it contains the explicit definitions of the changes which are more likely to happen or that are expected by the parties. Moreover, the methodologies can also use the conditions pre-defined in the SLAs to adjust the load of the system. This process is complex and requires multi-objective solutions to find the optimal (or a better) scenarios for such cases since the possibilities in large scale are numerous. For example, even if a consumer requests a large number of new VMs, the provider can avoid violations of SLAs by removing VMs from other consumers, by e.g., providing a discount to them.

Service and infrastructure *Monitoring* are essential for the decision-making and SLA management. With dynamic SLAs, this process needs to adapt the knowledge generation methods to use the collected data before and after the changes. Finally, management systems must track the changes in the SLA for billing purposes and for legal reasons (e.g., in case of disputes).

References

1. SLAC: A Formal Service-Level-Agreement Language for Cloud Computing (2016). http://sysma.imtlucca.it/tools/slac/
2. Breiman, L.: Random forests. Mach. Learn. **45**(1), 5–32 (2001)
3. Di Modica, G., Regalbuto, V., Tomarchio, O., Vita, L., Doria, V.A.: Dynamic re-negotiations of SLA in service composition scenarios. In: SEAA, pp. 359–366. IEEE (2007)
4. Di Modica, G., Tomarchio, O., Vita, L.: Dynamic SLAs management in service oriented environments. J. Syst. Softw. **82**(5), 759–771 (2009)
5. Djemame, S.S.K.: Enabling service-level agreement renegotiation through extending WS-Agreement specification. SOCA **9**, 177–191 (2015)

6. Galati, A., Djemame, K., Fletcher, M., Jessop, M., Weeks, M., Hickinbotham, S., McAvoy, J.: Designing an SLA protocol with renegotiation to maximize revenues for the CMAC platform. In: Haller, A., Huang, G., Huang, Z., Paik, H., Sheng, Q.Z. (eds.) WISE 2011 and 2012. LNCS, vol. 7652, pp. 105–117. Springer, Heidelberg (2013)
7. Garg, R., Saran, H., Randhawa, R., Singh, M.: A SLA framework for QoS provisioning and dynamic capacity allocation. In: IWQoS, pp. 129–137. IEEE (2002)
8. Green, L.: Service level negotiation in a heterogeneous telecommunication environment. In: I4CT. IEEE (2004)
9. Lee, C.A., Sill, A.F.: A design space for dynamic service level agreements in OpenStack. J. Cloud Comput. **3**(1), 17 (2014)
10. Nanduri, R., Maheshwari, N., Reddyraja, A., Varma, V.: Job aware scheduling algorithm for mapreduce framework. In: CloudCom, pp. 724–729. IEEE (2011)
11. Omezzine, A., Tazi, S., Bellamine, N., Saoud, B., Drira, K., Cooperman, G.: Towards a dynamic multi-level negotiation framework in cloud computing. In: CloudTech. IEEE (2015)
12. Parkin, M., Kuo, D., Brooke, J., MacCulloch, A.: Challenges in EU grid contracts. In: Exploiting the Knowledge Economy: Issues, Applications and Case Studies, pp. 67–75. IOS Press (2006)
13. Parkin, M., Hasselmeyer, P., Koller, B.: An SLA re-negotiation protocol. In: NFPSLA-SOC (2008)
14. Pichot, A., Wäldrich, O., Ziegler, W., Wieder, P.: Towards dynamic service level agreement negotiation: an approach based on WS-Agreement. In: WEBIST, pp. 107–119. SCITEPRESS (2009)
15. Reiss, C., Wilkes, J., Hellerstein, J.L.: Google cluster-usage traces: format + schema. Technical report, Google Inc. November 2011. http://googleclusterdata. googlecode.com/files/Googlecluster-usagetraces-format+schema(2011.10. 27external).pdf
16. Shen, W., Li, Y., Ghenniwa, H., Wang, C.: Adaptive negotiation for agent-based grid computing. JASA **97**(457), 210–214 (2002)
17. Uriarte, R.B., Tiezzi, F., De Nicola, R.: SLAC: a formal service-level-agreement language for cloud computing. In: UCC, pp. 419–426. IEEE (2014)
18. Uriarte, R.B., Tsaftaris, S., Tiezzi, F.: Service clustering for autonomic clouds using random forest. In: CCGrid, pp. 515–524. IEEE (2015)
19. Uriarte, R.B., Westphall, C.B.: Panoptes: a monitoring architecture and framework for supporting autonomic clouds. In: NOMS. IEEE (2014)

Adaptation

Reinforcement Learning Techniques
for Decentralized Self-adaptive Service Assembly

M. Caporuscio[1], M. D'Angelo[1], V. Grassi[2], and R. Mirandola[3(✉)]

[1] Linnaeus University, Växjö, Sweden
{mauro.caporuscio,mirko.dangelo}@lnu.se
[2] Università di Roma Tor Vergata, Rome, Italy
vgrassi@info.uniroma2.it
[3] Politecnico di Milano, Milan, Italy
raffaela.mirandola@polimi.it

Abstract. This paper proposes a self-organizing fully decentralized solution for the service assembly problem, whose goal is to guarantee a good overall quality for the delivered services, ensuring at the same time fairness among the participating peers. The main features of our solution are: (*i*) the use of a gossip protocol to support decentralized information dissemination and decision making, and (*ii*) the use of a reinforcement learning approach to make each peer able to learn from its experience the service selection rule to be followed, thus overcoming the lack of global knowledge. Besides, we explicitly take into account load-dependent quality attributes, which lead to the definition of a service selection rule that drives the system away from overloading conditions that could adversely affect quality and fairness. Simulation experiments show that our solution self-adapts to occurring variations by quickly converging to viable assemblies maintaining the specified quality and fairness objectives.

1 Introduction

We consider a distributed peer-to-peer scenario, where a large set of peers cooperatively work to accomplish specific tasks. In general, each peer possesses the know-how to perform some tasks (offered services), but could require services offered by other peers to carry out these tasks. Scenarios of this type can be typically encountered in pervasive computing application domains like ambient intelligence or smart transportation systems, where several (from tens to thousands) services cooperate to achieve some common objectives [13].

A basic functional requirement for this scenario is to match required and provided services, so that the resulting assembly makes each peer able to correctly deliver its service(s). Besides this functional requirement, we also assume the existence of non functional requirements concerning the quality of the delivered service, expressed in terms of several quality attributes referring to different quality domains (e.g., performance, dependability, cost).

M. Aiello et al. (Eds.): ESOCC 2016, LNCS 9846, pp. 53–68, 2016.
DOI: 10.1007/978-3-319-44482-6_4

Our goal is to devise a self-assembly procedure among the peers, aimed at fulfilling both functional and non functional requirements. For the latter, we aim in particular to maximize some notion of global utility expressed in terms of the quality attributes of the services delivered by peers in the system, ensuring at the same time fairness (i.e., no peer should be excessively favored or penalized with respect to others). Challenges to be tackled to achieve this goal include: (1) the presence of several functionally equivalent services, with different values of their quality attributes, which makes non trivial determining the "best" selection of offered services to be bound to required services; (2) the intrinsic dynamism of a large distributed system, with peers entering/exiting the system, or changing the value of their quality attributes, which require to dynamically adapt the assembly to the changing system configuration; (3) the lack of global knowledge, which is difficult to achieve and maintain in a large distributed system with autonomous peers; this makes centralized service assembly policies hardly usable; (4) the need of devising a service selection and assembly procedure that scales with increasing system size (up to hundreds or thousands of services/peers); (5) the possibly load-dependent nature of service quality attributes. This obviously holds for attributes in the performance domain (e.g., response time), where load has a negative impact on their value; it may also hold for other domains like the dependability domain, where increasing load could increase the likelihood of failures [8], or the cost domain, for example in case of cost schemes based on congestion pricing [11]. Load-dependent quality attributes rule out simple greedy service selection policies, as they could easily lead to service overloading, and consequent worsening of the overall delivered quality.

To cope with these challenges we propose in this paper a self-adaptive fully decentralized solution for the service assembly problem, whose main features are: (i) the adoption of an unstructured peer-to-peer approach for dynamic service discovery, based on the use of a gossip protocol that guarantees resilience through self-adaptation to dynamic changes occurring in the system, and scalability with respect to the system size, thanks to the bounded amount of information maintained and exchanged among peers; (ii) the use of a reinforcement learning approach to make each peer able to dynamically learn from its experience the service selection rule to be followed, thus overcoming the lack of global knowledge; (iii) the explicit consideration of load-dependent quality attributes, which leads to the definition of a service selection rule that drives the system away from service overloading conditions.

The paper is organized as follows. In Sect. 2 we give an overview of the main features of the adopted approach. In Sect. 3 we define the system model and state the problem we intend to solve. In Sect. 4 we detail the core elements of our approach. In Sect. 5 we present experimental results obtained through simulation. In Sect. 6 we survey related work, while in Sect. 7 we present conclusions and hints for future work.

2   Adopted Approach Overview

Self-adaptive systems have been proposed to cope with the dynamic environment where large software-intensive systems typically operate, for example because of changes in the availability or quality of the resources they rely on [2].

A self-adaptive system typically consists of a *managed system* that implements the system business logic, and a *feedback loop* that implements the adaptation logic for the managed system. General architecture for the feedback loop is the MAPE-K model, with *Monitor* (M), *Analyze* (A), *Plan* (P) and *Execute* (E) activities, plus a *Knowledge* (K) that maintains relevant information for the other components (e.g., system state, adaptation rules) [17].

In our setting, *Monitor* aims at collecting information about candidate services and their quality attributes, whereas *Analyze* and *Plan* aim at selecting, among the set of known candidates, those services that best serve to resolve existing dependencies and fulfill non functional requirements. Finally, *Execute* actually implements the bindings with the selected services, so leading to the construction (and maintenance) of the required assembly. However, how the MAPE-K activities are actually architected and implemented must take into account the specific characteristics of the managed system and its operating environment. In the rest of this section, we outline the main characteristics of the approach we have adopted to this end, highlighting how it deals with the challenges described in the Introduction.

MAPE-K information sharing architectural pattern – In large distributed settings a single MAPE-K loop is hardly adequate to manage the whole system, and *monitor, analyze, plan,* and *execute* are implemented by multiple MAPE-K loops that coordinate with one another. According to the *information sharing pattern* [17], each peer self-adapts locally by implementing its own MAPE-K loop, but requires state information from other peers in the system. Apart from information sharing, peers do not coordinate other activities. Hence, this pattern supports autonomous adaptation decisions at each node, and enables scalability thanks to the loose coordination required, limited to state information exchange.

Gossip based monitoring – According to the information sharing pattern, information collected by the *monitor* at each peer is shared with other peers in the system. In the scenario we are considering, this information mainly concerns offered services the peer is aware of, and their functional and non-functional properties. To cope with some of the challenges we have outlined in the introduction, this coordinated monitoring activity should scale with increasing system size, and be able to quickly react to changes occurring in the system (e.g., new offered services, variations of their quality). To this end, we adopt a gossip-based approach [1], which exploits epidemic protocols to achieve reliable information exchange among large sets of interconnected peers, also in presence of network volatility (e.g., peers join/leave the system suddenly). Specifically, in a gossip communication model, each peer in the system periodically exchanges information with a dynamically built peer set, and spreads information epidemically, similar to a virus in biological communities. This guarantees quick, decentralized and scalable information dissemination, and makes gossip-based communication well suited for our purposes. We detail the applied algorithm in Sect. 4.1.

TD-learning based analysis and planning – *Analyze* and *Plan* are local at each peer, and do not require any explicit coordination with other peers. In our setting, these activities aim at selecting, within the set of candidates built by the monitoring activity, the offered services to resolve the dependencies of local services, trying at the same time to maximize the system quality and ensure fairness (see Sect. 3). In the dynamic scenario we are considering, fixed selection rules are hardly able to achieve satisfactory results. Indeed, we make peers learn on their own the selection rule to be applied, using a reinforcement learning approach where the learner is not told which actions to take, as in most forms of machine learning, but instead must discover which actions yield the most reward by trying them [15]. These features fit well with the considered scenario, where peers do not know each other (and the services they offer) in advance, but discover themselves dynamically. Moreover, services can have multiple dependencies to be resolved, and are characterized by multiple load-dependent quality attributes. To this end, we focus on temporal-difference (TD) learning methods [15], which can learn directly from raw experience without a model of the environment's dynamics and are implemented in an on-line, fully incremental fashion. In particular, we base the learning on two kinds of knowledge that are incrementally acquired by each peer: information about the existence of offered services and their advertised quality, achieved through the gossip-based monitoring activity, and the direct experience of the services' quality, acquired by each peer after actually binding to the selected services. We use the second kind of knowledge to balance through a *trust model* the advertised quality with the actually experienced quality, building to this end a two-layer TD-learning model. We detail this model in Sect. 4.2.

3   System Model

In this section we define the model of the system we are considering and introduce the terminology and notation used in the rest of the paper.

We consider a set of N distributed services $\mathbf{S} = \{S_1, \ldots, S_N\}$ hosted by peer nodes communicating each other through a network. A service S is a tuple $\langle Type, Deps, In_t, Out_t, \mathbf{u}, \mathbf{U}_t \rangle$, where:

- $S.Type \in \mathbf{T}$ denotes the type of the provided interface (we say that $S.Type$ is the type of S). We assume $w \geq 1$ different service types $\mathbf{T} = \{T_1, \ldots, T_w\}$.
- $S.Deps \subseteq \mathbf{T}$ is the set of required dependencies for S: for each $d \in S.Deps$, S must be bound to a service S' such that $d = S'.Type$, in order to be executed. If $S.Deps = \emptyset$, then S has no dependencies. We assume that $S.Deps$ is fixed for each service and known in advance.
- $S.In_t \subseteq \mathbf{S}$ is the set of services S is bound to at time t, to resolve its dependencies.

- $S.Out_t \subseteq \mathbf{S}$ is the set of other services that are bound to S at time t, to resolve one of their dependencies.
- $\mathbf{u} \subseteq \mathbb{R}^m$ is a vector of m "local quality" attributes (e.g., reliability, cost, response time), which express the quality of the service S, depending only on internal characteristics of S and of the node hosting it. If S has a non empty set of dependencies, then $\mathbf{u}$ gives only a partial view of the overall quality of S, which also depends on the quality of the services used to resolve them. For example, in case of a completion time attribute, the corresponding $\mathbf{u}$ entry could represent the execution time in isolation of S internal code on the hosting node, without considering the completion time of the called services.
- $\mathbf{U}_t \subseteq \mathbb{R}^m$ is a vector of m "overall quality" attributes, which express the quality of the service S at time t, depending on both local quality of S and the quality of the services it is bound to to resolve its dependencies. We show below (see Eq. 1) how $\mathbf{U}_t$ is expressed in terms of both these factors.

At each time point $t \in \mathbb{N}$ a service is either *fully resolved* or *partially resolved*. A service S is *fully resolved* if either: (i) S has no dependencies ($S.Deps = \emptyset$); or (ii) for all $d \in S.Deps$ there exists a fully resolved service $S' \in S.In_t$ such that $d = S'.Type$. On the other hand, a *partially resolved* service S has a non empty list of dependencies, and at least one dependency is either not matched, or is matched by a partially resolved service.

Given these definitions, the overall quality for a service S is defined as follows:

$$\mathbf{U}_t(S) = \begin{cases} \mathbf{L}(\mathbf{u}(S), S.Out_t), & \text{if } S.Deps = \emptyset \\ \bot & \text{if } S \text{ is partially resolved} \\ \mathbf{C}\left(\mathbf{L}(\mathbf{u}(S), S.Out_t), \mathbf{U}_t(S_1), \ldots, \mathbf{U}_t(S_k)\right) \\ \quad \text{if } S \text{ fully resolved, with } S.In_t = \{S_1, \ldots, S_k\} \end{cases} \tag{1}$$

In Eq. (1) if S has no dependencies ($S.Deps = \emptyset$), then S is by definition fully resolved, and $\mathbf{U}_t(S)$ is calculated by means of a suitable function $\mathbf{L} : \mathbb{R}^m \times 2^{\mathbf{S}} \to \mathbb{R}^m$, which, given the local quality $\mathbf{u}(S)$ and the set $S.Out_t$ of services currently bound to S, returns the actual load-dependent $\mathbf{U}_t(S)$ at time t. In order to keep the model as general as possible, we use the set $S.Out_t$ to define the load-dependent nature of $\mathbf{L}$, without explicitly specifying information such as request rate and job size [12], which is application specific. However, $\mathbf{L}$ can be easily extended and instantiated to account for further specific information, without affecting our notion of overall quality. Instead, if S has a nonempty set of dependencies ($S.Deps \neq \emptyset$) and is not fully resolved, $\mathbf{U}_t(S)$ is set to $\bot$, i.e., the special value that is guaranteed to be "worse" than the quality of any fully resolved instance of S. Finally, if S has a nonempty set of dependencies and is fully resolved, $\mathbf{U}_t(S)$ is computed using a function $\mathbf{C} : \mathbb{R}^{(1+|S.In_t|)m} \to \mathbb{R}^m$, which combines the local load-dependent quality $\mathbf{L}(\mathbf{u}(S), S.Out_t)$ with the overall quality of all S dependencies. The general equation (1) can be instantiated for specific quality attributes as described, for example, in [1].

Problem formalization – Our goal is to maximize the quality globally delivered by the services hosted in the system, ensuring at the same time fairness among services. To this end, we must define our notion of global quality and fairness.

For the former, the vector $\mathbf{U}_t(S)$ details the overall quality delivered by a specific service S in terms of a set of distinct quality attributes. To facilitate dealing with multiple and possibly conflicting quality attributes, we transform $\mathbf{U}_t(S)$ into a single scalar value, using the Simple Additive Weighting (SAW) technique [18]. According to SAW, we redefine the service quality of S as a weighted sum of its normalized quality attributes, as follows:

$$GU_t(S) = \sum_{i=1}^{m} w_i \frac{V_i^{max} - U_{i,t}(S)}{U_{i,t}(S) - V_i^{min}} \tag{2}$$

where $U_{i,t}(S)$ denotes the i-th entry of $\mathbf{U}_t(S)$, V_i^{max} and V_i^{min} denote, respectively, the maximum and minimum value of $U_{i,t}$, and $w_i \geq 0$, $\sum_{i=1}^{m} w_i = 1$, are weights for the different quality attributes expressing their relative importance.

$$\xi_t = \frac{1}{|\mathbf{S}_t^{full}|} \sum_{S \in \mathbf{S}_t^{full}} GU_t(S) \tag{3} \qquad \zeta_t = \frac{(\sum\limits_{S \in \mathbf{S}_t^{full}} GU_t(S))^2}{|\mathbf{S}_t^{full}| \sum\limits_{S \in \mathbf{S}_t^{full}} GU_t(S)^2} \tag{4}$$

Now, let $\mathbf{S}_t^{full} \subseteq \mathbf{S}$ be the set of fully resolved services at time t. Equation 3 defines the *global system quality* as the average quality offered by services in $\mathbf{S}_t^{full}$. Furthermore, in order to measure the *uniformity of quality* delivered in the system, we make use of the *Jain's fairness index* [6], defined as in Eq. 4.

In our load-dependent setting, the more uniform is the quality, the more uniform the load distribution tends to be. Hence, our goal can be stated as the definition of a self-adaptive assembly procedure that: (i) maximizes ξ_t, thus optimizing *quality*, and (ii) maximizes ζ_t, thus optimizing *fairness*.

To this end, next section describes the system operations for service discovery and selection that drive the system towards the achievement of this goal.

4 System Operations

This section describes the implementation of the MAPE-K information sharing pattern that drives the self-adaptive assembly process, focusing in particular on the monitoring (Sect. 4.1), and analyzing and planning (Sect. 4.2) activities.

4.1 Gossip Based Monitoring

Algorithm 1 describes the general gossip-based scheme [7] that implements the monitoring activity (M). It includes two concurrent threads: an active thread that starts an interaction by sending a message to a random set of peers[1], and a passive thread that reacts to messages received from other peers.

Every Δt time units, the *active thread* reads monitored information I_K from the knowledge base (K) (line 4), and sends a message $\mathbf{m}$ containing I_K to the current *peer set* (line 6). Specifically, $I_K = Hosted \cup Known$ contains information

---

[1] Provided by an underlying peer sampling protocol, e.g. NEWSCAST [16].

Algorithm 1. Gossip based information sharing

```
 1: procedure ACTIVETHREAD
 2:     loop
 3:         Wait Δt
 4:         I_K ← READ_K()
 5:         for all S_i ∈ GETPEERS() do
 6:             SEND ⟨I_K⟩ to S_i
 7: procedure PASSIVETHREAD
 8:     loop
 9:         Wait for message ⟨m⟩
10:         for all S_i ∈ m do
11:             UPDATE_K(S_i)
12: function UPDATE_K(in S ∈ S)
13:     if ∃S̄ ∈ Hosted|S.Type ∈ S̄.Deps  then
14:         if |Known| < N_K then
15:             Known ← Known ∪ {S}
16:         else
17:             m ← min_j{GU_t(S_j) | S_j ∈ Known ∧ S_j.Type = S.Type}
18:             Known ← Known \ {S_m} ∪ {S}
```

about the set of services hosted locally and monitored by M, and the set of other known services discovered by means of message gossiping, respectively.

On the other hand, the *passive thread* listens for messages gossiped by other peers and, upon receiving a new message **m**, it invokes the function UPDATE_K() for each S_i contained in **m**. The function UPDATE_K() is in charge of updating the knowledge K with the received information. Indeed, referring to Algorithm 1, UPDATE_K() updates the set *Known* (stored in K) that collects the currently known N_K (or less) "best" services solving at least one dependency for the hosted services[2]. In particular, if the size of *Known* is exceeded, the S_j with the smallest $GU_t(S)$ (i.e., S_m) is replaced by the newly discovered $S_i \in$ **m**.

As a consequence, the total amount of exchanged information between a pair of peer nodes is upper bounded by $O(N_K \cdot |\text{GETPEERS}()|)$. This makes scalable the information sharing procedure, as its complexity at each round grows at most linearly with the number of nodes in the system, assuming that GETPEERS() returns a set of peers whose cardinality is independent of the system size.

4.2   TD-learning Based Analysis and Planning

As introduced in Sect. 2, the *analysis* and *planning* activities are locally implemented at each peer. The goal of these activities is to (i) analyze the information kept by the knowledge K (i.e., the set of service candidates *Known*), and (ii) select the services of interest that resolve the dependencies of local services (i.e., *Hosted*), trying to maximize the global system quality ξ_t and the fairness ζ_t.

Algorithm 2 outlines the *analysis* implementation. It consists of a thread that actively checks, every Δ_t time units, the knowledge K. Whenever the analysis performed by CHECK_K() notices a variation in K, then a new plan is required by calling SELECT_K() that implements the P activity.[3] SELECT_K() implements a

---

[2] The upper bound N_K is a system parameter.

[3] For the sake of simplicity, we omit the details of CHECK_K(), which strictly depends on the specific implementation of K.

Algorithm 2. TD-learning based analysis and planning

```
 1: procedure ACTIVETHREAD
 2:     loop
 3:         Wait Δt
 4:         b ← CHECK_K()
 5:         if b = true then
 6:             for all S_i ∈ Hosted do
 7:                 SELECT_K(S_i)
 8: function SELECT_K(inout S ∈ S)
 9:     for all d ∈ S.Deps do
10:         m ← arg max_j{H_t(S_j) | S_j ∈ Known ∧ S_j.Type = d}
11:         if (∃S_k ∈ S.In_t − S_k.Type = d) then
12:             if H_t(S_k) < H_t(S_m) then
13:                 S.In_t ← S.In_t \ {S_k} ∪ {S_m}
14:         else
15:             S.In_t ← S.In_t ∪ {S_m}
```

---

selection rule that, among the set of service candidates contained in K, properly chooses the set of services of interest that best achieve the goal stated in Sect. 3, as explained below.

The service selection rules are defined by means of a TD-learning method [15] that calculates, based on historical data, a *value function* that expresses how good a particular action is in a given situation. Indeed, *value functions* are used to properly select the action that provides the best possible *reward*, in a given situation. The general formulation of a TD method is:

$$E_t \leftarrow E_{t-1} + \alpha[R_t - E_{t-1}] \tag{5}$$

where E_t is the estimated value function at step t, $\alpha \in (0, 1]$ is the learning-rate parameter, R_t is the reward obtained by taking the action, and E_{t-1} is the value function calculated at the previous step – i.e., the *historical data*. In simple incremental averaging estimation methods [15], the learning-rate parameter α changes at every step and is calculated as $1/k$, where k is the number of accumulated rewards at step t.

Its rationale is to increasingly give more weight to the accumulated experience. TD methods are well suited in our context, since they can learn from raw experience, without relying on any predefined model of the environment. Indeed, the variability is faced on-line, in a fully incremental fashion. Specifically, we adopt a service selection rule implementing a *Two-layer* Hierarchical Reinforcement Learning (2HRL) [3] technique, which considers both data monitored locally, and data shared by the monitoring activities (M) of other peers.

Learning from local data – First layer aims at learning the behaviour of service candidates in $Known$ by relying on direct experience, without considering the information shared by other peers.

Let $GU_t^R(S_j)$ be the quality obtained while interacting with a given S_j at time t. This value is used to predict the quality $GU_{t+1}^E(S_j)$ expected from the same S_j at the next time step (i.e., at time $t + 1$). Specifically, at any given time t, the planning activity P calculates for all $S_j \in Known$, the expected quality $GU_t^E(S_j)$ by instantiating Eq. 5:

$$GU_t^E(S_j) = GU_{t-1}^E(S_j) + \alpha_j[GU_t^R(S_j) - GU_{t-1}^E(S_j)] \tag{6}$$

where $GU_t^E(S_j)$ is the estimated quality (i.e., value function) at time t, $\alpha_j \in (0, 1]$ is the learning-rate, $GU_t^R(S_j)$ is the quality (i.e., the reward) obtained by directly interacting with S_j at time t, and $GU_{t-1}^E(S_j)$ is the quality estimated at the previous step – i.e., the historical data.

As in Eq. 5, the learning-rate parameter α_j could be calculated as $\alpha_j \leftarrow 1/SR(S_j)$, where $SR(S_j)$ is the number of times that S_j has been invoked. However, while this averaging method is appropriate for stationary environments, it is not well suited for dealing with highly dynamic environments such as the one considered here. In fact, it would make the method not able to promptly react to sudden changes. In these cases, literature suggests to use a constant step-size parameter $\overline{\alpha}$ to be defined at design-time [15].

We introduce instead the notion of *learning-window*, i.e., a fixed time-window of size z, in which we apply TD technique. The idea is to subdivide the non-stationary problem into a set of smaller stationary problems, which can be solved by applying the averaging method. Indeed, calculating α_j as $\alpha_j \leftarrow 1/[SR(S_j) \bmod z]$ provides us with the flexibility of averaging methods while preventing long-past rewards to be overweighted.

Learning from shared data – Second layer aims at integrating into the learning process of each peer the information remotely monitored and shared by other peers. As described in Sect. 4.1, each M activity continuously monitors the local set of hosted services $Hosted$ and for each $S \in Hosted$, gossips every Δ_t information about it, e.g., $S.In_t$, $S.Out_t$, and $GU_t(S)$. However, since the gossip-based communication is epidemic, the data sent by a given peer p_i might be outdated when received by the other peers in the system. Indeed, monitored data is strongly time- and load-dependent (see Sect. 3), and might quickly change over time, due to highly dynamic changes occurring in the system. In this scenario, understanding how much the P activity of a peer can trust the received data is crucial for selecting the services $S_j \in Known$ that best fit the goal of maximizing ξ_t and ζ_t (see Sect. 3).

To this end, let $\mathbf{m}_{\overline{t}}$ be a message received by activity P at time $\overline{t} < t$, and let $GU_{\overline{t}}(S_j)$ be the quality advertised for each $S_j \in \mathbf{m}_{\overline{t}}$, i.e., $GU_{\overline{t}}(S_j)$ is the last quality value known for S_j. We estimate the *level of trust* $\tau_t(S_j)$ of the quality advertised by S_j by instantiating Eq. 5:

$$\tau_t(S_j) = \tau_{t-1}(S_j) + \alpha_j[F_t(S_j) - \tau_{t-1}(S_j)] \tag{7}$$

where $\tau_t(S_j)$ is the estimated *level of trust* (i.e., value function) at time t, $\alpha_j \in (0, 1]$ is the learning-rate calculated within the *learning-window*, and $F_t(S_j)$ (i.e., reward) measures how much accurate is the data received about S_j. Specifically, the *accuracy* is calculated as 1 minus the relative error between the value $\overline{GU}_t^R(S_j)$ at time t and the value $GU_{\overline{t}}(S_j)$ advertised at time $\overline{t}$:

$$F_t(S_j) = 1 - \frac{|\overline{GU}_t^R(S_j) - GU_{\overline{t}}(S_j)|}{|GU_{\overline{t}}(S_j)|} \tag{8}$$

where $\overline{GU}_t^R(S_j) = min(GU_t^R(S_j), GU_{\bar{t}}(S_j))$ is the normalized value of $GU_t^R(S_j)$, which forces $F_t(S_j) \in [0,1]$.

Finally, the two TD-learning layers are combined in a new function H that, given a service $S_j \in Known$, computes its expected quality at time t:

$$H_t(S_j) = \tau_t(S_j) \cdot GU_{\bar{t}}(S_j) + (1 - \tau_t(S_j)) \cdot GU_t^E(S_j) \tag{9}$$

Informally, if trust is high (i.e., $\tau_t(S_j) \approx 1$) then shared data $GU_{\bar{t}}(S_j)$ is considered highly relevant in the evaluation of S_j. Viceversa, whenever the trust in shared data is low (i.e., $\tau_t(S_j) \approx 0$), then local experience $GU_t^E(S_j)$ is considered more relevant than shared data for evaluating S_j.

Function $\textsc{Select}_K$ in Algorithm 2 shows how the 2HRL technique is used to build, for a given $S \in Hosted$, the set of bindings $S.In_t$ that achieves the global goal: maximizing ξ_t and ζ_t. The algorithm checks, for all dependences $d \in S.Deps$, what is the service $S_m \in Known$ that matches the dependency d and evaluates the maximum value of H_t (line 10). If a service S_k matching d is already in $S.In_t$, then S_m replaces S_k only if the former provides a better H_t than the latter (line 13). On the other hand, if $S.In_t$ does not contain any service matching d, then S_m is added to $S.In_t$ (line 15).

5   Experimental Evaluation

In this section we present a set of simulation experiments to assess the effectiveness of our approach. To this end, we implemented a large-scale simulation model for the PeerSim simulator [9]. PeerSim is a free Java package designed to efficiently simulate peer-to-peer protocols, which provides a cycle-based engine implementing a time-stepped simulation model. The cycle-based engine is well suited to evaluate peer-to-peer protocols, where the most important metric is the convergence speed measured as the number of rounds (message exchanges) that are needed to reach a desired configuration. Such a performance metric (number of interactions) has the advantage of being independent of the details of the underlying hardware and network infrastructure.

Model Parameters – We consider a system with N services and w different interface types $\mathbf{T} = \{T_1, \dots, T_w\}$. For the sake of simplicity, we assume that each network node hosts a single service; hence the number of nodes inside the network is equal to the number of services, i.e., N. We create $\lfloor N/w \rfloor$ services of each type and, for each service S we randomly set the number of its dependencies. Specifically, to avoid loops in the dependency graph, we allow a service S to only depend on services of type strictly greater than $S.Type$. Therefore, for each service S we initialize the dependency set

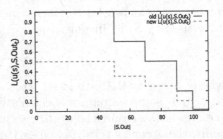

Fig. 1. Local quality functions

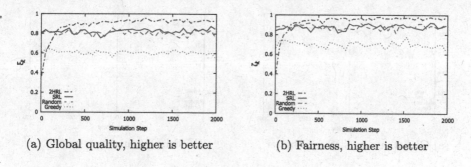

(a) Global quality, higher is better   (b) Fairness, higher is better

Fig. 2. Static scenario

$S.Deps$ as a random subset of $\{S.Type + 1, S.Type + 2, ..., w\}$. Note that, according to this rule, services of type T_w have no dependencies. Finally, we assume that the load-dependent quality function $L()$ (see Sec. 3) of each service S is defined by the solid line in Fig. 1, and the *global quality* $GU_t(S)$ is defined such that it returns values in the range $(0, 1]$. Furthermore, other parameters of our HRL approach are set as follows: (i) the learning-window parameter z is set to 5, and (ii) for all $S_i \in \mathbf{S}$ the initial trust $\tau_0(S_i)$ is set to 0.95.

Performance Measures – As stated in Sect. 3 we evaluate the performance of our approach by means of the *global system quality* ξ_t, and the *fairness* ζ_t. In particular, ξ_t is computed as the average quality of all fully resolved services at step t, and ζ_t is computed as Jain's fairness index. Both ξ_t and ζ_t are higher-is-better metrics whose upper-bound is 1. All experiments are run by considering $N = 1000$ services, $w = 10$ interface types, and 2000 simulation steps. All results are computed by taking the average of 50 independent simulation runs.

5.1 Simulation Results

Hereafter we report the simulation results obtained in different scenarios. To show the effectiveness of the proposed approach, we compare the results obtained by our approach with a set of state-of-the-art techniques based on different selection rules. Specifically, we experimented the following alternative selection rules: (i) a *Random* algorithm, which does not consider quality values but randomly selects, among the available services, those services that satisfy the required functional dependencies; (ii) a *Greedy* algorithm, which selects among the available services, those services with maximum quality; and (iii) a single-layer reinforcement learning (SRL) algorithm, which exploits past experience to predict the behavior of known services [12]. All the experiments show that our solution outperforms the results provided by these alternative selection rules.

Static scenario – This experiment considers a static scenario involving $N = 1000$ services of $w = 10$ different types. Figure 2 shows how ξ_t and ζ_t, calculated on the fully resolved assembly resulting from the application of different selection rules, vary in function of time t. In particular, it shows how our 2HRL approach

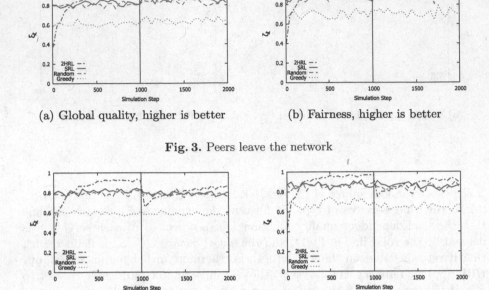

(a) Global quality, higher is better   (b) Fairness, higher is better

Fig. 3. Peers leave the network

(a) Global quality, higher is better   (b) Fairness, higher is better

Fig. 4. Peers join the network

outperforms other selection rules by building a fully-resolved assembly whose ξ_t and ζ_t tend to upper-bound (see Fig. 2a and b). Next experiments aim at assessing the ability of 2HRL to self-adapt to changes that might happen in the networking environment. Indeed, open-end collections of distributed peer-to-peer nodes are necessarily prone to failures since autonomous nodes might suddenly leave/join the network at any time, as well as change their local quality.

Peers leave the network – This experiment considers a dynamic scenario where a number of nodes unexpectedly leave the networking environment. In particular, starting from the previous experimental setting – i.e., $N = 1000$ services of $w = 10$ different interface types – we randomly remove 500 nodes after $t = 1000$ simulation steps. Figure 3 reports how the different selection rules react to the environmental change. In particular, it shows how the 2HRL selection rule allows services to promptly react and to self-organize into fully-resolved assemblies that improve the global system quality. In fact, drastically removing half of the services (i.e., from 1000 to 500) from the network reduces the total load in the network and makes the 2HRL converging towards an optimal configuration evaluating $\xi_t \approx 1$ (see Fig. 3a) and $\zeta_t \approx 1$ (see Fig. 3b).

Peers join the network – On the other hand, this experiment considers a dynamic scenario where a number of new nodes join the networking environment. In particular, starting from the initial experimental setting – i.e., $N = 1000$

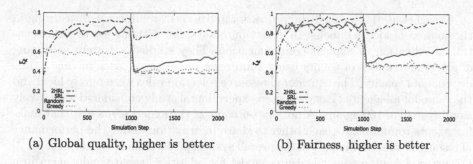

(a) Global quality, higher is better   (b) Fairness, higher is better

Fig. 5. Peers change the local quality function

services of $w = 10$ different interface types – we randomly add 500 new nodes
at simulation step $t = 1000$. Figure 4 reports how the different selection rules
react to the new environmental change. In this case, after an initial drop of ξ_t
at time step $t = 1000$ the 2HRL selection rule allows services to learn from the
new environment setting and to self-organize into fully-resolved assemblies that
gradually re-establish a good level of global quality (see Fig. 4a) and fairness
(see Fig. 4b). The initial drop of ξ_t at time step $t = 1000$ is mainly caused by
the fact that the trust value $\tau_0(S) = 0.95$ makes the algorithm to select newly
added services, which are evaluated better than the older ones. However, the
2HRL selection rule quickly learns from the new setting and converges towards
a new optimal configuration within a few steps. Setting the initial trust $\tau_0(S)$
to a lower value – e.g., $\tau_0(S) = 0.5$ – would mitigate such an issue by allowing
2HRL to behave more conservatively while evaluating new discovered services.

Peers change the local quality function – Finally, this experiment considers
a dynamic scenario where 500 randomly chosen services change at time step
$t = 1000$ their quality function $L(\mathbf{u}(S), S.Out_t)$, as depicted by the dashed line
in Fig. 1. Figure 5 reports how the different selection rules react to the new
setting. Also in this case, we can notice that after an initial drop of ξ_t at time
step $t = 1000$ the 2HRL selection rule allows services to quickly self-organize
into fully-resolved assemblies that re-establish good level of global quality (see
Fig. 5a) and fairness (see Fig. 5b).

6   Related Work

In this section we focus exclusively on approaches based on reinforcement learning. This methodology has been already used in literature to tackle service selection and load balancing problems [4,5,14,19]. Some of them (e.g.,[5,14]) are
based on the approach previously presented in [12]. All these papers consider
scenarios with a single type of dependency, and where the agents already know
the full set of available resources. On the contrary, we assume that each peer does
not know in advance the other peers (and the services they offer) in the environment, but discover them dynamically. Moreover, our services can have multiple
dependencies, and we consider multiple load-dependent quality attributes.

Shaerf et al. [12] studied the process of multi-agent reinforcement learning in the context of load balancing in a distributed system, without use of either central coordination or explicit communication. They studied a system consisting of a certain number of agents using a finite set of resources, each having a time dependent capacity. The considered resource selection rules were purely local and the same for all agents. The presented experimental study considered a relatively small system of 100 agents. A notable outcome of the experiments was that making agents communicate each other to share information about the performance of resources was detrimental to the overall system performance. Galstyan et al. [4] presented a reinforcement learning model for adaptive resource allocation in a multi-agent system. The learning scheme is based on minority games on networks. Each agent learns over time the best performing strategies and use them to select the resource to be used. Zhang et al. [19] propose a multi-agent learning algorithm and apply it for optimizing online resource allocation in cluster networks. The learning is distributed to each cluster, using local information only and without access to the global system reward. Sugawara et al. [14] investigate multi-agent systems where agents can't identify the states of all other agents to assign tasks. The selection is done according to local information about the other known agents; however this information is limited and may contain uncertainty. Parent et al. [10] apply reinforcement learning for the dynamic load balancing of parallel data-intensive applications. Viewing a parallel application as a one-state coordination game in the framework of multi-agent reinforcement learning they are able to improve the classic job farming approach.

7   Conclusion

In this paper we have presented a self-organizing fully decentralized approach for the dynamic assembly of services in distributed peer-to-peer scenarios, whose goal is to guarantee a good overall quality for the delivered services, ensuring at the same time fairness among the participating peers. The core element of the proposed solution is the combined use of gossip protocols and reinforcement learning techniques. Gossip supports the decentralized information dissemination and decision making, whereas reinforcement learning enables each peer to dynamically learn from its experience the service selection rule to be followed, thus overcoming the lack of global knowledge. Besides, we explicitly take into account load-dependent quality attributes, which leads to the definition of a service selection rule that drives the system away from overloading conditions that could adversely affect quality and fairness. Thanks to these features, the system is able to build and maintain in a fully decentralised way an assembly of services that, besides functional requirements, fulfils global QoS requirements. Moreover, a set of simulation experiments shows how our solution self-adapts to occurring variations and quickly converges to feasible assemblies, which maintains the specified quality and fairness objectives.

Future work encompasses the extension of the experimental part with the inclusion of different real-world scenarios and other possible definitions of fairness. We also intend to extend 2HRL to cyber-physical systems, where a new set of challenging quality concerns have to be managed under severe resource constraints, e.g., energy consumption, real-time responsiveness.

References

1. Caporuscio, M., Grassi, V., Marzolla, M., Mirandola, R.: GoPrime: a fully decentralized middleware for utility-aware service assembly. IEEE Trans. Softw. Eng. **42**(2), 136–152 (2016)
2. Cheng, B.H.C., et al.: 08031 - software engineering for self-adaptive systems: a research road map. In: Dagstuhl Seminar Proceedings Software Engineering for Self-Adaptive Systems, vol. 08031. IBFI (2008)
3. Erus, G., Polat, F.: A layered approach to learning coordination knowledge in multiagent environments. Appl. Intell. **27**(3), 249–267 (2007)
4. Galstyan, A., Kolar, S., Lerman, K.: Resource allocation games with changing resource capacities. In: Proceedings of the Second International Joint Conference on Autonomous Agents and Multiagent Systems AAMAS 2003, pp. 145–152 (2003)
5. Ghezzi, C., Motta, A., Panzica La Manna, V., Tamburrelli, G.: QoS driven dynamic binding in-the-many. In: Heineman, G.T., Kofron, J., Plasil, F. (eds.) QoSA 2010. LNCS, vol. 6093, pp. 68–83. Springer, Heidelberg (2010)
6. Jain, R.K., Chiu, D.M.W., Hawe, W.R.: A quantitative measure of fairness and discrimination for resource allocation in shared computer systems. Technical report DEC-TR-301, Digital Equipment Corporation, September 1984
7. Jelasity, M., Voulgaris, S., Guerraoui, R., Kermarrec, A.M., van Steen, M.: Gossip-based peer sampling. ACM Trans. Comput. Syst. **25**(3) (2007). Article No. 8
8. Jiang, L., Xu, G.: Modeling and analysis of software aging and software failure. J. Syst. Softw. **80**(4), 590–595 (2007)
9. Montresor, A., Jelasity, M.: PeerSim: a scalable P2P simulator. In: Proceedings of the 9th International Conference on Peer-to-Peer (P2P 2009), Seattle, WA, pp. 99–100, September 2009
10. Parent, J., Verbeeck, K., Lemeire, J., Nowe, A., Steenhaut, K., Dirkx, E.: Adaptive load balancing of parallel applications with multi-agent reinforcement learning on heterogeneous systems. Sci. Program. **12**(2), 71–79 (2004)
11. Paschalidis, I.C., Tsitsiklis, J.N.: Congestion-dependent pricing of network services. IEEE/ACM Trans. Netw. **8**(2), 171–184 (2000)
12. Schaerf, A., Shoham, Y., Tennenholtz, M.: Adaptive load balancing: a study in multi-agent learning. J. Artif. Intell. Res. **2**, 475–500 (1995)
13. Schuhmann, S., Herrmann, K., Rothermel, K., Boshmaf, Y.: Adaptive composition of distributed pervasive applications in heterogeneous environments. ACM Trans. Auton. Adapt. Syst. (TAAS) **8**(2), 10:1–10:21 (2013)
14. Sugawara, T., Fukuda, K., Hirotsu, T., Sato, S., Kurihara, S.: Adaptive agent selection in large-scale multi-agent systems. In: Yang, Q., Webb, G. (eds.) PRICAI 2006. LNCS (LNAI), vol. 4099, pp. 818–822. Springer, Heidelberg (2006)
15. Sutton, R.S., Barto, A.G.: Reinforcement Learning: An Introduction. MIT Press, Cambridge (1998)
16. Voulgaris, S., Jelasity, M., van Steen, M.: A robust and scalable peer-to-peer gossiping protocol. In: Moro, G., Sartori, C., Singh, M.P. (eds.) AP2PC 2003. LNCS (LNAI), vol. 2872, pp. 47–58. Springer, Heidelberg (2004)

17. Weyns, D., Schmerl, B., Grassi, V., Malek, S., Mirandola, R., Prehofer, C., Wuttke, J., Andersson, J., Giese, H., Göschka, K.M.: On patterns for decentralized control in self-adaptive systems. In: de Lemos, R., Giese, H., Müller, H.A., Shaw, M. (eds.) Software Engineering for Self-Adaptive Systems. LNCS, vol. 7475, pp. 76–107. Springer, Heidelberg (2013)
18. Yoon, K.P., Hwang, C.L.: Multiple Attribute Decision Making: An Introduction, vol. 104. Sage Publications, Thousand Oaks (1995)
19. Zhang, C., Lesser, V., Shenoy, P.: A multi-agent learning approach to online distributed resource allocation. In: Proceedings of Twenty-First International Joint Conference on Artificial Intelligence (IJCAI 2009), vol. 1, pp. 361–366 (2009)

Situation-Aware Execution and Dynamic Adaptation of Traditional Workflow Models

Kálmán Képes[1([⊠])], Uwe Breitenbücher[1], Santiago Gómez Sáez[1],
Jasmin Guth[1], Frank Leymann[1], and Matthias Wieland[2]

[1] Institute of Architecture of Application Systems,
University of Stuttgart, Stuttgart, Germany
kalman.kepes@iaas.uni-stuttgart.de
{breitenbucher,gomezsaez,guth,leymann}@informatik.uni-stuttgart.de
[2] Institute for Parallel and Distributed Systems,
University of Stuttgart, Stuttgart, Germany
wieland@informatik.uni-stuttgart.de

Abstract. The continuous growth of the Internet of Things together
with the complexity of modern information systems results in several
challenges for modeling, provisioning, executing, and maintaining systems that are capable of adapting themselves to changing situations in
dynamic environments. The properties of the workflow technology, such
as its recovery features, makes this technology suitable to be leveraged in
such environments. However, the realization of situation-aware mechanisms that dynamically adapt process executions to changing situations
is not trivial and error prone, since workflow modelers cannot reflect
all possibly occurring situations in complex environments in their workflow models. In this paper, we present a method and concepts to enable
modelers to create traditional, situation-independent workflow models
that are automatically transformed into situation-aware workflow models that cope with dynamic contextual situations. Our work builds upon
the usage of workflow fragments, which are dynamically selected during
runtime to cope with prevailing situations retrieved from low-level context sensor data. We validate the practical feasibility of our work by a
prototypical implementation of a Situation-aware Workflow Management
System (SaWMS) that supports the presented concepts.

Keywords: Workflow technology · Situation-aware workflow
execution · Workflow adaptation · Workflow transformation · Workflow
fragments

1 Introduction

The significant increase of devices with network capabilities allows the integration of such into large software systems, which enables paradigms such as the
Internet of Things [3]. One fundamental aspect of such a paradigm is the existence of multiple sensors that continuously emit data representing the context

© IFIP International Federation for Information Processing 2016
Published by Springer International Publishing Switzerland 2016. All Rights Reserved
M. Aiello et al. (Eds.): ESOCC 2016, LNCS 9846, pp. 69–83, 2016.
DOI: 10.1007/978-3-319-44482-6_5

of physical or virtual entities and running applications, e.g., temperature data of physical machines or the utilization of virtual machines that run software. Dynamic contextual changes have a severe impact on the application behavior, which must be able to cope with and to adapt themselves to different situations, e.g. opening or closing room windows to regulate its temperature. The existence of a wide spectrum of possibly occurring situations across different application domains, however, arises several challenges to developers regarding the tasks of designing, implementing, and provisioning all necessary software artifacts to realize complex processes that provide the required runtime flexibility.

The workflow technology enables the modeling and executing of process models that describe the desired behavior of information systems [15]. Workflow models typically comprise a set of interconnected activities that are executed by a runtime environment to achieve a business goal. However, these models are not situation-aware by nature. For example, the usage of standardized workflow languages, such as BPEL [18] or BPMN [19], requires the explicit modelling of every individual behavior to cope with each and every possible environmental change. If a workflow model describes the steps of a production process, and one machine of this process breaks during execution, the overall workflow must be adapted to achieve the business goal, e.g. by adding activities that repair the machine or move the process to another machine. Unfortunately, if all possibly occurring situations must be considered, this leads to several issues at both modeling and runtime levels, as (i) modeling all possibly occurring situations leads to extensive and complex workflow models that are hard to create and even harder to maintain. In addition, (ii) process modelers may not have the complete knowledge about all possibly arising situations, and (iii) most of the existing standard-compliant workflow engines are currently not capable of handling the dynamic nature of frequently changing situations. Moreover, using standard-compliant technologies to realize workflows that adapt themselves to changing situations is a non-trivial issue. In contrast, existing situation-aware workflow management systems often employ custom, non-standardized workflow languages, which reduces the portability of workflow models between different runtimes.

In this paper, we tackle these issues. We present the *ProSit Method* that enables creating traditional process models, which are then automatically transformed into situation-aware workflow models, which can be executed by any standard-compliant runtime environment without requiring an extension of the employed workflow system. This transformation is achieved by searching workflow fragments in the original process, replacing each of them by a single activity whose execution is handled by a situation-aware service bus that dynamically selects an appropriate fragment that provides the original functionality for the currently prevailing situation during runtime. This supports the creation of dynamic, self-adaptive processes using the standard-compliant workflow technology and reduces the required expertise regarding possibly occurring situations. Moreover, we present an architecture of a situation-aware workflow management system called *ProSit System*, and validate its practical feasibility by a prototypical implementation. Finally, we conduct a case study to evaluate the approach.

The remainder of this paper is structured as follows. In Sect. 2, we motivate our approach while Sect. 3 presents a life-cycle of situation-aware workflows and the overall method. The architecture and implementation of the *ProSit System* is introduced in Sect. 4, which is subsequently evaluated in Sect. 5 using a case study. Section 6 discusses related works, Sect. 7 concludes the paper.

2   Motivation and Background

The workflow technology has considerably influenced the development of software, as it allows the robust and reliable automation of business processes [15]. The foundations of this technology have contributed to the creation of several standards, such as BPEL and BPMN. Due to the standardization, these languages enable creating portable process models that can be executed by different standard-compliant runtimes, therefore avoiding vendor lock-in. However, these languages do not support an efficient means to handle changing situations and to model situation-aware behavior without polluting the respective models with extensive and heterogeneous situation handling logic.

Several works have targeted the workflow adaptation in supply chain and pervasive environments, e.g., [2,8,24]. More specifically, the enhancement of process models with context information and the usage of process fragments as a means to dynamically adapt workflows have been the major research contributions of these works. However, these approaches do not support the development of standard-compliant workflow models that automatically become situation-aware during their execution, which is the major research goal of the ProSit-Method. In addition, due to large amounts of sensors propagating low-level heterogeneous data, there is a need to integrate mechanisms for detecting aggregated high-level situations that provide well-defined semantics.

To overcome these issues, in the SitOPT project[1], we aim at providing a *Situation-aware workflow Management System (SaWMS)* capable of aggregating low level sensor data to high level situations and using these situations for dynamic workflow adaptation [25]. In the following, we describe the necessary concepts of this architecture that are required to understand the contributions of this paper. Figure 1 depicts the overall SitOPT architecture, consisting of three main layers: *Sensing Layer*, *Situation Recognition Layer*, and *Situation-aware Workflow Layer*. The Sensing Layer comprises the set of domain-specific sensors, which are basically responsible for reading context parameters and propagating data samples to the upper layers. The Situation Recognition layer filters, aggregates, and processes the contextual data retrieved from the different objects. The data aggregation and processing tasks are driven by the Situation Recognition middleware, which is mainly responsible for receiving the low level sensor data and mapping this data to high level situations. The existence of multiple *Sensor Adapters* enable the data processing and aggregation from different domain-specific sensors.

---

[1] https://www.ipvs.uni-stuttgart.de/abteilungen/as/forschung/projekte/SitOPT.

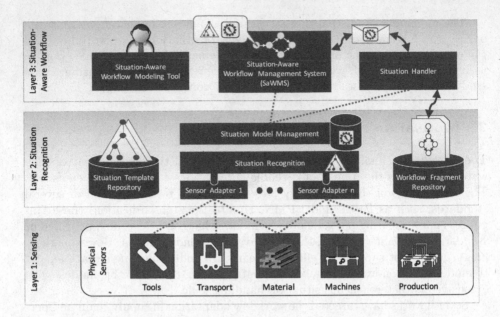

Fig. 1. Overview of the SitOPT architecture and its three layers [25]

The situation-aware workflow adaptation is handled by the SaWMS and the *Situation Handler*. The SaWMS is responsible for executing workflows and passing all service invocations to the Situation Handler, which mainly acts as a situation-aware service bus regarding the contributions of this paper. If a request is received by the Situation Handler, it selects an appropriate workflow fragment (stored in the *Workflow Fragment Repository*) that is capable of executing the requested operation in awareness of the currently prevailing situation. The *Situation-Aware Workflow Modeling Tool* supports creating workflow models by suggesting activities and operations, respectively, which can be adapted dynamically for different situations. In this paper, we extend the SaWMS by a method and concepts to enable automatically transforming traditional, situation-unaware workflow models in situation-aware models that are dynamically adapted using the Situation Handler.

3   Situation-Aware Execution of Workflow Models

As described in the previous sections, the current workflow technology is not situation-aware by nature. In this section, we (i) introduce a life-cycle for situation-aware workflows and (ii) present the ProSit-Method for the transformation of traditional workflow models into situation-aware workflows afterwards.

3.1   Situation-Aware Workflow Model Life-Cycle

In Fig. 2, we introduce a life-cycle encompassing the (i) modeling, (ii) provisioning, and (iii) execution of situation-aware workflows using workflow fragments as

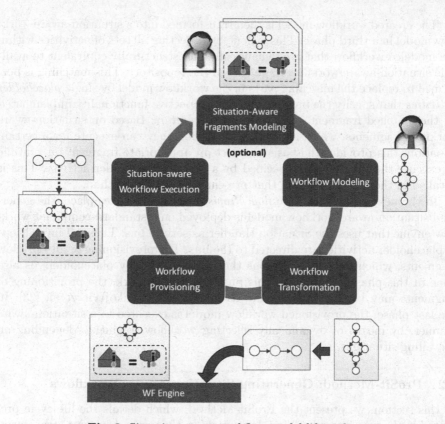

Fig. 2. Situation-aware workflow model life-cycle

the basis for the dynamic runtime adaptation. This life-cycle defines the context and basis for the ProSit-Method that is introduced in the next section.

In a first phase, situation-aware workflow fragment models that implement a certain action for a concrete situation are developed. For example, in the smart home domain, a fragment model is developed that can reduce the temperature in a room if the temperature outside the room is lower. Another fragment may implement the same action for another situation, e.g. for the situation that the temperature outside the room is higher. While the first fragment opens a window to reduce the temperature, the second activates the air conditioner. These fragment models are typically modeled by domain experts and can be used by different processes. However, their suitability differs depending on the prevailing situation. Since the repository of available generic situation-aware workflow fragment models grows over time, this first phase may be skipped if the modeler decides that the available fragments, i.e. the possible adaptations, are sufficient for the workflow to be created. Therefore, this phase is optional.

In a second phase, the workflow model is created, describing the set of activities that must be performed and the data flow between them. To increase the efficiency of modeling, and to avoid errors, available workflow fragments should be used since they have been developed by domain experts.

The created workflow model is then transformed into a situation-aware work-flow model in a third phase. This is done by detecting all sets of activities within the modeled workflow that are semantically and structurally equivalent to available situation-aware workflow fragments in the repository. This matching is performed to replace the matching parts in the workflow model by single *placeholder activities* that specify the invocation of the respective functionality implemented by the matched fragment, e.g., *Reduce Temperature*. Based on situation-aware workflow fragments, which all specify the action they can execute for a certain situation, this provides the basis to select an appropriate fragment on runtime to execute the functionality specified by a certain placeholder activity. This is detailed in the next subsection that presents the ProSit-Method.

In the next phase, the *Workflow Provisioning* phase takes place: the generated situation-aware workflow model is deployed on a standard-compliant work-flow engine that uses the Situation Handler as service bus. Thus, all invocations of placeholder activities are directed to the bus. The provisioning of all workflow fragments, which implement actions that are specified by placeholders, is also done in this phase. To improve this phase, in future work, the provisioning of fragments may be done on-demand, as presented by Vukojevic et al. [23]. In the last phase, the provisioned workflow model is executed in a situation-aware manner, by means of dynamically selecting workflow fragments depending on prevailing situations.

3.2   ProSit-Method: Generating Situation-Aware Workflows

In this section, we present the ProSit-Method, which details the life-cycle presented in the previous subsection. In particular, the method supports transforming traditional, situation-unaware workflow models into situation-aware work-flow models that contain placeholder activities for the invocation of actions that shall be dynamically adapted based on the prevailing situations. The method is depicted in Fig. 3 and consists of six steps that are presented in this section.

The first step of the method, *Workflow Modeling*, corresponds to the second phase in the life-cycle and, therefore, consists of modeling the desired workflow model. In this paper, we focus on imperative, graph-based workflow languages as described by Pichler et al. [20], e.g. using BPEL or BPMN. In the second step, the *Fragment Detection*, all available situation-aware workflow fragment models are structurally and semantically matched against the workflow model. More specifically, the main objective of this step is to detect *subworkflow models*, as defined in [14], that are equivalent to a certain workflow fragment model. Since every workflow fragment model describes (i) the action it implements as well as (ii) the situation for which it can be executed, this matching enables detecting the semantics of certain parts of the workflow model. For example, if the fragment matches the model that reduces the temperature of a room by opening the window, the action *Reduce Temperature* has been recognized. It is fundamental to denote that this step does not restrict the techniques to be used to determine neither the semantic nor the structural equivalence. For example, subgraph isomorphism algorithms can be used to match the control flows of the workflow model and workflow fragment model as well the respective

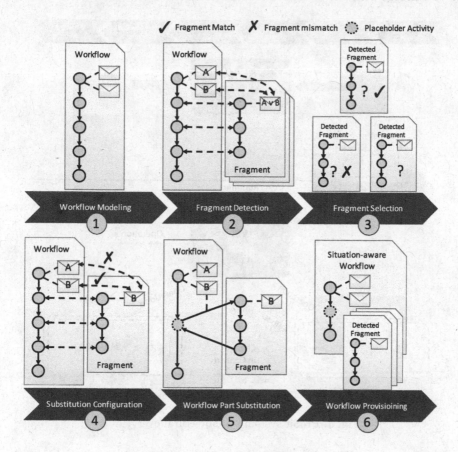

Fig. 3. The ProSit method

data flows [7]. The semantic equivalence of activities mainly depends on the domain and can be realized, for example, by matching the labels of activities. In our prototype, we defined equivalence rules and implemented the described matching for the language BPEL, (see Sect. 4). If the workflow modeling in the first step uses available fragments, the probability of finding matching fragments increases.

After detecting matching fragments in the workflow model, some of them may be overlapping. For resolving such overlaps, the *Fragment Selection* step enables to manually select the fragment that shall replace the placeholder activities. However, if the matching is unique or the selection shall be done by the system, a fully automated approach can be realized, too.

The *Substitution Configuration* step configures the data flow, if necessary. This step is required, if the data flow of the original workflow and the selected workflow fragment(s) do not uniquely match. More specifically, the matching among the workflow variables and the input and output messages of the workflow fragment is driven. If necessary, this step can also target the semantic checking among existing data variables in the original workflow and their equivalent

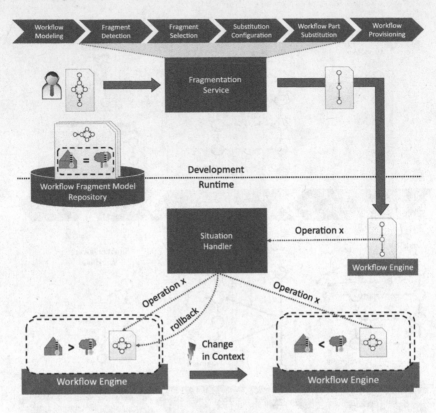

Fig. 4. ProSit system - architectural overview

variables in the workflow fragment model. After this step, it is ensured that the workflow model part to be replaced is matched by at least one proper fragment that is equivalent in control flow, data flow, and semantics.

Once the data flow compatibilities are resolved, the *Workflow Part Substitution* step replaces each matched part inside the workflow model with a single placeholder activity, therefore transforming the original workflow model into a situation-aware workflow model. The inserted activities are responsible for executing the specified action, e.g., *Reduce Temperature*, depending on the currently prevailing situation. Our architecture presented in the next section supports this by discovering and selecting appropriate workflow fragments for each placeholder activity and invoking them. Thus, the situation-aware placeholder activity prescribes the use of *late binding* [21], since the overall system provides a set of workflow fragments for which it is specified under which situations they are allowed to be executed. The ProSit method does not restrict on the mechanism and technological support for the execution of a placeholder activity, such as inside the running workflow instance itself, as presented in [8], or through an external service bus. However, the latter is realized in our architecture.

Finally, the situation-aware workflow model is provisioned. The provisioning mechanism is not restricted by the method, since it depends on the implementation.

4   Architecture and Realization

In this section, we present the conceptual architecture of the ProSit-System, which realizes the ProSit-Method and the introduced life-cycle. Figure 4 depicts the architecture. The system is tailored towards two main environments: *Development* and *Runtime*. In the *Development Environment*, the workflow model and workflow model fragment developers create the respective models. Workflow fragment models are persisted in the *Workflow Fragment Model Repository*, which persists a set of tuples, each one containing the (i) fragment model, (ii) deployment artifacts required for deploying and executing the model fragment, and (iii) the situation and goal descriptions that each workflow fragment model is adequate for.

The *Fragmentation Service* enables the transformation of standard-compliant, situation-unaware workflow models into fragmented situation-aware workflow model variants by means of performing matching operations of workflow fragment models in the traditional model, as described in the previous section. The output of the *Fragmentation Service* is a situation-aware workflow model containing concrete executable activities and situation-aware placeholder activities, which are later bound to a certain implementation during the execution phase, such as a workflow fragment model. Situation-aware workflow models are then provisioned on a standard-compliant workflow engine that is capable of executing workflow models specified in a standard workflow language. Since the original, traditional, workflow model has been transformed and changed in terms of replacing activities by placeholder activities, these placeholder activities need to be handled. In particular, this means that for each placeholder activity an invocation of the Situation Handler is defined. Thus, all actions that need to be executed are sent to this handler that is responsible for executing the specified action while monitoring the current prevailing situation. To serve such requests, the handler discovers and invokes an appropriate workflow model fragment, i.e., a fragment that is capable of executing the requested action and that specifies the current prevailing situation for such an action (see Fig. 4 *Operation X*). Thus, the Situation Handler acts as a *Situation-Aware Service Bus* that discovers appropriate services, which are implemented as workflow fragments, and handles the interconnection among them. To enable this, workflow fragments must be complete workflow models that can be executed standalone.

To allow the Situation Handler to find appropriate workflow fragments, these are registered in a repository. This repository contains the workflow fragment models including all meta-data, e.g., which action it implements for which situation, and *situational endpoints*, which are endpoints referencing already deployed fragments that can be invoked directly. Compensation tasks, e.g. due to failures, are also handled by the Situation Handler, by means of rolling back the execution of a workflow model fragment if the originally prevailing situation changes. In this case, a rollback message is sent to the endpoint and a new feasible endpoint is selected. Details about this rollback, as well as about the architecture and prototype of the described Situation Handler can be found in Fürst [6].

We implemented the presented architecture and matchmaking concepts in the scope of the SitOPT Workflow Management Environment [4, 10, 25].

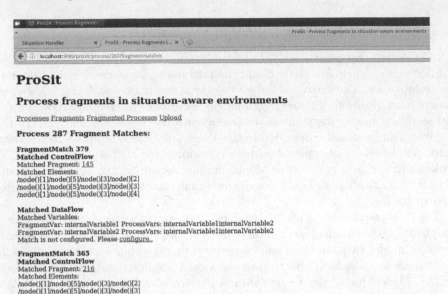

Fig. 5. ProSit component showing the matched fragments against a workflow model

With respect to the implementation of our approach, in the modeling environment, workflow developers use the Eclipse based BPEL Designer[2] for the modeling of workflow and workflow fragment models. For the persistence and discovery of workflow fragment models, i.e. for implementing the Workflow Fragment Model Repository shown in Fig. 4, we used the Fragmento repository presented by Schumm et al. [22]. In the scope of this paper, we implemented the ProSit Transformation Service as a RESTful API that allows to process BPEL workflow fragment models and BPEL workflow models. When BPEL workflows are processed, the matching against Single-Entry-Single-Exit-based fragments is started, where we use the library JGraphT [12] to transform these models into graph-representations for solving an subgraph isomorphism between the models. The results of each of the steps are stored as XML data inside the Fragmento repository to be accessable by external clients to additionally configure certain aspects, such as selection of fragments for replacement (see Fig. 5). Details about the mapping of control flow, data flow, and activity semantics regarding BPEL can be found in Képes [13]. The Situation Handler is developed as a RESTful service that allows adding situational endpoints and to register on occurrences of situations (see Fürst [6] for more information). Concrete situational endpoint data is persisted as interface descriptors according to the WSDL standard (see Fig. 6). The routing mechanism in the Situation Handler is handled through the Apache Camel [11].

---

[2] BPEL Designer: https://eclipse.org/bpel/.

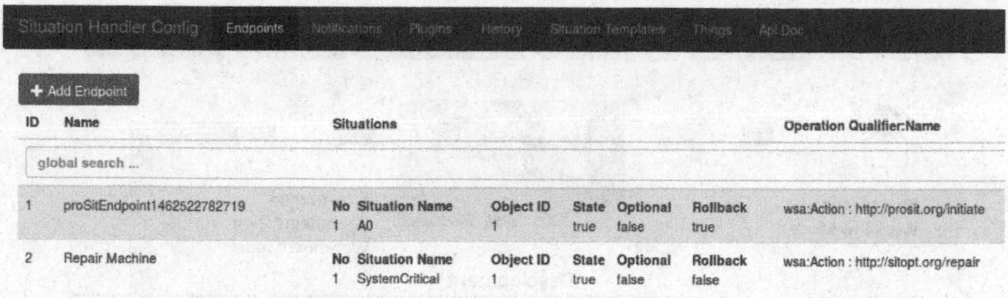

| Situation Handler Config | Endpoints | Notifications | Plugins | History | Situation Templates | Things | Api Doc |

+ Add Endpoint

ID	Name	Situations						Operation Qualifier:Name
	global search ...							
1	proSitEndpoint1462522782719	**No** **Situation Name** 1 A0	**Object ID** 1	**State** true	**Optional** false	**Rollback** true		wsa:Action : http://prosit.org/initiate
2	Repair Machine	**No** **Situation Name** 1 SystemCritical	**Object ID** 1	**State** true	**Optional** false	**Rollback** false		wsa:Action : http://sitopt.org/repair

Fig. 6. The situation handler web UI to add situational endpoints

5 Case Study

The evaluation of our approach has been performed by means of conducting a case study from the SitOPT project. More specifically, we implemented a room temperature regulation mechanism using situation-aware workflows as the basis, as depicted in Fig. 7. The evaluation presented in this section consists of (i) transforming a *RoomRegulation* workflow into a situation-aware workflow, by means of using the *Fragmentation Service*, and the *OpenWindow* and *RegulateClimate* fragments, which are subsequently (ii) provisioned, executed, and adapted using the standard-compliant workflow engine WSO2 BPS.

A first step in our validation consists of modeling a set of workflow fragment models, i.e. *OpenWindow* and *RegulateClimate*, which are two actions that can be performed to regulate a room's temperature. Subsequently, the modeling of the *RoomRegulation* workflow comprises the set of necessary tasks to regulate the temperature in a smart room. Subsequently to the modeling phase, the *Fragmentation Service* transforms the original *RoomRegulation* into a situation-aware workflow by substituting its logic with situation-aware placeholder activities (see step 2 in Fig. 7). This substitution is performed taking the potential situational workflow fragment models persisted in the Workflow Fragment Model Repository into consideration.

After the provisioning of the *RoomRegulation*, the execution phase takes place. When a variation of temperature in the room occurs, an instance of the *RoomRegulation* workflow invokes the operation *reduceTemperature* in the *Situation Handler* (see step 3 in Fig. 7), which determines the outside temperature by invoking the SitOPT situation recognition system *SitRS* [10]. This allows the Situation Handler to determine which workflow fragment to use for serving the original *reduceTemperature* request (see steps 4 and 5 in Fig. 7). In our scenario, the room temperature is lower than outside, so opening the windows won't suffice to achieve the goal of reducing temperature. Therefore, once a workflow fragment model is discovered, the *Situation Handler* selects the *RegulateClimate* fragment which activates the climate control to serve the *reduceTemperature* request. Once the temperature is regulated, the *RegulateClimate* continues its execution, potentially waiting until the temperature is stabilized.

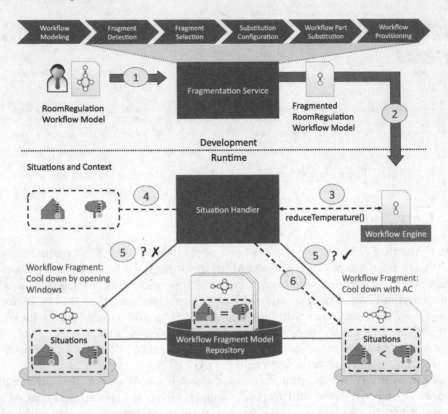

Fig. 7. Room temperature regulation case study

6 Related Work

This section presents related work in the domains of workflow flexibility, and context- and situation aware applications. Refinement of processes has been widely studied in other works. Context-aware process injection (CAPI) is introduced as a concept for the execution of process fragments during runtime [17], by means of enabling the design of processes that adapt themselves into specified process regions based on the actual context. Fragments are executed if a specified region of the process model is reached. Context-aware annotated fragments can be executed sequential or parallel, and once or multiple times. Although this approach represents a language extension, it is not standard compliant. Bucchiarone et al. [5] enable the usage of processes fragments to refine context-aware abstract activities, in order to react to contextual conditions. While this approach is highly flexible, it is neccessary to have detailed knowledge of the domain and processes running in it. Developers have to define entities with their possible states, fragments with annotated goals, preconditions, effects and compensation effects.

The concept of *Worklets* is introduced in [1], which partially or completely implements a context-aware process. A collection of subprocesses are conflated using *Ripple Down* rules, which evaluate activities and discover which *Worklet* matches to a specific context. While the approach is flexible in selecting work-flows (Worklets) when activating a task that needs to be substituted, it is missing changes at runtime of such workflows, e.g. the context changes and the activities in the substituting workflow isn't appropriate anymore. Aligned with such an approach, Wieland et al. introduce Context4BPEL, which consists of a language extension for BPEL 2.0 [24]. It focusses on precise context information, which are used for modelling within activities and control flow. Breitenbücher et al. intro-duce SitME, a concept that enables the modelling of situations on the workflow tier [4]. Within a start activity, a workflow can receive occurring situations to start the execution of a workflow. Additionally, *Situational Scopes* can be defined within a workflow, which can only be executed if specified situations prevail. The approach presented in [24] works on the workflow instance level. Therefore, intro-ducing an huge burden in performance when handling fine-grained sensor data inside the workflow engine. [4] transforms the defined situation-aware constructs to native elements of the target workflow language.

Modafferi et al. [16] introduce a concept for developing context-aware work-flows, by selecting alternative subprocesses based on context data. To react on changes within the context, the standard behavior of workflow engines, i.e., the rollback/compensation of activities, is used. Counteracting the expensive roll-back, Modafferi et al. define edges between subprocesses, which can be evalu-ated during runtime. If an edge is existent, the workflow engine can switch to the alternative subprocess without any rollback. Similar to the SitME concept, this approach represents a language extension. In González and Ortiz [9], the usage of a context-aware Enterprise Service Bus (ESB) is proposed to adapt service calls based on complex events. The main idea is that ESBs are responsi-ble for transforming, routing, etc. messages between participants in the system. González et al. define high-level situations based on CEP rules that when are processed by a *Context Reasoner* to adapt specific parts of the message.

7 Conclusion

The emergence of network-capable devices has raised a number of challenges in the last years related to how to aggregate and process massive amounts of data retrieved from multiple interconnected sensors, and react accordingly to envi-ronmental changes. Applications utilizing such devices must be context-aware by nature, and must provide agile and flexible mechanisms to react to different situations.

This work focuses on how to build and execute such applications using the well established workflow technology as the basis. As the workflow technology is not situation-aware by nature, we focus in this paper on enhancing such tech-nology to support the situation-aware adaptability features required by context-aware application systems. For such a purpose, a life-cycle for situation-aware workflows is firstly presented. The life-cycle phases related to the (i) transformation of traditional into situation-aware workflow models, and the (ii) execution of such situation-aware workflows, are covered by the ProSit method and architectural support. Situation-aware workflows can be generated by discovering, matching, and replacing workflow fragments in traditional workflow models. Situation-aware workflows can then be executed and adapted based on retrieved situations. The evaluation of our approach is performed in the scope of the SitOPT project, by means of using a smart home case study as the basis.

Future works are aligned with exploring the usage of workflow fragments of more complex shapes as the Single-Entry-Single-Exit, where only one start and end activity are specified. Moreover, we plan to evaluate our approach using further case studies in the IoT domain, as well as investigating the usage of our approach in Cloud scenarios, i.e. for the situation-aware management of Cloud resources.

Acknowledgments. This work is partially funded by the BMWi German Projects "SePiA.Pro" (01MD16013F) and "SmartOrchestra" (01MD16001F), and the DFG German Project "SitOPT" (610872).

References

1. Adams, M., ter Hofstede, A.H.M., Edmond, D., van der Aalst, W.M.P.: Worklets: a service-oriented implementation of dynamic flexibility in workflows. In: Meersman, R., Tari, Z. (eds.) OTM 2006. LNCS, vol. 4275, pp. 291–308. Springer, Heidelberg (2006)
2. Ardissono, L., Furnari, R., Goy, A., Petrone, G., Segnan, M.: Context-aware workflow management. In: Baresi, L., Fraternali, P., Houben, G.-J. (eds.) ICWE 2007. LNCS, vol. 4607, pp. 47–52. Springer, Heidelberg (2007)
3. Atzori, L., Iera, A., Morabito, G.: The internet of things: a survey. Comput. Netw. **54**(15), 2787–2805 (2010)
4. Breitenbücher, U., Hirmer, P., Képes, K., Kopp, O., Leymann, F., Wieland, M.: A situation-aware workflow modelling extension. In: Proceedings of iiWAS 2015, pp. 478–484. ACM (2015)
5. Bucchiarone, A., Marconi, A., Pistore, M., Raik, H.: Dynamic adaptation of fragment-based and context-aware business processes. In: Proceedings of the 19th International Conference on Web Services (ICWS), pp. 33–41. IEEE (2012)
6. Fürst, S.: Konzept und Implementierung eines Situation Handlers. Master thesis, University of Stuttgart, IAAS (2015)
7. Gallagher, B.: Matching structure and semantics: a survey on graph-based pattern matching. AAAI FS **6**, 45–53 (2006)
8. Gómez Sáez, S., Andrikopoulos, V., Hahn, M., Karastoyanova, D., Weiß, A.: Enabling reusable and adaptive modeling, provisioning & execution of BPEL processes. In: Proceedings of SOCA 2015. IEEE (2015)
9. González, L., Ortiz, G.: An event-driven integration platform for context-aware web services. J. UCS **20**(8), 1071–1088 (2014)
10. Hirmer, P., Wieland, M., Schwarz, H., Mitschang, B., Breitenbücher, U., Leymann, F.: SitRS - a situation recognition service based on modeling and executing situation templates. In: Proceedings of the 9th Symposium and Summer School On Service-Oriented Computing, pp. 113–127. IBM Research Report (2015)

11. Ibsen, C., Anstey, J.: Camel in Action, 1st edn. Manning Publications Co., Greenwich (2010)
12. JGraphT Team: JGraphT - a free Java Graph Library (2016). http://jgrapht.org/
13. Képes, K.: Erkennung und dynamische Ersetzung von Fragmenten in Workflow-Modellen. Master thesis, University of Stuttgart, IAAS (2016)
14. Kopp, O., Eberle, H., Leymann, F., Unger, T.: The subprocess spectrum. In: Proceedings of the Business Process and Services Computing Conference (BPSC 2010), vol. P-177, pp. 267–279. Gesellschaft für Informatik e.V. (GI) (2010)
15. Leymann, F., Roller, D.: Production Workflow: Concepts and Techniques. Prentice Hall PTR, Upper Saddle River (2000)
16. Modafferi, S., Benatallah, B., Casati, F., Pernici, B.: A methodology for designing and managing context-aware workflows. In: Krogstie, J., Kautz, K., Allen, D. (eds.) MOBIS'05. IFIP, vol. 191, pp. 91–106. Springer, New York (2005)
17. Mundbrod, N., Grambow, G., Kolb, J., Reichert, M.: Context-aware process injection: enhancing process flexibility by late extension of process instances. In: Debruyne, C., Panetto, H., Meersman, R., Dillon, T., Weichhart, G., An, Y., Ardagna, C.A. (eds.) OTM 2015. LNCS, vol. 9415, pp. 127–145. Springer, Heidelberg (2015)
18. OASIS: Web Services Business Process Execution Language (WS-BPEL) Version 2.0. Organization for the Advancement of Structured Information Standards (OASIS) (2007)
19. OMG: Business Process Model and Notation (BPMN) Version 2.0. Object Management Group (OMG) (2011)
20. Pichler, P., Weber, B., Zugal, S., Pinggera, J., Mendling, J., Reijers, H.A.: Imperative versus declarative process modeling languages: an empirical investigation. In: Daniel, F., Barkaoui, K., Dustdar, S. (eds.) BPM Workshops 2011, Part I. LNBIP, vol. 99, pp. 383–394. Springer, Heidelberg (2011)
21. Schonenberg, H., Mans, R., Russell, N., Mulyar, N., van der Aalst, W.: Process flexibility: a survey of contemporary approaches. In: Dietz, J.L.G., Albani, A., Barjis, J. (eds.) Advances in Enterprise Engineering I. LNBIP, vol. 10, pp. 16–30. Springer, Heidelberg (2008)
22. Schumm, D., Karastoyanova, D., Leymann, F., Strauch, S.: Fragmento: advanced process fragment library. In: Pokorny, J., Repa, V., Richta, K., Wojtkowski, W., Linger, H., Barry, C., Lang, M. (eds.) Information Systems Development, pp. 659–670. Springer, New York (2011)
23. Vukojevic-Haupt, K., Gómez Sáez, S., Haupt, F., Karastoyanova, D., Leymann, F.: A middleware-centric optimization approach for the automated provisioning of services in the cloud. In: Proceedings of CloudCom 2015, pp. 174–179. IEEE (2015)
24. Wieland, M., Kopp, O., Nicklas, D., Leymann, F.: Towards context-aware workflows. In: CAiSE 2007, pp. 577–591 (2007)
25. Wieland, M., Schwarz, H., Breitenbücher, U., Leymann, F.: Towards situation-aware adaptive workflows: SitOPT a general purpose situation-aware workflow management system. In: Proceedings of PerCom 2015, pp. 32–37. IEEE (2015)

SLA-Aware Services

Subsumption Reasoning for QoS-Based Service Matchmaking

Kyriakos Kritikos[(✉)] and Dimitris Plexousakis

ICS-FORTH, 70013 Heraklion, Greece
{kritikos,dp}@ics.forth.gr

Abstract. Service-orientation has revolutionized the way applications are constructed and provisioned. To this end, a proliferation of web services is being increasingly available. To exploit such services, an accurate service discovery process is required with a suitable performance focusing both on functional and quality of service (QoS) aspects. In fact, QoS is the main distinguishing factor for the plethora of functionally-equivalent services available in the internet. Accuracy in service discovery comes via exploiting formal techniques and ontologies in particular. Satisfactory performance levels can be reached via using smart methods that intelligently organise the service advertisement space. In this paper, we propose smart ontology-based QoS-aware service discovery algorithms that exploit ontology subsumption as a means of matching QoS requests and offers. These algorithms exploit a variety of methods to structure the service advertisement space. Based on the empirical evaluation conducted, our proposed algorithms outperform the state-of-the-art in certain circumstances. To this end, ontology-based subsumption is indeed a promising technique to realise QoS-based service matchmaking.

Keywords: Service · Matchmaking · Discovery · QoS · Ontology · Subsumption

1 Introduction

Service-orientation has revolutionized the way web applications and processes are constructed, provisioned and evolved. With the advent of cloud computing, which delivers extra advantages, a proliferation of available services has been achieved covering various types of functional capabilities. To exploit such services and rapidly build added-value functionality, there is a need for accurate and fast service discovery algorithms focusing both on functional and quality-of-service (QoS) aspects. The state-of-the-art in functional service discovery exploits either ontology-based [9], information retrieval [?] or a mixture of such techniques [7] to perform service matching. It has been proven that only when ontology-based techniques are involved [7], higher accuracy levels can be attained.

© IFIP International Federation for Information Processing 2016
Published by Springer International Publishing Switzerland 2016. All Rights Reserved
M. Aiello et al. (Eds.): ESOCC 2016, LNCS 9846, pp. 87–101, 2016.
DOI: 10.1007/978-3-319-44482-6_6

However, functional service discovery alone cannot enable the service designer to discover those services satisfying all requirement aspects. On the contrary, QoS has been deemed as the aspect enabling the differentiation between the plethora of functionally-equivalent services currently available. In fact, QoS can play a significant role in all phases of the service lifecycle [3]. To this end, various types of QoS-based service discovery approaches have been proposed. To increase the accuracy in the service discovery results, some of these types do exploit either ontology-based techniques [11] alone or constraint solving techniques as well [5]. Those approaches exploiting solely ontology-based techniques use ontology-based subsumption to perform the matching but have relied on wrong ontology constructs to specify QoS-based service specifications. As such, their applicability is quite limited. On the other hand, mixed-based approaches have a wider applicability and have been shown to exhibit much better performance.

In this paper, we propose a pure ontology-based approach which exploits ontologies in a correct way via more suitable constructs enhancing the respective applicability. In addition, we propose smart algorithms which intelligently organise the service offer space so as to perform service matchmaking via ontology subsumption on a subset of all offers. By considering the two main disadvantages of a mixed-based approach which are the ontology to constraint specification transformation and the solving of multiple constraint models to infer the matching between a pair of a service QoS offer and demand, our empirical evaluation shows that our proposed algorithms outperform mixed-based state-of-the-art ones in certain circumstances. This is a proof that ontology subsumption alone can be considered as a promising technique for QoS-based service matchmaking.

The rest of the paper is structured as follows. Section 2 reviews the related work. Section 3 provides background knowledge enabling to better understand the paper propositions. Section 4 analyses the proposed approach and the algorithms realising it. Section 5 discusses the experimental evaluation results. Finally, Sect. 6 concludes the paper and draws further research directions.

2   Related Work

2.1   QoS-Based Service Description

A plethora of languages have been proposed for describing QoS-based offers and requests. According to the survey in [3], these languages can be distinguished according to their formality, expressiveness and complexity. From these languages, OWL-Q [4], a modular and semantic-based service description language, seems to be the most promising, especially in terms of expressiveness as it covers in a rich manner all possible aspects of QoS-based service description. Based on OWL-Q, a mid-level ontology is available which provides a common vocabulary of QoS terms which can be used to populate QoS-based service specifications, such as domain-independent QoS attributes and metrics (e.g., *response time*). Due to the above unique advantages, the approach proposed in this paper exploits OWL-Q along with its mid-level ontology.

2.2   QoS-Based Service Discovery

Various QoS-based service matchmaking approaches have been proposed that can be categorised in three main types. Ontology-based approaches [11] rely on ontology subsumption to perform the service specification matching. These approaches are able to support only unary-based service specifications, i.e., involving one QoS term per constraint (QoS capability or requirement). Constraint-based approaches [1] assume the existence of a common QoS term vocabulary through which constraint models can be specified mapping to the actual service QoS offers and requests. Then, they exploit constraint solving techniques and specific matchmaking metrics to perform the matching of the constraint models. In comparison to ontology-based approaches, constraint-based ones operate over n-ary specifications and have a much better performance. Finally, mixed based approaches [5] attempt to exploit the best of both worlds. This means that they operate over semantic QoS specifications by first aligning them according to their QoS terms and then transforming them into constraint models which can then be matched based on the second type of approaches. In comparison to the former two types, this type can operate on n-ary specifications, it exhibits better accuracy levels due to the alignment of the specifications that goes beyond using subsumption reasoning and exhibits almost equivalent performance levels with respect to the constraint-based approach type.

Apart from the above approach categorisation, recently some new mixed approaches [6] have been proposed able to speed up the service matching time by cleverly organising the QoS service offer space. These approaches create a QoS offers subsumption hierarchy. As such, when a QoS request subsumes a hierarchy node, it subsumes all its descendants. Thus, these descendants do not have to be matched with the QoS request and matching time gets reduced.

The approach proposed in this paper belongs to the first type. As such, it suffers from the disadvantage of handling only unary constraints. However, this disadvantage is not crucial as most, if not all, of existing QoS service specifications in the real world are unary. Moreover, to speed up the matchmaking time, we propose different algorithms which attempt to similarly organise the offer space as in the recent approaches. In this way, we do not only reduce the matchmaking time but are able to outperform these recent approaches in certain cases for the following two reasons: (a) our approach does not require transforming ontology-based QoS specifications to a different form and (b) ontology subsumption can be faster than constraint-based matching even for a pair of a QoS offer and demand due to the way constraint matching metrics are realised. Thus, the use of pure ontology-based approaches in QoS-based service matching is not only feasible but also quite practical in certain cases. We believe that the prospective practitioners will benefit from the proposal and findings of this paper.

3   Background

In this section, we first explain why the current realisation of the pure ontology-based approach type is not appropriate and what is our proposal for solving

(A) Offer in QRL	(B) Offer in DAML-QoS	(C) Offer in OWL-Q

using QoS;
 	
guarantees{
AvgRtTime>=2 and
        AvgRtTime<=10;
ATHR>=100 and ATHR<=120
}
	Advert ≡ QoSProfile
	n (≤10responseTime.AVGRespTMetric)
	n (≥2responseTime.AVGRespTMetric)
	n (≥100throughput.AVGThrMetric)
	n (≤ 120throughput.AVGThrMetric)
		Advert ≡ Specification and (hasTerm
		some
		(MeanResponseTime and (value some
		int[>= "2"^^int, <= "10"^^int]))) and
		(hasTerm some
		(MeanThroughput and (value some
		int[>= "100"^^int, <= "120"^^int])))

	Advert ≡ Specification and (hasTerm some (MeanResponseTime and (value some int[<= "-2"^^int, >= "-10"^^int]))) and (hasTerm some (MeanThroughput and (value some int[>= "100"^^int, <= "120"^^int]))) (D) Offer in OWL-Q (with negate)	

Fig. 1. The example QoS offer in different forms

this issue. Then, we highlight what is the process for adding and matching QoS offers for both ontology-based approach types as this paper focuses on their comparison.

3.1 Realisation Issues

Suppose we have the example QoS offer in Fig. 1A in QRL [1]-like syntax indicating that *average response time* will be less or equal to 10 and greater than 2 seconds while *average throughput* will be between 100 and 120 requests per second inclusive. In the pure ontology-based approach type, the two metrics will originate from a mid-level ontology specifying domain-independent QoS terms. Indeed, this is the case of the approach in [11] which maps both metrics to sub-classes of *CompositeMetric*, thus connecting the upper-level ontology proposed to the mid-level one. However, the latter approach will then rely on a misuse of OWL cardinality constraints to specify the constraints of the specifications as indicated in Fig. 1B. In particular, it will indicate that the cardinality of the value-based properties (e.g., *responseTime*) of these metrics will be in accordance to the ranges in Fig. 1A. This wrong QoS constraint modelling has two main disadvantages: (a) only a specific type of QoS terms can be addressed mapping to non-negative integers – as such, terms like availability cannot be catered as their value types map to real numbers; (b) this modelling can also lead to an error that is at maximum one-half of the QoS term unit. Apart from the wrong modelling, the respective QoS ontology language exploited is quite limited with respect to the capabilities and richness of OWL-Q.

The above modelling issue is solved via the rationale in Fig. 1C. While there are again terms mapping to a composite metric class, we actually restrict the range of the *value* datatype property for them based on the desired limits. As such, we can model different value types for these terms; either concrete XSD[1] types (e.g., *integer*) or specialisations of them (e.g., constrained integers). By also exploiting OWL-Q, our QoS modelling is correct, richer and more extensive.

---

[1] http://www.w3.org/TR/xmlschema11-1/.

using QoS;
 	
quarantees{
AvgRtTime>=1 and
    AvgExTime<=12;
ATHR>=80 and ATHR<=140
}
 	
(A) Demand in QRL
	Advert ≡ Specification and (hasTerm some
	(MeanResponseTime and (value some int{<= "-1"^^int, >= "-12"^^int}))) and
	(hasTerm some
	(MeanThroughput and (value some int{>= "80"^^int, <= "140"^^int})))
	
	(B) Demand in OWL-Q (with negate)
		using QoS;
		
		quarantees{
		X₁>=2 and X₁ <=10;
		X₂>=100 and X₂ <=120;
		X₁ <1
		}
		
		(C) 1ˢᵗ Constraint Problem

using QoS;
 	
quarantees{
X₁>=2 and X₁<=10;
X₂>=100 and X₂<=120;
X₁>12
}
 	
(D) 2ⁿᵈ Constraint Problem
	using QoS;
	
	quarantees{
	X₁>=2 and X₁<=10;
	X₂>=100 and X₂<=120;
	X₂<80
	}
	
	(E) 3ʳᵈ Constraint Problem
		using QoS;
		
		quarantees{
		X₁>=2 and X₁<=10;
		X₂>=100 and X₂<=120;
		X₂>140
		}
		
		(F) 4ᵗʰ Constraint Problem

Fig. 2. The QoS demand and the 4 matchmaking problems

However, there is still a specific issue. Subsumption reasoning caters mainly for positively monotonic QoS terms. This can be understood from the example QoS demand in Fig. 2B which needs to be matched with the aforementioned QoS offer. While it is apparent that the QoS offer is more specific than the QoS demand and there is a match, the *average response time* is a negatively monotonic metric. As such, any ontology reasoner will never infer that the QoS offer is subsumed by the QoS demand.

The solution to this problem is to negate the constraints on negatively monotonic metrics. This is equivalent to considering a new, positively monotonic term equal to the negation of the original term. In this way, both the QoS offer and demand will be expressed as in Figs. 1D and 2B and their matching will be derived through an ontology reasoner, like Pellet[2] [8]. This treatment of QoS specifications has the following alternative concequences: (a) either the modeller should specify the QoS constraints as well as the QoS terms in the newly prescribed way taking special case on negatively monotonic terms or (b) the respective tools enabling the editing of the QoS specifications should be realised to transform internally the modeller constraints in the appropriate format or pre-processing of QoS specification via transformation tools is performed before the actual registration or matching of the specification is performed.

3.2   Ontology-Based QoS Specification Management Process

In a pure ontology-based approach, the QoS offer management process is quite simple. The existence of a semantic repository is assumed where the support for a specific ontology language like OWL is offered. Obviously, on top of OWL, a QoS-based service description language like OWL-Q lies via which the offers are actually specified. As indicated in [6], a mixed-based approach requires a QoS term (needed for their alignment) and a constraint model repository. As such, extra storage requirements are imposed.

---

[2] https://github.com/Complexible/pellet/.

QoS Offer Registration. In an ontology-based approach, QoS offers to be registered are first loaded in order to check whether they are consistent. This maps to creating a small knowledge base (KB) out of this offer and checking if this KB is consistent by evaluating whether any concept is subsumed by OWL *Nothing.* In a mixed-based approach, apart from consistency checking, the ontology needs first to be realised and validated and then to be transformed into a constraint model. Thus, it is expected that the offer registration time is faster in an ontology-based approach.

By considering the previous sub-section's example, the mixed-based approach will map the QoS offer in Fig. 1B into a constraint model similar to that of Fig. 1A where each unique QoS term will be mapped to a specific variable.

QoS Request Matching. A QoS request passes the same sub-process when issued as it must be checked for consistency. Then, it must be matched with all the QoS offers stored in the respective repository. In the pure ontology-based approach, the QoS request is entered into the existing KB and then classification is performed such that all subsumption relations are discovered between this request and all QoS specifications. As such, the QoS request is matched with all QoS offers that it subsumes. Please note that matchmaking as conformance or subsumption is the main matching metric in all approach types.

For the rest of the approach types, there is a matching of two constraint models mapping to the QoS request and offer when the solution space of the latter is included in the solution space of the former. This is translated in solving one or more constraint problems depending on the constraint arity of the QoS specifications. In case of unary constraints, specification conformance maps to checking M (mapping to the offer's number of constraints) constraint problems constructed by the offer's constraint model and a negation of each demand's constraint. If all problems are infeasible, then there is a match between the QoS offer and request. In case of n-ary constraints, only one constraint problem needs to be solved constructed from the QoS offer and the negation of the QoS demand. A match is inferred if the latter problem is infeasible. In the first case, more steps must be performed with respect to the pure ontology-based approach whose timing depends on the number of constraints involved. In the second case, one complicated step is performed but has no counterpart in the pure ontology-based approach as the latter can address unary constraints only.

In a mixed-based approach, the QoS request of the previous subsection will be first mapped to the constraint model in Fig. 2D. Then, four constraint problems need to be solved as depicted in Figs. 2C and F.

4   Proposed Approach

4.1   Architecture

Figure 3 depicts the proposed approach architecture by visualising both the respective components and their interactions. There are five main components involved. The *Semantic Repository* is an ontology-based repository able to store all QoS offers. The *Matcher* is a web service (WS) taking as input a QoS request

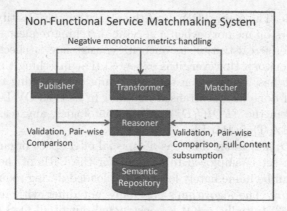

Fig. 3. Non-functional service matchmaking system architecture

which is then matched with all QoS offers stored. This WS internally realises one or more matching algorithms so it can be configured to operate based on one of them. The *Publisher* is also a WS enabling service providers to publish their QoS offers in the semantic QoS-based matchmaking system. Similarly to *Matcher*, it can be configured to operate a specific (de-)publication algorithm mapping to the approach followed for matchmaking. Both the *Publisher* and *Matcher* exploit two other components: (a) the *Transformer* which loads the specification and then transforms the constraints for negatively-monotonic terms, when users do not model them as expected; (b) the *Reasoner* which performs different types of tasks: (a) ontology-based specification validation, (b) pair-wise specification comparison and (c) (incremental) subsumption over full repository content. Invalid specifications are returned back to their issuers with a suitable error message.

The semantic QoS-based matchmaking system currently operates solely on OWL-Q based specifications. In the future, it will include extra transformation functionality to support original specifications in different QoS-based service specification languages which will be injected in the *Transformer*'s existing capabilities. Distribution of content will also be examined to cater for better scalability levels. Due to the nature of the proposed algorithms, such distribution is quite easy and natural to realise without any implication on algorithm accuracy.

4.2   Algorithms

In the following, we are going to analyse the four main algorithms that we have realised and are included in the capabilities of the *Matcher* component. We focus on the two main processes supported: *QoS offer registration* and *QoS request matching*. For each algorithm, the presentation starts with the main rationale, it then explicates the way the offer space is organised, next the algorithm core is analyzed and finally its complexity analysis is supplied.

Naive. *Rationale.* The main rationale of the algorithm, also justifying its name, is to load all offers on memory when a specific matching request is issued. This facilitates an offer's registration as once its consistency is checked, it is just stored in the repository. However, it is expected that matching time will not be appropriate as it has been proven that subsumption reasoning does not scale well, especially if done in a centralised manner. In fact, as OWL-Q along with its mid-level lies in the *SROIQ(D)* family of ontologies, any reasoning task is decidable but NExpTime-Hard.

Offer Space Organisation. There is no special offer space organisation. Only one specific hash set is employed to account for the URIs of the offers stored such that they can be immediately located and loaded during request matching.

Algorithm Core. The algorithm's core does not differ with respect to that sketched in Sect. 3. Initially, a KB is constructed out of all QoS offers and the QoS request and then classification is performed. Finally, a query on the KB is performed to obtain all offers subsumed by the request.

Complexity Analysis. Suppose that a specification usually has 4–5 QoS terms and 4–5 constraints on them, all wrapped into a single class definition. As such, we expect that the specification loading time will be more or less constant and equal to L_{spec}. Thus, the time needed to check the request's consistency (similar as loading) as well as construct a KB out of N offers and 1 QoS request will be $O(L_{spec} * (N + 2))$. If we further assume that the time to classify $N + 1$ specifications is S_{N+1}, such that the classification depends on the specification number, the overall matching time would be $O(L_{spec} * (N + 1)) + S_{N+1}$. We expect that usually $O(S_{N+1})$ takes much longer than $O(L_{spec} * (N + 2))$, especially when the specification number becomes bigger, so we will have a final complexity of $O(S_{N+1})$ for matchmaking. Offer registration, on the other hand, takes $O(N * L_{spec})$ time as each offer is just loaded and checked for consistency.

Incremental. *Rationale.* The naive approach does not incrementally build the KB but constructs it on demand. As such, as incremental classifiers are available, it might be better to employ incremental classification to save time when classifying a temporal extension of the KB encompassing the request.

Offer Space Organisation. The previous algorithm's hash set is preserved to account for the offers already stored. KB is the other organisation medium constantly updated. The classification tree constructed contains all possible subsumption connections between the specifications involved.

Algorithm Core. During offer registration we discovered that it is a little bit costly to run classification each time an offer must be registered. As such, we run classification only every X offers, where X is a configuration parameter for the algorithm. In each registration, the offer is loaded, checked for consistency and then stored in the KB.

For request matching, after consistency checking, we temporarily include the request in the KB and then we perform incremental classification. We then query the KB to find the offers subsumed by the request.

Complexity Analysis. Suppose that S_X^Y is the incremental classification time when X specifications are added to the KB and Y specifications are already loaded. Then, the offer registration time for N offers will be $O\left(L_{spec} * N + \sum_{Y=1}^{N} {}^X_{X} S_X^{Y*X}\right)$.

On the other hand, the request matching time will take at most $O\left(L_{spec} + S_1^N\right)$ as we will have to check the request consistency and incrementally classify only the temporal addition of the request in the existing KB.

Subsumes. *Rationale.* As a naive approach does not scale well in practice and driven by the fact that even the incremental algorithm might also exhibit similar performance problems, we decided to rely on the method in the *SubMIPMM* algorithm [6] and create our own subsumes offer hierarchy to be matched against any issuing request. In such hierarchy, if the request subsumes a node, then it also subsumes its descendants so some comparisons are avoided.

Offer Space Organisation. We do not construct a complete subsumes hierarchy as this requires connecting a new offer to all parents that subsume it and the registration time would be highly increased. The main trick as followed in [6] is to connect the offer to the first tree in the hierarchy forest in which it is matched.

Algorithm Core. The registration process is simple. We first match the new offer with all hierarchy's top offers. In case of a match, we check subsumption direction. If the new offer subsumes one or more top nodes, it becomes a top node itself and the matched nodes its children. If the offer is subsumed by one or more top nodes, we take the first one and check where to place the new offer in its own tree. So, the same matching procedure is followed until either the new offer subsumes some nodes in the selected tree or becomes this tree's leaf.

Concerning request matching, we match the request with all top-nodes in the subsumption hierarchy. In case the request subsumes a top-most node, we add this node along with its descendants in the matching offers set. Otherwise, we need to go down a top-most node's subtree similarly to the way top-matching is performed to find matching offers. The latter is due to the fact even if the request does not match the top-node, as we descend the tree, the offers becomes stricter with a smaller solution space and thus the probability that they finally match the request becomes higher.

For both processes, if pair-wise subsumption reasoning takes less than pair-wise constraint-based matching, this algorithm will be faster than *SubMIPMM*.

Complexity Analysis. Concerning offer registration, we need first to check offer consistency. Then, different cases can occur. In the best case, the offer is equivalent to the first top-most node so we do not need to check anything else. The time complexity will then become: $O\left(L_{spec} + S_2\right)$. In the worst case, the hierarchy maps to a tree and we have to put the new offer as a child of the rightmost leaf node. This means that we will have to compare the new offer with all offers stored. In this case, the time complexity is $O\left(L_{spec} + N * S_2\right)$ which can be reduced to $O\left(N * S_2\right)$. In the average case, B trees more or less balanced will exist and the time complexity will become: $O\left(L_{spec} + \frac{N+B^2}{2*B} * S_2\right)$ which can be reduced to $O\left(\frac{N+B^2}{2*B} * S_2\right)$.

Different cases map to request matching. The best one occurs when the hierarchy maps to a tree and the request subsumes the root node. The time complexity will be: $O\left(L_{spec} + S_2\right)$. The worst case occurs when the request must be compared with all tree nodes (as it does not subsume any offer or just the rightmost leaf one). The time complexity will be: $O\left(L_{spec} + N * S_2\right)$ which can be reduced to $O\left(N * S_2\right)$. In the average case, we assume that P offers will be subsumed and that there will be at least a two-level hierarchy between the subsumed offers. As such, the time complexity will be $O\left(L_{spec} + N * \left(1 - \frac{P}{2}\right) * S_2\right)$ which is reduced to $O\left(N * \left(1 - \frac{P}{2}\right) * S_2\right)$.

SubsumesFrag. *Rationale.* The previous algorithm constructed the hierarchy in an incremental manner and used ontology-based reasoning only when pair-wise comparisons of specifications were performed. As many pair-wise comparisons may have to be made, the current algorithm's rationale is to construct a bigger KB involving C specifications and not just 2 as we expect that this will take less time than having to reason over $C - 1$ KBs of size 2 (if we assume that always the first specification is constant, i.e., the request). Moreover, we use incremental classification to construct the offer hierarchy as this might be deemed better than having to construct this hierarchy in a pair-wise manner. As such, we expect that this algorithm will be faster than the previous one.

Algorithm Core. In offer registration, for each X offers stored, we perform incremental classification over the KB and store the classification hierarchy in main memory. Rationale is again that it is better to incrementally do this every time a specific number of incoming offers is issued rather than running incremental classification on-demand for each incoming offer to be registered.

Matchmaking follows a similar rationale as in the previous algorithm. The sole exception lies on the fact that now the classification is more complete but also contains new offers (less than X) that have not yet been classified and are considered top-nodes. Due to the classification completeness, we also need to keep track of the nodes visited so as not to revisit them again. The matching process starts by matching the top-nodes in the classification hierarchy in chunks of C nodes each time (see *Rationale* paragraph). If a top-node is subsumed, we do not follow its descendants but just add them in the matching offers set. We also mark this node and its descendants as visited. Otherwise, we need to go down the top-node's tree to find matches again similarly to top-node matching.

Complexity Analysis. Offer registration is equivalent to the case of the incremental classification algorithm. Thus, its time complexity is: $O\left(L_{spec} * N + \sum_{Y=1}^{\frac{N}{X}} S_X^{Y*X}\right)$.

Request matching has 3 cases. In the best case, the request matches a left top-node in the 1st subsumption chunk taking: $O\left(L_{spec} + S_C\right)$. In the worst case, we must match the request with all nodes. This takes $O\left(L_{spec} + \frac{N}{C} * S_C\right)$, further reduced to $O\left(\frac{N}{C} * S_C\right)$. In the average case, we make the same assumptions as in previous algorithm. The time complexity is: $O\left(L_{spec} + \frac{N*\left(1-\frac{P}{2}\right)}{C} * S_C\right)$, further reduced to $O\left(\frac{N*\left(1-\frac{P}{2}\right)}{C} * S_C\right)$.

5   Experimental Evaluation

The experimental evaluation aims at comparing the proposed algorithms with the *subMIPMM* mixed-based one to identify cases that these algorithms prevail. This evaluation relied on the experimental framework in [6]. It also exploits the second real dataset from WS-Dream collection [10] and one randomly constructed in a controlled manner. The main comparison metric is average execution time for both registration and matchmaking. Accuracy has not been considered as all algorithms are perfect in this aspect [6] by completely realising the matchmaking metric of specification conformance [1]. In the following, we first shortly explain the way experiments have been performed and then present each experiment's results along with their respective analysis.

Please note that Pellet was used for ontology subsumption in the algorithms while the Ibex constraint solving framework (www.ibex-lib.org/) was exploited for constraint matching in *SubMIPMM*.

5.1   Experiment Set-Up

All experiments were performed in a laptop with a 64bit OS, a 6GB main memory and a multicore CPU of 2.4 GHz frequency. For each experiment, we have conducted a series of steps to produce the respective average measurements of the algorithms considered. Each step maps to specific fixed or dynamic values of the control parameters and a series of 30 runs from which the average was calculated in order to alleviate for interferences at the OS level.

Real or randomised input was used in the experiments. In case of WS-Dream dataset, depending on the offer number (given as a control parameter value), we randomly selected an equal number of measurements from around 4500 available ones which were transformed into respective ontology-based offers mapping to the two main terms exploited, i.e., *response time* and *throughput*. The corresponding request was randomly selected again from the 4500 measurements. In case of the randomised dataset, the offers were randomly created based on current values of the control parameters. More details about this can be found in [6]. The respective randomised request was constructed again based on the control parameter values so as to match a specific percentage of offers.

5.2   1st Experiment

In this experiment, we exploited the randomised dataset and considered that half of the offers will be matched by each request issued. The number of offers was linearly increasing from 40 to 640 with a step of 100. The respective experiment results are visualised in Figs. 4a and b.

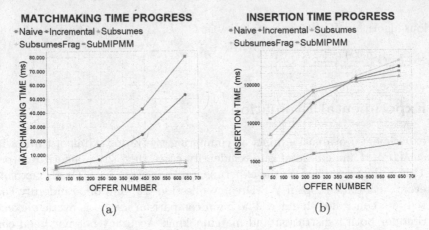

Fig. 4. (a) shows matching time results for 1st experiment while (b) shows registration time results for 1st experiment

Concerning matching time, it is clear that *SubMIPMM* algorithm is the best, followed by *Subsumes*. *SubsumesFrag* comes next while in the end we have *Incremental* and *Naive*. These matchmaking results were not expected especially between the two ontology-based subsumes algorithms while *SubMIPMM* prevailance possibly indicates that there is a bound in the variable number always leading to constraint-based matchmaking being faster than ontology subsumption. Please note that there is a speedup with respect to incremental reasoning which is not great as the removal of a previous request and the addition of a new one (based on the way the experiment was conducted) in the existing KB requires performing subsumption over a great number of offers.

Concerning registration time, it was obvious that *Naive* will be the best while *subMIPMM* the last. However, the second expectation was not realised as there is a specific breakpoint in *SubsumesFrag* performance because incremental reasoning is not efficient due to the nature of specifications and subsumption's exponential complexity. The order change between *Subsumes* and *SubMIPMM* is due to the fact that the latter performs two (complex) constraint solvings per comparison in registration in contrast to just one for matchmaking while obviously the former performs just one classification per comparison constantly.

5.3   2nd Experiment

In this experiment, we exploited again the randomised dataset with almost similar control parameter values but: (a) the offer number is now constant (300) and (b) we linearly increase the QoS term number in the specifications from 10 to 60 with a step of 10. Our main goal is to show that as the QoS term number increases, the constraint number in each QoS specification also increases; as such the number of constraint problems to be solved by *subMIPMM* also increases. In this sense, we expect that there will be a specific bound on the

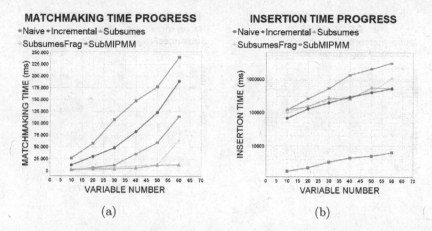

Fig. 5. (a) shows matching time results for 2nd experiment while (b) shows registration time results for 2nd experiment

QoS term number beyond which subsumption reasoning will be quicker than pair-wise constraint-based matching. Figure 5 shows the experiment results.

Concerning matching time, the results are in accordance to the previous experiment ones for the same initial variable number. However, as soon as the variable number goes to 20, we clearly see that *SubMIPMM*'s performance gets worse and less than that of the ontology-based subsumes algorithms whose performance order is not altered throughout the experiment. The order between *Naive* and *Incremental* is also not altered with respect to the previous experiment, something quite expected.

Concerning registration time, it is clear that *SubMIPMM* is the worst algorithm as it has to increasingly solve a much higher number of constraint problems per offer registration when the number of QoS variables and respective constraints increases. The order between the two ontology-based subsumes algorithms is almost the same which is evident also by the theoretical complexity analysis. As in the previous experiment, the order and performance of the rest of the ontology-based algorithms is not modified.

5.4 3rd Experiment

In this experiment, we exploit the real dataset and increase the offer number from 100 to 600. So, similar settings as in 1st experiment apply with two exceptions: (a) the QoS term number is 2 and not 10; (b) it is expected that the QoS offer number to be matched is small and thus much more work is expected for all subsumes-based algorithms. The main goal is to stress-test the algorithms in real situations and inspect whether the last algorithm can outperform the rest as it will have to perform less subsumption checking pieces of work. Figures 6a and b visualise the respective results.

Concerning matching time, the results validate the complexity analysis as all subsumes algorithms exhibit a linear behaviour while the rest an exponential one.

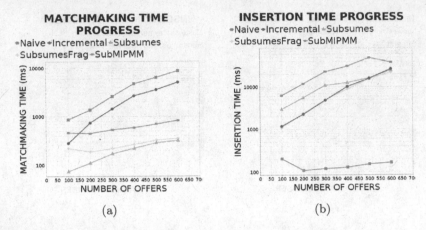

Fig. 6. (a) shows matching time results for 3rd experiment while (b) shows registration time results for 3rd experiment

We also see a difference with respect to the 1st experiment results as a much better algorithm performance is exhibited. This can be possibly due to the fact that the variable number is less so each matchmaking piece of work takes less time. In addition, we now see that *SubMIPMM* is worse than the ontology-based approaches from which *Subsumes* is still the best.

Concerning registration time, the results are expected based on our assumptions as *SubsumesFrag* is the best among all subsumes algorithms followed by *Subsumes* and then *SubMIPMM*. The behaviour of *SubsumesFrag* and *Incremental* coincides, as expected. Obviously, the *Naive* algorithm has constantly the best performance in all experiments according to this aspect.

Two main derivations must be highlighted from the above results: (a) a smart ontology-based approach can outperform a constraint-based one under real circumstances and (b) *Subsumes* seems to be the best algorithm in the long run for both registration and matchmaking – this can be seen from the breakpoint at 500 in the x-axis for registration beyond which this algorithm is better than *SubsumesFrag*. The latter also reveals the main weakness of even an incremental reasoner due to the nature of the specifications that it has to address and the exponential complexity in subsumption.

6 Conclusions

This paper has presented a pure ontology-based approach in QoS-based service matchmaking. This approach is realised by a naive and two clever algorithms which intelligently organise the service advertisement space. The latter two algorithms significantly outperfom the naive one in matching time and even compete with recent state-of-the-art QoS-based service matching algorithms. This is clearly shown in the randomised and realistic experimental evaluation where the cases in which our novel algorithms prevail are detected. Based on our propositions and findings, we showcase that a pure ontology-based approach when assorted with smart algorithms and techniques can really compete with other QoS-based service matching approach types. So, we provide guidance to practitioners under which circumstances an ontology-based approach can be exploited.

Concerning future work, the following directions are planned. First, further investigation of new algorithms which more cleverly organise the advertisement space. Second, checking the modification of the normal subsumption reasoning process in order to cater for: (a) not requiring the modification of negatively monotonic QoS terms to positive ones and (b) for more cleverly matching QoS-based service specifications. Third, performing a more thorough evaluation with the state-of-the-art to detect additional cases where a pure ontology-based approach should be recommended. Fourth, coupling the novel approach proposed with a semantic functional matchmaker in order to realise a complete ontology-based service discovery system. Such coupling could also lead to cleverly and concurrently organising and matching the offer space according to both specification aspects to further speed up the overall matchmaking time.

Acknowledgments. This research has received funding from the European Community's Framework Programme for Research and Innovation HORIZON 2020 (ICT-07-2014) under grant agreement number 644690 (CloudSocket).

References

1. Cortés, A.R., Martín-Díaz, O., Toro, A.D., Toro, M.: Improving the automatic procurement of web services using constraint programming. Int. J. Coop. Inf. Syst. **14**(4), 439–468 (2005)
2. Dong, X., Halevy, A., Madhavan, J., Nemes, E., Zhang, J.: Similarity search for web services. In: VLDB 2004: Proceedings of the Thirtieth International Conference on Very Large Data Bases, Toronto, Canada, pp. 372–383. VLDB Endowment (2004)
3. Kritikos, K., Pernici, B., Plebani, P., Cappiello, C., Comuzzi, M., Benbernou, S., Brandic, I., Kertész, A., Parkin, M., Carro, M.: A survey on service quality description. ACM Comput. Surv. **46**(1), 1 (2013)
4. Kritikos, K., Plexousakis, D.: Semantic QoS metric matching. In: ECOWS, pp. 265–274. IEEE Computer Society (2006)
5. Kritikos, K., Plexousakis, D.: Requirements for QoS-based web service description and discovery. IEEE Trans. Serv. Comput. **2**(4), 320–337 (2009)
6. Kritikos, K., Plexousakis, D.: Novel optimal and scalable nonfunctional service matchmaking techniques. IEEE Trans. Serv. Comput. **7**(4), 614–627 (2014)
7. Plebani, P., Pernici, B.: URBE: web service retrieval based on similarity evaluation. IEEE Trans. Knowl. Data Eng. **21**(11), 1629–1642 (2009)
8. Sirin, E., Parsia, B., Grau, B.C., Kalyanpur, A., Katz, Y.: Pellet: a practical OWL-DL reasoner. J. Web Sem. **5**(2), 51–53 (2007)
9. Sycara, K.P., Paolucci, M., Soudry, J., Srinivasan, N.: Dynamic discovery and coordination of agent-based semantic web services. IEEE Internet Comput. **8**(3), 66–73 (2004)
10. Zhang, Y., Zheng, Z., Lyu, M.R.: WSPred: a time aware personalized QoS prediction framework for web services. In: ISSRE (2011)
11. Zhou, C., Chia, L.T., Lee, B.S.: DAML-QoS ontology for web services. In: ICWS, p. 472. IEEE Computer Society (2004)

Towards Combined Functional
and Non-functional Semantic Service Discovery

Kyriakos Kritikos[✉] and Dimitris Plexousakis

ICS-FORTH, 70013 Heraklion, Greece
{kritikos,dp}@ics.forth.gr

Abstract. Service-orientation is increasingly adopted by application
and service developers, leading to a plethora of services becoming increasingly available. To enable constructing applications from such services,
respective service description and discovery must be supported by considering both functional and non-functional aspects as they play a significant role in the service management lifecycle. However, research in service
discovery has mainly focused on one aspect and not both of them. As
such, this paper investigates the issues involved in considering both functional and non-functional aspects in service discovery. In particular, it
proposes different ways via which aspect-specific algorithms can be combined to generate a complete service discovery system. It also proposes
a specific unified service discovery architecture. Finally, it evaluates the
proposed algorithms' performance to give valuable insights to the reader.

Keywords: Service · Discovery · Matchmaking · Semantics · Ontology · Performance · Evaluation · Functional · Non-functional · QoS ·
Architecture

1 Introduction

Nowadays, modern applications and business processes adopt service-orientation
due to the many advantages it delivers, including loose coupling, re-usability,
increased performance and cost reduction. To construct such applications, the
services from which they are built need to be described appropriately, discovered
and finally composed. Concerning service discovery, the state-of-the-art can be
split into approaches that either focus on functional or non-functional aspects.

Functional service discovery work [8] matches user's functional requirements by exploiting various types of techniques from information retrieval and
the semantic web [9,16]. Functional requirements and capabilities are mainly
described via service IO while some work [7] covers behavioral aspects via service
preconditions and effects which are however not available in real service advertise-
ments. Most work nowadays exploits semantic techniques to exhibit better accuracy levels and other techniques to achieve performance speedup. However, the
discovery accuracy is imperfect due to non-consideration of behavioural aspects.

© IFIP International Federation for Information Processing 2016
Published by Springer International Publishing Switzerland 2016. All Rights Reserved
M. Aiello et al. (Eds.): ESOCC 2016, LNCS 9846, pp. 102–117, 2016.
DOI: 10.1007/978-3-319-44482-6_7

Non-functional service discovery work [10] can be split into three main categories. Ontology-based approaches [19] employ subsumption techniques to infer the matching between ontology-based non-functional service descriptions but are suitable for unary-constrained specifications. Constraint-based approaches [5] exploit n-ary specifications as models, including quality terms drawn from common vocabularies, and particular metrics which involve solving one or more constraint (combined) models to infer the matchmaking. Mixed approaches [10] combine the best of both worlds by exploiting ontology-based specifications to cover the non-functional semantics and align the quality terms involved as well as the metrics in the previous approach type to perform the service matchmaking.

While each aspect is more or less well covered in literature, very few approaches [2,6] deal with both aspects concurrently. Such approaches, however, do not adopt the best possible algorithm for each aspect, do not capture service semantics, and do not have a suitable performance and accuracy level. Moreover, they have not explored the possible ways the two different types of matching can be best combined to infer the best possible one. In fact, most of these approaches employ a simplistic approach to account for non-functional user requirements and preferences which will never be adopted by respective practitioners.

As such, this paper first proposes a unified architecture explicating how different-aspect algorithms can be integrated to support a complete service discovery process by also accommodating for semantics capturing. Then, the paper proposes different combinations of aspect-specific algorithms attempting to accelerate the overall matching performance by not compromising discovery accuracy. Some combinations might be naturally applied and easily realised while others attempt to intelligently organise the service advertisement space to reduce the matchmaking time. These combined algorithms are finally evaluated by a semi-randomised framework according to their performance so as to provide particular insights on which is the preferred one in different circumstances.

The rest of the paper is structured as follows. Section 2 reviews the related work. Section 3 presents the unified architecture. Section 4 analyses the proposed combined' algorithms. Section 5 presents the performance evaluation results. Finally, Sect. 6 concludes the paper and draws directions for further research.

2   Related Work

As we focus on combined service discovery, we only consider combined approaches. For aspect-based discovery analysis, the reader can refer to [8,10].

QoS Ranking. By reviewing related work, it seems that most approaches [12–14] first functionally match the service request and then rank the respective matches based on the user's non-functional preferences. Non-functional ranking usually relies on considering utility functions that depend on the respective quality term monotonicity while the overall rank is produced via a weighted sum of the application of the utility functions over the match's promised quality term values. Based on the above, it seems that all such approaches neglect the fact that a user may pose non-functional requirements which must be respected such that the functional matches are further filtered before they are ranked.

The approach in [14] caters for ontology encoding and fast reasoning issues. It attempts to smartly organise the functional advertisement space by exploiting two advertisement relations that seem to map to well-known functional degrees of match. However, the second relation seems not to be suitable based on the formal notion of subsumption. After cleverly matching a request, the functional matches produced are just ranked based on their non-functional degree of match.

The sequential approach in [13] starts by discovering services that functionally match the request and have an appropriate distance from the user to minimise network latency. Then, the expected execution time of each matched service is computed based on performance ratings which is finally exploited to rank the matched services and select the top one for dynamic adaptation reasons.

QoS Threshold-Based Filtering. A small improvement over the previous category comes via threshold-based filtering of functional matches [6,15]. However, it is questionnable whether a simple threshold can be enough to respect the semantics of all non-functional requirements posed. It rather seems as a trial-and-error approach towards attempting not to overwhelm users with irrelevant results not satisfying their non-functional requirements. What makes the approach in [6] more interesting with respect to the rest in this category is that it attempts to enable a unified semantic service description and considers various types of information to infer the ranking, including QoS, business policies and context.

Combined. [2] proposes a sequential combined algorithm coupled with service ranking based on non-functional preferences. This algorithm actually resembles *SeqOnTheFly* (see Sect. 4) as it attempts to match on the fly each functional result with the user's non-functional requirements. However, this work is not assorted with specification validation mechanisms and does not employ specification alignment, thus relying on a common quality term vocabulary. It does not also check how sequential matching can be enhanced for better performance.

In [3], a three step discovery process is proposed. First, functional matching is performed by exploiting subsumption hierarchy and predicate-based inferencing. Second, functional matches are clustered based on QoS via the average linkage clustering and squared Euclidian distance metrics. Third, the best cluster's matches are ranked based on each match's distance from the cluster centroid. This approach is regarded as combined as it performs a kind of filtering on the functional match space. However, it is questionnable whether such a filtering is suitable if we also consider performance aspects. In addition, semantics for QoS terms are neglected. Functional matching seems also to be wrongly performed.

3   Architecture

Figure 1 depicts the architecture of a complete and unified service discovery system by also showing the interactions between the respective components and their ordering in terms of basic discovery system operations. The architecture

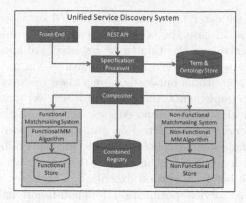

Fig. 1. The architecture of the unified service discovery system

comprises 10 main components: 2 constitute entry points, 4 map to the main discovery logic and 4 relate to the respective individual and combined registries.

Front-end is the first entry point, a web-based UI interacting with a human user, either a service provider or requester. It visualises information assisting the respective interaction, such as forms to specify functional and non-functional requests or to enable providers to upload, register or update service descriptions.

The *REST-API* is a service-based component enabling programmatic interaction with automated agents acting on behalf of users. It exposes the functionality expected in a service discovery system, like registering, updating and matching service specifications. It also offers utilities that validate the specifications before being registered. Service provider-related functionalities are only available to registered users, while discovery ones are publicly available with additional features only offered to registered users, like the ability to retrieve all matchmaking results and provide customised algorithms for service selection.

Once one operation starts execution, the respective specifications are passed to *Specification Processor* which loads and processes them to check their syntactic and semantic validity as well as to align them if they refer to equivalent but differently described terms. Constraint-based consistency is also checked for non-functional specifications. In case of a validation error, an error message is relayed to the user. Otherwise, operation passes to the core discovery component, the *Compositor*. Specification alignment is performed by consulting a *Term and Ontology Store* which includes a common set of basic terms via which alignment can be rapidly performed (see [10]) as well as the domain ontologies encountered.

Compositor realises the composition logic with respect to the individual aspect-specific algorithms exploited. It also guarantees the consistency of the information being registered in these algorithms. This is achieved via the *Combined Registry* storing the mappings between functional and non-functional specifications of service providers. This integration approach enables decoupling the aspect-specific discovery functionality and independence from any service specification language. Language adoption is coupled with selecting an aspect-specific algorithm. As such, we cater for using either unified or aspect-specific service description languages. In case the latter language type is used, consistency is maintained via the entries of the *Combined Registry*. We aim at semantic languages for which any service profile kind is identified via a *URI*. This enables using only semantic algorithms but leads to increased discovery accuracy.

The *Compositor* implements the combined service matching logic with respect to the main algorithms proposed (see Sect. 4). It also guarantees the transactionality of service (de-)registration and update operations. This means that if an operation fails when executed via a specific aspect-specific sub-system, and is successful with respect to the other sub-system, we have to roll-back to the previous state before operation execution. The latter maps, e.g., to de-registering a functional service specification if its non-functional counterpart fails to be registered. This transactionality type is enabled by realistically assuming that each respective aspect-specific sub-system provides aspect-specific operations that return either boolean values indicating the operation outcome (e.g., non-registration as functional service specification already exists) or exceptions when errors occur. The respective suite of functionally-equivalent service operations is obviously already available in each aspect-specific system.

Each aspect-specific sub-system should provide an entry point via which aspect-specific interactions can be performed (either a programmatic REST-API or a specific component). For the two main aspects, we name the respective components as *Functional Service Discovery* and *Non-Functional Service Discovery*. We do not unveil their structure as it can be specific to the sub-system selected. We just unveil that each sub-system logically has a (functional / non-functional) store in which aspect-specific service specifications are stored.

Concerning implementation details, all system code was realised in Java as it is the main implementation language for almost all matchmakers. *Front-End* implementation is on-going while the *REST-API* was realised via Jersey. The *Specification Processor* exploits different loading and validation techniques. The Pellet reasoner [17] is exploited for ontology-based loading and consistency checking. The Ibex (www.ibex-lib.org) finite constraint and Choco (http://www.choco-solver.org/) constraint programming solvers are exploited for constraint-based consistency checking. The *Combined Registry* is a serialisable Java object which exposes different methods related to manipulating aspect-specific specifications (e.g., registering a functional and non-functional service URI pair or an additional non-functional profile for an existing service).

Alive Matchmaker [4] was selected as a state-of-the-art functional matching sub-system which exhibits high performance levels due to applying smart structures via which the matching of semantic I/O concepts can be performed while also catering for domain ontology evolution. The *Unary* algorithm of the discovery system in [10] was selected for hybrid non-functional service matching as it is scalable, exhibits high performance levels and has perfect accuracy.

4   Algorithm Analysis

Combining aspect-oriented matching algorithms was explored under different criteria. The first one concerns the expected way to combine two functionalities, where two possible ways exist: (a) each functionality is performed in sequence or (b) both functionalities are executed in parallel and their results are integrated.

Concerning (a), we chose to execute first the functional discovery algorithm as this more naturally depicts the process executed by humans who first seek to satisfy their functional requirements and then the non-functional ones. Functional service discovery can also be considered more restrictive than non-functional one. This can be due to the fact that when performing non-functional matching, domain-independent metrics are usually considered leading to obtaining many functionally irrelevant results out of the respective domain scope. As such, when no results are discovered in the first discovery form, there is no reason to continue with the non-functional one spending unnecessary resources.

Solution (b) attempts to execute the aspect-specific discovery algorithms in parallel to save time. Compared to the first approach, it may spend more resources but it will be surely faster, provided that when one aspect-based discovery algorithm ends earlier with not result, we can stop the other one.

The second criterion explored exploiting different structures to smartly organise the service advertisement space to speed-up service matching. By relying on the approach in [10], we have considered combined subsumes relations between different service discovery offers (where a discovery offer maps to one functional and non-functional offer pair for one service) enabling us to not browse the whole advertisement space but stop at certain places without requiring to go down in respective subsumes branches. Figure 2 depicts the notion of a subsumes service advertisement hierarchy via a small forest of 4 offers. Offer O_1 subsumes offers O_{11} and O_{12} for different reasons. Offer O_{11} is subsumed due to its functional part (its non-functional part is equivalent) while offer O_{12} is subsumed due to its non-functional part (its functional part is equivalent). Offer O_2 is not related to the tree's offers as it possesses an unrelated functional part. This also highlights the definition of the combined subsumes relation: $comb\_subsumes\,(S_1, S_2) \equiv func\_subsumes\,(S_1, S_2) \wedge nonfunc\_subsumes\,(S_1, S_2)$

By exploiting this subsumption relation, we speed up the service matching process. For example, assume that request R is issued. We will first compare it with offer O_1. If R subsumes O_1, it also subsumes its descendants. As such, we do not have to go deeper into the respective tree. However, we need to also check other trees in the forest which could be partially related to each other. There are two relation kinds to be exploited: *subsumes* and the opposite one, *subsumedBy*. Based on the empirical evaluation in [10], the first relation is more suited when more than 30 percent of the offers match a request. Otherwise, the second relation is more suitable. By combining functional and non-functional service matching, we expect that the percentage of matched offers can be lower than in the case of aspect-specific matching. In this way, it might be preferrable to exploit the *subsumedBy* relation in the end, especially for a highly populated service registry

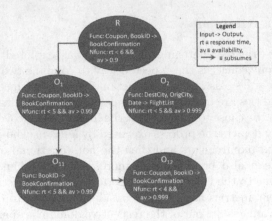

Fig. 2. The subsumption forest with request R subsuming a root tree node

spanning multiple domains as each request is expected to be specific to just one domain and thus lead to matching of a quite low offer percentage.

In the sequel, a small section is first provided explaining the main symbols and assumptions made. The next four subsections shortly analyse the proposed algorithms' functionality for service registration and discovery by also providing a respective complexity analysis. Other operation types (e.g., deletion and updating) are not considered as they tend to map either to similar actions as in case of registration (i.e., deletion) or to a two actions sequence (i.e., updating by combining deletion and insertion). Finally, the last section discusses the expected performance of the proposed algorithms based on the complexity analysis.

4.1 Symbols and Assumptions

We assume that one functional and non-functional part comprise the service request. We also assume that S service offers have been registered. This means that around $\frac{S}{3}$ functional offers are to be registered in a functional matchmaker and S non-functional offers in the non-functional one as each functional offer is expected to be accompanied by 3 non-functional offers for the same service, mapping to gold, silver and bronze classes of customers. Functional offer preprocessing takes $O(1)$ while for a non-functional offer takes $O(2M + M * T_z)$, where the first part maps to the offer's consistency checking and the second to its alignment; M represents the number of the offer's quality terms. The latter can be reduced to $O(M * T_z)$ constituting the total pre-processing time. Finally, we assume that each non-functional offer comprises at most $2M$ constraints mapping to the upper and lower bounds given for each quality term.

4.2 Sequential Algorithm

Analysis. *Matchmaking.* We propose two main algorithm variations named as: *Sequential* and *SeqOnTheFly*. The first version first performs functional service discovery; then it fetches the respective non-functional offers from the functional results, registers them to the non-functional matchmaker and matches them with the non-functional request part. Finally, it returns back the ending results to the user and clears the non-functional matchmaker. On the other hand, the second version checks on the fly whether the non-functional offers mapping to the matched functional ones are subsumed by the request's non-functional part. We expect that the first version is more suitable when non-functional offers are great in number as the total registration time will be compensated by the fast matching via the matchmaker's smart structures. Otherwise, the second version should be preferred. Section 5 will explore which is the amount of non-functional offers that represents the break point between choosing one over the other version.

Registration. Both algorithm versions follow the same registration process by registering the functional offer in the functional matchmaker and inserting the respective combined entry in the *Combined Registry.* Non-functional-based registration is not needed due to the way the non-functional matchmaker is exploited. The pre-requisite processing step for specifications controls their validity and transactionally rolls back the combined registration, if needed.

Complexity Analysis. *Matchmaking.* We rely on the complexity analysis of the aspect-specific matchmakers and on the fact that the request validity has to be checked. Pre-processing as already stated takes $O\left(M * T_Z\right)$.

The functional matching part [4] requires $O\left(R_O * \frac{S}{3} * R_{AO} + M_{FO} * I_S^{Mean}\right)$, where R_O, R_{AO} represent the number of input and acceptable inputs of the request, respectively, $\frac{S}{3}$ represents the number of functional service offers registered, M_{FO} the number of matched services based on their output and $I_{M_{FO}^{mean}}$ the mean number of inputs of each matched service. The latter can be reduced to $O\left(R_O * S * R_{AO}\right)$ as $\frac{S}{3}$ is expected to be much bigger than M_{FO} and I_S^{Mean} could be at most 3. Non-functional matching time depends on the combined algorithm version. For each version, we assume that $O\left(k * M_{FO}\right)$ non-functional offers must be matched, k non-functional offers for each functional match, based on our assumption for the mapping between functional and non-functional offers.

For normal non-functional matching, in the worst case, covering both registration and matching of non-functional offers, the time will be $O\left(M * (M_{FO} + 2 * log_{M_{FO}})\right)$. For on the fly non-functional matching, $O\left(2M * M_{FO}\right)$ time is needed as we must check each constraint of a non-functional offer with the request non-functional part's respective constraint. Thus, in the end, the matchmaking time for *Sequential* will be $O(R_O * S * R_{AO} + (M * (M_{FO} + 2 * log_{M_{FO}})) + M * T_Z)$. If we consider that M is small and cannot go beyond 10 quality terms and that S is much bigger than M_{FO}, the complexity formula can be reduced to: $O\left(R_O * S * R_{AO} + T_Z\right)$.

For *SeqOnTheFly*, the matching time will be $O(R_O * S * R_{AO} + (2M * M_{FO}) + M * T_Z)$ which can be similarly reduced to $O(R_O * S * R_{AO} + T_Z)$. Thus, in the end, the matching complexity for both algorithm versions coincides.

Registration. One functional and its respective 3 non-functional offers are to be registered. Thus, we need to pre-process 4 specifications and only register via the functional matchmaker the functional offer. Pre-processing takes again $O(M * T_Z)$ as in matchmaking. Functional registration takes $O(S_C)$ as in the worst case is dominated by the time needed to infer the subsumption hierarchy of the domain ontology mapping to the service I/O, where S_C represents this time for an ontology of C concepts. Thus, registration time for both algorithm versions will be $O(T_Z + S_C)$.

4.3   Parallel Algorithm

Analysis. Matchmaking is performed, after user request is pre-processed and aligned, by exploiting in parallel the functional and non-functional matchmakers and then concatenating their results. The exploitation of the *Combined Registry* to map functional matches to their non-functional counter-parts (which can be 3 times their number) guarantees the concatenation of the same type of objects.

For registration, we register in parallel the functional offer and non-functional part in the functional and non-functional matchmakers, respectively. The respective consistency is achieved by informing the *Combined Registry*.

Time Complexity Analysis. *Matchmaking.* Pre-processing as in the previous algorithm takes $O(M * T_Z)$. Functional matching, as already stated, takes $O(R_O * S * R_{AO})$. Non-functional matching takes $O(M * (S + log_S))$. Concatenating the different result types takes: $O(M_{FO})$. In the end, the total matchmaking time will be: $O(\max(R_O * S * R_{AO}, M * (S + log_S)) + M_{FO} + M * T_Z)$ which can be further reduced to: $O(S + T_Z)$.

Registration. Functional registration takes $O(S_C)$ as indicated in the previous algorithm. Non-functional registration takes $O(M * log_S)$. Thus, total registration time will be $O(\max(S_C, M * (log_S + T_Z)))$ which can be reduced to $O(\max(S_C, log_S + T_Z))$.

4.4   Subsumes Algorithm

Analysis. *Matchmaking.* It is recursively performed [10]. The offer is matched with each root node. If it subsumes the node, it also subsumes its children. As such, we just consider this node and its descendants as matches. Otherwise, we must descend this hierarchy recursively to find respective matching nodes. All matching results for each root node search (including recursive calls) are finally collected to be returned to the user.

Registration. It is recursively performed [10]. First, each root node is checked with the offer to be matched. If the offer is equivalent to the node, it is entered into the node's represented offers and registration ends. If the offer subsumes the node, it becomes its parent. If the root node subsumes the offer, the same checking is performed recursively at the node's children. When at the root node's subsumption hierarchy the offer is subsumed by one node but does not subsume its children, the offer is entered as a child of this parent node.

Complexity Analysis. *Matchmaking.* 3 cases hold [10]. In the worst case, we perform functional and non-functional subsumption checking for all forest nodes. In functional subsumption checking, we expand each output concept of the functional offer with respect to its ancestor concepts in $O(1)$ step and check if each output concept of the functional request is inside one of the expanded lists. This takes $O(R_O * S_O)$ for each functional offer. For non-functional subsumption checking, we check if each offer constraint is more restrictive that the respective demand constraint. This takes $O(2 * M)$ as for each offer constraint, we immediately find the request counter part. So, individual subsumption checking takes $O(R_O * S_O + 2M)$. By visiting all S nodes and accounting processing time, total matching time is: $O(S * (R_O * S_O + 2M) + M * T_Z)$. As both R_O and S_O tend to be small and M is less than 10, this reduces to just $O(S + T_Z)$.

In the best case, only the sole root node is matched (forest reduced to a tree) which takes $O(S + T_Z)$. In the average case, we expect that the tree is more or less balanced, a percentage of P nodes is subsumed and there is always a pair of parent-child offers. In this case, total matching will take: $O\left(S * \left(1 - \frac{P}{2}\right) + T_Z\right)$.

Registration. Three cases are also considered. For all cases, we need to do preprocessing but also account for ontology subsumption-based structure updating. This maps to $O(S_C + T_Z)$. In the best case, the first root node compared with the new offer is equivalent to it. This ends up doing two comparisons (one for node-to-offer subsumption and one for offer-to-node subsumption) and translates to $O(2 * (S * (R_O * S_O) + 2M))$. Thus, in total, the time will be $O(S_C + T_Z)$.

In the worst case, we have a single tree and the offer has to be inserted in the rightmost leaf. This maps to performing twice the subsumption checking over all tree nodes which will map to $O(S + S_C + T_Z)$ in the end.

In the average case, we will have B balanced trees and the offer has to be inserted in the middle of the median tree. This will map to $\frac{S+B^2}{2B}$ subsumption checks which will then map in the end to a total time of: $O\left(\frac{S+B^2}{2B} + S_C + T_Z\right)$.

4.5   SubsumedBy Algorithm

Analysis. *subsumedBy* is opposite to *subsumes*. We organise the offer hierarchy in this way to cater for the case that a very small offer number matches a request to be placed in the hierarchy's leaves (as subsumption maps to something more restricted or specific so less matches means more restricted matches).

Matchmaking. It is performed by matching the request with the root nodes based on the *subsumes* relation. If there is no match, there is no need to go down the root node's hierarchy (as either there is no relation at all or the request is *subsumedBy* the root node). Otherwise, we include the root node in the final matches and visit its children recursively. All matching results from each (recursive) root node search are finally collected and returned to the user.

Registration. It is symmetric to *Subsumes*. We check first the root nodes. An offer equivalent to a root node is included in the offers represented by the node and registration ends. If the offer is subsumed by this node, it becomes the node's parent. If it subsumes the node, we go recursively to the node children. The offer finally becomes a child of a root node descendant or a forest root (in case it is unrelated to any root node or subsumed by one or more root nodes).

Complexity Analysis. *Matchmaking.* The same complexity as in *Subsumes* holds for the best and worst cases. The sole exception is the conditions mapping to these cases. In the best case, the sole root node is not subsumed by the request. In the worst case, all non-subsumed nodes by the request lie in the forest leaves and do not represent more than one offer. In average, the same assumptions hold as in *Subsumes*. This, however, maps to matching the request with $O\left(S * \frac{P+1}{2}\right)$ nodes which finally maps to the total matching time of: $O\left(S * \frac{P+1}{2}\right) + T_Z$

Registration. This process is identical to that of *Subsumes* concerning the best and worst cases, so the respective time complexity is the same. The same holds for the conditions mapping to worst, best and average cases.

4.6 Discussion

Concerning matchmaking, based on the time complexity analysis, it seems that in the worst case the *Parallel* algorithm is the best followed by *Sequential* and then the *subsumes*-based algorithms. However, in the average case, if there is some kind of subsumption hierarchy between the different nodes, it might be the case that the *subsumes*-based algorithms have the best possible performance and the best algorithm can depend on the percentage of offers being matched.

Concerning registration time, the performance order seems to be clearer as the *Parallel* algorithm must have the best performance followed by the sequential and then the *subsumes-based* algorithms. So, there is a clear winner plus a performance trade-off between matchmaking and registration for the second place where different algorithms are nominated as best for different operations.

5 Evaluation

The evaluation was performed via the experimental framework in [10], covering the non-functional aspect and being able to generate in a controlled manner both randomised and real non-functional service specifications, as well as the OWLSTC framework, covering the functional aspect with real or realistic functional service specifications along with ways to measure functional discovery accuracy. The main goal was to evaluate the algorithms' average matchmaking and registration performance. Accuracy is neglected due to the following reasons: (a) non-functional matchmakers have perfect accuracy [10]; (b) accuracy results will be identical to those of the functional matchmaker exploited that have already been reported. The target is to discover those circumstances that the selection of a specific algorithm from those proposed is recommended. We also consider the *AliveMM* functional matchmaker so that we are enabled to compare the overall matchmaking time with respect to the functional part and unveil the degree in which the latter influences the former.

In the sequel, we explicate the way the sole experiment was conducted based on the experimental framework and then discuss the experiment results.

5.1 Experiment Set-Up and Control

Unified Framework Features. By combining aspect-specific experimental frameworks, we generate an overall framework with the capabilities to create in a controlled manner both functional and non-functional specifications. Functional specifications can either rely on the OWLSTC collection, to be as realistic as possible, or can be produced randomly [11] via a domain ontology's concepts combined to produce the service I/O. Non-functional specifications rely on the WS-Dream [18] and QWS [1] datasets or on generating randomised unary specifications that can include integer or real-valued metrics of different types and semantics. In the experiment conducted, we relied on OWLSTC and the randomised generation of non-functional specifications. Our choice for the non-functional aspect relates to the fact that the WS-Dream dataset is big but quite limited in the metric number while QWS is smaller. However, we desire to generate a much greater non-functional offer set with an increased metric number such that respective requests can also match a particular offer percentage.

Offer Generation. For each functional service offer, three non-functional offers were generated in a controlled manner. This resulted in generating around 3150 service offers (functional and non-functional pairs) provided that OWLSTC contains around 1050 functional service specifications. This also supports our main real-world assumption that each service can be associated to three non-functional offers catering for gold, silver and bronze customer classes. The offer number considered in each experiment step depended on a specific configuration parameter given as input to the specification generator. For instance, if this number is 100, we randomly take 100 functional offers from OWLSTC and couple each to 3 non-functional offers randomly generated such that the next non-functional offer has an increased performance and price with respect to the previous one to map to the different customer classes.

Experiment Set-Up. The experiment was conducted in a Windows 7 SSD-based machine with 2 GHz dual-core CPU and 6 GB of RAM. It included conducting a set of steps in which one configuration parameter varied (the offer number) according to a specific range (50 to 1050 with an increase step of 200 for the functional offers). Each step was executed 30 times to produce the respective average matchmaking and registration time values of the considered algorithms such that any possible interference at the OS level is diminished.

5.2 Experiment Results

Figure 3 depicts the experiment results for matchmaking and registration time.

Concerning matchmaking time, the best algorithm is *Parallel*. The order for the rest is not stable. Initially, the sequential algorithms are better than the subsumes; this is reversed when the functional offer number is equal or above 650.

This means that beyond a specific offer number, the offer hierarchy becomes more structured such that matching time can be really saved via a subsumes-based approach. This matches exactly our expectations for the subsumes algorithms.

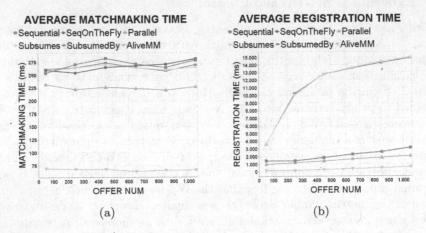

Fig. 3. (a) shows the experiment service matchmaking results while (b) the service registration ones

The partial order between the sequential algorithms is also unstable. Initially, as the number of non-functional offers to filter is small, *SeqOnTheFly* is slightly faster. However, beyond 650 functional offers, this is reversed as it becomes better to employ a non-functional matchmaker to register and match the non-functional offers rather than employ pair-wise non-functional filtering.

The subsumes algorithms are equivalent apart from the initial step where probably the matched offer number is quite small thus favouring *SubsumedBy*. This needs further investigation as we need to discover those circumstances that one algorithm prevails over the other to assist practitioners in their selection.

The results produced validate the complexity analysis (especially with respect to the algorithm order) due also to corresponding OWLSTC features. In particular, a more or less stable algorithm performance is seen due to the small matched offer percentage and the small output parameter number per service. This leads to a more or less stable matching performance for the functional matchmaker as depicted in the results. Moreover, while the number of non-functional offers to be matched is greater in each step, the scalable non-functional matchmaker used enabled to reach almost equivalent performance levels. So, these matchmakers combination also leads to a stable matching performance.

Non-functional matching time takes more with respect to functional one. This is proven by comparing the functional matchmaker and *Parallel* algorithm performance. Thus, non-functional matching has still space for further optimisation. This also indicates that it is always proper for a sequential matchmaker to first filter based on the functional aspect and then the non-functional one. This is an interesting result to be accounted by researchers and practitioners.

Concerning registration time, the best algorithm is again *Parallel* followed by the sequential ones. The difference between these algorithms is small but is big with respect to the subsumes ones. The complexity analysis also validated this. This means that probably the subsumes algorithms should not be used in cases when a high offer number is constantly registered or updated. However, it can also be acceptable in the rest of the cases. So, the use of these algorithms depends on the registry provider's preferences and constraints especially with respect to the main requirements of its clients, i.e., service providers and requesters.

No ordering between sequential and between subsumes algorithms can be inferred from the results. This is natural as the sequential algorithms rely on the same registration process. For the subsumes algorithms, by also relying on the matchmaking results, it seems that the structures produced are more or less similar, leading to almost the same registration time.

To conclude, we stress that the *Parallel* algorithm seems to be the best for both matchmaking and registration so it is undoubtly recommended as the ideal algorithm for service registry realisation. In case that a different algorithm is needed or preferred, then the recommendation will be towards the subsumes algorithms despite the fact that their behavior with respect to registration is the worst. However, for highly dynamic environments, it seems that the best choice will be the sequential algorithms as an alternative to *Parallel* due to their capability to also deal with the dynamicity in service updating.

6 Conclusions and Future Work

This paper has presented four algorithms which attempt to combine in a different way the facilities of functional and non-functional state-of-the-art service discovery algorithms. We believe that this investigation is genuine and really assists practitioners in choosing the algorithm that best matches their current situation. The respective algorithm evaluation has unveiled the circumstances in which each algorithm prevails based on performance aspects. Apart from these 4 novel algorithms proposed, we have also implemented an unified service discovery architecture covering both the functional and non-functional aspects. Such an architecture comprises components that not only perform core service discovery tasks but also specification validation and alignment. It also includes components that enable both a visual and a programmatic interaction with a human or software agents, respectively. The algorithm combination is performed such that transactionality of offer registration and updating is achieved.

Concerning future work, the following directions will be pursued. First, more thorough validation of the proposed algorithms to produce even more interesting performance insights. Second, completing the development of the service discovery architecture. Third, extending functional matching towards covering the service functional behaviour to further increase discovery accuracy in case respective formal service descriptions are in place. Finally, integrating the service discovery system in an existing service composition framework to enable a faster and more accurate service composition process.

Acknowledgments. This research has received funding from the European Community's Framework Programme for Research and Innovation HORIZON 2020 (ICT-07-2014) under grant agreement number 644690 (CloudSocket).

References

1. Al-Masri, E., Mahmoud, Q.H.: Investigating web services on the world wide web. In: WWW, pp. 795–804. ACM, Beijing (2008)
2. Benaboud, R., Maamri, R., Sahnoun, Z.: Agents and owl-s based semantic web service discovery with user preference support. Int. J. Web Semant. Technol. **4**(2), 57–75 (2013)
3. Charrad, M., Ayadi, N.Y., Ahmed, M.B.: A semantic and QoS-aware broker for service discovery. J. Res. Pract. Inf. Technol. **44**(4), 387–399 (2012)
4. Cliffe, O., Andreou, D.: Service Matchmaking Framework. Public Deliverable D5.2a, Alive EU Project Consortium. http://www.ist-alive.eu/index.php?option=com_docman&task=doc_download&gid=28&Itemid=49. Accessed 10 Sept 2009
5. Cortés, A.R., Martín-Díaz, O., Toro, A.D., Toro, M.: Improving the automatic procurement of web services using constraint programming. Int. J. Coop. Inf. Syst. **14**(4), 439–468 (2005)
6. Jiang, S., Aagesen, F.A.: An approach to integrated semantic service discovery. In: Gaiti, D., Pujolle, G., Al-Shaer, E.S., Calvert, K.L., Dobson, S., Leduc, G., Martikainen, O. (eds.) AN 2006. LNCS, vol. 4195, pp. 159–171. Springer, Heidelberg (2006)
7. Klein, M., König-Ries, B.: Coupled signature and specification matching for automatic service binding. In: Zhang, L.-J., Jeckle, M. (eds.) ECOWS 2004. LNCS, vol. 3250, pp. 183–197. Springer, Heidelberg (2004)
8. Klusch, M.: Semantic web service coordination. In: Schumacher, M., Schuldt, H., Helin, H. (eds.) CASCOM: Intelligent Service Coordination in the Semantic Web, pp. 59–104. Springer, Berlin (2008)
9. Klusch, M., Fries, B., Sycara, K.: OWLS-MX: a hybrid semantic web service matchmaker for OWL-S services. Web Semant.: Sci. Serv. Agents World Wide Web **7**(2), 121–133 (2009)
10. Kritikos, K., Plexousakis, D.: Novel optimal and scalable nonfunctional service matchmaking techniques. IEEE Trans. Serv. Comput. **7**(4), 614–627 (2014)
11. Kritikos, K., Plexousakis, D., Paternò, F.: Task model-driven realization of interactive application functionality through services. TiiS **3**(4), 25 (2014)
12. Lemos, F., Grigori, D., Bouzeghoub, M.: Adding non-functional preferences to service discovery. In: Brambilla, M., Tokuda, T., Tolksdorf, R. (eds.) ICWE 2012. LNCS, vol. 7387, pp. 299–306. Springer, Heidelberg (2012)
13. Makris, C., Panagis, Y., Sakkopoulos, E., Tsakalidis, A.: Efficient and adaptive discovery techniques of web services handling large data sets. J. Syst. Softw. **79**(4), 480–495 (2006)
14. Mokhtar, S.B., Preuveneers, D., Georgantas, N., Issarny, V., Berbers, Y.: EASY: Efficient semAntic Service discoverY in pervasive computing environments with QoS and context support. J. Syst. Softw. **81**(5), 785–808 (2008)
15. Pathak, J., Koul, N., Caragea, D., Honavar, V.G.: A framework for semantic web services discovery. In: WIDM, pp. 45–50. ACM, New York (2005). http://doi.acm.org/10.1145/1097047.1097057

16. Plebani, P., Pernici, B.: URBE: web service retrieval based on similarity evaluation. IEEE Trans. Knowl. Data Eng. **21**(11), 1629–1642 (2009)
17. Sirin, E., Parsia, B., Grau, B.C., Kalyanpur, A., Katz, Y.: Pellet: a practical OWL-DL reasoner. J. Web Sem. **5**(2), 51–53 (2007)
18. Zhang, Y., Zheng, Z., Lyu, M.R.: WSPred: a time-aware personalized QoS prediction framework for web services. In: ISSRE (2011)
19. Zhou, C., Chia, L.T., Lee, B.S.: DAML-QoS ontology for web services. In: ICWS, p. 472. IEEE Computer Society (2004)

Declarative Elasticity in ABS

Stijn de Gouw[1], Jacopo Mauro[3(✉)], Behrooz Nobakht[2],
and Gianluigi Zavattaro[4]

[1] Fredhopper, Amsterdam, Netherlands
[2] Leiden University, Leiden, Netherlands
[3] University of Oslo, Oslo, Norway
jacopom@ifi.uio.no
[4] University of Bologna/INRIA, Bologna, Italy

Abstract. Traditional development methodologies that separate software design from application deployment have been replaced by approaches such as continuous delivery or DevOps, according to which deployment issues should be taken into account already at the early stages of development. This calls for the definition of new modeling and specification languages. In this paper we show how deployment can be added as a first-class citizen in the object-oriented modeling language ABS. We follow a declarative approach: programmers specify deployment constraints and a solver synthesizes ABS classes exposing methods like `deploy` (resp. `undeploy`) that executes (resp. cancels) configuration actions changing the current deployment towards a new one satisfying the programmer's desiderata. Differently from previous works, this novel approach allows for the specification of incremental modifications, thus supporting the declarative modeling of elastic applications.

1 Introduction

Software applications deployed and executed on cloud computing infrastructures should flexibly adapt by dynamically acquiring or releasing computing resources. This is necessary to properly deliver to the final users the expected services at the expected level of quality, maintaining an optimized usage of the computing resources. For this reason, modern software systems call for novel engineering approaches that anticipate the possibility to reason about deployment already at the early stages of development.

Modeling languages like TOSCA [21], CloudML [16], and CloudMF [13] have been proposed to specify the deployment of software artifacts, but they are mainly intended to express deployment of already developed software. An integration of deployment in software modeling is still far from being obtained in the current practices. To cover this gap, in this paper we address the problem of

Supported by the EU projects FP7-610582 *Envisage: Engineering Virtualized Services* (http://www.envisage-project.eu) and H2020-644298 *HyVar: Scalable Hybrid Variability for Distributed, Evolving Software Systems* (http://www.hyvar-project.eu).

M. Aiello et al. (Eds.): ESOCC 2016, LNCS 9846, pp. 118–134, 2016.
DOI: 10.1007/978-3-319-44482-6_8

extending the ABS (Abstract Behavioural Specification) language [2] with linguistic constructs and mechanisms to properly specify deployment. Following [9] our approach is declarative: the programmer specifies deployment constraints and a solver computes actual deployments satisfying such constraints. In previous work [10] we presented an external engine able to synthesize ABS code specifying the initial static deployment; in this paper we fully integrate this approach in the ABS language allowing for the declarative specification of the incremental upscale/downscale of the modeled application depending, e.g., on the monitored workload or the current level of resource usage.

ABS is an object-oriented modeling language with a formally defined and executable semantics. It includes a rich tool-chain supporting different kinds of analysis (like, e.g., logic-based modular verification [11], deadlock detection [15], and cost analysis [3]). Executable code can be automatically obtained from ABS specifications by means of code generation. ABS has been mainly used to model systems based on asynchronously communicating concurrent objects, distributed over Deployment Components corresponding to containers offering to objects the resources they need to properly run. For our purposes, we adopted ABS because it allows the modeling of computing resources and it has a real-time semantics reflecting the way in which objects consume resources. This makes ABS particularly suited for modeling and reasoning about deployment.

Our initial proposal for the declarative modeling of deployment into ABS [10] was based on three main pillars: (i) classes are enriched with annotations that indicate functional dependencies of objects of those classes as well as the resources they require, (ii) a separate high-level language for the declarative specification of the deployment, (iii) an engine that, based on the annotations and the programmer's requirements, computes a fully specified deployment that minimizes the total cost of the system. The computed deployment is expressed in ABS and can be manually included in a main block.

The work in [10] had two main limitations: (i) there was no way to express incremental deployment decisions like, e.g., the need to upscale or downscale the modeled system at run-time and (ii) there was no real integration of the code synthesized by the engine in the corresponding ABS specification. In this paper we address these limitations by promoting the notion of deployment as a first-class citizen of the language. During a pre-processing phase, the new tool Smart-Depl generates classes exposing the methods deploy and undeploy to upscale and downscale the system. The deployment requirements can now also reuse already deployed objects just specifying which existing objects could be used, and how they should be connected with new objects to be freshly deployed. This has been the fundamental step forward that allowed us to support incremental modification of the current deployment. Moreover, other relevant contributions of this paper are (i) a more natural high-level language for the specification of requirements that now supports universal and existential quantifiers, and (ii) the usage of the delta modules and the variability modeling features of the ABS framework [7] to automatically and safely inject the deployment instructions into the existing ABS code.

Our ABS extension and the realization of the corresponding SmartDepl tool have been driven by Fredhopper Cloud Services, an industrial case-study of the

European FP7 Envisage project. The Fredhopper Cloud Services offer search and targeting facilities on a large product database to e-Commerce companies. Depending on the specific profile of an e-Commerce company Fredhopper has to decide the most appropriate customized deployment of the service. Currently, such decisions are taken manually by an operation team which decides customized, hopefully optimal, service configurations taking into account the tension among several aspects like the level of replications of critical parts of the service to ensure high availability. The operators manually perform the operations to scale up or down the system and this usually causes the over-provision of resources for guaranteeing the proper management of requests during a usage peak. With our extension of ABS, we have been able to realize a new modeling of the Fredhopper Cloud Services in which both the initial deployment and the subsequent up- and down-scale is expected to be executed automatically. This new model is a first fundamental step towards a new more efficient and elastic deployment management of the Fredhopper Cloud Services.

Structure of the paper. Section 2 describes the Fredhopper Cloud Services case-study. Section 3 reports the ABS deployment annotations that we already defined in [10]. Section 4 presents the new high-level language for the specification of deployment requirements while Sect. 5 discusses the corresponding solver. Finally, the application of our technique to the Fredhopper Cloud Services use-case is reported in Sect. 6. Section 7 discusses the related literature while in Sect. 8 we draw some concluding remarks.

2   The Fredhopper Cloud Services

Fredhopper provides the Fredhopper Cloud Services to offer search and targeting facilities on a large product database to e-Commerce companies as services (SaaS) over the cloud computing infrastructure (IaaS). The Fredhopper Cloud Services drives over 350 global retailers with more than 16 billion in online sales every year. A customer (service consumer) of Fredhopper is a web shop, and an end-user is a visitor of the web shop.

The services offered by Fredhopper are exposed at endpoints. In practice, these services are implemented to be RESTful and accept connections over HTTP. Software services are deployed as *service instances*. Each instance offers the same service and is exposed via Load Balancer endpoints that distribute requests over the service instances.

The number of requests can vary greatly over time, and typically depends on several factors. For instance, the time of the day in the time zone where most of the end-users are plays an important role (typical lows in demand are observed between 2 am and 5 am). Figure 1 shows a real-world graph for a single day (with data up to 18:00) plotting the number of queries per second (y-axis, ranging from 0–25 qps, the horizontal dotted lines are drawn at 5, 10, 15 and 20 qps) over the time of the day (x-axis, starting at midnight, the vertical dotted lines indicate multiples of 2 h). The 2 am–5 am low is clearly visible.

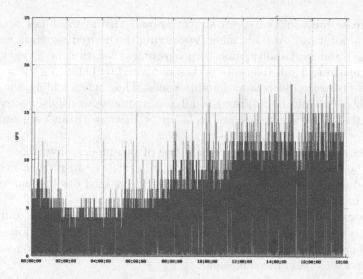

Fig. 1. Number of queries per second (in green the query processing time). (Color figure online)

Peaks typically occur during promotions of the shop or around Christmas. To ensure a high quality of service, web shops negotiate an aggressive Service Level Agreement (SLA) with Fredhopper. QoS attributes of interest include query latency (response time) and throughput (queries per second). For example, based on the negotiated SLA with a customer, services must maintain 100 queries per seconds with less than 200 ms of response time over 99.5 % of the service uptime, and 99.9 % with less than 500 ms.

Previous work reported in [10] aimed to compute an optimal initial deployment configuration (using the size of the product catalogue, number of expected visitors and cost of the required virtual machines). The computation was based on an already available model of the Fredhopper Cloud Services written in the ABS language. In this paper we address the problem of maintaining a high quality of service after this initial set-up by taking dynamic factors into account, such as fluctuating user-demand and unexpectedly failing virtual machines.

The solution that we propose is based on a tool named SmartDepl that, when integrated in the ABS model of the Fredhopper Cloud Services, enables the modeling of automatic upscaling or downscaling. When the decision to scale up or down is made, SmartDepl indicates how to automatically evolve the deployment configuration. This is not a trivial task: the desired deployment configuration should satisfy various requirements, and those can trigger the need to instantiate multiple service instances that furthermore require proper configuring to ensure they function correctly.

The requirements can originate from both business decisions or technical reasons. For instance, for security reasons, services that operate on sensitive customer data should not be deployed on machines shared by multiple customers. Below we list some of these requirements.

– To increase fault-tolerance, we aim to spread virtual machines across geographical locations. Amazon allows specifying the desired region (a geographical area) and availability zone (a geographical location in a region) for a virtual machine. Fault tolerance is then increased by balancing the number of machines between different availability zones. Thus, when scaling, the number of machines should be adjusted in all zones simultaneously. Effectively this means that with two zones, we scale up or down with an even number of machines.
– Each instance of a Query service is in one of two modes: 'live' mode to serve queries, or 'staging' mode to serve as an indexer (i.e., to publish updates to the product catalogue). There always should be at least one instance of Query service in staging mode.
– The network throughput and latency between the PlatformService and indexer is important. Since the infrastructure provider gives better performance for traffic between instances in the same zone, we require the indexer and PlatformService to be in the same zone.
– Installing an instance of the QueryService requires the presence of an instance of the DeploymentService on the same virtual machine.
– For performance reasons and fault tolerance, load balancers require a dedicated machine without other services co-located on the same virtual machine.

3 Annotated ABS

The ABS language is designed to develop executable models. It targets distributed and concurrent systems by means of concurrent object groups and asynchronous method calls. Here, we will recap just the specific linguistic features of ABS to support the modeling of the deployment; for more details we refer the interested reader to the ABS project website [2] and [10] for the cost annotations.

The basic element to capture the deployment in ABS is the *Deployment Component* (DC), which is a container for objects/services that, intuitively, may model a virtual machine running those objects/services. ABS comes with a rich API that allows the programmer to model a cloud provider of deployment components.

```
1 CloudProvider cProv = new CloudProvider("Amazon");
2 cProv.addInstanceDescription(Pair("c3",
3   InsertAssoc(Pair(CostPerInterval,210),
4     InsertAssoc(Pair(Memory,7500),
5       InsertAssoc(Pair(Cores,4), EmptyMap)))));
6 DeploymentComponent dc = cProv.prelaunchInstanceNamed("c3");
7 [DC: dc] Service s = new QueryServiceImpl();
```

In the ABS code above, the cloud provider "Amazon" is modeled as the object cProv of type CloudProvider. The fact that "Amazon" can provide a virtual machine of type "c3" is modeled by calling addInstanceDescription in Line 2. With this instruction we also specify that c3 virtual machines cost 0,210 cents per hour, provide 7.5 GB of RAM and 4 cores. In Line 5 an instance of "c3" is

launched and the corresponding deployment component is saved in the variable
dc. Finally, in Line 6, a new object of type QueryServiceImpl (implementing
interface Service) is created and deployed on the deployment component dc.

ABS supports declaring interface hierarchies and defining classes implementing them.

```
interface Service { ... }
interface IQueryService extends Service { ... }
class QueryServiceImpl(DeploymentService ds, Bool staging)
  implements IQueryService { ... }
```

In the excerpt of ABS above, the IQueryService service is declared as an interface that extends Service, and the class QueryServiceImpl is an implementation
of this interface. Notice that the initialization parameters required at object
instantiation are indicated as parameters in the corresponding class definition.

Classes can be annotated with the cost and requirements of an object of that
class.

```
[Deploy: scenario[Name("staging"), Cost("Cores", 2),
 Cost("Memory",7000), Param("staging", Default("True")),
 Param("ds", Req)] ]
[Deploy: scenario[Name("live"), Cost("Cores", 1),
 Cost("Memory",3000), Param("staging", Default("False")),
 Param("ds", Req)] ]
```

The above two annotations, to be included before the declaration of the
class QueryServiceImpl in the above ABS code, describe two possible deployment
scenarios for objects of that class. The first annotation models the deployment
of a Query Service in staging mode, the second one models the deployment in
live mode. A Query Service in staging mode requires 2 cores and 7 GB of RAM.
In live mode, 1 core and 3 GB of RAM suffices. Creating a Query Service object
requires the instantiation of its two initialization parameters ds and staging.
The second parameter should be instantiated with True or False depending on
the deployment scenario. The first parameter is required (keyword Req in the
annotation): this means that the Query Service requires a reference to an object
of type DeploymentService passed via the ds initialization parameter.

4   The Declarative Requirement Language DRL

Computing a deployment configuration requires taking into account the expectations of the ABS programmer. For example, in the Fredhopper Cloud Services,
one initial goal is to deploy with reasonable cost a given number of Query Services and a Platform Service, possibly located on different machines to improve
fault tolerance, and later on to upscale (or subsequently downscale) the system according to the monitored traffic. Each desiderata can be expressed with
a corresponding expression in *Declarative Requirement Language* (DRL): a new
language for stating constraints a configuration to be computed should satisfy.

Table 1. DRL grammar.

```
 1 b_expr : b_term (bool_binary_op b_term )* ;
 2 b_term : ('not')? b_factor ;
 3 b_factor : 'true' | 'false' | relation ;
 4 relation : expr (comparison_op expr)? ;
 5 expr : term (arith_binary_op term)* ;
 6 term : INT                                              |
 7   ('exists' | 'forall') VARIABLE 'in' type ':' b_expr  |
 8   'sum' VARIABLE 'in' type ':' expr                     |
 9   (( ID | VARIABLE | ID '[' INT ']' ) '.')? objId       |
10   arith_unary_op expr                                   |
11   '(' b_expr ')'                                        ;
12 objId :  ID | VARIABLE | ID '[' ID ']' | ID '[' RE ']';
13 type : 'obj' | 'DC' | RE ;
14 bool_binary_op : 'and' | 'or' | 'impl' | 'iff' ;
15 arith_binary_op : '+' | '-' | '*' ;
16 arith_unary_op : 'abs' ; // absolute value
17 comparison_op : '<=' | '=' | '>=' | '<' | '>' | '!=' ;
```

As shown in Table 1, that reports an excerpt of the DRL grammar,[1] a desiderata is a (possibly quantified) Boolean formula b_expr obtained by using the usual logical connectives over comparisons between arithmetic expressions. An atomic arithmetic expression is an integer (Line 6), a sum statement (Line 8) or an identifier for the number of deployed objects (Line 9). The number of objects to deploy using a given scenario is defined by its class name and the scenario name enclosed in square brackets (Line 12). For example, the below formula requires deploying at least one object of class QueryServiceImpl in staging mode.

```
QueryServiceImpl[staging] > 0
```

The square brackets are optional (Line 12 - first option) for objects with only one default deployment scenario. Regular expressions (RE in Line 12) can match objects deployed using different scenarios. The number of deployed objects can be prefixed by a deployment component identifier to denote just the number of objects defined within that specific deployment component. As an example, the deployment of only one object of class DeploymentServiceImpl on the first and second instance of a "c3" virtual machine can be enforced as follows.

```
c3[0].DeploymentServiceImpl = 1 and
    c3[1].DeploymentServiceImpl = 1
```

---

[1] The complete grammar defined using the ANTLR compiler generator is available at https://github.com/jacopoMauro/abs_deployer/blob/smart_deployer/decl_spec_lang/DeclSpecLanguage.g4.

Here the 0 and 1 numbers between the square brackets represent respectively the first and second virtual machine of type "c3". To shorten the notation, the [0] can be omitted (Line 9).[2]

It is possible to use also quantifiers and sum expressions to capture more concisely some of the desired properties. Variables are identifiers prefixed with a question mark. As specified in Line 13, variables in quantifiers and sums can range over all the objects ('obj'), all the deployment components ('DC'), or just all the virtual machines matching a given regular expression (RE). In this way it is possible to express more elaborate constraints such as the co-location or distribution of objects, or limit the amount of objects deployed on a given DC.[3] As an example, the constraint enforcing that every Query Service has a Deployment Service installed on its virtual machine is as follows.

```
forall ?x in DC: (
  ?x:QueryServiceImpl['.*'] > 0   impl
  ?x.DeploymentServiceImpl > 0 )
```

Here impl stands for logical implication. The regular expression '.*' allows us to match with both deployment modalities for the Query Service (staging and live). Finally, specifying that the load balancer must be installed on a dedicated virtual machine (without other Service instances) can be done as follows.

```
forall ?x in DC: (
  ?x.LoadBalancerServiceImpl > 0   impl
  (sum ?y in obj: ?x.?y) = ?x.LoadBalancerServiceImpl )
```

5 Deployment Engine

SmartDepl is the tool that we have implemented to realize automatic deployment. The key idea of SmartDepl is to allow the user on the one hand to declaratively specify the desired deployments and, on the other hand, to develop its program abstracting from concrete deployment decisions. More concretely, deployment requirements are specified as program annotations. SmartDepl processes each of these annotations and generates for each of them a new class that specifies the deployment steps to reach the desired target. Then this class can be used to trigger the execution of the deployment, and to undo it in case the system needs to downscale.

As an example, imagine that an initial deployment of the Fredhopper Cloud Services has been already obtained and that, based on a monitor decision, the

---

[2] We assume that every deployment desiderata expressed in DRL deals with only a bounded number of deployment components (the bound is a configuration parameter for SmartDepl). Notice that this does not mean that the total number of deployment components in an application is bound, as the deployment can be repeated an unbounded number of times.

[3] DRL improves on the specification language presented in [10] because the addition of the quantifiers and sums allow to write the desiderata more concise and naturally.

Table 2. An example of a deployment annotation.

```
1  { "id": "AddQueryDeployer",
2    "specification": "QueryServiceImpl[live] = 1",
3    "obj": [ { "name": "platformObj",
4             "provides": [ {
5               "ports": [ "MonitorPlatformService",
6                          "PlatformService" ],
7             "num": -1 } ],
8             "interface": "PlatformService" },
9           { "name": "loadBalancerObj",
10            "provides": [ {
11              "ports": [ "LoadBalancerService" ],
12              "num": -1 } ],
13            "interface": "LoadBalancerService" },
14          { "name": "serviceProviderObj",
15            "provides": [ {
16              "ports": [ "ServiceProvider" ],
17              "num": -1 } ],
18            "interface": "ServiceProvider" } ],
19    "DC": [] }
```

user wants to add a Query Service instance in live mode. The annotation that describes this requirement is the JSON object defined in Table 2.[4]

In Line 1, the keyword `"id"` specifies that the name of the class with the deployment code, to be synthesized by SmartDepl, is `AddQueryDeployer`. As we will see later, this class exposes methods to be invoked to actually execute deployment actions that modifies the current deployment according to the requirements in the deployment annotation. The second line contains the declarative specification of the desired configuration in DRL. Deploying a new instance of the Query Service may involve other relevant objects from the surrounding environment, such as the `PlatformService` or a `LoadBalancerService`. Which objects are relevant may come from business, security or performance reasons, thus in general it may be undesirable to select or create automatically a Service instance of the right type. SmartDepl is flexible in this regard: the user supplies the appropriate ones. By using the keyword `"obj"`, Lines 3–18 list the appropriate objects. Since these object are already available, they need not be deployed again. The names of these objects are specified with the keyword `"name"` (Lines 3, 9, 14), the provided interfaces with the keyword `"port"` (Lines 5–6, 11, 16) with the amount of services that can use it (keyword `"num"` in Lines 7, 12, 17 — in this case a −1 value means that the object can be used by an unbounded number of other objects), and the object interface with keyword `"interface"` (Lines 8, 13, 18). Finally, with the keyword `"DC"`, the user specifies if there are existing deployment

---

[4] To facilitate the interoperability between ABS and SmartDepl we have adopted a JSON syntax for the deployment annotations. For the interested reader the formal specification of the JSON annotations is defined in https://github.com/jacopoMauro/abs_deployer/blob/smart_deployer/spec/smart_deploy_annotation_schema.json.

components with free resources that can be used to deploy new objects. In this case, for fault tolerance reasons the user wants to deploy the Query Service in a new machine and therefore the "DC" is empty (Line 19).

Once the annotation is given, the user may freely use this class. For instance, the below ABS code scales the system up or down based on a monitor decision.

```
1  while ( ... ) {
2    if ( monitor.scaleUp() ) {
3      SmartDeployInterface depObj = new AddQueryDeployer(
4        cProv, platformService, loadBalancerService, serviceProvider);
5      depObj.deploy();
6      depObjList = Cons(depObj,depObjList);
7    } else if ( (monitor.scaleDown()) && (depObjList != Nil) ) {
8      SmartDeployInterface depObj = head(depObjList);
9      depObjList = tail(depObjList);
10     depObj.undeploy(); } }
```

Every time an upscale is needed, an object of class AddQueryDeployer (the name associated with the annotation previously discussed) is created. The idea is to store the references to these deployment objects in a list called depObjList. We now discuss the initialization parameters for such objects. The first parameter is the cloud provider, as defined for instance in Sect. 3. The next parameters are the objects already available for the deployment that do not need to be re-deployed. These are given according to the order they are defined in the annotation in Table 2. The generated class implements the SmartDeployInterface with: (i) a deploy method to realise the deployment of the desired configuration, (ii) an undeploy method to undo the deployment gracefully by removing the virtual machine created with the deploy method, (iii) getter methods to retrieve the list of new objects and deployment components created by running the deploy method (e.g., a call depObj.getIQueryService() retrieves the list of all the Query Services created by depObj.deploy()). The actual addition of the Query Service is performed in Line 5 with the call of the deploy method. If the monitor decides to downscale (Line 7), the last deployment solution is retrieved (Line 8), and the corresponding deployment actions are reverted by calling the undeploy method.[5]

Technically, SmartDepl is written in Python ($\sim$1k lines of code) and relies on Zephyrus2, a configuration optimizer that given the user desiderata and a universe of components, computes the optimal configuration satisfying the user needs.[6] The cost annotations (see Sect. 3) are used to compute a configuration

---

[5] Since ABS does not have an explicit operation to force the removal of objects the undeploy procedure just removes the references to these objects leaving the garbage collector to actually remove them. The deployment components created by the deploy methods are removed instead using an explicit kill primitive provided by ABS.

[6] SmartDepl uses Zephyrus2 (freely available at https://bitbucket.org/jacopomauro/zephyrus2.git) since it allows the use of a now expressive language and because it relies on MiniSearch [24], a new efficient and flexible framework for planning the search strategies. Zephyrus2 is a completely new re-engineering of the previous Zephyrus solver [8,9].

that satisfies the constraints, minimizes the cost of the deployment components that need to be created and, in case of ties, minimizes the number of created objects. The user is notified if no configuration exists that satisfies the desiderata. Once a configuration is obtained, SmartDepl uses topological sorting to take into account all the object dependencies and computes the sequence of deployment instructions to realise the desirable configuration. SmartDepl exploits Delta Modeling [7] to generate the code of the classes and methods to inject into the interface. SmartDepl also notifies the user when it is unable to generate a sequence of deployment actions due to mutual dependencies between the objects.[7]

As an example the deploy code generated by SmartDepl for the annotation defined in Table 2 is the following.

```
 1 Unit deploy() {
 2   DeploymentComponent c3_0 = cloudProvider.prelaunchInstanceNamed("c3");
 3   ls_DeploymentComponent = Cons(c3_0,ls_DeploymentComponent);
 4   [DC: c3_0] DeploymentService oDef___DeploymentServiceImpl_0_c3_0 =
 5     new DeploymentServiceImpl(platformObj);
 6   ls_DeploymentService = Cons(oDef___DeploymentServiceImpl_0_c3_0,
 7     ls_DeploymentService);
 8   [DC: c3_0] IQueryService olive___QueryServiceImpl_0_c3_0 = new
 9     QueryServiceImpl(oDef___DeploymentServiceImpl_0_c3_0, False);
10   ls_IQueryService = Cons(olive___QueryServiceImpl_0_c3_0, ls_IQueryService);
11   ls_Service = Cons(olive___QueryServiceImpl_0_c3_0, ls_Service);
12   ls_EndPoint = Cons(olive___QueryServiceImpl_0_c3_0, ls_EndPoint);
13 }
```

At Line 3, a new deployment component c3_0 is created. In Lines 4–5 an object of class DeploymentService is created, since every Query Service requires a corresponding Deployment Service (it is one of the required parameters, cf. Sect. 3) to be deployed before the Query Service. In Lines 8–9 the desired object of class IQueryService is created. Both objects are deployed on c3_0.

Even though for the sake of the presentation this is just a simple example, it is immediately possible to notice that SmartDepl alleviates the user from the burden of the deployment decisions. Indeed, she can specify the desired configuration without worrying about the dependencies of the various objects and their distributed placement for obtaining the cheapest possible solution.

SmartDepl is open source, available at https://github.com/jacopoMauro/abs_deployer/tree/smart_deployer and to increase its portability it can be installed also by using the Docker container technology [12]. As illustrated in Fig. 2, Smart-Depl has also been integrated into the ABS toolchain,[8] an IDE for a collection of tools for writing, inspecting, checking, and analyzing ABS programs developed within the Envisage European project.

---

[7] This occurs when the creation of an object requires the execution of a complex protocol, such as what happens for the boostrapping of Linux distributions [1].

[8] http://abs-models.org/installation/.

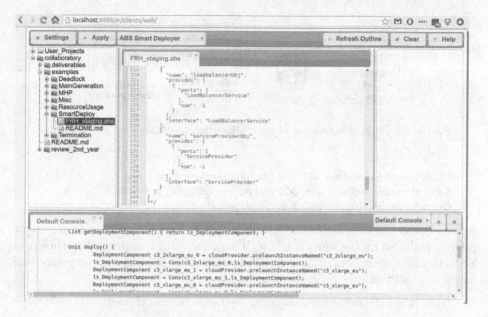

Fig. 2. SmartDepl execution within the ABS toolchain IDE.

6   Application to the Fredhopper Use Case

In this section we report on the modeling with SmartDepl of the concrete deployment requirements of the Fredhopper Cloud Services, previously introduced in Sect. 2. We decided to apply our techniques to the Fredhopper Cloud Services use case because it was already modeled in ABS, and thanks to extensive profiling of the in-production system, the cost of its services are known.

SmartDepl was used twice: to synthesize the initial static deployment of the entire framework and to add (and later remove) instances of the Query Service if the system needs to scale. Since the Fredhopper Cloud Services uses Amazon EC2 Instance Types, we used two types of deployment components corresponding to the "xlarge" and "2xlarge" instances of the Compute Optimized instances (version 3)[9] of Amazon. For fault tolerance and stability, Fredhopper Cloud Services uses instances in multiple regions in Amazon (regions are geographically separate areas, so even if there is a force majeure in one region, other regions may be unaffected). We model the instance types in different regions as follows: "c3_xlarge_eu", "c3_xlarge_us", "c3_2xlarge_eu", "c3_2xlarge_us" ("eu" refers to a European region, "us" is an American region).

The static deployment of the Fredhopper Cloud Services requires deploying a Load Balancer, a Platform Service, a Service Provider and 2 Query Services with at least one in staging mode. This is expressed as follows.

---

[9] https://aws.amazon.com/ec2/instance-types/.

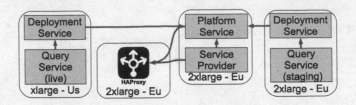

Fig. 3. Example of automatic objects allocation to deployment components.

LoadBalancerServiceImpl = 1 and PlatformServiceImpl = 1 and
ServiceProviderImpl = 1 and QueryServiceImpl[staging] > 0 and
QueryServiceImpl[staging] + QueryServiceImpl[live] = 2

For the correct functioning of the system, a Query Service requires a Deployment
Service installed on the same machine. This constraint is expressed as shown in
Sect. 4. The requirement that a Service Provider is present on every machine
containing a Platform Service is expressed by:

forall ?x in DC: (?x.PlatformServiceImpl > 0 impl ?x.ServiceProviderImpl > 0)

Not all services can be freely installed on an arbitrary virtual machine. To
increase resilience, we require that the Load Balancer, the Query/Deployment
Services, and the Platform Service/Service Provider are never co-located on the
same virtual machine. The end of Sect. 4 shows how this is expressed.

To handle catastrophic failures, the Fredhopper Cloud Services aim to balance the Query Services between the regions (see Sect. 2). This is enforced by
constraining the number of the Query Services in the different data centers to
be equal. In DRL this is expressed with regular expressions as follows.

(sum ?x in '.*_eu': ?x.QueryServiceImpl['.*']) =
(sum ?x in '.*_us': ?x.QueryServiceImpl['.*'])

As described in Sect. 4, for performance reasons, the Query Service in Staging
mode should be located in the zone of the Platform Service, since Amazon connects instances in the same region with low-latency links. For the European
data-center this is expressed by:

(sum ?x in '.*_eu': ?x.QueryServiceImpl[staging]) > 0) impl
(sum ?x in '.*_eu': ?x.PlatformServiceImpl) > 0)

From this specification SmartDepl computes the initial configuration in Fig. 3,
which minimizes the total costs per interval. It deploys the Load Balancer, Platform Service and one staging Query Service on three "2xlarge" instances in
Europe, and deploys a live Query service on an "xlarge" instance in US.

After this initial deployment, the Cloud engineers of Fredhopper Cloud Services rely on feedback provided by monitors to decide if more Query Services in
live mode are needed. Figures 4 and 5 show some of the main metrics for a single
customer used to determine the scaling. The timescale in the figures is 1 day,
but this can be adjusted to see trends over longer periods, or zoom in on a short

period. The figures show that the number of queries served per second (qps, first graph of Fig. 4) is relatively high and the requests (Fig. 4, second graph) are fairly low, so requests are not queuing. Furthermore the CPU usage (Fig. 4, third graph) and memory consumption with small swap space used (Fig. 5, second and third graphs) look healthy. Hence, no scaling is needed.

If we would have needed to scale up, *two* Query Service instances are added: one in an EU region, and one in an US region for balancing across regions. In contrast, if there is unnecessary overcapacity, the most recent ones can be shut down. Since the Cloud operations team currently manually decides to scale, and Fredhopper has very aggressive SLAs, the team is typically conservative with down-scaling, leading to potential over-spending. The ability of SmartDepl to deploy in the programming language (ABS) itself allows to leverage the extensive tool-supported analyses available for ABS [3, 11, 15, 25]. For example, by using monitors to track the quality of services, SmartDepl allows to reason on a rigorous basis on the scaling decisions and their impact on the SLA agreed with the customers.

Furthermore, while the operations team currently use ad-hoc scripts to configure newly added or removed service instances, and these scripts are specific to

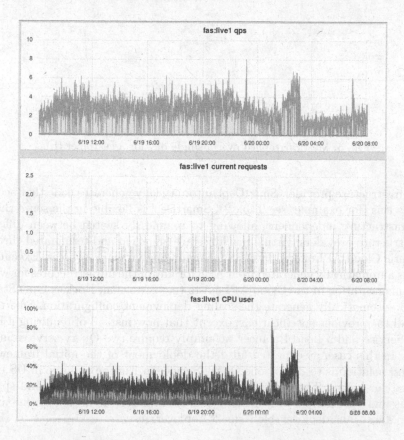

Fig. 4. Metrics graphed over a single day for a customer (a).

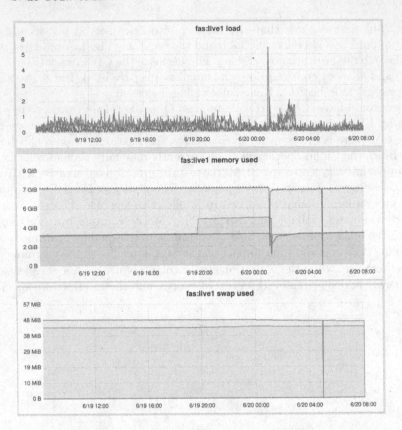

Fig. 5. Metrics graphed over a single day for a customer (b).

the infrastructure provider, SmartDepl automatically generates code that accomplishes this (for example, see Table 2). SmartDepl is flexible in the sense that it is infrastructure independent, allowing to seamlessly switch between different infrastructure providers: virtual machines are launched and terminated through a generic Cloud API offered by ABS for managing virtual resources. Executable code is automatically generated from ABS for any of the infrastructures for which an implementation of the Cloud API exists (e.g., Amazon, Docker, OpenStack).

To automatically generate the scaling deployment configuration, SmartDepl uses all the previous specifications, except that now instead of requiring a Platform Service and a Load Balancer we simply require two Query services in live mode. In this case, as expected after the deployment of the initial framework, the best solution is to deploy one Query Service in Europe and one in US using "xlarge" instances. The ABS model used with all the annotations and specifications and an example of generated code is available at https://github.com/jacopoMauro/abs_deployer/blob/smart_deployer/test/.

7   Related Work

Many management tools for bottom-up deployment exist, e.g., CFEngine [6], Puppet [19], MCollective [23], and Chef [22]. Such tools allow for the declaration of components, by indicating how they should be installed on a given machine, together with their configuration files, but they are not able to automatically decide where components should be deployed and how to interconnect them for an optimal resource allocation. The alternative holistic approach allows modeling the entire application and derives the deployment plan top-down. In this context, one prominent work is represented by the TOSCA (Topology and Orchestration Specification for Cloud Applications) standard [21]. Following a similar philosophy, we can mention Terraform [17], JCloudScale [26], Apache Brooklyn [4], and tools supporting the Cloud Application Management for Platforms protocol [20]. A first attempt to combine the holistic and bottom-up approaches is reported in [5]: a global deployment plan expressed in TOSCA is checked for correctness against local specifications of the deployment lifecycle of the single components.

Similarly to our approach, ConfSolve [18] and Engage [14] use a solver to plan deployment starting from the local requirements of components, but these approaches were not incorporated in fully-fledged specification languages (including also behavioral descriptions as in our case with ABS).

8   Conclusions

We presented an extension of the ABS specification language that supports modeling deployment in a declarative manner: the programmer specifies deployment constraints, and a solver synthesizes ABS classes with methods that execute deployment actions to reach an optimal deployment configuration that satisfies the constraints. Our approach, which is inspired by [9] and significantly improves our initial work [10], can be easily applied to any other object-oriented language that offers primitives for the acquisition and release of computing resources.

As a future work we plan to investigate the possibility to invoke at run time the external deployment engine. In this way, it could be possible to dynamic redefine the deployment constraints by means of a dynamic tuning of the engine. Nevertheless, dynamically computing the deployment steps may require additional elements such as the support of new reflection primitives to get a snapshot of the running application, and possibly the use of sub-optimal solutions when computing the optimal configuration takes too much time.

References

1. Abate, P., Johannes, S.: Bootstrapping software distributions. In: CBSE 2013 (2013)
2. Abstract behavioral specification language. http://www.abs-models.com/
3. Albert, E., Arenas, P., Flores-Montoya, A., Genaim, S., Gómez-Zamalloa, M., Martin-Martin, E., Puebla, G., Román-Díez, G.: SACO: static analyzer for concurrent objects. In: ETAPS (2014)

4. Apache Software Foundation: Apache Brooklýn. https://brooklyn.incubator.apache.org/

5. Brogi, A., Canciani, A., Soldani, J.: Modelling and analysing cloud application. In: Dustdar, S., Leymann, F., Villari, M. (eds.) ESOCC 2015. LNCS, vol. 9306, pp. 19–33. Springer, Heidelberg (2015)

6. Burgess, M.: A site configuration engine. Comput. Syst. **8**(2), 309–337 (1995)

7. Clarke, D., Muschevici, R., Proença, J., Schaefer, I., Schlatte, R.: Variability modelling in the ABS language. In: Aichernig, B.K., de Boer, F.S., Bonsangue, M.M. (eds.) FMCO 2010. LNCS, vol. 6957, pp. 204–224. Springer, Heidelberg (2011)

8. Cosmo, R.D., Lienhardt, M., Mauro, J., Zacchiroli, S., Zavattaro, G., Zwolakowski, J.: Automatic application deployment in the cloud: from practice to theory and back. In: CONCUR (2015)

9. Cosmo, R.D., Lienhardt, M., Treinen, R., Zacchiroli, S., Zwolakowski, J., Eiche, A., Agahi, A.: Automated synthesis and deployment of cloud applications. In: ASE (2014)

10. de Gouw, S., Lienhardt, M., Mauro, J., Nobakht, B., Zavattaro, G.: On the integrationof automatic deployment into the ABS modeling language. In: Dustdar, S., Leymann, F., Villari, M. (eds.) ESOCC 2015. LNCS, vol. 9306, pp. 49–64. Springer, Heidelberg (2015)

11. Din, C.C., Bubel, R., Hähnle, R.: KeY-ABS: a deductive verification tool for the concurrent modelling language ABS. In: CADE (2015)

12. Docker Inc.: Docker. https://www.docker.com/

13. Ferry, N., Chauvel, F., Rossini, A., Morin, B., Solberg, A.: Managing multi-cloud systems with CloudMF. In: NordiCloud (2013)

14. Fischer, J., Majumdar, R., Esmaeilsabzali, S.: Engage: a deployment management system. In: PLDI (2012)

15. Giachino, E., Laneve, C., Lienhardt, M.: A framework for deadlock detection in core ABS. CoRR (2015)

16. Gonçalves, G.E., Endo, P.T., Santos, M.A., Sadok, D., Kelner, J., Melander, B., Mångs, J.: CloudML: an integrated language for resource, service and request description for D-Clouds. In: CloudCom (2011)

17. HashiCorp: Terraform. https://terraform.io/

18. Hewson, J.A., Anderson, P., Gordon, A.D.: A declarative approach to automated configuration. In: LISA (2012)

19. Kanies, L.: Puppet: next-generation configuration management. ;login: the USENIX magazine (1) (2006)

20. OASIS: Cloud Application Management for Platforms. http://docs.oasis-open.org/camp/camp-spec/v1.1/camp-spec-v1.1.html

21. OASIS: Topology and Orchestration Specification for Cloud Applications (TOSCA) Version 1.0. http://docs.oasis-open.org/tosca/TOSCA/v1.0/cs01/TOSCA-v1.0-cs01.html

22. Opscode: Chef. http://www.opscode.com/chef/

23. Puppet Labs: Marionette collective. http://docs.puppetlabs.com/mcollective/

24. Rendl, A., Guns, T., Stuckey, P.J., Tack, G.: MiniSearch: a solver-independent meta-search language for MiniZinc. In: CP (2015)

25. Wong, P.Y.H., Bubel, R., de Boer, F.S., Gómez-Zamalloa, M., de Gouw, S., Hähnle, R., Meinke, K., Sindhu, M.A.: Testing abstract behavioral specifications. STTT **17**(1), 107–119 (2015)

26. Zabolotnyi, R., Leitner, P., Hummer, W., Dustdar, S.: JCloudScale: closing the gap between IaaS and PaaS. ACM Trans. Internet Technol. **15**(3), 10 (2015)

Job Placement

Interplay of Virtual Machine Selection and Virtual Machine Placement

Zoltán Ádám Mann[(✉)]

paluno – The Ruhr Institute for Software Technology,
University of Duisburg-Essen, Essen, Germany
zoltan.mann@gmail.com

Abstract. Previous work on optimizing resource provisioning in virtualized environments focused either on mapping virtual machines to physical machines (i.e., virtual machine placement) or mapping computational tasks to virtual machines (i.e., virtual machine selection). In this paper, we investigate how these two optimization problems influence each other. Our study shows that exploiting knowledge about the physical machines and about the virtual machine placement algorithm in the course of virtual machine selection leads to better overall results than considering the two problems in isolation.

1 Introduction

As cloud data centers are serving an ever growing demand for computation, storage, and networking, their efficient operation has become a high priority. On one hand, the operation of data centers incurs huge costs and environmental impact. According to a recent study, data center electricity consumption in the USA alone will increase to 140 billion kWh per year by 2020, costing US businesses 13 billion USD annually in electricity bills and emitting nearly 100 million tons of CO_2 per year [25]. On the other hand, servers often run with low utilization – in fact, a significant percentage of running servers do not do any useful work [1].

Virtualization has been widely adopted in data centers to consolidate workload on the necessary number of physical machines (PMs), with the aim of achieving high utilization and switching off unused PMs to save energy. For this purpose, virtual machines (VMs) are used as the virtual infrastructure for running the workload. Live migration technology makes it possible to migrate a running VM from one PM to another one without noticeable downtime. This way, data center operators can react to changes in the workload and always use the appropriate number of turned-on PMs to accommodate the active VMs, taking into account their current resource needs. However, too aggressive consolidation must be avoided because overloading physical resources leads to performance degradation. Furthermore, live migration of VMs incurs increased resource consumption, so that the number of migrations must be limited.

© IFIP International Federation for Information Processing 2016
Published by Springer International Publishing Switzerland 2016. All Rights Reserved
M. Aiello et al. (Eds.): ESOCC 2016, LNCS 9846, pp. 137–151, 2016.
DOI: 10.1007/978-3-319-44482-6_9

Optimization relating to the management of VMs has received considerable attention in the last couple of years because of its impact on costs, application performance and carbon emission [29]. As shown in our recent survey [21], most previous research efforts fall into one of two categories: VM placement and VM selection. The goal of *VM placement* is to determine a mapping of VMs to PMs with the objective of minimizing energy consumption while obeying performance constraints and keeping the number of VM migrations low [23]. On the other hand, *VM selection* is concerned with assigning computational tasks to VMs.

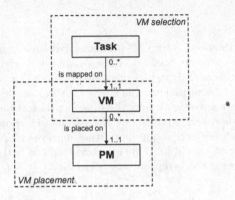

Fig. 1. Overview of VM selection and VM placement

The separation between the VM placement problem and the VM selection problem (see Fig. 1) is rooted in the fact that the two kinds of optimization are performed by different actors: VM placement is carried out by cloud providers, whereas VM selection is done by cloud users. Moreover, the two problems are quite different: VM placement is about physical resources, power consumption, and live migration, whereas VM selection is typically concerned with lease costs and application-level performance metrics. The central notion that connects the two perspectives is the VM.

Although VMs play an important role, we argue that VMs are just a tool for mapping users' tasks to PMs in a safe and manageable fashion. Users' main objective is to find hosts for their tasks, providers' objective is to utilize their infrastructure by accommodating workload that is valuable for users. VMs can be seen as wrappers around tasks that make all this possible, at the price of some overhead. In this respect, VM placement and VM selection are just two sides of the same coin. Most importantly, the two problems influence each other.

A simplified example is shown in Fig. 2. Here, we consider PMs of capacity 1 (for this conceptual example, the exact metric is unimportant) and six tasks with resource need 0.3 each. Further, we assume that a VM adds an overhead of 0.05 to the size of the contained task(s) in terms of resource consumption. The three subfigures show the effect of different VM selection algorithms on VM placement. In Fig. 2(a), the VM selection algorithm selects a dedicated VM for

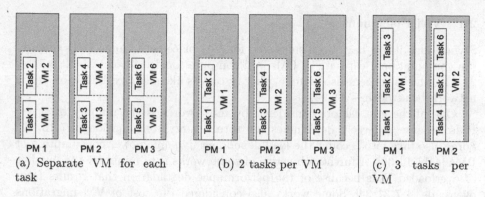

Fig. 2. Examples of the impact of VM selection decisions on the possibilities of VM placement

each task, resulting in 6 VMs of size 0.35 each, the placement of which requires at least 3 PMs. In Fig. 2(b), tasks are grouped pairwise into VMs, resulting in 3 VMs of size 0.65 each, the placement of which again requires 3 PMs. In Fig. 2(c), groups of 3 tasks are mapped to VMs, resulting in 2 VMs of size 0.95 each, and these can be hosted by 2 PMs. Therefore, this third scenario leads to approximately 33 % energy savings. However, if we continue this line of thought and map 4 tasks into a single VM, this would result in a VM of size 1.25, which cannot be accommodated by the available PMs (or, if we map such a VM to one of the available PMs, this will lead to severe resource overload).

As demonstrated by this example, VM selection influences VM placement in a non-trivial way. Therefore we argue that, at least in a private cloud setting, where VM selection and VM placement are in the hand of the same organization, the two kinds of optimization should be carried out in a closely coupled way. Even in a public cloud setting, it is important to understand the inter-dependence of the two optimization problems, so that the provider can motivate users (by means of appropriate pricing mechanisms) to use VM sizes that allow good placement. So, the main question that this paper addresses can be summarized as follows: how to perform VM selection in such a way that the resulting VMs allow an advantageous VM placement?

In particular, we show that incorporating knowledge about the capacity of the PMs into the VM selection algorithm already leads to substantial improvement compared to PM-oblivious VM selection. Further improvement is possible if the VM selection algorithm also exploits knowledge about the current placement of VMs on PMs as well as about the VM placement optimization algorithm.

2   Previous Work

As shown in our recent survey [21], most previous research efforts on VM mapping problems fall into one of two categories: VM placement is concerned with mapping VMs to PMs in a data center, while VM selection considers the problem of mapping tasks to VMs.

2.1   VM Placement

Several algorithms have been suggested for VM placement. Some focus only on the computational capacity of PMs and computational load of VMs [2,4,7,14, 22,34], whereas others also include other resources like memory, I/O, storage, or network bandwidth [5,11,24,31].

One of the cost factors considered by most works is the number of active PMs because it largely determines the total energy consumption [3,7,13,34]. Some also take into account the load-dependent dynamic power consumption of PMs [4,11,14,30]. A further objective of some works is to minimize the number of overloaded PMs because of the performance degradation that results from overloads [4,7,31,34]. Some works also considered the cost of VM migrations [4,7,13,30].

The special case of the VM placement problem in which a single resource type is considered and the only objective is to minimize the number of used PMs is equivalent to the well-known bin-packing problem. On the one hand, this means that the VM placement problem is strongly NP-hard so that the existence of an efficient exact algorithm is very unlikely. On the other hand, simple packing heuristics like First-Fit (FF), Best-Fit (BF), Worst-Fit (WF) and First-Fit-Decreasing (FFD) are known to perform very well on bin-packing. Hence, several authors proposed to adopt such heuristics to the VM placement problem [2–4,14,19,31,34].

2.2   VM Selection

Concerning VM selection, also many different problem models have been suggested. Similarly to the VM placement problem, most works focus on computational power [8,20,27,35] but some consider also other resource types like memory [18,26]. The main optimization objective is to find the best trade-off between performance and VM lease costs, which typically means that either the minimum required performance is given and costs must be minimized or the acceptable costs are constrained and performance must be maximized.

Several different models have been investigated also in terms of VM lease costs. Most works consider costs proportional to VM usage time [6,15,20,32,33,35], but some also add fees depending on consumed resource usage [18,26] or discounts for long-term VM rental [12,18].

Existing VM selection algorithms assume that VMs have fixed rental fees and fixed capacities. However, in a private cloud, VM capacities can be arbitrarily chosen and also changed, and instead of rental fees, real operations costs have to be minimized, which are incurred at the level of PMs.

2.3   Inter-dependence of VM Placement and VM Selection

In contrast to the works cited above, we do not handle VM placement or VM selection in isolation, but are interested in their interplay. We are aware of two papers that have a somewhat similar aim. The recent work of Piraghaj et al. [28]

focuses on selecting optimal VM sizes based on the characteristics of the tasks to be allocated. The objective is to reduce energy consumption by minimizing resource wastage. Each VM is assumed to have a fixed size irrespective of its workload, and the difference between the VM's size and the total size of its workload is wasted.

In contrast, we assume that a VM's real size (what is taken into account by the provider in VM placement decisions) follows the resource requirements of its workload. The rationale is that resource usage is most of the time significantly below the peak, yielding a great opportunity for consolidating VMs based on their current load and continuously adapting the placement accordingly, always using just the necessary number of active PMs [30,34]. Another important difference is that the work of Piraghaj et al. did not consider migrations, whereas we do. Through these differences we arrive at a more realistic model, in which the sought trade-offs and the objectives are also different (consolidation through migration versus minimization of wastage through sizing).

Ganesan et al. [10] consider a Software-as-a-Service provider that wants to allocate the components of its applications to VMs. The focus of the work is on VM sizing, namely, determining the dedicated and shared capacity for the VMs, based on past observations of the applications' workload. Their algorithm also outputs *recommendations* for VM placement, like which VMs can be placed statically and which ones need dynamic placement. However, the actual allocation of VMs to PMs is not carried out; they assume that it is done by some external algorithm. In contrast, we are interested in the impact of sizing on placement; it is unfortunately not possible to tell how good that approach is in this respect. Another limitation of that paper is the assumption that each application component is mapped to a separate VM, whereas we also allow to co-locate multiple tasks in the same VM.

3   Problem Model

VM selection and VM placement are difficult problems on their own, so combining them results in a very complex problem. In this paper, we focus on the following aspects, related to performance and costs (and leave further aspects, such as security and fault tolerance, for future research):

- Energy consumption of the PMs, which depends on the number and load of turned-on PMs
- Overhead (extra resource consumption) of virtualization
- Overhead (extra time) associated with launching new VMs
- Overhead (extra resource consumption) of VM migrations
- Performance degradation resulting from PM overloads

It is important to note that the impact of these aspects are conflicting: e.g., because of the overheads of virtualization, it would be advantageous to combine into a single VM as many tasks as possible; on the other hand, too big VMs limit the consolidation possibilities, thus potentially leading to higher energy consumption and/or more PM overloads.

We consider d resource types; for example, if CPU and memory are considered, then $d = 2$. Each task j has a size $s(j) \in \mathbb{R}_+^d$ describing its resource need according to the considered resource types. Similarly, the size of a VM v is $s(v) \in \mathbb{R}_+^d$, the vector of its resource needs. Each task must be mapped to exactly one VM; a VM may accommodate multiple tasks. For a task j, $v(j)$ denotes its hosting VM; for a VM v, $T(v)$ denotes the set of tasks that it hosts. The size of a VM is determined by the size of the tasks it hosts:

$$s(v) = s_0 + \sum_{j \in T(v)} s(j), \tag{1}$$

where $s_0 \in \mathbb{R}_+^d$ is the size of an empty VM, representing the overhead of virtualization, in terms of extra resource consumption. This overhead stems from the (load-independent) resource needs of the guest operating system, hence a constant overhead is a good approximation, although for some resource types more sophisticated models of the virtualization overhead might be more realistic.

Each PM p has a capacity $c(p) \in \mathbb{R}_+^d$. Each VM v must be hosted by exactly one PM $p(v)$; a PM p may host multiple VMs and their set is denoted by $V(p)$. To guarantee the required level of performance, the following capacity constraint must hold:

$$s(p) = \sum_{v \in V(p)} s(v) \leq c(p). \tag{2}$$

Note that here "$\leq$" means that in each dimension the left-hand side must be less than or equal to the right-hand side.

The power consumption of a PM is a function of its CPU load. As in several previous works [2,11,17,30], we use a linear approximation, i.e., the power consumption of a PM with CPU capacity c and CPU load x is given by

$$W(x) = W_{min} + (W_{max} - W_{min}) \cdot x/c, \tag{3}$$

where W_{min} and W_{max} are the minimum and maximum power consumption of the PM, respectively.

To simplify the presentation, we assume that each PM has the same capacity and the same power consumption characteristics.

The following decision points – and hence optimization opportunities – exist:

- VM selection:
    - If a new task arrives, it must be mapped to a VM. For this purpose, either one of the existing VMs must be selected or a new VM must be created.
    - If a VM becomes empty, it can be destroyed or kept for later reuse.
- VM placement:
    - If a new VM is created, it must be mapped to a PM. For this purpose, either one of the turned-on PMs must be chosen or a new PM must be turned on.
    - A VM can be migrated from its old PM to a new one.
    - If a PM becomes empty, it can be switched off.

Note that the VM placement can be re-optimized again and again with live migrations; in contrast, a task is mapped to one VM for its entire life[1].

The aim is to make these decisions in such a way that the performance of the system is as high as possible (requiring the number of migrations, the number of PM overloads and the number of VM launches to be minimized) and its cost is as low as possible (requiring the number of turned-on PMs and their energy consumption to be minimized).

4   VM Selection and VM Placement Algorithms to Assess

Our aim is to investigate the interplay between VM selection and VM placement. For both subproblems, several algorithms are conceivable, leading to a huge number of possible combinations. To keep the number of experiments manageable, we chose to fix an algorithm for VM placement and consider a series of algorithms for VM selection that differ in how much knowledge they exploit about the underlying VM placement.

Specifically, we use the algorithm of Beloglazov et al. for VM placement as a representative example of previously proposed VM placement algorithms, which was shown to achieve a good trade-off between energy consumption, number of migrations, and number of PM overloads [2]. Whenever a new VM is requested, the first PM that has sufficient free capacity is chosen to host it or a new PM is turned on if no such PM could be found. Moreover, the VM placement is re-optimized at regular time intervals, consisting of the following steps:

1. From each overloaded PM, a minimal set of VMs is removed so that the PM is not overloaded anymore. (A PM is overloaded if its load exceeds its capacity in at least one dimension.)
2. From each underloaded PM, all its VMs are removed. (A PM p is underloaded if $s(p) \leq \lambda \cdot c(p)$, i.e., its load is below λ times its capacity in each dimension, where $0 < \lambda < 1$ is a given constant.)
3. The list of removed VMs is sorted in decreasing order of CPU load.
4. For each removed VM, the first PM with sufficient free capacity is chosen.
5. Emptied PMs are switched off.

Next, the considered VM selection algorithms are presented. We start with the ones that are completely oblivious of the underlying PMs and the VM placement algorithm, and then gradually increase the exploited knowledge:

- **Simple.** This approach creates a new VM for each task, like in [10].
- **Multiple(k).** Tasks are assigned to VMs in groups of k, where $k \in \mathbb{Z}_+$ is a given constant. In the order as tasks arrive, a VM is created for task 1, which is then used for tasks $2, \ldots, k$ as well. For task $k + 1$, a new VM is created, which is used for tasks $k + 2, \ldots, 2k$ as well, and so on.

---

[1] Although some applications may support the migration of individual tasks, but this cannot be assumed in general.

- **Maxsize(μ).** In contrast to the previous algorithms, this one exploits some knowledge about the PMs. The idea here is to ensure that the size of each VM is at most $\mu \cdot c$, where $0 < \mu \leq 1$ is a given constant and c is the capacity vector of the PMs. When a new task arrives, it is checked which of the existing VMs could host it without exceeding the $\mu \cdot c$ threshold. If no such VM exists, a new one is created. If multiple appropriate VMs exist, one of them is selected according to a *selection policy*, which can be one of FF, BF, WF. Since these policies work in a single dimension whereas VM and task sizes are multi-dimensional, a *selection metric* is used to convert a d-dimensional vector to a number. Possible metrics are the sum, product, maximum, or minimum of the coordinates, the length of the vector, or the imbalance of the vector, defined as the difference between the maximum and minimum coordinate.
- **Consolidation-friendly.** This algorithm exploits not only knowledge about the PMs but also about the current VM placement and the VM placement algorithm. When a new task arrives, it is first checked whether there is a PM that is not underloaded and has enough free capacity to accommodate the new task. Such PMs are preferred because in this case, no overhead nor a PM overload is generated, and also no consolidation opportunity is obstructed. When there are multiple such PMs, one of them is selected using an appropriate PM selection heuristic and metric, similarly as in the Maxsize algorithm. When no such PM exists, then one of the underloaded PMs is selected with the same policy and metric. In this case, a consolidation opportunity is obstructed, but still no overhead is generated. In any case, after a PM has been chosen, one of its VMs has to be selected using a selection policy and metric, and the new task is mapped to this VM. Finally, if no appropriate PM could be found, then a new VM is created to accommodate the new task.

The Simple, Multiple, and Maxsize algorithms are used as representatives of the class of previously proposed VM selection algorithms. However, the Maxsize algorithm is already more advanced than the existing algorithms because existing algorithms just assume some given VM size limit without considering how this size limit should relate to the PMs' capacity. The Consolidation-friendly algorithm was designed by us specifically to show how detailed knowledge about the underlying VM placement algorithm can be exploited during VM selection.

5   Empirical Results

All the proposed algorithms were implemented in a simulation framework in C++, which is freely available from https://sourceforge.net/p/vm-alloc/task_vm_pm/. To obtain practically relevant results, we used real-world test data. For the tasks, we used a real workload trace from the Grid Workloads Archive, namely the AuverGrid trace, available from http://gwa.ewi.tudelft.nl/datasets/gwa-t-4-auvergrid. From the trace, we used the first 10,000 tasks that had valid CPU and memory usage data. The simulated time (i.e., the time between the start of the first task and the end of the last one) is a bit over 29 days, thus giving sufficient exposure to practical workload patterns.

As PMs, we simulated HP ProLiant DL380 G7 servers with Intel Xeon E5640 quad-core CPU and 16 GB RAM. Their power consumption varies from 280 W (zero load) to 540 W (full load) [16]. Throughout the experiments, we focus on two resource types: CPU and memory, i.e., $d = 2$. For memory sizes, absolute values are used in MB. For CPU capacities and loads, relative values are used, where 100 % is the capacity of one physical CPU core. Concerning virtualization overhead, previous work reported 5–15 % for the CPU [36] and 107–566 MB for memory [9]. In our experiments, we use 10 % CPU overhead and 200 MB memory overhead. The parameter of the VM placement algorithm, λ, is set to 0.4 as in [2]. The VM placement is re-optimized every 5 min.

For each evaluated algorithm, the following *quality metrics* were measured:

- Total energy consumption
- Average number of turned-on PMs
- Maximum number of turned-on PMs
- Maximum number of concurrently used VMs (as indication of the necessary number of VM launches)
- Number of migrations
- Number of PM overloads

For each quality metric, smaller numbers are better.

First, the Simple and Multiple(k) algorithms are evaluated. Note that Multiple(1) is exactly the Simple algorithm.

The results are shown in Fig. 3. As can be seen, the total energy consumption and the average and maximum number of turned-on PMs all show a similar pattern with an increase at the beginning, maximum at $k = 2$, and decrease afterwards. This can be attributed to two conflicting effects. With increasing k, the average VM size grows and the number of VMs decreases, which leads on the one hand to less consolidation opportunities, on the other hand to a decrease of the resource consumption overhead.

Based on these metrics, higher values of k seem preferable. However, from Fig. 3(e) and (f) it can be seen that the number of PM overloads skyrockets at $k = 17$ and the number of migrations is exorbitantly large already for $k \geq 4$. Although there is a slow decrease of the number of migrations afterwards (thanks to the decreasing number of consolidation opportunities), but an acceptable level is reached only for very high values of k, where the number of overloads is already prohibitively large. Thus, the best compromise seems to be the case $k = 3$.

The biggest problem with the Multiple(k) algorithm is that the value of k at which the sudden explosion of the number of migrations and number of overloads takes place cannot be predicted nor controlled. This depends on several factors, like the capacity of the PMs and the workload's characteristics. Therefore, this algorithm is dangerous. Small values of k are safer but lead to higher costs (higher energy consumption) and lower performance (more VMs need to be launched).

Next, we evaluated the Maxsize(μ) algorithm. More precisely, this is a family of algorithms, characterized by the value of μ, the used selection policy, and selection metric. We tested 6 different values for μ (0.25, 0.3, 0.5, 0.6, 0.9, 1.0),

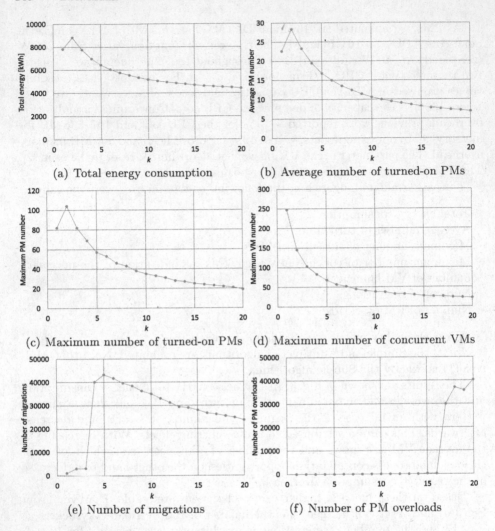

Fig. 3. Results of the Multiple(k) algorithm for different values of k

3 selection policies (FF, BF, WF), and 6 selection metrics (sum, product, maximum, minimum, imbalance, length). The effect of μ on the different quality metrics is shown in Fig. 4 (each data point corresponds to one value of μ and the average according to the two other parameters).

In contrast to the previous experience with the Multiple(k) algorithm, these figures show no sudden large increases in any quality metric. This is a big advantage: apparently, the knowledge of the PMs' capacity allows the algorithm much better control of the PMs' utilization, leading to safer operation. Only the number of migrations (Fig. 4(e)) and the number of PM overloads (Fig. 4(f)) show some seemingly significant oscillations; however, when compared with the corresponding results of the Multiple(k) algorithm, we can see that these oscillations span actually a quite small range.

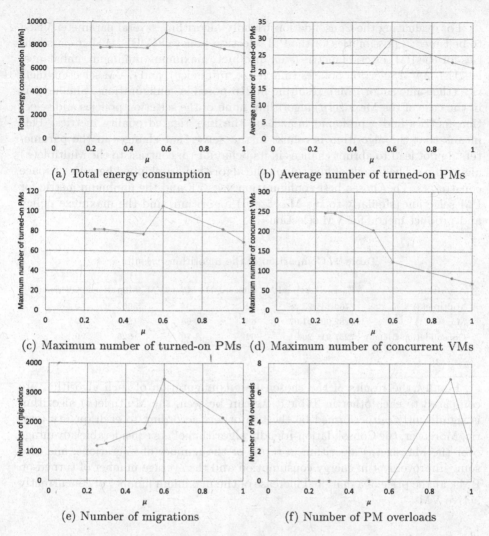

Fig. 4. Results of the Maxsize(μ) algorithm for different values of μ

Looking at the details, it can be observed that $\mu = 0.6$ leads to significantly worse performance than $\mu = 0.5$ according to most quality metrics. This is logical, since VMs of size at most $0.5 \cdot c$ can be pairwise consolidated to a PM, but if their size can go somewhat beyond this limit, then the opportunities for consolidation decrease. This shows once again the importance of PM-level knowledge in VM selection. According to most quality metrics, $\mu = 1$ is the best choice.

The effect of the selection policy and selection metric on the considered quality metrics is much smaller than the effect of μ. Therefore, to save space, these results are not shown (but they can also be found in our online repository mentioned above). The FF policy and the minimum metric were chosen as best, although their advantage over the others is small.

For evaluating the Consolidation-friendly algorithm, several parameters need to be tuned: 3 possibilities for the PM selection policy (FF, BF, WF), 6 possibilities for the PM selection metric (sum, product, maximum, minimum, imbalance, length), 2 VM selection policies (maximize, minimize), and 6 VM selection metrics (the same as for PMs), resulting in 216 possible configurations. Similarly as in the case of the Maxsize(μ) algorithm, none of the selection policies and selection metrics had a profound impact on the investigated quality metrics. This means that the algorithm is robust in the sense that changes in the parameters do not lead to abrupt changes in its behavior (in contrast to the Multiple(k) algorithm). The details of fine-tuning the algorithm are skipped because of space constraints. The chosen best configuration uses FF and the minimum metric for PM selection (similarly to the Maxsize(μ) algorithm) and the maximize policy and product metric for VM selection.

Table 1. Comparison of the algorithms' results

Algorithm	Energy	Avg #PM	Max #PM	Max #VM	Migrations	Overloads
Multiple(3)	7766.14	23.28	82	103	3062	0
Maxsize(1)	7282.90	21.07	68	68	1209	0
Consolidation-friendly	7257.91	20.91	68	70	826	0

Finally, the results of the chosen best configuration of each algorithm are compared to each other in Table 1. As can be seen, the Multiple(k) algorithm is significantly outperformed by the two others according to each quality metric. Moreover, the Consolidation-friendly algorithm offers considerable advantage over the Maxsize(μ) algorithm in terms of the number of migrations, and also some improvement in energy consumption and the average number of turned-on PMs, at the price of a marginal increase of the maximum number of concurrently active VMs.

6   Conclusions

In this paper, we analyzed the interplay of VM selection and VM placement algorithms. By fixing the VM placement algorithm and considering a series of VM selection algorithms that exploit an increasing amount of knowledge about the underlying PMs and the VM placement, we showed the importance of such information. Specifically, already the knowledge of the PMs' capacity makes VM selection more efficient in terms of cost and also much more resilient to the negative impact of inappropriate parameter choices. Adding more knowledge about the details of the VM placement algorithm leads to a further improvement, especially in terms of the number of migrations.

This insight can be used especially in a private cloud setting, where all details of the PMs and the VM placement are available. In this case, exploiting this knowledge in the sizing of VMs and the mapping of tasks to VMs leads to considerable improvements. In a public cloud setting, the provider who has the knowledge about the PMs and the VM placement should shape usage-based pricing schemes in such a way that it corresponds to the real costs, so that users are incentivized to use actual VM sizes that lead to good consolidation.

Directions for future research include the investigation of further aspects that make the interplay of VM selection and VM placement even more complex, such as data transfer among the tasks or security and reliability considerations. Moreover, a software engineering challenge is how to design the interface between VM selection and VM placement tools so that they can exchange the necessary pieces of information.

Acknowledgments. A part of this work was carried out when Z.Á. Mann was with Budapest University of Technology and Economics. This work was partially supported by the Hungarian Scientific Research Fund (Grant Nr. OTKA 108947) and the European Union's 7th Framework Programme (FP7/2007–2013) under grant agreement 610802 (CloudWave).

References

1. Anthesis Group: 30% of servers are sitting "comatose" (2015). http://anthesisgroup.com/30-of-servers-are-sitting-comatose/
2. Beloglazov, A., Abawajy, J., Buyya, R.: Energy-aware resource allocation heuristics for efficient management of data centers for cloud computing. Future Gener. Comput. Syst. **28**, 755–768 (2012)
3. Beloglazov, A., Buyya, R.: Energy efficient allocation of virtual machines in cloud data centers. In: 10th IEEE/ACM International Conference on Cluster, Cloud and Grid Computing, pp. 577–578 (2010)
4. Beloglazov, A., Buyya, R.: Optimal online deterministic algorithms and adaptive heuristics for energy and performance efficient dynamic consolidation of virtual machines in cloud data centers. Concurr. Comput. Pract. Exp. **24**(13), 1397–1420 (2012)
5. Biran, O., Corradi, A., Fanelli, M., Foschini, L., Nus, A., Raz, D., Silvera, E.: A stable network-aware VM placement for cloud systems. In: Proceedings of the 12th IEEE/ACM International Symposium on Cluster, Cloud and Grid Computing (CCGRID 2012), pp. 498–506. IEEE Computer Society (2012)
6. Bittencourt, L.F., Madeira, E.R., da Fonseca, N.L.: Scheduling in hybrid clouds. IEEE Commun. Mag. **50**(9), 42–47 (2012)
7. Breitgand, D., Epstein, A.: SLA-aware placement of multi-virtual machine elastic services in compute clouds. In: 12th IFIP/IEEE International Symposium on Integrated Network Management, pp. 161–168 (2011)
8. Candeia, D., Araújo, R., Lopes, R., Brasileiro, F.: Investigating business-driven cloudburst schedulers for e-science bag-of-tasks applications. In: 2nd IEEE International Conference on Cloud Computing Technology and Science, pp. 343–350 (2010)
9. Chang, C.R., Wu, J.J., Liu, P.: An empirical study on memory sharing of virtual machines for server consolidation. In: IEEE 9th International Symposium on Parallel and Distributed Processing with Applications, pp. 244–249 (2011)

10. Ganesan, R., Sarkar, S., Narayan, A.: Analysis of SaaS business platform workloads for sizing and collocation. In: IEEE 5th International Conference on Cloud Computing (CLOUD), pp. 868–875 (2012)
11. Gao, Y., Guan, H., Qi, Z., Hou, Y., Liu, L.: A multi-objective ant colony system algorithm for virtual machine placement in cloud computing. J. Comput. Syst. Sci. **79**, 1230–1242 (2013)
12. Genez, T.A.L., Bittencourt, L.F., Madeira, E.R.M.: Workflow scheduling for SaaS/PaaS cloud providers considering two SLA levels. In: Network Operations and Management Symposium (NOMS), pp. 906–912. IEEE (2012)
13. Gmach, D., Rolia, J., Cherkasova, L., Kemper, A.: Resource pool management: reactive versus proactive or let's be friends. Comput. Netw. **53**(17), 2905–2922 (2009)
14. Guazzone, M., Anglano, C., Canonico, M.: Exploiting VM migration for the automated power and performance management of green cloud computing systems. In: Huusko, J., de Meer, H., Klingert, S., Somov, A. (eds.) E2DC 2012. LNCS, vol. 7396, pp. 81–92. Springer, Heidelberg (2012)
15. Hoenisch, P., Hochreiner, C., Schuller, D., Schulte, S., Mendling, J., Dustdar, S.: Cost-efficient scheduling of elastic processes in hybrid clouds. In: IEEE 8th International Conference on Cloud Computing, pp. 17–24 (2015)
16. HP: Power efficiency and power management in HP ProLiant servers (2012). http://h10032.www1.hp.com/ctg/Manual/c03161908.pdf
17. Jung, G., Hiltunen, M.A., Joshi, K.R., Schlichting, R.D., Pu, C.: Mistral: dynamically managing power, performance, and adaptation cost in cloud infrastructures. In: IEEE 30th International Conference on Distributed Computing Systems, pp. 62–73 (2010)
18. Lampe, U., Siebenhaar, M., Hans, R., Schuller, D., Steinmetz, R.: Let the clouds compute: cost-efficient workload distribution in infrastructure clouds. In: Vanmechelen, K., Altmann, J., Rana, O.F. (eds.) GECON 2012. LNCS, vol. 7714, pp. 91–101. Springer, Heidelberg (2012)
19. Li, W., Tordsson, J., Elmroth, E.: Virtual machine placement for predictable and time-constrained peak loads. In: Vanmechelen, K., Altmann, J., Rana, O.F. (eds.) GECON 2011. LNCS, vol. 7150, pp. 120–134. Springer, Heidelberg (2012)
20. Li, W., Tordsson, J., Elmroth, E.: Modeling for dynamic cloud scheduling via migration of virtual machines. In: Proceedings of the 3rd IEEE International Conference on Cloud Computing Technology and Science, pp. 163–171 (2011)
21. Mann, Z.A.: Allocation of virtual machines in cloud data centers - a survey of problem models and optimization algorithms. ACM Comput. Surv. **48**(1) (2015). Article No. 11
22. Mann, Z.A.: Rigorous results on the effectiveness of some heuristics for the consolidation of virtual machines in a cloud data center. Future Gener. Comput. Syst. **51**, 1–6 (2015)
23. Mann, Z.A.: A taxonomy for the virtual machine allocation problem. Int. J. Math. Models Methods Appl. Sci. **9**, 269–276 (2015)
24. Mishra, M., Sahoo, A.: On theory of VM placement: anomalies in existing methodologies and their mitigation using a novel vector based approach. In: IEEE International Conference on Cloud Computing, pp. 275–282 (2011)
25. Natural Resources Defense Council: Scaling up energy efficiency across the data center industry: evaluating key drivers and barriers (2014). http://www.nrdc.org/energy/files/data-center-efficiency-assessment-IP.pdf

26. Oliveira, D., Ocana, K.A.C.S., Baiao, F., Mattoso, M.: A provenance-based adaptive scheduling heuristic for parallel scientific workflows in clouds. J. Grid Comput. **10**, 521–552 (2012)

27. Pandey, S., Wu, L., Guru, S.M., Buyya, R.: A particle swarm optimization-based heuristic for scheduling workflow applications in cloud computing environments. In: 24th IEEE International Conference on Advanced Information Networking and Applications (AINA), pp. 400–407. IEEE (2010)

28. Piraghaj, S.F., Dastjerdi, A.V., Calheiros, R.N., Buyya, R.: Efficient virtual machine sizing for hosting containers as a service. In: IEEE World Congress on Services, pp. 31–38 (2015)

29. Sáez, S.G., Andrikopoulos, V., Hahn, M., Karastoyanova, D., Leymann, F., Skouradaki, M., Vukojevic-Haupt, K.: Performance and cost trade-off in IaaS environments: a scientific workflow simulation environment case study. In: Helfert, M., Muñoz, V.M., Ferguson, D. (eds.) Cloud Computing and Services Science. CCIS, vol. 581, pp. 153–170. Springer, Heidelberg (2015)

30. Svärd, P., Li, W., Wadbro, E., Tordsson, J., Elmroth, E.: Continuous datacenter consolidation. In: IEEE 7th International Conference on Cloud Computing Technology and Science (CloudCom), pp. 387–396 (2015)

31. Tomás, L., Tordsson, J.: An autonomic approach to risk-aware data center overbooking. IEEE Trans. Cloud Comput. **2**(3), 292–305 (2014)

32. Tordsson, J., Montero, R.S., Moreno-Vozmediano, R., Llorente, I.M.: Cloud brokering mechanisms for optimized placement of virtual machines across multiple providers. Future Gener. Comput. Syst. **28**(2), 358–367 (2012)

33. Tsamoura, E., Gounaris, A., Tsichlas, K.: Multi-objective optimization of data flows in a multi-cloud environment. In: Proceedings of the Second Workshop on Data Analytics in the Cloud, pp. 6–10 (2013)

34. Verma, A., Dasgupta, G., Nayak, T.K., De, P., Kothari, R.: Server workload analysis for power minimization using consolidation. In: Proceedings of the 2009 USENIX Annual Technical Conference, pp. 355–368 (2009)

35. Villegas, D., Antoniou, A., Sadjadi, S.M., Iosup, A.: An analysis of provisioning and allocation policies for infrastructure-as-a-service clouds. In: 12th IEEE/ACM International Symposium on Cluster, Cloud and Grid Computing (CCGrid), pp. 612–619 (2012)

36. Zhou, Y., Zhang, Y., Liu, H., Xiong, N., Vasilakos, A.V.: A bare-metal and asymmetric partitioning approach to client virtualization. IEEE Trans. Serv. Comput. **7**(1), 40–53 (2014)

An Auto-Scaling Cloud Controller Using Fuzzy Q-Learning - Implementation in OpenStack

Hamid Arabnejad[1], Pooyan Jamshidi[2], Giovani Estrada[3], Nabil El Ioini[4], and Claus Pahl[4(✉)]

[1] IC4, Dublin City University, Dublin, Ireland
[2] Imperial College London, London, UK
[3] Intel, Leixlip, Ireland
[4] Free University of Bozen-Bolzano, Bolzano, Italy
`claus.pahl@unibz.it`

Abstract. Auto-scaling, i.e., acquiring and releasing resources automatically, is a central feature of cloud platforms. The key problem is how and when to add/remove resources in order to meet agreed service-level agreements. Many commercial solutions use simple approaches such as threshold-based ones. However, providing good thresholds for auto-scaling is challenging. Recently, machine learning approaches have been used to complement and even replace expert knowledge. We propose a dynamic learning strategy based on a fuzzy logic algorithm, which learns and modifies fuzzy scaling rules at runtime without requiring prior knowledge. The proposed algorithm is implemented and evaluated as an extension to the OpenStack cloud platform, integrating it with the Heat and Ceilometer components for orchestration and monitoring, respectively, using Heat Orchestration Templates. We specifically focus on implementation and experimentation aspects here. Our auto-scaling approach can handle various load traffic situations, delivering resources on demand while reducing infrastructure and management costs. The experimentals show promising performance in terms of resource adjustment to optimize SLA compliance (response time) while reducing cloud provider's costs.

Keywords: Cloud computing · Orchestration · Controller · Fuzzy logic · Q-learning · OpenStack

1 Introduction

Cloud computing allows easy deployment of elastic applications. Our focus is on Infrastructure as a Service (IaaS), which allows customers to increase or decrease their computational and storage resources on the fly. The consumer does not manage or control the underlying cloud infrastructure, but has control over operating systems, storage, and deployed applications [12]. IaaS provides virtualization, which enables running multiple operating system (OS) instances, called virtual machines (VMs), on the same physical server.

© IFIP International Federation for Information Processing 2016
Published by Springer International Publishing Switzerland 2016. All Rights Reserved
M. Aiello et al. (Eds.): ESOCC 2016, LNCS 9846, pp. 152–167, 2016.
DOI: 10.1007/978-3-319-44482-6_10

Important concepts of cloud computing are elasticity and dynamism. Managing physical and virtual resources is a key challenge in the IaaS model. However, it allows applications to acquire and release resources dynamically, but deciding the correct number of resources to be released/acquired is the challenging concern. *Auto-scaling* is a process that automatically scales the number of resources and maintains an acceptable Quality-of-Service (QoS). The scaling process can be either vertical or horizontal. Vertical scaling involves modifying the amount of resources assigned to each VM (CPU and memory, mostly). Horizontal scaling involves acquiring or releasing of VMs. In most common operating systems, altering CPU core, memory or disk of the VM which it runs, is not possible without rebooting; for this reason, most cloud provider only offer horizontal scaling.

To address auto-scaling in IaaS infrastructures, we utilise FQL4KE, a technique for dynamic resource allocation, presented in [9]. The advantage of FQL4KE is that we do not need to rely on the knowledge provided by the users anymore, FQL4KE can start adjusting application resources with no a priori knowledge. We focus here on the implementation and evaluation of FQL4KE as an extension to the OpenStack cloud platform, integrating it with the Heat and Ceilometer components for orchestration and monitoring, respectively, using Heat Orchestration Templates for orchestration specification. Previously in [9], we performed the experiments on PaaS cloud platform whereas in this research, we specifically focus on architecture, implementation and experimentation aspects in OpenStack as an industry-standard IaaS cloud platform (we have documented the applicability to other platforms such as Azure elsewhere [8,9]. New here is the in-depth implementation and experimental evaluation coverage. We also cover a wider range of workload patterns. We demonstrate that this auto-scaling approach can handle various load traffic situations, delivering resources on demand while reducing infrastructure and management costs. The experimental results show promising performance in terms of resource adjustment to optimize SLA compliance and response time while reducing cloud provider's costs.

The paper is organized as follows. Section 2 describes auto-scaling process briefly and discusses on related research in this area, Sect. 3 describes the OpenStack architecture and orchestration, Sect. 4 describes our approach in detail followed by implementation in Sect. 5 and evaluation in Sect. 6.

2   Background and Related Work

The aim of auto-scaling approaches is to acquire and release resources dynamically while maintaining an acceptable QoS [10]. The auto-scaling process is usually represented and implemented by a IBM's MAPE-K (Monitor, Analyze, Plan and Execute phases over a Knowledge base) control loop [7].

Threshold-based rules. Threshold-based rules are supported by many cloud solutions such as EC2, Azure, or OpenStack. Conditions and rules in threshold-based approaches can be defined based on one or more performance metrics, such as CPU load, average response time or request rate. Each rule includes an *upper* and a *lower* threshold that defines bound values for applying auto-scaling.

Dutreilh et al. [3] investigate horizontal auto-scaling using threshold-based and reinforcement learning techniques. In [5], the authors describe an approach that operates fine-grained scaling at resource level in addition to VM-level scaling in order to improve resource utilization while reducing cloud providers' costs. Hasan et al. [6] extend the typical two threshold bound values and add two levels of threshold parameters and use the three domains (CPU loads, response time and network link bandwidth) in making scaling decisions. Chieu et al. [2] propose a strategy for dynamic scalability of PaaS and SaaS applications based on the number of active sessions and scaling the number of VMs if all instances with active sessions exceed thresholds. The advantage is simplicity. However, the performance depends on the quality of the thresholds.

Reinforcement Learning (RL). RL [17] is learning process for an agent to maximize its rewards. Here, the agent is an auto-scaler, the action is scaling up/down, the context is the target application and the reward is the performance improvement after applying the action. The goal of RL is how to choose an action in response to current state to maximize the rewards. The most used approach is Q-learning. It learns estimates of Q-values $Q(s, a)$, which map all system states s to the best action a. We initialise all $Q(s, a)$ and, during learning, choose an action a for state s based on an ϵ-greedy policy and apply it to the target platform. Then, we observe the new state s' and reward r and update the Q-value of the last state-action pair $Q(s, a)$ with respect to the observed outcome state (s') and reward (r). Tesauro et al. [18] propose a hybrid learning system for dynamic server allocation maximize the profits. Their approach combines a queuing network model (for online management) and reinforced learning using the SARSA approach (for offline training), making resource allocation decisions based on application workload and response time. Rao et al. [15] introduce VCONF, a reinforcement learning approach in the context of neural networks, for dynamic VM autoconfiguration according to the application requirements, i.e., it automatically changes VM configurations in order to achieve good performance for hosted applications.

In RL, there is no need of prior knowledge. It has the ability to online learn and update environmental knowledge by actual observations. However, there are some drawbacks in this approach such as taking long time to converge to optimal or near optimal solution for solving large real world problems and requiring good initialization of the Q-function.

Control Theory. Control theory deals with influencing the behaviour of dynamical systems by monitoring output and comparing it with reference values. By using the feedback of the input system (the difference between actual and desired output level), the controller tries to align actual output to the reference. For auto-scaling, the reference parameter, i.e., an object to be controlled, is the targeted SLA value. The system is the target platform and system output are parameters to evaluate system performance (response time or CPU load).

Ali-Eldin et al. [1] use queueing theory to model a service. Two adaptive hybrid reactive/proactive controllers estimate future load in order to support elasticity. Padala et al. [13] propose a feedback resource control system that automatically adapts to dynamic workload changes to satisfy service level objectives. They use an online model estimator to dynamically maintain the relationship between applications and resources, and a two-layer multi-input, multi-output (MIMO) controller that allocates resources to applications dynamically.

3   OpenStack Orchestration

OpenStack is an open-source platform, mostly deployed as an IaaS and used for building public and private clouds. The platform consists of interrelated components that control hardware pools of processing, storage, and networking resources through a data center. Users either manage it through a web-based dashboard, through command-line tools, or through a RESTful API. Figure 1 overviews the OpenStack core services. The important components here are:

- **Neutron:** is a system for managing networks and IP addresses and handles creation and management of a virtual networking infrastructure and gives users self-service ability over network configurations. It provides frameworks to mange and deploy advanced services such as load balancing.
- **Nova:** is the primary computing engine behind OpenStack. It provides deploying and managing virtual machines and other instances to handle computing tasks as the main part of an IaaS system.
- **Glance:** provides discovery, registration, and delivery services for disk and server images. It allows to use stored images as templates for new servers.
- **Heat:** is a service for managing the infrastructure needed for cloud applications to run. It provides templates to create and manage cloud resources such as storage, networking, instances, or applications. Templates are used to create stacks, which are collections of resources.
- **Ceilometer:** provides telemetry services to collect metering data. The collected data can be used for billing, system monitoring, or alerts.
- **Keystone:** provides user/service/endpoint authentication and authorization. Calling the API function requires authentication by Keystone.

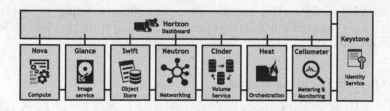

Fig. 1. An OpenStack block diagram

OpenStack orchestration allows managing the infrastructure required by a cloud application for its entire lifecycle. Orchestration automates processes which provision and integrate cloud resources such as storage, networking, instances to deliver a service defined by policies. Heat, as OpenStack's orchestration component, implements an engine to launch multiple composite cloud applications

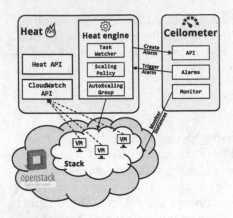
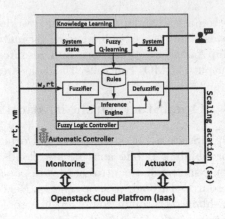

Fig. 2. Heat/Ceilometer architecture.   **Fig. 3.** Logical FQL4KE architecture.

described in text-based templates. Heat templates are used to create stacks, which are collections of resources such as compute instance, floating IPs, volumes, security groups or users, and the relationship between these resources. Heat along with ceilometer can create an auto-scaling service. By defining a scaling group (such as compute instance) alongside using monitoring alerts (such as CPU utilization) provided by Ceilometer, Heat can dynamically adjust resource allocation, i.e., launching resources to meet application demand and removing them when no longer required. Figure 2 shows the heat and ceilometer components. Heat executes HOT (Heat Orchestration Template) templates.

4   Auto-Scaling Algorithm

In [8,9] we proposed an elasticity controller, which is the basis of this investigation for OpenStack. This is an online learning mechanism by combining fuzzy control and fuzzy Q-learning (FQL) [4], called FQL4KE. The fuzzy Q-learning and control is a self-adaptive mechanism where the fuzzy control facilitates reasoning at a higher level of abstraction and the Q-learning allows to adjust the controller. The fuzzy rules are continually tuned through learning from the data collected. Here, we describe the implemention and evaluation in OpenStack.

4.1   FQL4KE Building Blocks

A fuzzy model is a qualitative model constructed from a set of fuzzy-rules to represent the relationship between system input and output [16]. However, there are some issues for defining rules at design-time such as: (i) whole knowledge or some parts of it may be available; (ii) knowledge is not an optimized model (existence of redundancy or ineffective rules); (iii) inaccuracy of some rules and (iv) instability of design-time rules requiring them to be changed at runtime. As a result, incomplete, inappropriate or not-optimized set of rules may lead to sub-optimal scaling decisions and loss of revenue for cloud application providers.

Figure 3 illustrates the building blocks of FQL4KE. During the application lifecycle, FQL4KE guides resource provisioning following the autonomic MAPE-K loop by monitoring continuously different characteristics of the application (workload and response time), checking the satisfaction of system goals and adopting resource allocation to satisfy goals.

The monitoring component collects required metrics such as workload (w), response time (rt) and number of VMs (vm) for both controller and learning component. The cloud controller is a fuzzy logic controller that takes the observed data, calculates the scaling action based on input monitored data and a set of rules, and as output returns the scaling action (sa) in terms of incrementing/decrementing the number of VMs. The learning component continuously updates the knowledge. Finally, the actuator issues adaptation commands from the controller at each control interval to the underlying platform.

4.2 Fuzzy Logic Controller

Fuzzy inference maps a set of control inputs to a set of control outputs through fuzzy rules. The first step is to partition the state space of each input variable into fuzzy sets through membership functions. Each fuzzy set is associated with a linguistic term such as "low" or "high". The membership function $\mu(x)$ quantifies the degree of membership of input signal x to the fuzzy set y. The membership functions, see Fig. 4, are triangular and trapezoidal [8]. Three fuzzy sets are defined for each input (workload and response time) to achieve a reasonable granularity in the input space while keeping the number of states small.

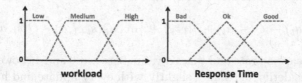

Fig. 4. Fuzzy membership functions for auto-scaling variables

For the inference mechanism, we define elasticity policies as rules: ''IF (w is *high*) AND (rt is *bad*) THEN ($sa+ = 2$)'', where the output function is a constant value that can be an integer in $\{-2, -1, 0, +1, +2\}$, which is associated to the change in the number of deployed nodes. Here, no a priori knowledge for defining the rules is assumed. FQL4KE finds the consequent Y for the rules.

Once the fuzzy controller is designed, controller execution comprises of three steps (cf. middle part of Fig. 3): (i) fuzzification of inputs, (ii) fuzzy reasoning and (iii) defuzzification of output. The fuzzifier projects the crisp data onto fuzzy information using membership functions. The fuzzy engine reasons based on a set of fuzzy rules and derives fuzzy actions. The defuzzifier reverts results back to crisp mode and activates an adaptation action. This result is enacted by issuing appropriate commands to the underlying platform fabric.

4.3 Fuzzy Q-Learning

The mechanism learns the policies at runtime, enabling knowledge evolution (i.e., KE in FQL4KE). As the controller has to take action in each control loop, it selects past actions taken which produced good (long-term cumulative) rewards:

$$R_t = r_{t+1} + \gamma r_{t+2} + \gamma^2 r_{t+3} + \cdots = \sum_{k=0}^{\infty} \gamma^k r_{t+k+1} \tag{1}$$

The discount rate γ determines the relative importance of future rewards. There is a trade-off (step 2 in Algorithm 1) between actions that have been tried (exploitation) and new actions that may lead to better rewards in the future (exploration).

In each control loop, the controller needs to take an action based on $Q(s, a)$, which is the expected cumulative reward that can be received by taking action a in state s. This value directly depends on the policy followed by the controller, thus determining the behavior of the controller. This policy $\pi(s, a)$ is the probability of taking action a from state s. As a result, the value of taking action a in state s following the policy π is defined as:

$$Q^{\pi}(s, a) = E_{\pi} \left\{ \sum_{k=0}^{\infty} \gamma^k r_{t+k+1} \right\} \tag{2}$$

where $E_{\pi}\{.\}$ is the expectation function under policy π. When an appropriate policy is found, the given learning problem is solved. Q-learning does not require any specific policy to evaluate $Q(s, a)$, therefore:

$$Q(s_t, a_t) \leftarrow Q(s_t, a_t) + \eta \left[r_{t+1} + \gamma \max_a Q(s_{t+1}, a) - Q(s_t, a_t) \right] \tag{3}$$

where η is the learning rate and takes a value between 0 and 1. Lower value for η means that considering old values slightly with every update and higher η gives more impact on recent rewards.

The policy adaptation is achieved by selecting a random action with probability ϵ and an action that maximizes Q in the current state with probability $1 - \epsilon$. The value of ϵ is determined by the exploitation/exploration strategy:

$$a(s) = \arg\max_a Q(s, k) \tag{4}$$

The fuzzy Q-learning is summarized in Algorithm 1[1]. For our use case, the state space is finite (i.e., 9 states as the full combination of 3×3 membership functions for fuzzy variables w and rt) and our controller has to choose a scaling action among 5 possible actions $\{-2, -1, 0, +1, +2\}$. However, the design methodology that we demonstrated in this section is general and can be applied for any possible state and action spaces. Note that the convergence is detected when the change in the consequent functions is negligible in each learning loop.

---

[1] A Matlab implementation: https://github.com/pooyanjamshidi/Fuzzy-Q-Learning.

Algorithm 1. Fuzzy Q-Learning

Require: discount rate (γ) and learning rate (η)
1: Initialize q-values:
2: Select an action for each fired rule:

$\qquad a_i = argmax_k q[i, k]$ with probability $1 - \epsilon$ $\qquad\qquad\qquad\qquad$ ▷ Eq 4

$\qquad a_i = random\{a_k, k = 1, 2, \cdots, J\}$ with probability ϵ

3: Calculate the control action by the fuzzy controller
4: Approximate the Q function from current q-values and firing level of the rules:

$$Q\big(s(t), a\big) = \sum_{i=1}^{N} \Big(\alpha_i(s) \times q[i, a_i] \Big)$$

$\qquad$ where $Q\big(s(t), a\big)$ is the value of the Q function for the state current state $s(t)$
$\qquad$ in iteration t and the action a

5: Take action a and let system goes to the next state $s(t + 1)$
6: Observe the reinforcement signal, $r(t+1)$ and compute the value for the new state:

$$V\big(s(t + 1)\big) = \sum_{i=1}^{N} \alpha_i\big(s(t + 1)\big).\max_a(q[i, q_k])$$

7: Calculate the error signal:

$\qquad \Delta Q = r(t + 1) + \gamma \times V_t\big(s(t + 1)\big) - Q\big(s(t), a\big)$ $\qquad\qquad\qquad$ ▷ Eq 3

8: Update q-values (where η is a learning rate):

$\qquad q[i, a_i] = q[i, a_i] + \eta.\Delta Q.\alpha_i\big(s(t)\big)$ $\qquad\qquad\qquad\qquad\qquad\qquad$ ▷ Eq 3

9: Repeat the process for the new state until it converges

4.4 Dynamic Resource Allocation by FQL4KE

For the *reward function*, the controller receives the current values of w and rt that correspond to the system state, $s(t)$ (step 4 in Algorithm 1). The control signal sa represents the action a that the controller takes in each iteration. We define the reward signal $r(t)$ based on two criteria: (i) SLA violations, and (ii) the amount of resources acquired, which directly determines the cost as follows:

$$r(t) = U(t) - U(t - 1) \tag{5}$$

where $U(t)$ is the utility value of the system at time t. Hence, if a controlling action leads to increased utility, it means that the action is appropriate. Otherwise, if the reward is close to zero, the action is not effective. A negative reward (punishment) makes the situation worse. The utility function is defined as:

$$U(t) = w_1.\Big(1 - \frac{vm(t)}{vm_{max}}\Big) + w_2.\Big(1 - H(t)\Big)$$

$$\tag{6}$$

$$H(t) = \begin{cases} \dfrac{rt(t) - rt_{des}}{rt_{des}}, & rt_{des} \le rt(t) \le 2.rt_{des} \\ 1, & rt(t) \ge 2.rt_{des} \\ 0, & rt(t) < rt_{des} \end{cases}$$

where $vm(r)$ and $rt(t)$ are workload and response time (actual & desired) of the system. w_1 and w_2 are their corresponding weights determining their relative importance in the utility function. In order to aggregate the individual criteria, we normalize them depending on whether they should be maximized or minimized.

For the *knowledge base update*, we start with controlling the allocation of resources with no a priori knowledge. After enough *explorations*, the consequents of the rules can be determined by selecting those actions that correspond to the *highest* q-value in each row of the Q-table. Although we do not rely on design-time knowledge, if even partial knowledge is available or there exists data regarding performance of the application, our solution can exploit such knowledge by initializing q-values (cf. step 1 in Algorithm 1) with more meaningful data. This implies a quicker learning convergence.

5 Implementation

We implemented `FQL4KE` in OpenStack. Orchestration and automation within OpenStack is handled by the Heat component. It provides a declarative structure for defining auto-scaling processes. A new OpenStack native standard has also been developed for providing templates for Orchestration called HOT (Heat Orchestration Template) which meant to replace the Heat CloudFormation-compatible format (CFN). Heat automatically provisions infrastructure (compute, network, storage) based on a YAML template file. The auto-scaling decisions made by Heat on when to scale application and whether scale up/down

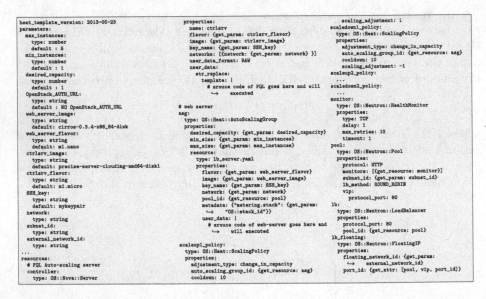

Fig. 5. Excerpts from OpenStack HOT Template, including resource boundaries and configurations, scaling policies and the integration of e.g. load balancer and monitoring tools, as part of the auto-scaling group (asg) definition.

should be applied, are determined based on collected metering parameters from platform. Collecting measurements in OpenStack is handled by Ceilometer.

A combination of Heat and Ceilometer is used (see Fig. 2). The main part of Heat is the stack, which contains resources such as compute instances, floating IPs, volumes, security groups or users, and the relationship between these resources. An exceprt of our Heat implementation, defined in YAML, is shown in Fig. 5. This YAML structure defines the required resources for auto-scaling process. Auto-scaling in Heat is done using three main resources:

- **auto-scaling group:** defined using type `OS::Heat::AutoScalingGroup` and is a resource type that is used to encapsulate the resource that we wish to scale, and some properties related to the scale process.
- **scaling policy:** defined using type `OS::Heat::ScalingPolicy` and is a resource type to define the effect a scaled process has on the resource.
- **alarm:** defined using type `OS::Ceilometer::Alarm` and is a resource type to define under which conditions the ScalingPolicy is triggered.

In the following, we describe the architectural integration of our controller with the OpenStack platform components – with turns out to be not straighforward.

In our implementation, the environment contains one or more VM instances that are members of a load balancer and defined as members in an AutoScalingGroup resource. Each instance (VM) includes a simple web server run inside of it after launching. The implemented server listens to an input port (here port 80) and return simple HTML pages as the response. The simple web server is created and coded as a part of the **user date** property of each VM. User data is the mechanism by which users can define their own pre-configuration as a shell script (the code of web server) that the instance runs on boot. The response time from each web server includes the VM instance's hostname. For the VM instance type, we used a minimal Linux distribution, `cirros`[2], an image that was designed for use as a test image on clouds such as OpenStack.

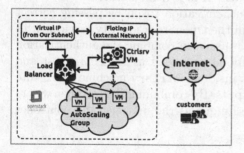

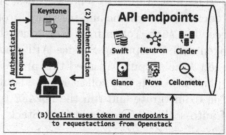

Fig. 6. System overview.   **Fig. 7.** cURL calling OpenStack API.

---

[2] CirrOS images, https://download.cirros-cloud.net/.

Generally, the native auto-scaling approach in OpenStack is designed by setting alarms based on threshold evaluations for a collection of metrics from Ceilometer. For this threshold approach, we can define actions to take if the state of the watched resource satisfies specified conditions. However, we replaced this by the FQL4KE algorithm, to control and manage scaling option. We added a resource type OS::Nova::Server to create an additional VM, named ctrlsrv, which acts as an auto-scaling server and enacts the scale up/down decision proposed the FQL learning algorithm. Figure 6 illustrates the implemented system in OpenStack. The created load-balancer distributes client HTTP requests across a set of web servers, i.e., auto-scaling group resources, collected in a load balancer pool. The algorithm used to distribute the load between members of the pool is ROUND_ROBIN. As shown, the ctrlsrv machine, by gathering information from the load-balancer and the current state of the AutoScalingGroup resource, decides which horizontal scaling, i.e., up or down, should applied in the target platform. The scale-up will launch a new server instance. which may take a few minutes as the instance needs to be started and added to the load-balancer pool. Once all preconfigured settings are installed, i.e., the defined user data file, it will go to active and receive or answer to requests sent by the load-balancer.

The proposed auto-scaling algorithm is coded in Python and runs inside the ctrlsrv machine. We added a complete fuzzy logic library. This is functionally similar to the respective matlab features and implements used our FQL4KE approach. However, for some parameters in the proposed algorithm, such as the current number of VM instances or workload, we used the OpenStack API command line. For example, command nova list shows a list of running instances. Due to the unavailability of direct access to the OpenStack API inside of ctrlsrv machine, we used the popular command line utility cURL to interact with a couple of OpenStack APIs. cURL allows transmitting and receiving HTTP requests and responses from the command line or a shell script, which enables working with the OpenStack API directly. For some OpenStack APIs, it is necessary to send additional data, such as authentication keys, as a header request. In Fig. 7, the process of using cURL to call OpenStack APIs is demonstrated.

The first step is to send a request authentication token by passing correct credentials (username and password) from the OpenStack identity service. After receiving Auth-Token from Keystone, the user can combine the authentication token and Computing Service API Endpoint and send as HTTP request and receive the output. We used this process inside of ctrlsrv machine to execute OpenStack APIs and collect required outputs. By combining the settings, we are able to inetgrate and run the FQL4KE technique as the manager and controller of auto-scaling processes in OpenStack.

6   Experimental Results and Discussion

The experimental evaluation is designed to show the effectiveness of proposed FQL4KE approach as part of the OpenStack platform. Furthermore, the cost improvement by proposed approach for cloud provider is demonstrated.

6.1   Experimental Setup and Benchmark

In our experiment, FQL4KE was implemented as a full working system and was tested on OpenStack. A web server was considered as target cloud application. Each server is configured and installed on one dedicated VM, which uses Cirros images (Linux distribution), and random response times between 0 and 1 sec. For the auto-scaling control server, due to the Impossibiliity of installing any additional package in the Cirros image, we considered a VM machine running a Linux Ubuntu precise server. The maximum and minimum number of VMs that are allowed to be available at the same time is set to 5 and 1, respectively.

The term workload refers to a number of concurrent user request arrival in different time. Workload is defined as the sequential of users accessing the target application that need to be handled by auto-scaler. According to [10,11], application workload types can be categorized in four representative patterns: (a) The *Predictable Bursting* pattern indicates the type of workload that is subject to periodic peaks and valleys such services with seasonality trends or high performance computing, (b) the *Variations* pattern reflects applications such as News&Media, event registration or rapid fire sales, (c) the *Fast Growth* pattern presents applications such as events, business growth and slashdot effect and (d) the *ON&OFF* pattern reflects applications such as analytics, bank/tax agencies and test environments. In all cases, we considered 10 and 100 as minimum and maximum number of concurrent users per second.

We used Siege[3] as our performance measuring tool. Siege is a HTTP load testing and benchmarking utility which simulates web browsers. It can generate concurrent user requests and measure performance metrics such as average response time. For each number N of concurrent users, we generate N request per second by Siege for 10 min. The learning rate is set to a constant $\eta = 0.1$ and the discount factor is set to $\gamma = 0.8$. Here, considered lower value for η causes to giving more impact on old rewards with every update. After sufficient epochs of learning, we update the controller's knowledge base (FIS rules) and decrease the exploration rate (ϵ) until a minimum value is reached, here 0.2. So, FQL starts with exploration phase and after a first learning convergence happens, it enters the balanced exploration-exploitation phase.

Additionally, we compare the FQL4KE approach with a base-line strategy. The results of comparing with fixed numbers of VMs equal to a minimum and maximum permitted value are also shown as based-line (benchmark) approaches, named $VM\#1$ and $VM\#5$, reflecting under- and over-provisioning strategies.

6.2   Performance

The metric to evaluate dynamic auto-scaling of resource allocation must represent response time in order to measure the QoS experienced by the users. To compare our approach with other approaches, we use the observed end-to-end response time for four workload patterns (Figs. 8(a) and (b)), here achieving the

---

[3] Siege, https://www.joedog.org/siege-home/.

system goals. Additionally, to evaluate the infrastructure provider's operational cost, we used the percentage number of used VMs as represented metrics to show proposed approach effectiveness in auto-scaling applications to meet their QoS requirements while reducing infrastructure providers cost (Figs. 9(a) and (d)).

6.3   Effectiveness of the FQL4KE Algorithm

Figures 8(a) and (b) show the fluctuation of the observed end-to-end response time for the workload patterns, e.g., Predictable Bursting (sine wave) or Variation. For each change of the input workload, i.e., the concurrent input request submitted by individual users, the corresponding response time varies between upper or lower bound, depending on current load balance and number of available VMs. FQL4KE monitors the target application and scales up/down the current number of VMs by detecting these fluctuation of the response time. In our experiment, the scaling process, up/down, can be completed in a few milliseconds, due to simplicity and fast booting of Cirros image.

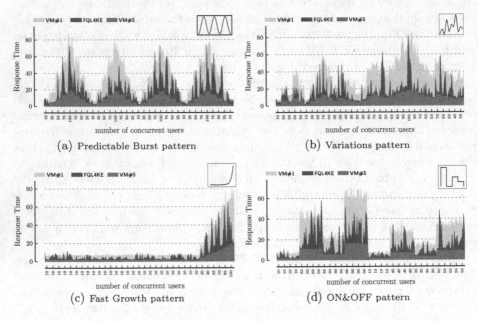

(a) Predictable Burst pattern

(b) Variations pattern

(c) Fast Growth pattern

(d) ON&OFF pattern

Fig. 8. The observed End-to-End response time for the four workload Patterns.

As shown in Fig. 8, FQL4KE demonstrates good performance compared with the base-line approaches, $VM\#1$ and $VM\#5$, which have a fixed number of VMs during the test. Firstly, performance of scaling actions produced by FQL4KE during the initial learning epochs at runtime may be poor. However, after some iterations and updating the knowledge base, the proposed approach adopts itself and is able to make more accurate decisions for the current status of system.

6.4   Cost-Effective Scaling by FQL4KE

Figs. 9(a) and (d) show the percentage of used VMs during the trial for all work-load patterns. Our approach depends on current workload and relative response time of the system at the current time, increasing the number of available VMs in scaling up and decreasing the number of idle VMs in scaling down. The FQL4KE algorithm conducts distributed-case scaling and allocates suitable numbers of VMs during the trail according to the workload. For example, the maximum number of VMs used is only in 19 % of time during our experiment. This implies our approach can meet the QoS requirements using a smaller amount of resources, which is an improvement on resource utilisation for applications in terms of hosting VMs. Thereby, FQL4KE can perform auto-scaling of application as well as save provider costs by increasing resource utilisation.

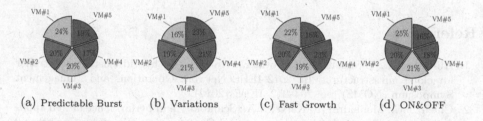

(a) Predictable Burst   (b) Variations   (c) Fast Growth   (d) ON&OFF

Fig. 9. Percentage numbers of VMs used by FQL4KE for 4 pattern types.

7   Conclusions and Future Work

We investigated VM-level scaling of cloud applications. In most real cases, no priori knowledge is available regarding elasticity policies that cloud controllers could exploit. A fuzzy Q-learning approach, called FQL4KE, that uses a fuzzy rule-based system combined with a reinforcement learning algorithm for learning optimal elasticity policies, has been implemented in OpenStack, an open-source IaaS platform. FQL4KE is capable of automatically updating the controller and learns to improve its performance simultaneously. Unlike supervised techniques, it does not require off-line training. FQL4KE can efficiently scale up/down cloud resources to meet the given QoS requirements while reducing cloud provider costs by improving resource utilisation. FQL4KE has been implemented in OpenStack platform to demonstrate the practical effectiveness of proposed approach has been successfully tested and presented.

A key contribution here is the demonstration of the architectural integration requirements that need to be overcome to actually implement an advanced autoscaling technique in an industrial setting. We have described the architectural challenges and solutions, including the successful evaluation in a real-world system. It reflects our experience in moveing a conceptual soliution that has been tested through simulations into a real setting. This includes how to use the platform mechanism to orchstrate the core tool like load balancer or networking, replacing the built-in controller and integrating this with identity management and the monitoring tools, which is critical in this context.

We plan to carry out further long-term experiments beyond the selected workload patterns induced. Conceptually, extensions are worth considering that extend the solution for environments which are partially observable. An exploration of different learning approaches, online and offline, is also planned. Here, possible dynamic changes in the fuzzy rule set need to be taken into account. A further direction is to investigate container virtualisation [14] and its workload and performance management.

Acknowledgement. This work was partly supported by IC4 (the Irish Centre for Cloud Computing and Commerce), funded by EI and the IDA.

References

1. Ali-Eldin, A., Tordsson, J., Elmroth, E.: An adaptive hybrid elasticity controller for cloud infrastructures. In: 2012 IEEE Network Operations and Management Symposium (NOMS), pp. 204–212. IEEE (2012)
2. Chieu, T.C., Mohindra, A., Karve, A.A.: Scalability and performance of web applications in a compute cloud. In: International Conference on e-Business Engineering (2011)
3. Dutreilh, X., Rivierre, N., Moreau, A., Malenfant, J., Truck, I.: From data center resource allocation to control theory and back. In: International Conference on Cloud Computing (CLOUD), pp. 410–417. IEEE (2010)
4. Glorennec, P.Y.: Fuzzy Q-learning and dynamical fuzzy Q-learning. In: Proceedings of the Third IEEE Conference on Fuzzy Systems, 1994, IEEE World Congress on Computational Intelligence, pp. 474–479. IEEE (1994)
5. Han, R., Guo, L., Ghanem, M.M., Guo, Y.: Lightweight resource scaling for cloud applications. In: 2012 12th IEEE/ACM International Symposium on Cluster, Cloud and Grid Computing (CCGrid), pp. 644–651. IEEE (2012)
6. Hasan, M.Z., Magana, E., Clemm, A., Tucker, L., Gudreddi, S.L.D.: Integrated and autonomic cloud resource scaling. In: Network Operations and Management Symposium (NOMS), pp. 1327–1334 (2012)
7. Huebscher, M.C., McCann, J.A.: A survey of autonomic computing degrees, models, and applications. ACM Comput. Surv. (CSUR) **40**(3), 7 (2008)
8. Jamshidi, P., Ahmad, A., Pahl, C.: Autonomic resource provisioning for cloud-based software. In: 9th International Symposium on Software Engineering for Adaptive and Self-Managing Systems, pp. 95–104. ACM (2014)
9. Jamshidi, P., Sharifloo, A., Pahl, C., Arabnejad, H., Metzger, A., Estrada, G.: Fuzzy self-learning controllers for elasticity management in dynamic cloud architectures. In: International ACM Sigsoft Conference on the Quality of Software Architectures QoSA'2016, ACM (2016)
10. Lorido-Botran, T., Miguel-Alonso, J., Lozano, J.A.: A review of auto-scaling techniques for elastic applications in cloud environments. J. Grid Comput. **12**(4), 559–592 (2014)

11. Mao, M., Humphrey, M.: Auto-scaling to minimize cost and meet application deadlines in cloud workflows. In: International Conference for High Performance Computing, Networking, Storage and Analysis, ACM (2011)
12. Mell, P., Grance, T.: The NIST definition of cloud computing (2011)
13. Padala, P., Hou, K.Y., Shin, K.G., Zhu, X., Uysal, M., Wang, Z., Singhal, S., Merchant, A.: Automated control of multiple virtualized resources. In: European Conference on Computer systems, pp. 13–26 (2009)
14. Pahl, C.: Containerisation and the PaaS Cloud. IEEE Cloud Comput. **2**(3), 24–31 (2015)
15. Rao, J., Bu, X., Xu, C.Z., Wang, L., Yin, G.: Vconf: a reinforcement learning approach to virtual machines auto-configuration. In: International Conference on Autonomic Computing, pp. 137–146 (2009)
16. Sugeno, M., Yasukawa, T.: A fuzzy-logic-based approach to qualitative modeling. IEEE Trans. Fuzzy Syst. **1**(1), 7–31 (1993)
17. Sutton, R.S., Barto, A.G.: Introduction to Reinforcement Learning, vol. 135. MIT Press, Cambridge (1998)
18. Tesauro, G., Jong, N.K., Das, R., Bennani, M.N.: A hybrid reinforcement learning approach to autonomic resource allocation. In: International Conference on Autonomic Computing, pp. 65–73 (2006)

FedUp! Cloud Federation as a Service

Paolo Bottoni$^{(\boxtimes)}$, Emanuele Gabrielli, Gabriele Gualandi,
Luigi Vincenzo Mancini, and Franco Stolfi

Cyber Intelligence and Information Security Research
Center Dipartimento di Informatica, Sapienza University of Rome, Rome, Italy
{bottoni,gabrielli,gualandi,mancini,stolfi}@di.uniroma1.it

Abstract. Current solutions for establishing federations of clouds require applications to be installed on the individual members of the federation, which have to devote a certain amount of resources to services for federation managing. Moreover, additional interoperability requirements may need to be satisfied by individual clouds in order to join a federation. This situation may negatively affect the decision whether to join a federation. In this paper we propose an alternative approach by viewing creation and management of a cloud federation as cloud services themselves, thus allowing a drastic simplification in the federation set-up process and the decoupling of the federation management services from the technologies adopted by the individual clouds, minimising technological complexity and intrusiveness in the individual cloud infrastructures, while increasing the flexibility and scalability of resources. We also point out that existing technologies, in particular containers, microservices, configurators, clusters and orchestrators, can be the basis for implementing a platform for generation and management of federations of individual clouds, in a way which facilitates optimisation of workload and scaling of applications via resource aggregation, and makes deploying and joining federations fast, easy, and transparent.

1 Introduction

In the last few years, cloud-based solutions have become of interest for public and private organizations, due to the possibilities they offer for achieving: (1) greater cost reductions, by moving part of the budget from fixed to variable costs; and (2) greater resilience, and by increasing the flexibility and scalability of resources in response to changing business needs. Nevertheless, some elements –such as customers' perception that they are losing control over infrastructure resources, or the risk of vendor lock-in, stemming from a pervasive use of provider's services– are still an obstacle to the use of cloud solutions.

In order to mitigate these problems, many organizations are trying other cloud computing strategies including the creation of federations of individual clouds, from which they expect optimization of workload, increased availability of resources, probably even at more competitive costs and on an as-needed basis, and high levels of security and quality of service, probably better calibrated on the needs of an individual cloud joining a federation [3].

© IFIP International Federation for Information Processing 2016
Published by Springer International Publishing Switzerland 2016. All Rights Reserved
M. Aiello et al. (Eds.): ESOCC 2016, LNCS 9846, pp. 168–182, 2016.
DOI: 10.1007/978-3-319-44482-6_11

Current approaches to the construction of federations of clouds, see e.g. Fogbow[1], Zentera[2], Reservoir [7], handle federation services through some specific applications or frameworks. Hence, specific components must be installed on the infrastructure of the federation members, which are required to provide a certain amount of resources to run these components. In addition, when federating heterogeneous individual clouds, one has to consider the presence of: (1) distinct domains; (2) different security policies and service levels; and (3) different repositories of accounts. Other issues include the technological compatibility between the framework and the infrastructure of the individual member clouds, which may require adaptation to join a federation. All of this brings increased time and cost, which could make joining a federation inconvenient or impossible.

Faced to these problems, we argue that *construction* and *management* of federations of individual clouds should be seen as cloud services in turn, thus allowing a drastic simplification in the federation set-up process, the decoupling of the federation management services from the technologies adopted by the individual clouds, and minimal technological complexity and intrusiveness in the individual cloud infrastructures, while increasing the flexibility and scalability of resources. A further advantage is that joining a federation and contributing or obtaining resources to and from a federation could be achieved at a fine grain directly by end-users or with reduced intervention of cloud administrators.

In this paper we outline the basic requirements and the available technologies –in particular containers, configurators and orchestrators– which allow us to introduce the **FedUp!** approach to lean deployment and management of federations of heterogeneous clouds, by devising some simple mechanisms for setting up a federation and for allowing individual clouds to join an existing federation.

Paper Organisation. After concluding the introduction with a brief overview of related work, Sect. 2 presents the requirements and features on which the approach is based. Section 3 discusses the organisation of the **FedUp!** platform as a collection of microservices, possibly allowing a same cloud to join different federations, or even to participate in one federation in multiple ways, with different levels of service, Sect. 4 provides a description of how the approach can be realised with current technologies. The interactions involved in the execution of the main services for creating and managing federations of clouds are described in Sect. 5. Finally, Sect. 6 provides conclusions and points to future work.

1.1 Related Work

A layered model was proposed for the management of applications in a federated cloud in [9], where communication among clouds in the federation occurs at the respective layers (SaaS, PaaS, and IaaS[3]). In their proposal, a service request to a cloud, for an application at the SaaS level, will traverse layers and contact

---

[1] http://www.fogbowcloud.org/.

[2] http://zentera.net/.

[3] Acronyms for [Software, Platform, and Infrastructure] as a Service.

brokers at the different layers as needed, but the model does not consider the offering of specific services at federation level.

Reference to the cloud layers is made in [2] to introduce a distinction between *horizontal* (same layer) and *vertical* (across layers) federations, focusing on horizontal ones, where two fundamental scenarios are considered, viz. *redundant deployment* of services and *service migration* from a cloud provider to another, the service becoming accessible through a different endpoint. They provide a reference architecture describing services to be offered by a federation, but do not discuss dynamic creation and join/leave on the individual cloud side

When considering federations of heterogeneous clouds with some common level of trust, the notion of community cloud arises, as proposed in [4] and elaborated on from the point of view of security in [6]. Here, each node in the participating clouds can play both the roles of producer and consumer, and a specific layer for coordination is proposed, including management of virtual machines, identity, networking, and transactions.

The kind of flexibility and the fine granularity that the **FedUp!** approach grants is also in the direction of Resources as a Service, as advocated at the cloud level in [1], where users could subscribe to the usage of resources maintained by a cloud for as much as needed, instead of declaring beforehand the amount of resources they expect to need. By making joining and leaving federations easy, shorter turnaround times can be achieved, thus enabling greater responsiveness by federations to the requests coming from individual clouds.

2   FedUp! Overview and Requirements

We are developing the **FedUp!** approach (and the homonymous platform) to setting up and managing federations of resources from individual clouds in a simple and non-intrusive way, based on cloud services, i.e. services (e.g. Paas, SaaS, and IaaS) made available to users on demand via the Internet and fully managed by a provider. In particular, **FedUp!** has been designed as a platform by which to create federations in a PaaS style, based on the following activities.

1. Manage the entire life cycle for a federation (creation, management of individual cloud membership, management of feature descriptions and of feature-based bidding and awarding of membership, dismissal). This will in turn exploit mechanisms based on cloud services, setting the basis for the new notion of *Federation as a Service*, thus enabling fastest federation start-up time, decoupling of services from technologies for service distribution, smaller intrusion in the technological choices for member clouds (though not completely technology-agnostic, the approach can be targeted to various implementations), greater flexibility in management of single federations.
2. Allow a cloud to: (1) become a member of several federations at a time (through multi-tenancy); (2) apply for becoming a member of any federation based on a description of the resources it can contribute and/or of the resources it needs to acquire; (3) easily migrate from one federation to

another. This will grant ample possibilities to individual clouds for choosing the federation to join, greater flexibility in managing the membership agreement, and a better appreciation of its resources.

3. Maintain a central repository storing the records concerning the generated federations. Each federation is described by a set of features (publicly represented in the form of *tags*). This will allow the generation of theme-based federations offering a set of specific services to the member clouds.

We state a list of requirements for lean mechanisms for establishing, managing and granting access to federated clouds, classified under three categories:

General (GR)   Overall view of the system
Federation (FR) Resource-sharing and management of the federation
Usability (UR) Point of view of the user of the framework, either as administrator or as end-user

Table 1 expresses the identified requirements for the two basic mechanisms of *generating* and of *managing* a federation with **FedUp!**.

Table 1. General requirements for generating and managing federations

GR1	**FedUp!** must support heterogeneous clouds
GR2	**FedUp!** must have low impact on the existing infrastructure of individual clouds
GR3	**FedUp!** must allow the generation and dismissal of federations in a transparent way with respect to individual clouds
FR1	**FedUp!** must support the join of new member clouds and their abandoning
FR2	**FedUp!** must support an automatic generation of federations
FR3	**FedUp!** must generate federations orchestrated by an automatic system
UR1	**FedUp!** must provide the generated federation with mechanisms to allow access control to federation resources
UR2	**FedUp!** must allow a generated federation owner to specify the values of a pre-defined set of tags

We argue that such requirements, especially **GR3**, **FR2** and **FR3**, are best met if the deployed Federations are realized via a microservice approach, thus automating both generation and management of federations (e.g. **FedUp!** can provide these functionalities as services). Table 2 collects the resulting requirements on implementation of Infrastructure Services composing a Federation.

Table 2. Specific features required on a microservice implementation

F1	In order to be realistically orchestrable, microservices must work in isolation without requiring a dedicated VM each
F2	In order to be efficiently orchestrable (e.g. to support redundancy or migration), microservices have to be properly defined, by separating different data domains into different services, as expected in a microservice scenario

3   Generating and Managing Federations with FedUp!

In this section we describe the main components and functionalities of the **FedUp!** platform and the naming conventions used in this paper.

FedUp! is an innovative solution for generating and managing multiple cloud federations using an approach based on cloud services. A federation is conceived as a set of contributions from individual clouds with the aim of sharing and optimizing their own resources, together with a number of services for the dynamic proposal, acquisition and withdrawal of these contributions.

We refer to any federation generated via the **FedUp!** platform as a *Federation*. The owner of the individual cloud or tenant starting the generation process for a Federation, is referred to the *Federation owner*.

The actors which may interact with the platform have been identified as:

- *FedUp! Administrator*, responsible for **FedUp!** platform management.
- *Cloud* or *tenant administrator*, using the **FedUp!** utilities to create a Federation, or to make an individual cloud (or tenant) join an existing Federation generated with **FedUp!**.
- *User* of a cloud member of a Federation, who can request resources or services made available to the Federation.

As **FedUp!** is based on cloud services, in order to avoid ambiguities, we call "Utilities" the services that manage **FedUp!**. Each utility consists of a set of operations named "Actions" (see Table 3). **FedUp!** presents two main utilities:

- FedUp.Fed: this utility supports the generation and management of the Federations created with the **FedUp!** platform. Each Federation can consist of the aggregation of specific features established by the Federation owner at creation time (e.g. based on requested or granted quality of service, the level of safety on economic factors of political, institutional, geographical, etc.). The Federation features are described as tags. A dictionary of accepted tags is defined by **FedUp!** and the owner can choose the tags with their associated values, characterizing the new Federation at creation time. Tags are used by search functions available for the individual clouds to select the federations that match the membership requirements.
- FedUp.Cloud: this utility supports the communication with individual clouds requesting to join a Federation. Each individual cloud can join a specific Federation or can apply to join any Federation that matches specific tags.

These utilities rely in turn on the following structures:

- FedUp.Registry maintains information on the generated Federations and on the individual clouds that want to offer or use services offered by **FedUp!**.
- FedUp.ServiceRegistry maintains the information on services in terms of configuration and set of microservices.
- FedUp.ContainerHub maintains the images of the containers relative to the various microservices.

Table 3. The list of utilities and actions in **FedUp!**

Utility and action	Description
FedUp.Fed	Services for federation management
FedUp.Fed.Create	To create a new Federation. The cloud creating the new Federation becomes the owner
FedUp.Fed.Update	To change/update a Federation features, tags included
FedUp.Fed.Dismiss	To dismiss a Federation. All clouds, except the owner, need to quit
FedUp.Fed.Acquire	To integrate a cloud that wants to adhere to a Federation
FedUp.Fed.Search	To search for active Federations that satisfy the requirements of an individual cloud. This option is available for clouds that are looking for Federations to adhere to
FedUp.Cloud	Services for cloud/tenant management
FedUp.Cloud.Join	To adhere to a named Federation or to Federations characterized by given tags
FedUp.Cloud.Join(target)	To adhere to a targeted Federation
FedUp.Cloud.Join(tags[])	To adhere to a Federation that matches the given requirements (tags)
FedUp.Cloud.Update	To change/update a cloud features, tags included
FedUp.Cloud.Leave	To allow a cloud to leave a Federation, releasing the resources that cloud allocated to that Federation
FedUp.Cloud.Search	To search for available clouds matching the requirements of a Federation that wants to acquire clouds

- FedUp.ConfiguratorMaster is responsible for ensuring that Federations generated with **FedUp!** be properly configured in terms of the presence of files, installed packages and services running to manage that Federation. More information about this component is given in Sect. 4.

  In particular, FedUp.Registry contains:

- Data on generated Federations together with the corresponding tags describing their main features. The tags are assigned by the Federation owner at generation time, but can be changed during its construction and are used by the search functions made available for the individual clouds to search for Federations matching the membership requirements of the individual cloud.
- References to the individual clouds that want to share resources through the **FedUp!** platform with the corresponding tags describing their main features. Tags are assigned by the cloud owner during the registration to **FedUp!** and are used by search functions made available for the Federations to select individual clouds matching the Federation membership requirements.

– The map of participant clouds to individual Federations and the map of clouds available to federate.

The information provided by `FedUp.ServiceRegistry` fully defines a Federation infrastructure service, in terms of the information necessary to a cluster manager to correctly deploy and maintain the service. In particular, the following queries are handled:

– given the *id* of a service, the *id*s of the microservices composing that service;
– given the *id* of a microservice, the *id* of a container image relative to that microservice.

Finally, `FedUp.ContainerHub` can be queried to retrieve, given the *id* of a microservice, the correspondent image of a container.

An overview of the proposed solution is drawn in Fig. 1, while more information about how its realization is given in Sect. 4.

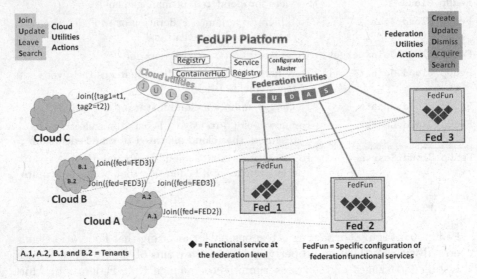

Fig. 1. A conceptual overview of the proposed solution

4   Implementation Aspects

In this section we provide some information about how to define a service configuration for a Federation and how to deploy the corresponding set of microservices using containers based on Docker[4], Saltstack[5] and Kubernetes[6] technologies.

We briefly introduce the following notions.

---

[4] https://www.docker.com/.
[5] http://saltstack.com/.
[6] https://github.com/kubernetes/kubernetes/blob/master/docs/design/README.md.

- *Microservice*: a term referring to a way of designing an architecture as a set of independently deployable services [5]. A single service can be thought as composed of a set of loosely-coupled microservices.
- *Configuration Management Engine*: a software responsible of ensuring that a remote Operating System is properly configured in terms of the presence of files, installed packages and running services.
- *Container*: an isolated, resource-controlled, portable operating environment.
- *Container Cluster Manager*: a software capable of orchestrating Containers among a set of nodes, managing a so called *Container Cluster*.

SaltStack is a well-known Configuration Management Engine based on a master-slave architecture [8]. It is also classifiable as a Remote Execution Engine since it allows the execution of remote executable files. The SaltStack master configures the Operative Systems of a set of machines (called *minions*) such that they comply with certain desired states. Among other configuration management engines, Saltstack is characterized by the use of asynchronous message queues. Containers are widely used to deploy software, since they are a more efficient alternative to virtual machines.

Docker is a common implementation of containers. Kubernetes is a Container Cluster Manager based on a master-slave architecture. It is defined as a system for managing containerized applications across multiple hosts, providing basic mechanisms for deployment, maintenance, and scaling of applications. Kubernetes automatically manages a cluster of containers by means of a scheduler, changing the state of the cluster to keep it consistent with respect to a set of declarative primitives, codified as YAML[7] formulas, and regarding topological, workload and policy aspects. Kubernetes organizes containers in a multi-level, hierarchical way. In Kubernetes terminology, a *cluster* is composed of a set of nodes, each *node* is composed of a set of pods, and a *pod* is composed of a set of containers. A *container* is intended to host a single microservice, realizing a part of the functionalities of a specific service. A service is not statically associated with a particular pod, but its traffic may be routed to different pods depending on the activities of the scheduler. This mechanism transparently decouples the containers from the services, providing robust availability.

The **FedUp!** platform is intended to automatically deploy *Federation Infrastructures* (which have been declaratively specified) via Kubernetes. This implies a possible coupling between the development of a Federation Infrastructure and Kubernetes, based on the following observations.

1. Kubernetes uses its own network models for inter-service communications. For example, it offers a DNS service as a pluggable component. This technique transparently masks the dynamic routing from a service to potentially different pods. As a consequence, differently from traditional models, services need to query the DNS service frequently.
2. Kubernetes needs a declarative proposition to be prepared for every single definition of a container, service or pod used by the infrastructure.

---

[7] YAML Ain't Markup Language, http://yaml.org/.

In order to decrease the coupling between the development of services and (specific versions of) Kubernetes, we exploit the flexibility of its network model. In particular, **FedUp!** adopts a traditional network model (i.e. using static IP address and ports). This is realized by defining a formalized model for the definition of a Federation Infrastructure, and an automatic generator of declarative primitives to be used for the deployment of a federation.

With this solution, the declarative propositions influencing a deployed Federation Infrastructure (e.g. numbers of replicas for pods, minimum policies for machines) need not be considered by the developers of a Federation Infrastructure. Given that reasonable declarative propositions can be chosen by **FedUp!**, developers are lifted from the burden of acquiring the necessary knowledge of, and re-implement services to fits to, a specific Kubernetes network model.

5   Federating Heterogeneous Clouds

In this section, we focus on the two basic mechanisms for creating a Federation and for the joining/acquisition of a cloud (actually a tenant) to a Federation. The other actions provided by **FedUp!** are realized in analogous ways. Figure 2 provides an activity diagram describing the fundamental phases involved in these two processes, which are then detailed in the following subsections.

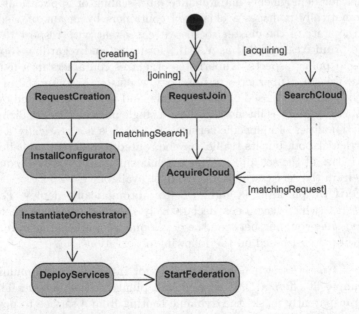

Fig. 2. An overview of the main processes in **FedUp!**.

While creation only involves the originator cloud and **FedUp!**, joining a Federation *Fed* is seen as a two-step process in which a cloud *Cld* (actually a tenant in a cloud) issues a request via the `Join` action, also providing information on what it can contribute, and *Cld* enters *Fed* when the latter accepts a specific request, via the `Acquire` action, or interrogates the **FedUp!** `Search` service about the presence of candidate clouds characterised by specific features. To support this kind of mechanisms, join and acquire requests are associated with a collection of tags expressing cloud features, e.g. the types and quantities of resources or services a cloud can contribute to a Federation, the SLAs of the contributed services, or even the intention to join a specific Federation. **FedUp!** will therefore publish a dictionary of managed tags and their admissible values. For example, in Fig. 1 in Sect. 3, we have indicated that clouds **A** and **B** had issued specific requests to participate in **Fed2** and **Fed3**, while cloud **C** has issued a request characterised by two specific values for two different tags.

Similarly, a Federation *Fed* can directly acquire a cloud, based on previous notifications of interest for some features, so that if a matching cloud issues a request to participate in *Fed*, it is automatically acquired. Criteria for accepting a new member are proper to any Federation and need not be public. For example, an initial set of governmental agencies can decide to set up a version of **FedUp!** and accept only clouds from other public agencies, while a European initiative for a federated cloud could accept only clouds managed by agencies at governmental level from EU nations.

Each cloud accepted in a Federation *Fed* will generate a partition of its resources to act as tenant for *Fed*. In principle a cloud can participate in several federations, e.g. in Fig. 1 cloud **A** participates both in **Fed2** and **Fed3**, and even present different tenants to the same Federation, e.g. cloud **B** participates in **Fed3** with two tenants, for example one for high performance resources and one for less stringent SLAs.

Given a single Federation, the shared resources can be partitioned into the *infrastructure resources* used to host the Federation itself, and the *cloud resources* that can be offered, or acquired, by the individual clouds. Unless differently specified, we use the term *resource* to refer to an infrastructure resource. Analogously, the term *service* refers to an infrastructure service rather than a service offered or acquired by the federation members. In this paper we are not specifically concerned with the implementation details of a Federation Infrastructure, but we just mention the following:

- A Federation Infrastructure is typically realized through a service named Workload Manager that interacts with a centralized registry, for storing and assigning cloud-resources and cloud-offerings.
- Services within the Federation Infrastructure may be relative to networking, monitoring, billing and authorization aspects.
- A Federation Infrastructure may be capable of federating heterogeneously in terms of the particular PaaS solutions used by the individual clouds.
- A Federation Infrastructure may have a (logically) centralized architecture.

Figure 3 shows the UML metamodel for dynamic, service-oriented, network Federation Infrastructures, using a containerized microservice architecture, in which the communication is realized over IP addresses/ports. In particular,

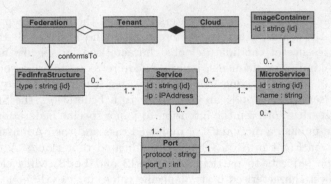

Fig. 3. The metamodel for the federation infrastructure

a *FedInfrastructure* is associated with a non-empty set of instances of *Service*, each described by a static IP address and one or more instances of *Port* to be used by other services. Each service results from the aggregation of a number of instances of *MicroService*, each in turn associated with a single port and with a single *ContainerImage*. The relation is also shown between the infrastructure metamodel and the general model of federations, which need to be conformant to some infrastructure and composed of tenants belonging to clouds.

A particular instance of this model can be translated into a proper set of declarative propositions: together with the declarative propositions provided by **FedUp!** (Sect. 4), they form the necessary information for a cluster manager to deploy and manage the federation. A Federation Infrastructure deployed by **FedUp!** has the following characteristics:

- A deployed Federation Infrastructure consists in a set of deployed services.
- A deployed service has network visibility among any other deployed service.
- A deployed service is composed of one or more microservices, each one deployed on a different container.

5.1 Creating a Federation

Figure 4 shows a sequence diagram presenting the fundamental steps for creating a federation. An administrator of a tenant *Ten1* in a cloud *Cld1* issues a request to `FedUp.Fed` (namely to its `Create` action) for creating a new Federation (arrow 1). The request contains the desired federation type (among the available Federation Infrastructure solutions) and the credentials usable to interact with *Cld1*'s IaaS Resource Manager. `FedUp.Fed` is capable of interacting with heterogeneous clouds trough a virtual interface exposed by an adapter service provided by **FedUp!** , using plugins associated to different IaaS solutions.

`FedUp.Fed` uses the received credentials to instantiate a Virtual Machine inside *Ten1* (arrow 2). This VM, named *Federation Configurator*, is a Salt-Stack slave of the `FedUp.ConfiguratorMaster`, located on the **FedUp!** side. The `FedUp.ConfiguratorMaster` remotely configures the *Federation Configurator* (arrow 3) so that it can in turn instantiate and configure inside *Ten1* a set of

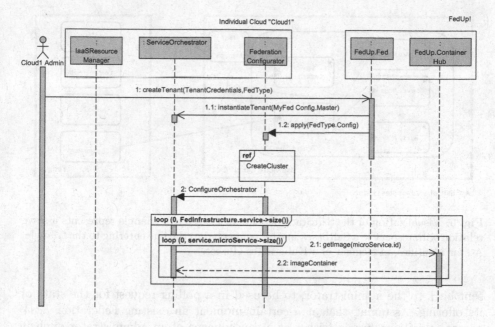

Fig. 4. The sequence diagram for creating a federation

virtual machines dedicated to form a Kubernetes cluster (through the operation
`Create Cluster`, not further detailed here). In particular, a *Service Orchestrator* VM is dedicated to host a Kubernetes Master, while the other ones are set
up to become Kubernetes nodes. The *Federation Configurator* is at the same
time a SaltStack slave of `FedUp.ConfiguratorMaster` and a SaltStack master
of the machines composing the cluster.

Figure 5 shows the considered SaltStack dependencies: a black triangle represents a slave relation with respect to a SaltStack master connected to the line
entering to the triangle, while a star represents a virtual machine which is part
of a Kubernetes Cluster. After the Kubernetes cluster is created, the *Service
Orchestrator* is remotely configured (arrow 4 of Fig. 4) to retrieve from **FedUp!**
the necessary files to deploy the Infrastructure Services. In particular, it is shown
how the `FedUp.ContainerHub` provides the containers relative to the microservices composing the Infrastructure Services. Similarly, the *Service Orchestrator*
retrieves the configuration files for the pods, containers and services (not shown)
from the `FedUp.ServiceRegistry`.

5.2   Joining a Federation

Figure 6 presents the fundamental steps for joining a federation, from the perspective of a new member. The administrator of a Tenant *Ten2* of cloud *Cld2*
(not federated yet) communicates the availability to join a federation, also providing a set of tags, describing its possible contributions. An ID `id_offer_x` is

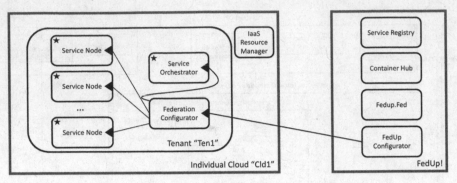

★ = part of a Kubernetes cluster

Fig. 5. Visualization of the SaltStack dependencies: a black triangle represents a slave relation with respect to a SaltStack master connected to the line entering to the triangle. A star identifies an element of a Kubernetes cluster.

sent back to the administrator, to be used in a polling request for the state of its offering. Assuming that at a certain moment an existing Federation *FedY* accepts this join offering (either as a consequence of an administrator explicit action, or of a standing search for matching offerings) and acquires the originator tenant, the ID of *FedY* will be returned to *Ten2* on the subsequent request.

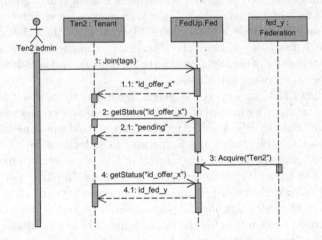

Fig. 6. The sequence diagram for a tenant joining a federation

Figure 7 shows the process for a *Federation Y*, identified by id_offer_y, to acquire a cloud *Cld2*. *Federation Y* looks up the FedUp.Registry for a set of acquirable tenants, based on a set of tags ("filter"). The set is populated based on an interaction between the registry and FedUp.Fed. In particular a subset of the available offerings, arranged into a list of IDs, ([...,id_offer_x,...])

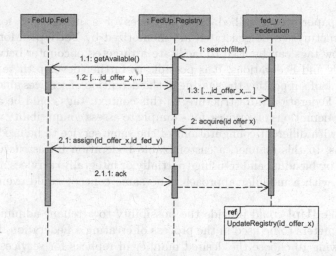

Fig. 7. The sequence diagram for a federation acquiring a tenant

is returned to the Federation. *Federation Y* can communicate its intention to acquire the offering identified by id_offer_x, which had been published by *Cld2*, to the Registry, which forwards the request to FedUp.Fed, that will complete the join process. An acknowledgement is sent back to *Cld2*, communicating id_offer_y.

6   Conclusions and Future Work

FedUp! provides a lean PaaS approach to the flexible deployment and management of federations of clouds, opening the way to the notion of Federation as a Service, whereby a central platform will maintain images of predefined configurations that an administrator can decide to install and activate on a managed portion of a cloud. In principle, any cloud user could exploit the resources obtained by joining a federation to federate them in turn within existing federations, or to start a new federation.

The platform relies on notions of containers, microservices, configurations and clusters made popular by technologies such as Docker, Kubernetes, and Saltstack, which are adopted in its current specification, but is in principle not tied to them, as it only requires that the tenant designated to start a federation will allow the installation of a virtual machine with an initial configurator, which will then execute the needed operations on the tenant. The current working prototype will be subject to extensive evaluation.

In this line, one can envision a marketplace of federation services, where also specific services that a single federation wants to offer can be defined and offered for configurations. For example, one could offer specific forms of workload management, or of data security across the different members of the federation.

In this paper we described how instances of a metamodel for Federation Infrastructures to be generated are memorized by **FedUp!**. Moreover, we described how tags can be used to facilitate a targeted encounter between individual clouds and Federations. It is possible to further develop these concepts. One can think of supporting the sharing of the definition of services among different types of Federation Infrastructure. In this context, tags could be associated with specific definitions of services, for example to assess compatibility with other services, or with different configurations of the same service to be used in different scenarios. In this manner, a customizable Federation Infrastructures could be deployed by blending and re-using (partially or integrally) services memorized by **FedUp!** with a modular approach. The same concept could even apply to microservices.

Finally, **FedUp!** could provide the possibility to a tenant administrator to specify parameters to be used in the process of creating a Federation. For example, by allowing to choose the desired number of replicas for services, the possibility would be offered to provide a parametric tuning of the robustness, in terms of availability, of the deployed services.

Acknowledgments. This work has been supported by the EU H2020 Programme under the SUNFISH project, grant agreement N. 644666.

References

1. Agmon Ben-Yehuda, O., Ben-Yehuda, M., Schuster, A., Tsafrir, D.: The rise of RaaS: the resource-as-a-service cloud. Commun. ACM **57**(7), 76–84 (2014)
2. Bermbach, D., Kurze, T., Tai, S.: Cloud federation: effects of federated compute resources on quality of service and cost. In: Proceedings of IC2E 2013, pp. 31–37 (2013)
3. Kertesz, A.: Characterizing cloud federation approaches. In: Mahmood, Z. (ed.) Cloud Computing: Challenges, Limitations and R&D Solutions, pp. 277–296. Springer, Berlin (2014)
4. Marinos, A., Briscoe, G.: Community cloud computing. In: Jaatun, M.G., Zhao, G., Rong, C. (eds.) Cloud Computing. LNCS, vol. 5931, pp. 472–484. Springer, Heidelberg (2009)
5. Newman, S.: Building Microservices. Designing Fine-Grained Systems. O'Reilly Media, Sebastopol (2015)
6. Nicanfar, H., Liu, Q., Talebifard, P., Cai, W., Leung, V.C.M.: Community cloud: concept, model, attacks and solution. In: Proceedings of CloudCom 2013, vol. 2, pp. 126–131, December 2013
7. Rochwerger, B., Breitgand, D., Levy, E., Galis, A., Nagin, K., Llorente, I.M., Montero, R.S., Wolfsthal, Y., Elmroth, E., Cáceres, J.A., Ben-Yehuda, M., Emmerich, W., Galán, F.: The reservoir model and architecture for open federated cloud computing. IBM J. Res. Dev. **53**(4), 4:1–4:11 (2009)
8. Sebenik, C., Hatch, T.: Salt Essentials. Fast Scalable, and Flexible Automation. O'Reilly Media, Sebastopol (2015)
9. Villegas, D., Bobroff, N., Rodero, I., Delgado, J., Liu, Y., Devarakonda, A., Fong, L., Sadjadi, S.M., Parashar, M.: Cloud federation in a layered service model. J. Comput. Syst. Sci. **78**(5), 1330–1344 (2012)

Compositionality

Service Cutter: A Systematic Approach to Service Decomposition

Michael Gysel[1], Lukas Kölbener[1], Wolfgang Giersche[2], and Olaf Zimmermann[1(✉)]

[1] University of Applied Sciences of Eastern Switzerland (HSR FHO), Oberseestrasse 10, 8640 Rapperswil, Switzerland
{michael.gysel, lukas.koelbener}@lifetime.hsr.ch,
ozimmerm@hsr.ch
[2] Zühlke Engineering AG, Wiesenstrasse 10a, 8952 Schlieren, Switzerland
wolfgang.giersche@zuehlke.com

Abstract. Decomposing a software system into smaller parts always has been a challenge in software engineering. It is particularly important to split distributed systems into loosely coupled and highly cohesive units. Service-oriented architectures and their microservices deployments tackle many related problems, but remain vague on how to cut a system into discrete, autonomous, network-accessible services. In this paper, we propose a structured, repeatable approach to service decomposition based on 16 coupling criteria distilled from the literature and industry experience. These coupling criteria form the base of Service Cutter, our method and tool framework for service decomposition. In the Service Cutter approach, coupling information is extracted from software engineering artifacts such as domain models and use cases and represented as an undirected, weighted graph to find and score densely connected clusters. The resulting candidate service cuts promise to reduce coupling between and promote high cohesion within services. In our validation activities, which included prototyping, action research and case studies, we successfully decomposed two sample applications with acceptable performance; most (but not all) test scenarios resulted in appropriate service cuts. These results as well as early feedback from members of the target audience in industry and academia suggest that our coupling criteria catalog and tool-supported service decomposition approach have the potential to assist a service architect's design decisions in a viable and practical manner.

Keywords: Functional partitioning · Loose coupling · Knowledge management · Microservices · Service interface design guidelines · Service granularity · Service quality

1 Introduction

In 1972, D. L. Parnas reflected "On the Criteria to Be Used in Decomposing Systems into Modules" [11]. Since then, functional decomposition has remained an important topic in software engineering. As software systems grew and became more complex, software engineers started to distribute modules and procedures over networks, e.g., as

© IFIP International Federation for Information Processing 2016
Published by Springer International Publishing Switzerland 2016. All Rights Reserved
M. Aiello et al. (Eds.): ESOCC 2016, LNCS 9846, pp. 185–200, 2016.
DOI: 10.1007/978-3-319-44482-6_12

remote objects, components or Web services [1]. Architectural styles such as *Service-Oriented Architecture (SOA)* aim at tackling the many design challenges of such distributed systems; however, designing service interface boundaries at the right level of granularity remained an important challenge for SOA practitioners [3, 17]. While partial solutions have been found, two of the related Research Problems (RP) remained open: (RP1) The *architecturally significant requirements* and *stakeholder concerns* to be addressed during service (de-)composition are still not understood fully and have not been documented consistently and comprehensively yet. (RP2) A requirements-driven, repeatable, and scalable *service decomposition method*, to be supported and partially automated by service design tools, has been missing until now.

In this paper, we collect architecturally significant requirements for service decomposition and introduce *Service Cutter*, our knowledge management method and supporting tool framework that assist software architects when they make service design decisions (note that we do not intend to fully automate this decision making process, but rather support it). The remainder of the paper presents our solutions to RP1 and RP2 as well as their validation in the following way: Sect. 2 scopes the context of our work and the research problems solved, and defines our basic service decomposition terminology. Section 3 presents our first research contribution, a coupling criteria catalog for service decomposition; Sect. 4 then defines a novel service decomposition process and an extensible tool architecture that integrates existing graph clustering algorithms to derive candidate service cuts from system specification artifacts. Section 5 presents an implementation of the tool architecture and our validation, which includes action research, two case studies, and performance measurements; Sect. 6 discusses strengths and weaknesses of Service Cutter and presents initial industry feedback. Section 7 concludes and highlights future work.

2   Context, Problem and Supporting Definitions

The impact of service boundary design is far-reaching. Loosely coupled, but highly cohesive services are crucial for the maintainability and scalability of software and allow architects and developers to choose a suitable technology independently for each particular business problem and context. Nevertheless, the decomposition of a monolithic application into services still is not fully understood, even with the rise of *microservices* [16], a contemporary incarnation of SOA principles and patterns combined with modern software engineering practices such as continuous, independent deployment. For instance, a popular introduction to microservices states that "deciding how to partition a system into a set of services is very much an art" [15].

Microservices advocates suggest leveraging *Domain-Driven Design (DDD)* [5] to obtain service boundaries: For instance, instances of the DDD pattern *aggregate* establish composed services that are aligned to consistency constraints, and services derived from *bounded contexts* are aligned to domain model boundaries or team organization structures. Both of these two DDD strategies are suitable approaches to service identification (assuming that one knows how to find aggregates and bounded contexts in the requirements). However, our collective industry experience and a literature review indicate that many more stakeholder concerns have to be taken into account during service decomposition – in particular, architecturally significant requirements including software quality attributes [2]. We believe that this process can and should be approached in a more structured way. This leads to our first hypothesis:

The driving forces for service decomposition can be presented to architects in a comprehensive and comprehensible coupling criteria catalog.

This criteria catalog, which will be introduced in the next section, assembles 16 decomposition criteria commonly used by architects to frame and guide their architectural decisions. We distilled it in an iterative and incremental way, leveraging consecutive project retrospectives, interviews, and a coupling criteria workshop.

A systematic collection of design knowledge can serve as the foundation for partial automation of analysis and design. This observation leads to our second hypothesis:

Based on the coupling criteria catalog, a system's specification artifacts can be processed in a structured and partially automated way to suggest service decompositions that promote loose coupling between and high cohesion within services.

To investigate whether these two hypotheses hold true, we conceptualized and developed *Service Cutter*, a tool framework architecture and prototype to analyze software engineering artifacts, including use cases and domain models, and to suggest candidate service decompositions.

Service Cutter and its presentation in this paper use the following terminology:

Definitions. The term *service* can be defined both on a logical and on a physical level:

1. A service is the technical authority for a specific business capability [3].
2. A service is accessed remotely through some invocation interface and communication protocol, either synchronously or asynchronously [6].

In order to provide capabilities, a service requires *resources*. We identified three types of resources that serve as the building blocks of services in our approach:

1. Data. A service may have ownership over a subset of a system's data [16]. It then is the only authority allowed to change this data, notifying other services on such changes. The data is often, but not always, stored in a database (then called application state); data exposed at the service interface constitutes its *published language* [5].

2. Operations. A service can encapsulate business rules and calculation (processing) logic. Operations are often, but not always, based on the data owned by the service.

3. Artifacts. An artifact is a snapshot of data or operation results transformed into a specific format. An example is a business report such as monthly sales figures by geography, which was assembled using operations and data.

To facilitate a systematic approach to service decomposition, we generalize these resources with the concept of a *nanoentity* shown in Fig. 1:

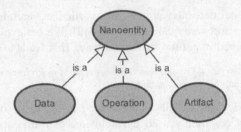

Fig. 1. Data, operations and artifacts generalized into the nanoentity concept.

Service decomposition then can be defined as the process of identifying a set of services and assigning all nanoentities to one (and only one) of these services. A *coupling criterion* represents a particular driving force for service decomposition; such criteria capture architecturally significant requirements and arguments why two nanoentities should or should not be owned and exposed by the same service. *Software System Artifacts (SSAs)* represent the analysis and design artifacts that contain information about coupling criteria; scoring *priorities* weigh the coupling criteria. A *service cut* is the output of a single execution of the service decomposition process.

3 Coupling Criteria Catalog

We conducted a literature review, reflected on past projects, and met for a workshop to assemble our collective, precompiled architecture design experience. We consolidated the results of these knowledge gathering activities in a *coupling criteria catalog* in an iterative and incremental manner. Our coupling criteria catalog aims at serving as a comprehensive, yet not complete collection of architecturally significant requirements and decision drivers for service decomposition. Note that we strived for consensus, clarity, and compactness; hence, not all candidate criteria made it into the catalog. Figure 2 lists the 16 Coupling Criteria (CC) in the final catalog version:

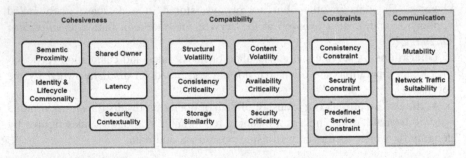

Fig. 2. Coupling Criteria (CC) catalog compiling 16 CC in four categories.

We grouped the CC into four categories in the catalog (to improve readability):

1. Cohesiveness: Criteria describing certain common properties of mutually related nanoentities that justify why these nanoentities should belong to the same service.

An example of a cohesiveness argument is that all nanoentities involved in the realization of a use case should belong to a single service to simplify use case execution.

2. Compatibility: Criteria indicating divergent characteristics of nanoentitics. A service should not contain nanoentities with incompatible characteristics. Examples of such characteristics are "high", "eventually", and "weak" for the criterion Consistency Criticality; these data consistency management options are mutually exclusive.

3. Constraints: Criteria specifying high-impact requirements that enforce that certain groups of nanoentities (a) must jointly constitute a dedicated service or (b) must be distributed amongst different services. The fact that a set of nanoentities has to be modified jointly and atomically, e.g. in the same database transaction, forms a strong requirement that justifies to be represented as constraint criterion in the catalog.

4. Communication: Criteria exclusively pertaining to the technical cost of remoting, e.g., *mutability*. Immutable resources do not require complex synchronization means.

All 16 CC are recorded in a common card layout inspired by pattern languages and agile practices. Table 1 introduces this *Coupling Criterion Card (C3)* template:

Table 1. A template for Coupling Criterion Cards (C3).

[Coupling Criteria Identifier and Name]	
Description	[A brief summary of the Coupling Criterion (CC) w.r.t. its impact on/usage of nanoentities]
System Specification Artifacts (SSAs)	[Requirements engineering input and software architecture concepts/deliverables pertaining to this coupling criterion]
Literature	[References to books, articles, and/or blog posts]
Type	Cohesiveness | Compatibility | Constraint | Communication
Characteristics	[Defines a set of possible values for this CC. Only applies to CC of type Compatibility. E.g., "critical", "normal", "low"]

The usage of such C3s makes the catalog structure recognizable and the catalog extensible. Tables 2 and 3 present two examples of filled-out C3 instances.[1]

Eliciting CC instances to reflect the non-functional requirements of a specific software product is a key aspect of analysis and design. Hence, software architects can leverage the CC catalog to establish a common terminology for their design discussions as well as architecture documentation. Moreover, our CC catalog can serve as the basis of a structured, repeatable way to identify, make, and capture related decisions [18]; it serves as *ubiquitous language* [5] for service decomposition.

---

[1] All 16 coupling criteria cards are published in full length in the Service Cutter wiki on GitHub, https://github.com/ServiceCutter/ServiceCutter/wiki/Coupling-Criteria.

Table 2. The "Identity and Lifecycle Commonality" CC.

CC-1 Identity and Lifecycle Commonality	
Description	Nanoentities that belong to the same identity and therefore share a common lifecycle (create, read, update, delete)
System Specification Artifacts (SSAs)	– Entity-Relationship Models – Domain-Driven Design Entity pattern instances
Literature	Entity definition in Domain-Driven Design [5]: *Some objects are not defined primarily by their attributes* *They represent a thread of identity that runs through time and often across distinct representations*
Type	Cohesiveness

Table 3. The "Semantic Proximity" CC.

CC-2 Semantic Proximity	
Description	Two nanoentities are semantically proximate when they have a semantic connection given by the business domain The strongest indicator for semantic proximity is coherent (joint) access of/to nanoentities within the same use case
System Specification Artifacts (SSAs)	– Coherent access to or updates of nanoentities in use cases (or user stories) – Aggregation or association relationships in an entity-relationship model
Literature	Single Responsibility Principle by Martin [9]: *Gather together the things that change for the same reasons* *Separate those things that change for different reasons* Richardson on microservice decomposition [15]: *There are number of strategies that can help [to partition a system into a set of services]. One approach is to partition services by verb or use case*
Type	Cohesiveness

4   Service Decomposition Concepts and Tool Architecture

To allow architects to leverage the CC catalog and receive service decomposition advice, we created the *Service Cutter* tool framework. Service Cutter derives *candidate service cuts* from user-prioritized coupling criteria (obtained from SSAs) to achieve loose coupling between services and high cohesion within services. To do so, additional design concepts are required, which will be introduced in this section.

Decomposition Input. The input to Service Cutter is a machine-readable representation of selected software engineering artifacts that represent intermediate stages of analysis and design. To represent these artifacts, we introduce *System Specification Artifacts (SSAs)*. SSAs serve as data sets from which the Service Cutter can extract the required coupling criteria information. Examples of SSA types are use cases, DDD entities/aggregates, and Entity-Relationship Models (ERMs); e.g., information about

CC-2 Semantic Proximity comes from these two SSA types. We designed additional SSA types to supply information that is not contained in existing ones (e.g., shared owner groups, predefined services, separated security zones and security access groups). The Service Cutter wiki provides detailed explanations and a reference of these nine types of SSAs (called "user representations" in the prototype).[2]

Figure 3 specifies the dependencies of coupling criteria and SSAs. For instance, information about CC-16, Security Constraint, can be obtained from the SSA "separated security zones". Security zones group nanoentities by their diverging privacy requirements, e.g. sensible personal information vs. unclassified, public data.

Decomposition Process. Figure 4 specifies the service cutting process in BPMN.

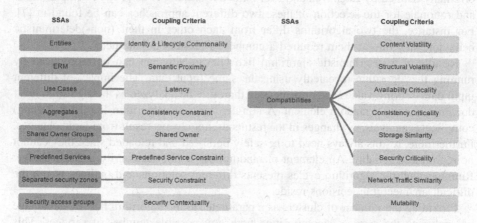

Fig. 3. Dependencies between System Specification Artifacts (SSAs) and CC.

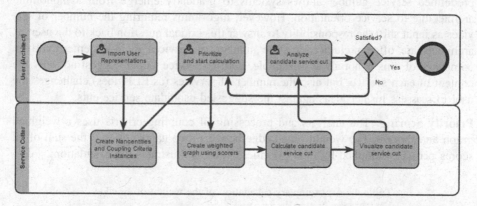

Fig. 4. Serving decomposition process (human vs. automated/tool-supported tasks).

---

[2] https://github.com/ServiceCutter/ServiceCutter/wiki/User-Representations.

Service Cutter processes the provided SSA instances and extracts nanoentities as well as coupling criteria instances from them. *Prioritized* coupling criteria and SSAs are transformed into an undirected, weighted graph; nodes represent nanoentities, and the weights of edges indicate how cohesive and/or coupled two nanoentities are.

Algorithm Integration. We then employ *clustering algorithms* on this graph to find candidate service cuts. Our concepts and tool architecture are designed to be general enough to allow the inclusion of multiple algorithms; e.g., a programming interface is provided which can be implemented for any clustering algorithm that is based on undirected, weighted graphs. At present, we included Java implementations of two algorithms, namely Girvan-Newman [10] and the Epidemic Label Propagation (ELP), originally defined by Raghavan and later refined by Leung et al. [14]. A comparison of and rationale for the selection of these two different approaches can be found in [7]. For instance, the two algorithms differ from each other in their (non-)deterministic behavior; only one of them required a number-of-clusters in parameter.

Results of a deterministic algorithm like Girvan-Newman can be reproduced by running the algorithm repeatedly using the same input data. The impact of different input data, scoring values and priorities can therefore be analyzed as the algorithm itself does not include a random element. A non-deterministic algorithm like ELP (Leung) complicates analysis, as changes in the results do not always result from input changes. Furthermore, results always need to be safely persisted and reloaded since they cannot be reproduced reliably. An element of randomness is not necessarily a disadvantage: Running multiple algorithm cycles presents different solutions and outlines where the difficult architectural decisions reside.

Providing the number of clusters as a parameter to the algorithm has the advantage of analyzing the service decomposition with any possible number of services. This feature can be used to better understand the structure and coupling between parts of the system when running the algorithm with varying input. Requesting a high number of services, for instance, may indicate how services can be decomposed further; a small predefined service number allows systems to gradually emerge from a monolithic architecture to service orientation. However, algorithms requiring the number of services as input shift the responsibility to answer this critical question back to the user; as architects are often prejudiced on the number of services their system should be composed of, this is not always desirable. Letting Service Cutter suggest not only the content of each service, but also the number of services (as ELP does) challenges the user to reassess his/her ideas against the suggested candidate service cuts.

Priority Scoring. The analysis and processing of coupling criteria uses a weighted graph and *scorers*. The weight on an edge between two nanoentities is the sum of all scores per CC multiplied by their priorities. Table 4 illustrates the calculation:

Table 4. An exemplary calculation of the weight of an edge.

Coupling criterion	Score	Priority	Result
CC-1: Semantic Proximity	4	1	$4 * 1 = 4$
CC-7: Availability Criticality	2.5	5	$2.5 * 5 = 12.5$
CC-9: Consistency Constraint	8	3	$8 * 3 = 24$
Total weight			$4 + 12.5 + 24 = 40.5$

The *score* is a number from −10 to +10. A score of +10 expresses that these two nanoentities should definitely reside in the same service according this coupling criterion. A score of −10 therefore represents the opposite extreme, i.e., that the nanoentities should be placed into different services.

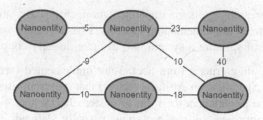

Fig. 5. Weighted edges representing the coupling connect the nanoentities.

The calculation is performed for every link between nodes with coupling information; Fig. 5 shows an example. The calculation depends on the involved coupling criteria; the scorers map coupling criteria to actual numbers used to construct the weighted graph. Table 5 maps CCs to the five types of scorers that differ in their calculation logic:

Table 5. Coupling criteria and the scorers calculating the weight of the edges.

Coupling criterion	Scorer type
Identity and Lifecycle Commonality *Shared Owner* *Latency* *Security Contextuality* *Consistency Constraint*	*Cohesive Group Scorer* Nanoentities in a cohesive group should remain together in one service. All relations between nanoentities in a group are scored +10
Semantic Proximity	*Semantic Proximity Scorer* The joint access to a pair of nanoentities is counted and mapped to an even distribution between 0 and 10
Structural Volatility *Consistency Criticality* *Storage Similarity* *Content Volatility* *Availability Criticality* *Security Criticality*	*Characteristics Scorer* To achieve homogenous services, this scorer sets a penalty of −1 to −10 to relations with diverging requirements
Security Constraint	*Separated Group Scorer* Sets a score of −10 to all nanoentities that belong to a group other than the current one
Predefined Service Constraint	*Exclusive Group Scorer* Same as Cohesive Group, but also adds a penalty of −10 to nanoentities not in the group
Mutability *Network Traffic* *Suitability*	Not defined and implemented yet

A detailed description of the scorers in Service Cutter can be found in [7].

5 Evaluation via Prototyping, Case Studies, Action Research

We validated our research results via implementation, case study, and action research. Service Cutter's current implementation supports a basic feature set that realizes the structured approach of splitting a system into discrete, loosely coupled services:

- 14 out of 16 coupling criteria from Sect. 3 are implemented (see Table 5).
- All nine System Specification Artifacts (SSAs) that represent user input (see Fig. 3 in Sect. 4) can be imported in the form of custom JSON files.
- Seven criteria priorities, in the prototype casually defined as "T-Shirt sizes" (IGNORE, XS, S, M, L, XL, XXL) allow users to characterize the context of a system by valuating the coupling criteria in relation to each other.
- The suggested candidate service cuts and their dependencies are visualized.
- The published language [5] of a service pair (including the data transferred to and from the invoked service) is exposed via the involved nanoentities.

Figure 6 features a candidate service cut for the "cargo tracking" domain model from [5]. This candidate service cut consists of three services A, B and C (larger squares), each owning a set of (cohesive) nanoentities represented as small squares:

Arrows between two services (e.g., Service A and Service B) indicate a dependency between them. The resulting published language, which characterizes the amount of coupling between these services in terms of the shared understanding about the nanoentities that are exposed at the service boundary, is also shown.

Release 1.1 of the Service Cutter implementation is available on GitHub[3]. This prototype consists of two components implemented in Java and JavaScript (using Spring Boot, Spring MVC, AngularJS, and JHipster), RESTful HTTP Web services wrapping the scoring logic, and a Web application for input and output visualization.

Validation Approach and Results. To further validate the implemented concepts, we assessed the candidate service cuts of the following two case studies:

1. A fictitious "Trading System" for which we forward-engineered the requirements, drawing on industry experience with financial services software.
2. The DDD sample application "Cargo Tracking" that accompanies the DDD book [5]; we reverse engineered the requirements for this scenario from the existing implementation that is available on SourceForge.[4]

To objectify the validation and have a comparison baseline, we defined expected service cuts for both systems according to our experience in service design; to reduce bias, we developed a service design checklist for this task.[5] Next, we defined three result categories in order to rate the candidate service cuts:

---

[3] https://github.com/ServiceCutter/ServiceCutter.

[4] https://sourceforge.net/projects/dddsample/.

[5] https://github.com/ServiceCutter/ServiceCutter/wiki/Decomposition-Questionnaire.

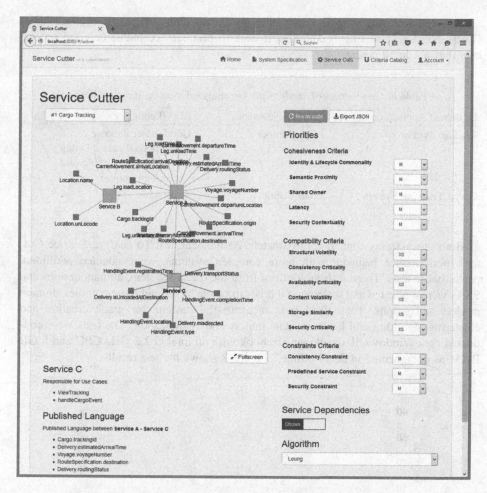

Fig. 6. Screenshot of Service Cutter presenting a candidate service cut.

A: Excellent service cut. The cut (i.e., suggested service decomposition) does not follow the way we expected, but we find reasons why the cut makes sense from an architect's perspective. It therefore improves our own view of the analysed system. *B: Expected service cut.* The cut meets and therefore validates our expectations. *C: Unreasonable service cut.* There is a mismatch between the cut and the expected one, and we do not find any reasons why this cut would be beneficial.

To be able to assess the quality of the output of Service Cutter, we use a four-level classification: An *excellent* output contains zero unreasonable service cuts and at least one excellent service cut (i.e., a cut in category A). A *good* output contains zero unreasonable service cuts (C). An *acceptable* output contains at most one unreasonable service cut (C). A *bad* output contains two or more unreasonable service cuts (C).

Table 6 summarizes the decomposition results for both systems. Both algorithms, Girvan-Newman and ELP (Leung), were able to produce acceptable or good service cuts (but not in all cases):

Table 6. Assessment of service cuts for analyzed systems (case studies).

Evaluated Application	Girvan-Newman	ELP (Leung)
Trading System	Good output	Good (note: in some exceptional cases, Leung produced acceptable *and* excellent output)
Cargo Tracking System	Bad output	Acceptable

Both test systems contain approximately 20 nanoentities. To analyze Service Cutter's performance behavior with more complex systems, we conducted additional performance tests. These tests are derived from the trading system; all nanoentities and SSAs were replicated and scaled up 60 times to create larger and more complex domain models and graphs. These load tests measure the runtime for graph creation and clustering algorithm and leave out data import and visualization. The tests were conducted on a Windows 10 developer notebook with an Intel i5 2.2 GHz CPU and 8 GB RAM as documented in detail online.[6] Figure 7 shows the test results.

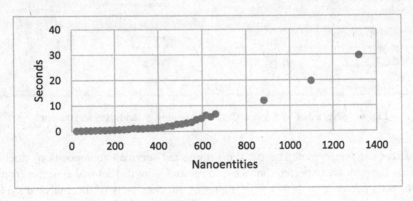

Fig. 7. Performance test results: service cut calculation (scaled up sample application)

The calculation for systems with up to 600 nanoentities is done in less than five seconds, which we consider reasonable. Around 75 % of the time used is consumed by graph creation whereas the clustering algorithm only uses around 25 % of the time. Hence, our Java code building the graph based on the imported data could be analyzed and improved to improve runtime performance even further.

---

[6] https://github.com/ServiceCutter/ServiceCutter/wiki/Runtime-Performance-Tests.

6 Discussion: User Feedback, Pros and Cons, Related Work

User Feedback. We presented the Service Cutter concepts and their implementation to more than 20 members of the target audience (i.e., software engineers and architects with experience in designing SOAs), and one of the authors of the paper applied Service Cutter to a single project case (as a form of technical action research). The systematic overall approach was appreciated and considered to be promising; it was pointed out that Service Cutter cannot only be used in an SOA context, but also be used to split modules without remote interfaces (with adjusted CC priorities).

The template-based coupling criteria cards were generally appreciated, but some of the current texts were assessed to be too terse (by one provider of feedback); a more elaborate, but not yet verbose wording was requested. The naming of some coupling criteria in our catalog also was challenged. An example is "CC-13 Network Traffic Suitability", which covers the more common and basic concept of *throughput* (which in turn is one facet of the top-level quality attribute *performance*). Furthermore, system and process assurance *audit compliance* [8] was suggested to be added as a compatibility criterion; further research is required to investigate how to integrate such a composite and complex, possibly even recursive criterion into Service Cutter.

Finally, our selection of two clustering algorithms was questioned, and it was suggested to only integrate deterministic algorithms that do not require the number of clusters as a parameter. This critique pertains to the current tool implementation only; the Service Cutter concepts from Sects. 3 and 4 do not rely on any particular algorithm. Due to the generality of our concepts and the modular, extensible architecture of their implementation, we expect the effort to integrate other algorithms into the Service Cutter framework to be in the range of a few person days per algorithm.

According to the feedback of our industry project partner, who leads an architect and developer community in professional services, Service Cutter and its underlying reasoning represent a sound framework to prepare and back architectural decisions. More specifically, it allows architects to study the impact of weight variations on the resulting candidate service cuts. Questions like "what, if security wasn't an issue here" can be answered easily by changing the respective scoring priority of criterion "security criticality". When used with care, Service Cutter can improve the credibility of architects involved in critical architecture assessments (evaluations) significantly. The SSAs and coupling criteria can also be used to educate junior architects or students on the driving forces of service decomposition.

Benefits. From our internal and external validation activities, we can conclude that Service Cutter offers a number of advantages to service architects: The coupling criteria catalog indeed collects relevant architecturally significant requirements and decision drivers for service decomposition, and it does so in an accessible, reusable, and extensible way. It therefore contributes to the body of reusable architectural decision knowledge as envisioned in our previous work [18].

Service Cutter suggests candidate service cuts that are obtained from commonly used analysis and design artifacts, such as use cases and domain models, via a nanoentity abstraction and the coupling criteria. By expecting several such analysis and design artifacts, Service Cutter challenges its users (i.e., service architects) to reflect which stakeholder input and non-functional quality characteristics are relevant for his/her system (and architecture design process). Hence, service architects might use these artifacts as a checklist and stimulus for the requirement engineering.

The candidate service cuts verify and/or challenge the architect's expectations regarding the number of services and their interface definitions. Both green field scenarios and iterative approaches for migrating a monolith to services are supported.[7]

Drawbacks and Liabilities. The benefits that we could observe during our evaluation activities come at a price; usage of Service Cutter concepts and their implementation during these activities has unveiled some (expected) drawbacks and liabilities.

Significant effort is required to enter SSAs (such as use cases and domain models) in JSON; in future versions, we plan to import them, e.g., from UML modeling tools.

We are aware of the risk of a "pseudo accuracy" effect. It is subject to debate whether service design work, dealing with rather diverse requirements (some of which are hard to quantify) can really be delegated to algorithms that look for an aggregated optimal solution. Architects traditionally apply their tacit knowledge and "gut feel" when making the relate decisions; they are biased. This discussion can be seen as the SOA variant of the more general discussion on "a rational design process: how and why to fake it" [12]. However, we believe our approach to be valuable even when being confronted with a healthy amount of skepticism – relevant design questions are asked and related criteria listed, and the relation between these concerns and the user input in SSAs is unveiled. Furthermore, a checklist effect occurs; discussions among collaborating architects are stimulated.

Other drawbacks and liabilities concern framework architecture design and extensibility. First and foremost, the clustering algorithms that are currently integrated possibly should be complemented with additional ones due to the only partially satisfying evaluation results. Algorithmic complexity is a major source of performance limitations and therefore has to be taken into account in any such future algorithm selection decisions; fortunately, clustering algorithms with linear complexity exist.

As the Service Cutter framework continues to evolve, additional validation and evaluation activities work will be required. For instance, it has to be verified that the tool performance does not degrade significantly when processing even larger amounts of user input that go beyond scaled up sample data and case studies (e.g., complex domain models from enterprise information systems).

Related Work. Quality attribute-driven design has been an important research topic in the software architecture community for many years [2, 11]; the specific requirements and constraints of service-oriented architectures and microservices have also been investigated and related methods proposed [4, 13, 17]. Such methods are complementary to the approach presented in this paper, providing an overall frame for the use of Service Cutter, as well as input for coupling criteria, SSAs, and priority scores.

Other research areas in service-oriented computing include service discovery and runtime topology lookup (e.g., in clouds), dynamic service matchmaking, service composition into business processes and workflows, quality-of-service awareness,

---

[7] Explained on GitHub: https://github.com/ServiceCutter/ServiceCutter/wiki/Usage-Scenarios.

policies, and agreement, as well as service management. These efforts have different goals than Service Cutter, which aims at assisting architects making design decisions; however, well-crafted service cuts can be seen as a prerequisite for the successful application of any advanced service-oriented computing concepts and technologies. In our future work, we therefore consider to include additional criteria and SSAs that represent the concepts from these research efforts as they mature.

7 Summary and Outlook

In this paper, we presented Service Cutter, a systematic approach to system decomposition, which has been a relevant problem since the very origins of program modularization and software engineering. Service Cutter advances the state of the art (a) with the concept of coupling criteria cards, (b) 16 instances of such cards (harvested from practical experience and the literature), and (c) an extensible service decomposition tool framework architecture that integrates graph clustering algorithms and features priority scoring starting from nanoentities and nine types of analysis and design specifications (including domain models and use cases). This structured and extensible combination of a criteria-driven method with supporting architectural knowledge and a design optimization and visualization tool paves the way towards the desired engineering approach to service interface and service granularity design.

We evaluated Service Cutter via implementation (integrating two existing graph clustering algorithms), a combination of action research and case study investigations, and load tests. The validation results and additional user feedback indicate that the proposed semi-automated approach to service decomposition works as designed and has the potential to benefit practitioners significantly. While the suggested service cuts did not always meet all early adopters' expectations, artifact input and coupling criteria were regarded adequate; the proposed decomposition process was appreciated.

While our early experiences with the presented structured, partially automated (i.e., tool supported) approach are promising, work remains to be done both on the conceptual (research) level, as well as on the implementation (engineering) level. For instance, further enhancements of Service Cutter may include seamless integrations of the analysis and design tool chain members so that SSAs can be extracted from other tools automatically. We discussed other directions for future work in Sect. 6; related development issues are tracked in the open source release of Service Cutter.

References

1. Alonso, G., Casati, F., Kuno, H.A., Machiraju, V.: Web Services – Concepts, Architectures and Applications. Data-Centric Systems and Applications. Springer, Heidelberg (2004)
2. Cervantes, H., Velasco, P., Kazman, R.: A principled way of using frameworks in architectural design. IEEE Softw. **30**(2), 46–53 (2013)
3. Dahan, U.: The Known Unknowns of SOA, Blog Post, November 2010. http://udidahan.com/2010/11/15/the-known-unknowns-of-soa/

4. Erradi, A., Anand, S., Kulkarni, N.: SOAF: an architectural framework for service definition and realization. In: Proceedings of SCC 2006. IEEE Computer Society (2006)
5. Evans, E.: Domain-Driven Design: Tackling Complexity in the Heart of Software. Pearson Education, Upper Saddle River (2003)
6. Fowler, M.: Inversion of Control Containers and the Dependency Injection Pattern, Online Article, January 2014. http://www.martinfowler.com/articles/injection.html
7. Gysel, M., Kölbener, L.: Service cutter – a structured way to service decomposition. Bachelor thesis, HSR Hochschule für Technik Rapperswil (2015). https://eprints.hsr.ch/476/
8. Julisch, K., Suter, C., Woitalla, T., Zimmermann, O.: Compliance by design – bridging the chasm between auditors and IT architects. Comput. Secur. **30**(6–7), 410–426 (2011). Elsevier
9. Martin, R.C.: Agile Software Development: Principles, Patterns, and Practices. Prentice Hall PTR, Upper Saddle River (2003)
10. Newman, M.E., Girvan, M.: Finding and evaluating community structure in networks. Phys. Rev. E **69** (2004). arXiv:cond-mat/0308217
11. Parnas, D.L.: On the criteria to be used in decomposing systems into modules. Commun. ACM **15**(12), 1053–1058 (1972)
12. Parnas, D.L., Clements, P.C.: A rational design process: how and why to fake it. IEEE Trans. Softw. Eng. **12**(2), 251–257 (1986)
13. Papazoglou, M., van den Heuvel, W.J.: Service-oriented design and development methodology. Int. J. Web Eng. Technol. (IJWET) **2**(4), 412–442 (2006). Inderscience Enterprises
14. Raghavan, U.N., Albert, R., Kumara, S.: Near linear time algorithm to detect community structures in large-scale network. Phys. Rev. E **76** (2007). arXiv:0709.2938
15. Richardson, C.: Microservices: Decomposing Applications for Deployability and Scalability. InfoQ article, May 2014. http://www.infoq.com/articles/microservices-intro
16. Zimmermann, O.: Microservices tenets: agile approach to service development and deployment. Overview and vision paper, SummerSoC 2016. J. Comput. Sci. Res. Dev. (CSRD), Springer (to appear)
17. Zimmermann, O., Krogdahl, P., Gee, C.: Elements of Service-Oriented Analysis and Design. IBM developerWorks, July 2004
18. Zimmermann, O., Wegmann, L., Koziolek, H., Goldschmidt, T.: Architectural decision guidance across projects. In: Proceedings of the 12th Working IEEE/IFIP Conference on Software Architecture (WICSA), pp. 85–92. IEEE Computer Society (2015)

Economic Aspects of Service Composition: Price Negotiations and Quality Investments

Sonja Brangewitz[✉] and Simon Hoof[✉]

Department of Economics and SFB 901, Paderborn University,
Paderborn, Germany
{sonja.brangewitz,simon.hoof}@upb.de

Abstract. We analyse the economic interaction on the market for composed services. Typically, as providers of composed services, intermediaries interact on the sales side with users and on the procurement side with providers of single services. Thus, in how far a user request can be met often crucially depends on the prices and qualities of the different single services used in the composition. We study an intermediary who purchases two complementary single services and combines them. The prices paid to the service providers are determined by simultaneous multilateral Nash bargaining between the intermediary and the respective service provider. By using a function with constant elasticity of substitution (CES) to determine the quality of the composed service, we allow for complementary as well as substitutable degrees of the providers' service qualities. We investigate quality investments of service providers and the corresponding evolution of the single service quality within a differential game framework.

Keywords: Service composition · Price negotiations · Quality investments · Nash bargaining solution · Differential games

1 Introduction

Service composition in cloud computing or on-the-fly computing environments is not just technically challenging, but also offers interesting questions that arise from an economic perspective. Strategic decisions with respect to service quality and prices influence the interaction between users, providers of composed services (also referred to as intermediaries), and providers of single services. A composed service with complementary single services as inputs requires negotiations with different service providers interdependently about prices and qualities.

This work was partially supported by the German Research Foundation (DFG) within the Collaborative Research Center "On-The-Fly Computing" (SFB 901). We thank Claus-Jochen Haake for constructive suggestions and comments.

© IFIP International Federation for Information Processing 2016
Published by Springer International Publishing Switzerland 2016. All Rights Reserved
M. Aiello et al. (Eds.): ESOCC 2016, LNCS 9846, pp. 201–215, 2016.
DOI: 10.1007/978-3-319-44482-6_13

However, the providers of single services strategically determine quality investments and thus the quality level to maximize their individual profits. Therefore, the intermediary selling the composed service has to pay the service providers accordingly to induce them to deliver the single services such that they fulfil the requirements to satisfy the users' demand. We propose a model that allows us to analyse the negotiations between the intermediary and the service providers and to investigate the evolution of service quality and the investments therein in a dynamic context using a differential game.

2   Literature

Formally, we combine models from cooperative bargaining theory and from noncooperative differential game theory to describe the interaction on the market for composed services. More precisely, for the price negotiations we use the well established Nash [9] bargaining solution. The use of multilateral Nash bargaining is inspired by the analysis in [6]. They investigate negotiations in vertical supply relationships between one manufacturer and two retailers and make use of the Nash bargaining solution to describe simultaneous and sequential price negotiations. In our model we add a dynamic variable by considering the demand of the end user and thus the negotiations depending on the qualities of the single services. We assume that simultaneous multilateral price negotiations take place at every instant in time. Using a differential game we investigate the dynamic evolution of the service quality. A comprehensive introduction into differential games is [5]. In particular, the evolution of service quality is modelled using the techniques for capital accumulation games [5, Chapter 9]. A similar game is also used to describe the evolution of quality in health care markets [4].

A systematic overview of the literature on service composition in cloud computing environments can be found in [8]. Here, the intermediary is also referred to as a "cloud service broker". They describe the analysis of "dynamically contracting service providers" as one of the "most remarkable challenges" for the cloud computing service composition problem [8, Sect. 4.2, p. 3813]. A comprehensive survey on the pricing of cloud services is [2]. Various pricing schemes and techniques are systematically presented and compared with respect to their advantages and disadvantages as well as fairness and implementation in practice. For cloud instance pricing, when jobs arrive sequentially following a specific stochastic process, two techniques such as fixed unit prices and spot markets have been explicitly investigated and compared in [1]. The authors provide evidence that a fixed unit price seems to dominate a combination of both pricing models in terms of expected revenue. Different approaches and protocols for bargaining-based negotiations of service level agreements in cloud computing are surveyed in [7, Sect. 4.2.1, p. 51:12f]. In particular, an application of cooperative bargaining theory to web services for bilateral negotiations between a user and a service provider is [10]. While the focus of these models is often primarily on the pricing or negotiation procedure, our model incorporates the interaction of different types of service providers that is required for trading composed services. A simple model describing the interaction between an intermediary and two service providers has already been analysed in [3]. However, the model was only able to capture two different quality levels of the composed and single services and the dynamic analysis was by means of a repeated game.

We extend this analysis here in the sense that the quality of a single service is a continuous state variable and the overall quality can range from complements to substitutes. This means that we include a parameter describing how the pure quality of a single service may or may not be compensated by the good quality of another single service. The investment decisions to change the quality level of the service providers are strategic. The differential game framework sets up a dynamic optimal control problem for each service provider and thus allows us to investigate the evolution of service quality over an infinite time horizon. Quality-dependent negotiations take place at every instant in time and are modelled by using cooperative bargaining theory.

3   Model

We study a market consisting of three types of market participants: users, intermediaries and service providers. An intermediary purchases single services and combines them, where the quality of the composed service depends on the qualities of the single services delivered by the service providers. Finally, the composed service is sold to the users. Here, we focus on the interaction between one intermediary as the seller of a composed service to the users and two service providers as the sellers of single services to the intermediary. Each of the service providers is assumed to produce one single service. These services are supposed to have complementary properties, i.e., the intermediary needs to bargain with both service providers and the overall quality depends on both single services. The economic interaction on the market for composed services is illustrated in Fig. 1. Time is indexed by $t \in \mathbb{R}_+ := [0, \infty)$. However, for ease of notation the time index is generally omitted.

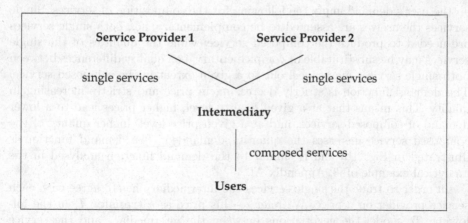

Fig. 1. Market interaction

4   Demand and Bargaining

The **quality of the composed service** is a function of the single services'
qualities

$$\Theta(\theta_1, \theta_2) := (\theta_1^\rho + \theta_2^\rho)^{\frac{1}{\rho}} \tag{1}$$

where $\theta_i \in \mathbb{R}_+$ denotes the quality of the single service produced by provider
$i = 1, 2$ and $\rho \in (-\infty, 1)$ is a measure of substitutability between the two single
services. Technically, the quality of the composed service as in (1) is determined
by a function with constant elasticity of substitution (CES) between the two
single services. For the limit cases we get some special functions, namely

$$\Theta(\theta_1, \theta_2) = \begin{cases} \min(\theta_1, \theta_2) & \text{for } \rho \to -\infty, \\ \theta_1 \theta_2 & \text{for } \rho \to 0, \\ \theta_1 + \theta_2 & \text{for } \rho \to 1. \end{cases} \tag{2}$$

For a given overall quality of the composed service Fig. 2(a) illustrates the special
cases. That is, for $\rho < 0$ the service qualities are complementary while for $\rho > 0$
they are substitutes.[1]

The **users' demand** for the composed services is modelled by a demand
function

$$D(\Theta, P) := \begin{cases} \dfrac{\Theta(\theta_1, \theta_2)}{P^2} & \text{if both services are provided} \\ 0 & \text{otherwise} \end{cases} \tag{3}$$

that describes the quantity the users are willing to purchase for a given price
$P \in \mathbb{R}_+$ and overall quality level $\Theta(\cdot)$ of the composed service. In addition, the
users' demand for a single service is supposed to be zero. These assumptions
on the user's demand imply the following for the composition of services: Single
services themselves are assumed to be complementary, i.e., both single services
are needed to produce the composed service; while the qualities of the single
services may be substitutable or complementary, i.e., quality differences between
both single services may cancel out to a given extent in the composed service.
The demand function is strictly decreasing in price and strictly increasing in
quality. This means that at a given quality level, higher prices lead to a lower
demand of composed services; and at a given price level, higher quality of the
composed service increases the quantity demanded. The demand function is
illustrated in Fig. 2(b) and is similar to the demand function analysed in the
analytical example of [3, Appendix A].

In order to trade the single services the intermediary has to agree with each
service provider on a price. We refer to this price as a **transfer** T_i in the following. To model the negotiations between the intermediary and the service

---

[1] Note that the elasticity of substitution can be denoted by $\sigma = \frac{1}{1-\rho}$. We may observe
$\sigma \to \{0, 1, \infty\}$ for $\rho \to \{-\infty, 0, 1\}$.

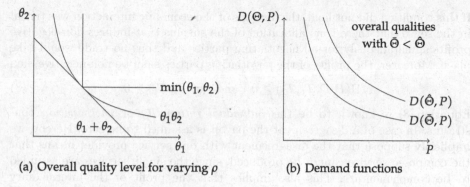

(a) Overall quality level for varying ρ **(b)** Demand functions

Fig. 2. Quality and demand of the composed service

providers we make use of cooperative bargaining theory (see [9]). We look at the individual profits from trading the single services. The intermediary is not only concerned with costs T_i, but must take into account the users' demand as well. The service provider on the other hand has revenues of T_i, but in addition production costs for supplying the single service. The overall **cost** function for each service provider i captures production as well as investment costs

$$C_i(\theta_i, I_i, D) := \frac{1}{2}\left(\alpha_i\theta_i^2 + \beta_i I_i^2\right) + \gamma_i D(\Theta, P) \tag{4}$$

with $\alpha_i, \beta_i, \gamma_i > 0$ and for $i = 1, 2$. Here I_i denotes the investment to improve the quality of service θ_i, i.e., one unit of investment comes with quadratic costs. In addition, production costs are linear increasing to cover a given demand and quadratic in the supplied quality level. The intermediary must pay some transfer T_i to each service provider to incentivise production. The **profits** of the three parties can now be stated as

$$\Pi(P, D, T_1, T_2) := P \cdot D(\Theta, P) - \sum_{i=1}^{2} T_i \tag{5}$$

$$\pi_i(T_i, C_i) := T_i - C_i(\theta_i, I_i, D) \tag{6}$$

where $\Pi(\cdot)$ is the profit of the intermediary, i.e., revenues from selling the composed service to the users minus transfers to the input suppliers. And $\pi_i(\cdot)$, for $i = 1, 2$, denotes the profit of the service providers, i.e. transfers from providing the single service minus total costs. The individual transfer schedule is the result of a simultaneous negotiation between the intermediary and the two service providers.

To ensure that **negotiations** actually take place we must assume that revenues of the intermediary exceed the production costs, i.e., there exists some surplus to be divided among the three parties

$$P \cdot D(\Theta, P) > \sum_{i=1}^{2} C_i(\theta_i, I_i, P). \tag{7}$$

If this condition did not hold, the analysis of the economic interaction was trivial in the sense that there is no allocation of the surplus that induces non-negative profits simultaneously for all negotiating parties and thus no trade would take place. Moreover, the profits of the negotiating parties shall be non-negative, i.e.,

$$\Pi(P, D, T_1, T_2) \geq 0 \quad \text{and} \quad \pi_i(T_i, C_i) \geq 0. \tag{8}$$

Equation (8) is known to be the *individual rationality* or *participation* constraints. In case of a disagreement the payoff is assumed to be zero. Hereby, we implicitly suppose that the disagreement with one service provider means that the composed service cannot be produced, since the single services are assumed to be complementary. This also implies that the profit of the intermediary cannot become positive when agreeing only with the other service provider as users do not demand single services.

We use the well-known **Nash bargaining solution** to explicitly determine these transfers [9]. The Nash bargaining solution has the advantage that it is characterized by some specific axioms[2] and leads to strictly positive profits of the intermediary as well as the service providers. Consider the negotiations between the intermediary and service provider i. The Nash bargaining solution then satisfies

$$T_i^N \in \arg\max_{T_i} \Pi(P, D, T_i, T_{3-i}) \cdot \pi_i(T_i, C_i) \quad \text{s.t. (8) holds.} \tag{9}$$

Note that the Nash product for the negotiations with service provider i in (9) as well as the participation constraint in (8) depend on the outcome of the negotiations between the intermediary and the other service provider $3 - i$. The complementarity of the single services is reflected by taking a zero disagreement payoff in case one of the negotiations fails.

The resulting transfer is then readily given by

$$T_i^N(P, D, C_i, T_{3-i}^N) = \frac{1}{2}\left(P \cdot D(\Theta, P) + C_i(\theta_i, I_i, D) - T_{3-i}^N(P, D, C_{3-i}, T_i^N)\right). \tag{10}$$

For $i = 1, 2$ we have two equations in two unknowns $T_i^N(\cdot)$. Hence, we may explicitly solve for the transfer and obtain

$$T_i^N(P, D, C_i, C_{3-i}) = \frac{1}{3}\left[P \cdot D(\Theta, P) + 2C_i(\theta_i, I_i, P) - C_{3-i}(\theta_{3-i}, I_{3-i}, P)\right]. \tag{11}$$

This means that the surplus that exists on the market for selling the composed service taking the service providers' costs into account is evenly split among the two service providers and the intermediary. Finally, the intermediary determines the sales price of the composed service. In every period the intermediary solves the following (static) program

$$P^* = \arg\max_P \Pi(P, D, T_1^N, T_2^N) = 2(\gamma_1 + \gamma_2). \tag{12}$$

---

[2] See [9] for further details.

Note that P^* is a datum determined by exogenous parameters, i.e., profits are given by

$$\Pi(P^*, D, T_1^N, T_2^N) = \pi_i(T_i^N, C_i) = \frac{1}{3}\left[P^* \cdot D(\Theta, P^*) - \sum_{i=1}^{2} C_i(\theta_i, I_i, P^*)\right].$$
(13)

Since every party earns the same profit, we may stick to one symbol π. After substituting (3), (4) and (12) into (13) one arrives at

$$\pi(\theta, I) = \frac{1}{6}\left[\frac{(\theta_1^\rho + \theta_2^\rho)^{\frac{1}{\rho}}}{2(\gamma_1 + \gamma_2)} - \left(\alpha_1\theta_1^2 + \alpha_2\theta_2^2 + \beta_1 I_1^2 + \beta_2 I_2^2\right)\right]$$
(14)

where $\theta = (\theta_1, \theta_2)$ and $I = (I_1, I_2)$. Note that costs of service composition may be easily introduced into the model. As the surplus resulting from the composed service is always evenly distributed among the negotiating parties we may include costs of service composition directly into Eqs. (5) and (7).

For the dynamic analysis it is crucial to note that the bargaining process takes place in every period. Therefore, (14) holds at every point in time $t \in \mathbb{R}_+$. This reduces the entire profit path $\{\pi(\theta(t), I(t)) : t \in \mathbb{R}_+\}$ into an expression which solely depends on the respective quality and investment level in each period where $\theta_i(t) : \mathbb{R}_+ \to \mathbb{R}_+$ and $I_i(t) : \mathbb{R}_+ \to \mathbb{R}$, respectively, are time-dependent functions. Next, we set up a differential game to investigate the dynamic interaction of both service providers and show how to determine the optimal investment decision and the associated path of the overall quality level.

5   Dynamics of Service Quality and Investments

In this section we analyse the service providers' incentives to invest into the quality of their single services. Each service provider i can govern the quality level over time by investing I_i (control variable). This means the next periods' quality is given by the current investment minus a loss in quality that appears over time (depreciation). The **law of motion** for the state variable can be modelled by a differential equation

$$\forall t \in \mathbb{R}_+ : \dot{\theta}_i = I_i - \delta\theta_i$$
(15)

where $\delta \in (0, 1]$ denotes depreciation of quality and we used the abbreviation $\dot{\theta}_i(t) := \frac{d\theta_i}{dt}(t)$. By introducing a depreciation of quality we assume that maintaining the service quality requires continuous investments. That is, I_i denotes gross investment. Here, the depreciation rate of quality captures that a service provider has to continuously take care of the quality of his service. For software services this is by continuously adapting the software to technological changes in the runtime environments, dependencies with other services or security requirements, for example. In our theoretical analysis, the depreciation rate remains a parameter of the model and may range from almost no reduction of quality over time to a complete reduction, making the software without investments in the extreme case useless. Equation (15) links the current quality and the investments into quality of a service provider. Thus, the optimization problem of service provider i boils down to choose a stream of investment levels $\{I_i(t) : t \in \mathbb{R}_+\}$ as to maximize his **discounted profits** with respect to the flow constraints and some given initial quality level

$$\max_{\{I_i(t)\}} \int_0^\infty e^{-rt}\pi(\theta, I)dt \tag{16}$$
$$\text{s.t. } \dot{\theta}_i = I_i - \delta\theta_i \quad \text{and} \quad \theta_i(0) > 0$$

where $r > 0$ denotes the time preference rate. Future profits are discounted since we presume that economic agents are impatient, i.e., they rather prefer to earn profits today than tomorrow.[3]

Next, the **best response** of a service provider is determined. The dynamic optimization problem is solved by applying the maximum principle [5, Theorem 4.2]. We set up the current value Hamiltonians for each service provider i by

$$H_i(\theta, I, \mu_i) = \pi(\theta, I) + \mu_i(I_i - \delta\theta_i). \tag{17}$$

where μ_i is the costate variable. The current value Hamiltonian measures current profits as well as future profits which arise by investing into the service quality. Note that each service provider faces an intertemporal trade-off when making an investment decision. Current investment instantly lowers profits due to investment costs, but also raises expectations of future gains from the investment due to an increase in the service quality. The costate variable is thus considered as a shadow price which translates gains of investment into current profits. Inserting the service provider's profit from (14), the 1. first order condition for optimal investment reads

$$\frac{\partial H_i}{\partial I_i}(\theta, I, \mu_i) = -\frac{\beta_i}{3}I_i + \mu_i = 0 \quad \Longleftrightarrow \quad I_i = \frac{3}{\beta_i}\mu_i. \tag{18}$$

The interpretation of (18) is straightforward: the larger the investment cost parameter given by β_i, the smaller the investment and the larger future gains of an increase in quality measured by the shadow price μ_i, the higher the investment. That is, current marginal costs of investment must be outweighed by future gains of current investment. The 2. first order condition gives the evolution of the costate over time

$$\dot{\mu}_i = \mu_i r - \frac{\partial H_i}{\partial \theta_i}(\theta, I, \mu_i) = \mu_i(r + \delta) + \frac{\alpha_i\theta_i}{3} - \frac{\theta_i^{\rho-1}\left(\theta_1^\rho + \theta_2^\rho\right)^{\frac{1-\rho}{\rho}}}{12(\gamma_1 + \gamma_2)}. \tag{19}$$

---

[3] From a technical point of view we must assume that $r > 0$, because otherwise the payoff integral may not converge.

Since we are rather interested in evaluating the dynamics in the (I_i, θ_i) space, we may differentiate (18) over time yielding

$$\dot{\mu}_i = \frac{\beta_i}{3}\dot{I}_i \tag{20}$$

and then combine it with (19) using (18) which gives us

$$\dot{I}_i = I_i(\delta + r) + \frac{\alpha_i}{\beta_i}\theta_i - \frac{\theta_i^{\rho-1}\left(\theta_1^\rho + \theta_2^\rho\right)^{\frac{1-\rho}{\rho}}}{4\beta_i(\gamma_1 + \gamma_2)}. \tag{21}$$

Considering both service providers, we now have a four-dimensional system of differential equations which is denoted by $\mathcal{D}(\dot{\theta}, \dot{I})$. The **dynamic equilibrium** or fixed point can be found by solving $\mathcal{D}(0,0)$ for I and θ and is given by[4]

$$\tilde{I}_i = \frac{\delta}{4(\gamma_1 + \gamma_2)\xi_i}\left(1 + \left(\frac{\xi_i}{\xi_{3-i}}\right)^{\frac{\rho}{2-\rho}}\right)^{\frac{1-\rho}{\rho}}, \tag{22}$$

$$\tilde{\theta}_i = \frac{\tilde{I}_i}{\delta} \tag{23}$$

with $\xi_i := \delta\beta_i(\delta + r) + \alpha_i$ and $\xi_{3-i} := \delta\beta_{3-i}(\delta + r) + \alpha_{3-i}$ for $i = 1, 2$. Note that for particular values of ρ we have[5]

$$\tilde{\theta}_i = \begin{cases} \dfrac{1}{4(\gamma_1 + \gamma_2)} \cdot \dfrac{1}{\xi_1 + \xi_2} & \text{for } \rho \to -\infty, \\[2mm] \dfrac{1}{4(\gamma_1 + \gamma_2)} \cdot \dfrac{1}{\xi_i} & \text{for } \rho \to 1. \end{cases} \tag{24}$$

If the qualities of the single services are complementary, then service provider i also takes into account the cost parameters of $3 - i$ and both providers will supply their single service in the same quality. This feature essentially captures the Leontief characteristics of the quality for the composed service. No service provider has an incentive to invest into quality of the single service if the overall quality is solely determined by the other provider. The dynamic equilibrium is in fact identical for both service providers for $\rho \to -\infty$. While if qualities are perfect substitutes, a service provider is concerned only about his firm-specific quality and investment costs. In addition, we see that the long-run quality level is unambiguously increasing in all exogenous parameters. The economic interpretation is as follows: Since α_i, β_i and γ_i are cost parameters for producing θ_i, we will observe a low long-run quality level for high production costs. If δ is high, then we will observe a low $\tilde{\theta}_i$, because quality depreciates rather rapidly

---

[4] Further details on the derivation are presented in Appendix A.1.

[5] At the discontinuity point $\rho = 0$, where the quality of the composed good switches from complementary to substitutable, one can show that the left- and right-hand side limits differ with $\lim_{\rho \to 0-} \tilde{\theta}_i = 0$ and $\lim_{\rho \to 0+} \tilde{\theta}_i = \infty$.

over time. To maintain some specific quality level the service provider must make large gross investments $\tilde{I}_i$, which are costly. Finally, $\tilde{\theta}_i$ is decreasing in r. That is, if the service provider is impatient and does not value future profits that much, he invests little and the long-run equilibrium is low as well.

The **stability** of the fixed point can be checked by evaluating the eigenvalues of the Jacobian matrix. It turns out that the eigenvalues are real and opposite in sign. That is, there are two positive and two negative eigenvalues, indicating that the system is saddle point stable.[6] There also exists a unique saddle path converging to the dynamic equilibrium.

6   Simulation

Since the problem is open loop[7] in nature, we are dealing with an initial value problem. That is, given $\theta_i(0)$ we are concerned only with determining optimal initial investment decisions $I_i(0)$, for $i = 1, 2$. The system dynamics are then fully characterized by the four differential equations $\mathcal{D}(\dot{\theta}, \dot{I})$. However, there are infinitely many possibilities to pick initial investment $I_i(0) \in \mathbb{R}$. To pin down the unique saddle path we make use of the 3. first order condition, namely the transversality condition

$$\lim_{t \to \infty} e^{-rt} \mu_i(t)\theta_i(t) = 0. \tag{25}$$

The transversality condition ensures that the system moves along the saddle path, because it rules out exploding paths which diverge from the dynamic equilibrium. Hence the transversality condition gives rise to a terminal condition. If investment is in steady state at some time instance $t = t_f$, then it has to be stuck there forever, i.e., $\lim_{t_f \to \infty} I_i(t_f) = \tilde{I}_i$ for $i = 1, 2$.

Now we are dealing with a 4D system of differential equations with two initial and two terminal conditions. We then use a numerical boundary value problem solver to simulate the system. To simulate the model we have to parametrize it. We used the following parameters throughout $\theta_1(0) = \theta_2(0) = 3$, $\delta = 1$, $r = 0.05$, $\alpha_1, \beta_1, \gamma_1 = 0.1$ and $\alpha_2, \beta_2, \gamma_2 = 0.2$. We vary $\rho \in \{-5, 0.9\}$ to emphasize the main feature of the model. That is, what the optimal quality level of a single service is if the overall quality of the composed service is either complementary or substitutable. The respective steady states are given by (23) and read

$$\rho = 0.9: \quad \tilde{\theta}_1 = \tilde{I}_1 = 4.3 \quad \text{and} \quad \tilde{\theta}_2 = \tilde{I}_2 = 2.3 \tag{26}$$

$$\rho = -5: \quad \tilde{\theta}_1 = \tilde{I}_1 = 1.3 \quad \text{and} \quad \tilde{\theta}_2 = \tilde{I}_2 = 1.2 \tag{27}$$

---

[6] The derivation can be found in Appendix A.2.

[7] Actually, here the cooperative as well as the open and closed loop solution coincide. Since profits are split evenly among the market participants they try to maximize the overall profit, which is basically the definition of a cooperative mood of play. In addition, the game is somehow linear-quadratic (LQ). That is, the law of motions are linear and the payoffs are quadratic with respect to the control and state variable. LQ games are known to have the same solution for open and closed loop strategies [5, Sect. 7.1].

If the services are substitutable ($\rho = 0.9$), then cost parameters drive the long-run equilibrium. Here the cost advantage of service provider 1 yields a higher investment and thus also a higher quality in the dynamic equilibrium. On the other hand, if services are complementary ($\rho = -5$), the cost advantage nearly vanishes and both service providers adjust quality towards some similar level. Figure 3 displays the respective time paths $\theta_i(t)$ and $I_i(t)$ over a time horizon of five periods $t \in [0, 5]$.

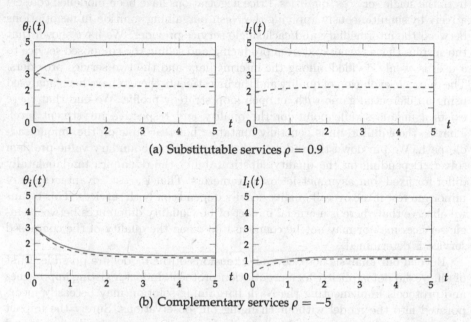

(a) Substitutable services $\rho = 0.9$

(b) Complementary services $\rho = -5$

Note: Quality and investment levels over five time periods $t \in [0, 5]$ for varying quality substitutability $\rho \in \{-5.0, 0.9\}$. Service provider 1 is indicated by solid red and provider 2 by dashed blue lines.

Fig. 3. Solution paths

Consider the case $\rho = 0.9$ (cf. Fig. 3(a)). Firm 1 invests slightly more than the long-run equilibrium level and thus increases quality over time $\dot{\theta}_1 > 0$. Service provider 2 on the other hand invests less and thus the quality decreases. Note that the time paths of quality steadily diverge from the common origin $\theta_1(0) = \theta_2(0)$. Consider the case $\rho = -5$ (cf. Fig. 3(b)). Even though the cost parameters did not change, the dynamics fundamentally differ with respect to the first case. Here the shape of the time path is congruent for both service providers. Service provider 1 now adjusts the quality towards the less efficient provider 2, i.e., both service providers decrease quality over time and reach some "close" equilibria due to the complementarity of the services. Now service provider 1 has no incentive to produce a high quality service, since the overall quality is strongly determined by the lower quality.

7   Conclusion

We introduced a model with an intermediary producing a composed service using two single services to investigate the dynamic interaction on the market for composed services. While considering in principal a composed service with two complementary single services as inputs, our analysis is valid for different assumptions on how the quality of the composed service is actually determined from the single services' qualities. Price negotiations have been modelled cooperatively by simultaneously applying the Nash bargaining solution in negotiations between the intermediary and each single service provider. We have shown that the surplus that is generated from producing and selling the composed service to a user is evenly divided among the intermediary and the two service providers. The dynamic evolution of quality and the investments therein have been analysed using a differential game with an open loop strategy profile. We find that there exists a unique saddle point for the quality and respective investment level. That is, the equilibrium is generally unstable, but reachable on the unique saddle path. We pin down the saddle path by applying a boundary value problem solver. Depending on the quality substitutability the dynamics fundamentally differ for fixed, but asymmetric cost parameters. That is, cost advantages are of minor interest if the overall quality heavily depends on both services. This means we observe that there is a crucial impact of how quality differences between single services may or may not be compensated when the quality of the composed service is determined.

Beyond our analysis here, several extensions of the model are possible. First of all, we did not explicitly fix a negotiation protocol. In fact, existing approaches and protocols implementing the Nash bargaining solution may be easily incorporated into the model without changing our observations. Surely the impact of competition between several intermediaries producing composed services and the use of more complex models of service composition are worth further investigation in future work. For instance, typically different alternative single services may be available for a composed service. Thus, besides complementary also substitutable single services may be considered. Competition between service providers may as well have an effect on the bargaining power of the intermediary. In addition, the comparison of different pricing models in an additional direction for further research.

A   Technical Appendix

A.1   Fixed Point

In this section we derive the unique fixed point of $\mathcal{D}(\dot{\theta}, \dot{I})$ denoted by $(\tilde{\theta}, \tilde{I})$. Instead of solving $\dot{I}_1 = \dot{I}_2 = \dot{\theta}_1 = \dot{\theta}_2 = 0$ simultaneously, we express the equilibrium investment level by means of the quality. Setting (15) equal to zero yields

$$\tilde{I}_i - \delta\tilde{\theta}_i = 0 \implies \tilde{I}_i = \tilde{\theta}_i\delta \quad \text{for } i = 1, 2. \tag{28}$$

We now solve the remaining equations for $\tilde{\theta}_1$ and $\tilde{\theta}_2$. Inserting (28) into (21) yields

$$\tilde{\theta}_i \delta \left(\delta + r + \frac{\alpha_i}{\beta_i \delta} \right) - \frac{\tilde{\theta}_i^{\rho-1} \left(\tilde{\theta}_1^\rho + \tilde{\theta}_2^\rho \right)^{\frac{1-\rho}{\rho}}}{4\beta_i(\gamma_1 + \gamma_2)} = 0. \tag{29}$$

Rearranging gives us

$$\tilde{\theta}_i^{2-\rho}(\beta_i \delta(\delta + r) + \alpha_i) = \frac{\left(\tilde{\theta}_1^\rho + \tilde{\theta}_2^\rho \right)^{\frac{1-\rho}{\rho}}}{4(\gamma_1 + \gamma_2)}. \tag{30}$$

Note that the right-hand side of (30) is identical for both providers, i.e., symmetric in the variables γ_1 and γ_2 as well as in $\tilde{\theta}_1$ and $\tilde{\theta}_2$. Thus, we know that

$$\tilde{\theta}_i^{2-\rho} \xi_i = \tilde{\theta}_{3-i}^{2-\rho} \xi_{3-i} \tag{31}$$

where we defined $\xi_i := \delta \beta_i(\delta + r) + \alpha_i$ for $i = 1, 2$. This yields a relationship between the two quality levels

$$\tilde{\theta}_{3-i} = \left(\frac{\xi_i}{\xi_{3-i}} \right)^{\frac{1}{2-\rho}} \tilde{\theta}_i =: \phi_i \tilde{\theta}_i. \tag{32}$$

Now, we plug (32) into (30) and obtain

$$\tilde{\theta}_i^{2-\rho} \xi_i = \frac{\left(\tilde{\theta}_i^\rho + (\phi_i \tilde{\theta}_i)^\rho \right)^{\frac{1-\rho}{\rho}}}{4(\gamma_1 + \gamma_2)}. \tag{33}$$

Solving according to $\tilde{\theta}_i$ yields

$$\tilde{\theta}_i = \frac{\left(1 + \phi_i^\rho \right)^{\frac{1-\rho}{\rho}}}{4(\gamma_1 + \gamma_2)\xi_i}. \tag{34}$$

A.2   Stability

The stability of the fixed point can be checked by evaluating the eigenvalues $\{\omega_n : n = 1, 2, 3, 4\}$ of the Jacobian matrix. We obtain

$$J_{\mathcal{D}} = \begin{bmatrix} \dfrac{\partial \dot{I}_1}{\partial I_1} & \dfrac{\partial \dot{I}_1}{\partial I_2} & \dfrac{\partial \dot{I}_1}{\partial \theta_1} & \dfrac{\partial \dot{I}_1}{\partial \theta_2} \\[2mm] \dfrac{\partial \dot{I}_2}{\partial I_1} & \dfrac{\partial \dot{I}_2}{\partial I_2} & \dfrac{\partial \dot{I}_2}{\partial \theta_1} & \dfrac{\partial \dot{I}_2}{\partial \theta_2} \\[2mm] \dfrac{\partial \dot{\theta}_1}{\partial I_1} & \dfrac{\partial \dot{\theta}_1}{\partial I_2} & \dfrac{\partial \dot{\theta}_1}{\partial \theta_1} & \dfrac{\partial \dot{\theta}_1}{\partial \theta_2} \\[2mm] \dfrac{\partial \dot{\theta}_2}{\partial I_1} & \dfrac{\partial \dot{\theta}_2}{\partial I_2} & \dfrac{\partial \dot{\theta}_2}{\partial \theta_1} & \dfrac{\partial \dot{\theta}_2}{\partial \theta_2} \end{bmatrix} = \begin{bmatrix} \varepsilon_{11} & 0 & \varepsilon_{13} & \varepsilon_{14} \\ 0 & \varepsilon_{22} & \varepsilon_{23} & \varepsilon_{24} \\ \varepsilon_{31} & 0 & \varepsilon_{33} & 0 \\ 0 & \varepsilon_{42} & 0 & \varepsilon_{44} \end{bmatrix} \tag{35}$$

with

$$\varepsilon_{11} = \varepsilon_{22} = \delta + r, \quad \varepsilon_{31} = \varepsilon_{42} = 1, \quad \varepsilon_{33} = \varepsilon_{44} = -\delta, \tag{36}$$

$$\varepsilon_{13} = \frac{\alpha_1}{\beta_1} + \frac{1-\rho}{4\beta_1(\gamma_1 + \gamma_2)} \theta_1^{\rho-2} \theta_2^{\rho} (\theta_1^{\rho} + \theta_2^{\rho})^{\frac{1}{\rho}-2}, \tag{37}$$

$$\varepsilon_{24} = \frac{\alpha_2}{\beta_2} + \frac{1-\rho}{4\beta_2(\gamma_1 + \gamma_2)} \theta_2^{\rho-2} \theta_1^{\rho} (\theta_1^{\rho} + \theta_2^{\rho})^{\frac{1}{\rho}-2}, \tag{38}$$

$$\varepsilon_{14} = -\frac{1-\rho}{4\beta_1(\gamma_1 + \gamma_2)} (\theta_1\theta_2)^{\rho-1} (\theta_1^{\rho} + \theta_2^{\rho})^{\frac{1}{\rho}-2}, \tag{39}$$

$$\varepsilon_{23} = -\frac{1-\rho}{4\beta_2(\gamma_1 + \gamma_2)} (\theta_1\theta_2)^{\rho-1} (\theta_1^{\rho} + \theta_2^{\rho})^{\frac{1}{\rho}-2}. \tag{40}$$

The eigenvalues are

$$\omega_{1,2} = \frac{1}{2} \left(\varepsilon_{11} + \varepsilon_{33} \pm \sqrt{(\varepsilon_{11} - \varepsilon_{33})^2 + 4\varepsilon_{13}} \right) = \frac{1}{2} \left(r \pm \sqrt{(r + 2\delta)^2 + 4\varepsilon_{13}} \right) \tag{41}$$

$$\omega_{3,4} = \frac{1}{2} \left(\varepsilon_{22} + \varepsilon_{44} \pm \sqrt{(\varepsilon_{22} - \varepsilon_{44})^2 + 4\varepsilon_{24}} \right) = \frac{1}{2} \left(r \pm \sqrt{(r + 2\delta)^2 + 4\varepsilon_{24}} \right). \tag{42}$$

Since $\varepsilon_{13} > 0$ and $\varepsilon_{24} > 0$ we must have $|r| < |\sqrt{(r + 2\delta)^2 + 4\varepsilon_{13}}|$ and $|r| < |\sqrt{(r + 2\delta)^2 + 4\varepsilon_{24}}|$. Hence two eigenvalues are positive and the remaining two are negative $\omega_{1,3} > 0 > \omega_{2,4}$ respectively. The system is thus said to be saddle point stable.

References

1. Abhishek, V., Kash, I.A., Key, P.: Fixed and market pricing for cloud services. In: 2012 IEEE Conference on Computer Communications Workshops (INFOCOM WKSHPS), pp. 157–162, March 2012
2. Al-Roomi, M., Al-Ebrahim, S., Buqrais, S., Ahmad, I.: Cloud computing pricing models: a survey. Int. J. Grid Distrib. Comput. **6**(5), 93–106 (2013)
3. Brangewitz, S., Haake, C.-J., Manegold, J.: Contract design for composed services in a cloud computing environment. In: Ortiz, G., Tran, C. (eds.) ESOCC 2014. CCIS, vol. 508, pp. 160–174. Springer, Heidelberg (2015)
4. Brekke, K.R., Cellini, R., Siciliani, L., Straume, O.R.: Competition and quality in health care markets: a differential-game approach. J. Health Econ. **29**(4), 508–523 (2010)
5. Dockner, E., Jørgesen, S., Long, N.V., Sorger, G.: Differential Games in Economics and Management Science. Cambridge University Press, Cambridge (2000)
6. Guo, L., Iyer, G.: Multilateral bargaining and downstream competition. Mark. Sci. **32**(3), 411–430 (2013)
7. Hani, A.F.M., Paputungan, I.V., Hassan, M.F.: Renegotiation in service level agreement management for a cloud-based system. ACM Comput. Surv. (CSUR) **47**(3), 51:1–51:21 (2015)

8. Jula, A., Sundararajan, E., Othman, Z.: Cloud computing service composition: a systematic literature review. Expert Syst. Appl. **41**(8), 3809–3824 (2014)
9. Nash, J.F.: The bargaining problem. Econometrica **18**(2), 155–162 (1950)
10. Zheng, X., Martin, P., Powley, W., Brohman, K.: Applying bargaining game theory to web services negotiation. In: 2010 IEEE International Conference on Services Computing (SCC), pp. 218–225, July 2010

Fault Tolerance

Fault-Aware Application Management Protocols

Antonio Brogi, Andrea Canciani, and Jacopo Soldani[✉]

Department of Computer Science, University of Pisa, Pisa, Italy
soldani@di.unipi.it

Abstract. We introduce *fault-aware management protocols*, which permit modelling the management behaviour of application components by taking into account the potential occurrence of faults, and we show how such protocols can be composed to analyse the behaviour of a multi-component application and to automate its management. We also illustrate a way to recover applications that are stuck because a fault was not properly handled and/or because a component is behaving differently than expected.

Keywords: Management protocols · Fault modelling · Finite state machines

1 Introduction

Automating the management of composite applications is currently one of the major concerns of enterprise IT [18]. Such applications typically integrate various heterogeneous components, whose deployment, configuration, enactment, and termination must be suitably coordinated.

A convenient way to represent the structure of a composite application is a topology graph [3], whose nodes represent the application components, and whose arcs represents the dependencies among such components. More precisely, each topology node can be associated with the requirements of a component, the operations to manage it, and the capabilities it features. Inter-node dependencies associate the requirements of a node with capabilities featured by other nodes.

In [4] we have shown how the management behaviour of topology nodes can be modelled by *management protocols*, specified as finite state machines whose states and transitions are associated with conditions defining the consistency of the states of a node and constraining the executability of management operations. Such conditions are defined on the requirements of a node, and each requirement of a node has to be fulfilled by a capability of another node. As a consequence, the management behaviour of a composite application can be easily derived by composing the management protocols of its nodes according to the dependencies defined in its topology.

[4] does not deal with deal with the potential occurrence of faults, which however must be considered when managing complex composite applications [9].

© IFIP International Federation for Information Processing 2016
Published by Springer International Publishing Switzerland 2016. All Rights Reserved
M. Aiello et al. (Eds.): ESOCC 2016, LNCS 9846, pp. 219–234, 2016.
DOI: 10.1007/978-3-319-44482-6_14

Indeed, an application component may be affected by faults caused by other components on which it relies (e.g., a component is shutdown or uninstalled while another component is relying on its capabilities).

In this paper we propose a *fault-aware* extension of management protocols, to permit modelling how nodes behave when faults occurs. We also illustrate how to analyse and automate the management of composite applications in a fault-resilient manner. Namely, we show how the fault-aware management behaviour of a composite application can be determined by simply composing the management protocols of its nodes according to the application's topology. We then describe how to determine whether a plan orchestrating the application management is valid, which are its effects (e.g., which capabilities are available after executing it, or whether it may generate faults while being executed), and how this also permits finding management plans from given application configurations to achieve specific goals.

Even if application components are described by fault-aware management protocols, the actual behaviour of components may differ from their described behaviour (e.g., because of some bug). We show how the unexpected behaviour of a component can be modelled by automatically completing its management protocol, and how this permits analysing the (worst possible) effects of a misbehaving component on the rest of an application. We also illustrate a way to recover applications that are stuck because a fault was not properly handled and/or because of misbehaving components.

The rest of the paper is organised as follows. Section 2 provides an example motivating the need for fault-aware management protocols. Section 3 illustrates such protocols and to compose them to analyse an application's management in presence of faults. Section 4 describes how to deal with faults caused by the unexpected behaviour of component(s), and how to recover stuck applications. Sections 5 and 6 discuss related work and draw some concluding remarks.

2   Motivating Example

Consider a toy application composed by a web-based front-end and a back-end, both deployed on an apache server, which in turn is installed on a debian operating system. Figure 1 illustrates the topology of such application, according to the TOSCA [21] graphical notation.

Each inter-node dependency is explicitly represented by a relationship connecting a node's requirement with another node's capability (e.g., the server requirements of front-end and back-end are connected with the app-rte capability of apache). A relationship can represent a *vertical* containment dependency (e.g., apache is installed on debian), or an *horizontal* dependency, specifying that a component requires another, without stating that the former is contained in the latter (e.g., front-end must connect to back-end's endpoint to work properly).

Suppose for instance that all nodes have been deployed, started, and properly connected each other (i.e., all components are in their *running* state). What happens if the stop operation of back-end is executed? The back-end application

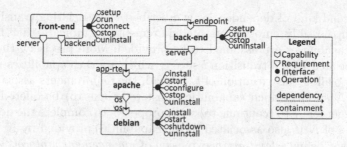

Fig. 1. Motivating example.

component is stopped, and this generates a fault in the front-end, which becomes unable to serve requests to its clients, simply because the connection dependency with back-end is not working any more. Furthermore, even if back-end is re-started, the front-end has to re-connect to the back-end.

Even worse is the case when a node presents an unexpected behaviour. Suppose again that the application is up and running, and that the apache server unexpectedly crashes. Such a crash results in faulting also the nodes contained in apache (viz., front-end and back-end), which are suddenly killed, and potentially enter in an inconsistent state that makes them unusable from there onwards.

Both the above mentioned cases fail because a node stops providing its capabilities while other nodes are relying on them to continue to work. In the first case this happens because of the invocation of a management operation that stops a node while other nodes are depending on it. In the second case a node unpredictably fails[1].

3   Modelling and Analysing Application Management in Presence of faults

3.1   Fault-Aware Management Protocols

Let N be a node modelling an application component. Management protocols [4] permit modelling the management behaviour of N by describing whether and how the management operations of N depend (i) on other operations of the same node, and/or (ii) on operations of other nodes providing the capabilities that satisfy the requirements of N.

The first kind of dependencies is described by specifying relationships between states and management operations of N. More precisely, to describe the order in which the operations of N can be executed, we employ a transition relation τ specifying whether an operation o can be executed in a state s, and which state is reached by executing o in s.

---

[1] Misbehaving components can be detected via monitoring (e.g., by exploiting watch-dogs or heartbeat services). We shall not deepen into details, as component monitoring is outside of the scope of this paper.

The second kind of dependencies is described by associating transitions and states with (possibly empty) sets of requirements to indicate that the corresponding capabilities are assumed to be provided. More precisely, the requirements associated with a transition t specify which are the capabilities that must be offered to allow the execution of t. Instead, the requirements associated with a state of N specify which capabilities must (continue to) be offered by other nodes in order for N to (continue to) work properly. To complete the description, each state s of N is also associated to the capabilities provided by N in s.

We hereby define a *fault-aware* extension of *management protocols* [4], to permit describing how N reacts when it is in a state assuming some requirements to be satisfied, and some other node(s) stop(s) providing the capabilities satisfying such requirements. We introduce a new transition relation φ to model the explicit fault handling of N, i.e. how N changes its state from s to s' when some of the requirements it assumes in s stop being satisfied.

Definition 1. *Let* $N = \langle S_N, R_N, C_N, O_N, \mathcal{M}_N \rangle$ *be a node, where* S_N, R_N, C_N, *and* O_N *are the finite sets of its states, requirements, capabilities, and management operations, and* $\mathcal{M}_N = \langle \overline{s}_N, \rho_N, \chi_N, \tau_N, \varphi_N \rangle$ *is a finite state machine defining the* fault-aware management protocol *of* N, *where*[2]:

- $\overline{s}_N \in S_N$ *is the initial state,*
- $\rho_N : S_N \to 2^{R_N}$ *is a function indicating which requirements must hold in each state* $s \in S_N$,
- $\chi_N : S_N \to 2^{C_N}$ *is a function indicating which capabilities of* N *are offered in a state* $s \in S_N$,
- $\tau_N \subseteq S_N \times 2^{R_N} \times O_N \times S_N$ *is a set of quadruples modelling the transition relation, i.e.* $\langle s, H, o, s' \rangle \in \tau_N$ *denotes that in state* s, *and if the requirements in* H *are satisfied,* o *is executable and leads to state* s', *and*
- $\varphi_N \subseteq S_N \times 2^{R_N} \times S_N$ *is a set of triples modelling the explicit fault handling for a node, i.e.* $\langle s, F, s' \rangle \in \varphi_N$ *denotes that the node will change its state from* s *to* s' *if the requirements in* F *stop being satisfied.*

Example 1. Figure 2 shows the management protocols of the nodes composing our motivating scenario (where thicker arrows represent τ, and lighter arrows represent φ).

Consider for instance the management protocol $\mathcal{M}_{\text{apache}}$, which describes the behaviour of the apache node. In its initial state (not-installed) apache does not require nor provide anything. In the installed and started states it instead assumes the os requirement to (continue to) be satisfied. If the os requirement is faulted, then apache returns to its initial state (thus requiring to be installed and started again). The started state is the only one where apache concretely provides its app-rte capability. Finally, note that all apache's operations can be performed only if the os requirement is satisfied.

---

[2] The constraints to ensure a deterministic semantics of fault-aware management protocols can be trivially formalised by extending those presented in [4]. In the following we consider management protocols that satisfy such requirements.

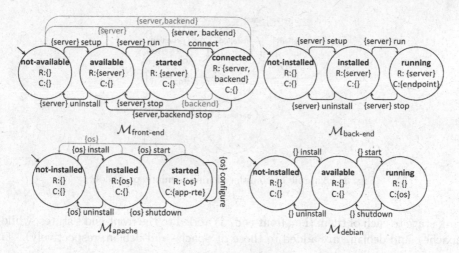

Fig. 2. Examples of management protocols.

Consider now the management protocol $\mathcal{M}_{\text{back-end}}$, which describes the behaviour of the back-end node. When back-end is installed or running, it assumes the capability satisfying its server requirement to (continue to) be provided. What happens if such capability stops being provided? □

The management protocol of a node may leave unspecified how the component will behave in case some requirements stop being fulfilled in some states. To explicitly model that, management protocols can be completed by adding transitions for all unhandled faults, all leading to a "sink" state $s_{\frac{1}{2}}$ (that requires and provides nothing)[3].

Definition 2. *Let* $N = \langle S_N, R_N, C_N, O_N, \mathcal{M}_N \rangle$ *be a node, where* $\mathcal{M}_N = \langle \overline{s}_N, \rho_N, \chi_N, \tau_N, \varphi_N \rangle$ *is its fault-aware management protocol. The management protocol* $\mathcal{M}_N$ *can be completed by replacing* S_N *and* φ_N *with:*

- $S'_N = S_N \cup \{s_{\frac{1}{2}}\}$*, with* $s_{\frac{1}{2}} \notin S_N$ *and* $\rho(s_{\frac{1}{2}}) = \chi(s_{\frac{1}{2}}) = \varnothing$*, and*
- $\varphi'_N = \varphi_N \cup \{\langle s, F, s_{\frac{1}{2}} \rangle \mid s \in S_N \wedge \varnothing \neq F \subseteq \rho(s) \wedge \nexists \langle s, F, s' \rangle \in \varphi_N\}$*.*

In the following we will assume fault-aware management protocols to be automatically completed as defined above.

Example 2. The completion of the management protocol $\mathcal{M}_{\text{back-end}}$ (Fig. 2) is shown in Fig. 3: We add a "sink state" back-end$_{\frac{1}{2}}$, and two transitions reacting to the unsatisfaction of the server requirement when back-end is in its installed or running states.

The extension of the other management protocols in Fig. 2 is even simpler: Since they handle all potential faults, their extension only consists in adding a

---

[3] It is easy to prove that the proposed completion preserves the determinism of a management protocol.

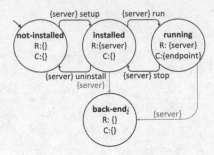

Fig. 3. Example of completed management protocol.

sink state to each of them (i.e., front-end$_\ell$ is added to the front-end's states, while apache$_\ell$ and debian$_\ell$ are added to those of apache and debian, respectively).   □

3.2   Composition of Fault-Aware Management Protocols

Let $A = \langle T, b \rangle$ be a generic composite application, where T is the finite set of nodes (application components) in the application topology[4], and where the connection among nodes is described by a (total) *binding* function

$$b : \bigcup_{N \in T} R_N \to \bigcup_{N \in T} C_N$$

associating each node's requirement with the capability satisfying it.

Since A defines a composition of the nodes in T that coordinate through the binding b among requirements and capabilities, we model the behaviour of A by simply composing the management protocols of the nodes in T.

First, we generalise the notion of global state of A [4] by introducing pending faults. To simplify notation, we shall denote with $\rho(G)$ the set of requirements that are assumed to hold by the nodes in T when A is in G, with $\chi(G)$ the set of capabilities that are provided by such nodes in G, and with $b(R)$ the set of capabilities bound to the requirements in R. Formally:

- $\rho(G) = \bigcup_{N \in T} \{ \rho_N(s) \mid s \in G \wedge s \in S_N \}$,
- $\chi(G) = \bigcup_{N \in T} \{ \chi_N(s) \mid s \in G \wedge s \in S_N \}$, and
- $b(R) = \bigcup_{r \in R} \{ b(r) \}$.

We define the global state of an application A as a set G containing the current state of each of its nodes. We also define a function P to denote the set of pending faults in G, which are the requirements that are assumed in G while the corresponding capabilities are not provided.

Definition 3. *Let* $A = \langle T, b \rangle$ *be a composite application, and let* $N = \langle S_N, R_N,$ $C_N, O_N, \mathcal{M}_N \rangle$. *A global state* G *of* A *is a set of states such that:*

$$G \subseteq \bigcup_{N \in T} S_N \ \wedge \ \forall N \in T \colon \exists! s \in G \cap S_N.$$

---

[4] For simplicity, and without loss of generality, we assume that, given two nodes in a topology, the names of states, requirements, capabilities, and operations are disjoint.

The set $P(G)$ of pending faults in G is defined as follows:

$$P(G) = \{r \in \rho(G) \mid b(r) \notin \chi(G)\}.$$

We denote by $\overline{G}$ the initial global state of A, where each node of T is in its initial state (viz., $\overline{G} = \bigcup_{N \in T} \{\overline{s}_N\}$).

The management behaviour of a composite application A is defined by a labelled transition system over its global states, which consists of two simple inference rules, *(op)* for operation execution and *(fault)* for fault propagation.

Definition 4. *Let $A = \langle T, b \rangle$ be a composite application, and let $N = \langle S_N, R_N, C_N, O_N, \mathcal{M}_N \rangle$ with $\mathcal{M}_N = \langle \overline{s}_N, \rho_N, \chi_N, \tau_N, \varphi_N \rangle$. The fault-aware management behaviour of A is modelled by a labelled transition system whose configurations are the global states of A, and whose transition relation is defined by the following inference rules:*

$$\frac{s \in G \quad \langle s, H, o, s' \rangle \in \tau_N \quad P(G) = \varnothing \quad b(H) \subseteq \chi(G)}{G \xrightarrow{o} (G - \{s\}) \cup \{s'\}} \ (op)$$

$$\frac{s \in G \quad \langle s, F, s' \rangle \in \varphi_N \quad F \subseteq P(G)}{G \xrightarrow{\perp} (G - \{s\}) \cup \{s'\}} \ (fault)$$

The *(op)* rule defines how the global state of A is updated when a node performs a transition $\langle s, H, o, s' \rangle$. Such transition can be performed when there are no pending faults (viz., $P(G) = \varnothing$), and the requirements needed to perform the transition are satisfied in G (viz., $b(H) \subseteq \chi(G)$). As a result, the global state G is updated with the new state of N (viz., $G' = (G - \{s\}) \cup \{s'\}$), potentially triggering faults to be handled (if $P(G') \neq \varnothing$).

The *(fault)* rule instead models fault propagation. It defines how the global state G of an application A is updated when executing a fault handling transition $\langle s, F, s' \rangle$ of a node N. Such transition can be executed if the faults it handles are pending in G (viz., $F \subseteq P(G)$), and its effects on the whole application A are the following: The state of N is updated (viz., $G' = (G - \{s\}) \cup \{s'\}$), novel faults may be triggered, while the faults in F are not pending any more.

3.3 Analysing an Application's Fault-Aware Management Behaviour

The management behaviour defined in Definition 4 permits analysing and automating the management of a composite application. For instance, we can easily define which sequences (or, more in general, which workflows) of management operations can be considered *valid* in a global state of an application.

Definition 5. *Let $A = \langle T, b \rangle$ be a composite application. The sequence $o_1 o_2 ... o_n$ of management operations in A is valid in a global state G_0 of A iff*

$$\exists G_1, G_2, ... G_n : G_0 \xrightarrow{o_1} G_1 \xrightarrow{o_2} G_2 \xrightarrow{o_3} ... \xrightarrow{o_n} G_n$$

where

$$\frac{G \overset{o}{\to} G'}{G \overset{o}{\mapsto} G'} \qquad \frac{G \overset{o}{\mapsto} G' \quad G' \overset{\perp}{\to} G''}{G \overset{o}{\mapsto} G''}$$

A *workflow* W *orchestrating the management operations in* A *is* valid *in* G_0 *iff all its sequential traces are valid in* G_0.

Example 3. Consider the workflow in Fig. 4(a), which permits restarting the back-end and front-end of our motivating application (Figs. 1 and 2). Suppose also that the application is in the following global state: debian is running, apache is started, back-end and front-end are running. It is easy to check that the workflow is valid in the considered global state since both its sequential traces are valid in such global state.

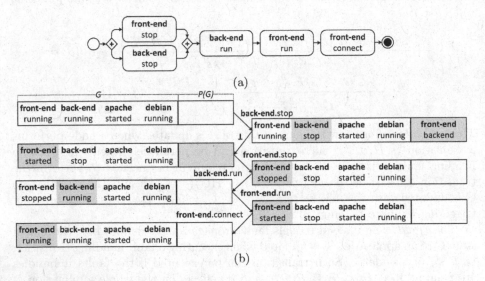

(a)

(b)

Fig. 4. Examples of (a) valid workflow and (b) valid sequence of operations.

Consider, for instance, the sequential trace performing back-end's stop before front-end's stop. Figure 4(b) shows the validity of such a sequential trace by illustrating the evolution of the application's global state. □

The modelling introduced in Sects. 3.1 and 3.2 can be exploited for various other purposes besides checking whether a plan is valid. For instance, validity may not be enough, as different sequential traces of a plan may reach different global states. It is thus interesting to characterise deterministic plans.

Definition 6. *Let* G *be a global state of a composite application* A. *A valid workflow plan* W *for* A *is* deterministic *from* G *if and only if all its sequential traces reach the same global state* G'.

The way to check whether a given plan is valid or deterministic is obviously a visit of the graph associated with the transition system of an application's management behaviour (Definition 4). It is worth highlighting that, thanks to the constraints on management protocols and to the way they are combined, such a graph is *finite* and thus its visit is guaranteed to terminate.

It is also interesting to compute the *effects* of a valid workflow W on the states of an application's components, as well as on the requirements that are satisfied and the capabilities that are available. Such effects can be directly determined from the global state(s) reached by performing the sequential traces of W.

Moreover, the problem of *finding* whether there is a workflow which starts from a global state G and achieves a specific goal (e.g., bringing some components of an application to specific states, or making some capabilities available) can also be solved with a visit of the graph associated with the transition system of an application's management behaviour.

Finally, our model allows to characterise an interesting property that an application may exhibit. If it is possible to reach the initial global state $\overline{G}$ from any global state G that is reachable from $\overline{G}$ itself, then it is always possible to generate a plan for any reachable goal from any reachable global state. This ensures an application's *recoverability*, meaning that whatever global state G we reach from the initial global state $\overline{G}$ (by executing whatever operation or performing whatever ⊥-transition), we can always get back to $\overline{G}$, thus always permitting to reset the application.

4 Modelling the Unexpected

4.1 Unexpected Behaviour of a Component

The analysis described in Sect. 3 assumes that each application component behaves according to its specified management protocol, thus not taking into account components that behave unexpectedly because of mismatches between their modelled and actual behaviour (e.g., because of bugs).

The unexpected behaviour of a component can be modelled by automatically completing its management protocol by adding a "crash" operation $\frac{1}{2}$ that leads the node to the sink state $s_{\frac{1}{2}}$.

Definition 7. *Let $N = \langle S_N, R_N, C_N, O_N, \mathcal{M}_N \rangle$ be a node, where $\mathcal{M}_N = \langle \overline{s}_N,$ $\rho_N, \chi_N, \tau_N, \varphi_N \rangle$ is its fault-aware management protocol. The management behaviour of N can be extended to include unexpected behaviour by replacing O_N and τ_N with:*

– $O'_N = O_N \cup \{\frac{1}{2}\}$, *and*
– $\tau'_N = \tau_N \cup \{\langle s, \rho(s), \frac{1}{2}, s_{\frac{1}{2}} \rangle \mid s \in S_N\}$[5].

---

[5] $\frac{1}{2}$ transitions can be fired only if the requirements in $\rho(s)$ are satisfied so as to ensure the well-formedness [4] of management protocols. Note that this is not a restriction since such requirements are satisfied are satisfied in s (by Definitions. 1 and 2).

The $\frac{\cdot}{2}$ operation, combined with the analyses presented in Sect. 3.3, permits analysing the management behaviour of an application also in presence of misbehaving components: Indeed, the possible unexpected behaviour of a node is modelled by $\frac{\cdot}{2}$ transitions which lead the nodes to their sink state $s_{\frac{\cdot}{2}}$, where we (pessimistically) assume that the node is not offering any capability any more. This permits us to analyse the (worst possible) effects of a misbehaving node on the rest of the application by simply observing whether and how the global state of the application changes.

Example 4. Consider the back-end's management protocol (Fig. 2), extended by adding back-end$_{\frac{\cdot}{2}}$ as illustrated in Example 2. The extension described in Definition 2 simply consists in adding "crash" transitions starting from not-installed, installed, and running, and leading to back-end$_{\frac{\cdot}{2}}$ (Fig. 5). The management protocols of front-end, apache and debian can be extended analogously.

The above extension permits, for instance, determining the effects of a "crashing" back-end when the whole application is up and running (Fig. 6). By invoking back-end's $\frac{\cdot}{2}$, the global state is changed by updating the state of back-end, and by filling the set of pending faults with the backend requirement of front-end (since it is assumed and connected to the back-end's endpoint capability, which is no more provided). The pending fault is then consumed by a $\perp$-transition, which updates front-end's state.   □

More interestingly, we may wish to recover an application having a component that is behaving unexpectedly. More precisely, from the global state reached after injecting a failure (by invoking the "crash" operation $\frac{\cdot}{2}$), we may wish to find a "recovery" plan whose execution permits reaching a given recovery goal (e.g., the global state in which the failure was injected). Notice that, such a

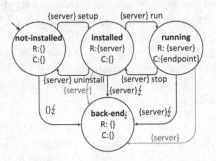

Fig. 5. Example of a management protocol including unexpected behaviour.

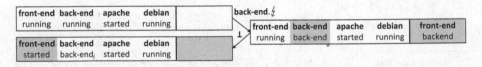

Fig. 6. Example of fault injection and subsequent global state update.

recovery plan cannot be determined by simply visiting of the graph associated with the labelled transition system modelling the management behaviour of an application, as the faulted node is stuck in its sink state (since no transition outgoes from such state).

4.2   Hard Recovery

Recovery plans can be generated automatically, and the underlying idea is quite simple. When a node N is stuck[6] in state $s_\downarrow$, it can be "hard reset" by the node N' in which it is contained (i.e., by the node in which it is installed or deployed). More precisely, by resetting the container node N', all nodes it contains (among which we have the stuck node N) are forcibly reset to their initial state and can be re-installed and started to return up and running.

Due to space limitations, we hereby show how to recover the global state directly on our motivating example after the fault injection of Example 4.

Example 5. Our objective is to enforce the hard reset of a node N stuck in its sink state $s_\downarrow$, by restarting the node in which N is contained. This can be naturally modelled with fault-aware management protocols, provided that the topology is extended with an alive capability to explicitly represent the node containment:

- Since front-end and back-end are contained in apache, (i) we add an alive requirement to front-end and back-end, (ii) we add an alive capability to apache, and (iii) we connect the alive requirements of front-end and back-end alive requirement with the alive capability of apache.
- Since apache is contained in debian, (i) we add an alive requirement to apache, (ii) we add an alive capability to debian, and (iii) we connect the alive requirement of apache to the alive capability of debian.

The updated topology permits to container nodes to witness whether they are still installed (by providing their alive capability), and to contained nodes to check whether they continue to be installed (by assuming their alive requirement). More precisely, it is possible to update the management protocols as shown in Fig. 7, which illustrates the updated protocols of back-end and apache[7]. In each state (other than the initial one), apache and back-end assume their alive requirement, i.e. they assume their containers to continue to be installed. apache is also providing its alive capability in such states, to witness to the nodes it contains (i.e., front-end and back-end) that it continue to be there. Additionally, whenever their alive requirement is removed, apache and back-end return to their initial state. This models the fact that, whenever a container is uninstalled, the nodes it contains are uninstalled along with it.

---

[6] In general, hard recovery can be exploited for recovering a desired global state whenever a node is stuck in its sink state.

[7] We omit the updated protocols of front-end and back-end due to space limitations, and since their update is analogous to that of back-end and apache.

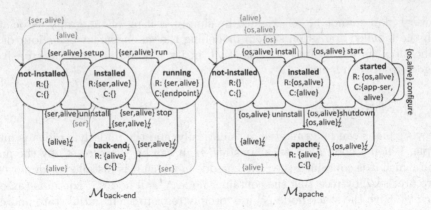

Fig. 7. Example of management protocols with alive requirements and capabilities.

With the above updates we are now able to recover the application from the stuck global state in Fig. 6. Essentially, back-end is stuck in back-end$_\notin$, and the only way to get out of it is to remove its alive requirement, which in turn means to shutdown and uninstall apache (to make it stop providing its alive capability). This results in killing also the front-end, which goes back to its initial state. Afterwards, we can re-install and start the apache server, setup and run the back-end and front-end nodes, and connect the front-end (to the back-end).

It can be easily verified that the above listed operations build up a valid workflow permitting the application to be again up and running from the global state reached in Example 4. As we already mentioned, such a plan can simply be determined with a visit of the graph associated with the transition system defined by management behaviour of the application. The only requirement is to use a modelling of the applications that is updated as we discussed at the beginning of this example.   □

5   Related Work

The problem of automating composite application management is one of the major trends in today's IT [18]. Our previous work [4,5], as well as Aelous [10], permit automatically deploying and managing multi-component cloud applications. The underlying idea of both approaches is quite simple: Developers describe the behaviour of their components through finite-state machines, and such descriptions can be composed to model the management behaviour of a composite application. Engage [12] is another approach for processing application descriptions to automatically deploy applications. The approach presented in this paper extends [4,5], and differs from [10,12], since it permits explicitly modelling faults and injecting failures in application components, analysing their effects, and reacting to them to restore a desired application state.

The rigorous engineering of fault-tolerant systems is a well-known problem in computer science [6], with many existing approaches targeting the design and analysis of such systems. For instance, [15] proposes a way to design object-oriented systems by starting from fault-free systems, and by subsequently refining such design by handling different types of faults. [2,22] instead focus on fault-localisation, thus permitting to redesign a system to avoid the occurrence of such a fault. These approaches differ from ours because they aim at obtaining applications that "never fail", since all potential faults have been identified and properly handled. Our approach is instead more recovery-oriented [7], since we focus on applications where faults possibly occur, and we permit designing applications capable of being recovered.

Similar considerations apply to [1,13,16], which however share with our approach the basic idea of modelling faults in single components and of composing the obtained models according to the dependencies between such components (i.e., according to the application topology).

[11] proposes a decentralised approach to deploy and reconfigure cloud applications in presence of failures. It models a composite applications as a set of interconnected virtual machines, each equipped with a configurator managing its instantiation and destruction. The deployment and reconfiguration of the whole application is then orchestrated by a manager interacting with virtual machine configurators. [11] shares with our approach the objective of providing a decentralised and fault-aware management of a composite application, by specifying the management of each component separately. However, it differs from our approach since it does permits specifying inter-component dependencies, but it is not possible to describe whether they are "horizontal" (i.e., a component requires another to be up and running) or "vertical" dependencies (i.e., a component is installed/deployed on another). Additionally, it focuses on recovering virtual machines that have been terminated because of environmental faults, while we also permit describing how components react to application-specific faults.

[19] proposes an approach to identify failures in a system whose components' behaviour is described by finite state machines. Even though the analyses are quite different, the modelling in [19] is quite similar to ours. It indeed relies on a sort of requirements and capabilities to model the interaction among components, and it permits "implicitly" modelling how components behave in presence of single/multiple faults. Our modelling is a strict generalisation of that in [19], since a component's state can change not only because of requirement unsatisfaction but also because of invoked operations, and since it permits "explicitly" handling faults (i.e., fault handling transitions are distinct from those modelling the normal behaviour of a component). Similar considerations apply to [8], whose modelling is also based on finite state machines with input and output channels (which permit fault communication and propagation by components).

UFIT [14] is a tool for verifying fault-tolerance of systems. It permits modelling systems' behaviour with timed automata, some of whose transitions explicitly represent how the system reacts to the occurrence of faults. Even if it models fault transitions in a way similar to ours, UFIT differs from our approach since it targets standalone systems and does not provide any mechanism to easily compose the automata modelling the behaviour of multiple systems.

Other approaches worth mentioning are [17,20]. The way in which our approach models fault-awareness by relying on the interactions between components,
as well as the idea of analysing/recovering faults through sequences of atomic
transactions (until a desired state is reached), are indeed inspired by [17]. Instead,
the idea of relying on fault injection to determine the effects of unpredictable
faults is inspired by [20].

In summary, to the best of our knowledge, the approach we propose in this
paper is the first that permits automatically orchestrating the management of
composite applications under the assumption that faults possibly occur during
such management, thus requiring to explicitly model how an application reacts
to their occurrence. It does so by following the common idea of modelling each
component separately, and of deriving the management behaviour of a composite
application by properly combining the behaviour of its components.

6   Conclusions

Management protocols [4] are a modular and reusable way to model the management behaviour of application components, and to automate the management
of a complex applications composed by multiple components.

In this paper we have extended management protocols by taking into account
the possibility of faults suddenly occurring, as well as of misbehaving components. More precisely, we have shown how to include faults in management protocols, and how to model components' unexpected behaviour. We have also shown
how to derive the fault-aware management of a composite application by simply composing the protocols of its components. Finally, we have discussed how
the proposed modelling permits automating various analyses (e.g., determining
whether a workflow orchestrating the management of an application is valid,
which are its effects, whether it generates faults, or recovering an application
that is stuck because of a faulted/misbehaving node).

The presented approach can be exploited for developing engines capable of
automatically orchestrating the management of composite application in a fault-
resilient manner. Indeed, given a desired application configuration, an orchestrator can automatically execute the sequence of operations needed to reach such
configuration, and it can maintain such configuration even if faults or unexpected
behaviours suddenly occur.

Please note that, even if some of the analyses we presented in Sects. 3 and
4 have exponential time complexity in the worst case, they still constitute a
significant improvement with respect to the state-of-the-art, as currently the
management of the components of a complex application is coordinated manually
(e.g., by developing ad-hoc scripts), and it is hardly reusable since it is tightly
coupled to such application.

It is important to observe that our approach can be easily adapted to cope
with applications whose topologies are dynamic. Indeed, to deal with applications whose components may dynamically (dis)appear, we only need to add

such components to the application topology, and to update the binding function relating requirements and capabilities. A formalisation of what above is in the scope of our immediate future work.

Another (obvious) extension for future work is to validate the approach we presented in this paper on concrete case studies. In this perspective, we plan to provide tools permitting to model and analyse fault-aware management protocols. More precisely, we plan to (i) properly extend BARREL [4], an open source tool exploiting management protocols for describing and analysing the management of composite TOSCA applications, and (ii) to develop a prototype automatically generating concrete workflows orchestrating the fault-aware management of TOSCA applications.

We also plan to extend the analyses that can be performed on fault-aware management protocols. For instance, we plan to devise techniques permitting to improve our analyses by determining fragments of the topology that can be managed independently from the rest of the topology. This would permit a smarter and more efficient reasoning, as the search space could be reduced by focusing only on the interested fragment(s).

Acknowledgements. This work has been partly supported by the project *Through the fog* (PRA_2016_64) funded by the University of Pisa.

References

1. Alhosban, A., Hashmi, K., Malik, Z., Medjahed, B., Benbernou, S.: Bottom-up fault management in service-based systems. ACM Trans. Internet Technol. **15**(2), 7:1–7:40 (2015)
2. Betin Can, A., Bultan, T., Lindvall, M., Lux, B., Topp, S.: Eliminating synchronization faults in air traffic control software via design for verification with concurrency controllers. Autom. Softw. Eng. **14**(2), 129–178 (2007)
3. Binz, T., Breitenbücher, U., Kopp, O., Leymann, F.: Automated discovery and maintenance of enterprise topology graphs. In: Proceedings of the 6th SOCA, pp. 126–134. IEEE (2013)
4. Brogi, A., Canciani, A., Soldani, J.: Modelling and analysing cloud application management. In: Dustdar, S., et al. (eds.) ESOCC 2015. LNCS, vol. 9306, pp. 19–33. Springer, Heidelberg (2015). doi:10.1007/978-3-319-24072-5_2
5. Brogi, A., Canciani, A., Soldani, J., Wang, P.: Modelling the behaviour of management operations in cloud-based applications. In: Moldt, D. (ed.) Proceedings of the International Workshop on Petri Nets and Software Engineering, PNSE 2015. CEUR Workshop Proceedings, vol. 1372, pp. 191–205. CEUR-WS.org (2015)
6. Butler, M., Jones, C., Romanovsky, A., Troubitsyna, E.: Rigorous Development of Complex Fault-Tolerant Systems. LNCS. Springer, Heidelberg (2007)
7. Candea, G., Brown, A.B., Fox, A., Patterson, D.: Recovery-oriented computing: building multitier dependability. Computer **37**(11), 60–67 (2004)
8. Chen, L., Jiao, J., Fan, J.: Fault propagation formal modeling based on stateflow. In: Proceedings of the 1st ICRSE, pp. 1–7. IEEE (2015)
9. Cook, R.I.: How Complex Systems Fail. University of Chicago, Chicago (1998)
10. Di Cosmo, R., Mauro, J., Zacchiroli, S., Zavattaro, G.: Aeolus: a component model for the cloud. Inf. Comput., 100–121 (2014)

11. Durán, F., Salaün, G.: Robust and reliable reconfiguration of cloud applications. J. Syst. Softw. (2015, in press)
12. Fischer, J., Majumdar, R., Esmaeilsabzali, S.: Engage: a deployment management system. In: Proceedings of the 33rd PLDI, pp. 263–274. ACM (2012)
13. Grunske, L., Kaiser, B., Papadopoulos, Y.: Model-driven safety evaluation with state-event-based component failure annotations. In: Heineman, G.T., Crnković, I., Schmidt, H.W., Stafford, J.A., Ren, X.-M., Wallnau, K. (eds.) CBSE 2005. LNCS, vol. 3489, pp. 33–48. Springer, Heidelberg (2005)
14. Hajisheykhi, R., Ebnenasir, A., Kulkarni, S.S.: UFIT: a tool for modeling faults in UPPAAL timed automata. In: Havelund, K., Holzmann, G., Joshi, R. (eds.) NFM 2015. LNCS, vol. 9058, pp. 429–435. Springer, Heidelberg (2015)
15. Johnsen, E., Owe, O., Munthe-Kaas, E., Vain, J.: Incremental fault-tolerant design in an object-oriented setting. In: Proceedings of 2nd APAQS, pp. 223–230 (2001)
16. Kaiser, B., Liggesmeyer, P., Mäckel, O.: A new component concept for fault trees. In: Proceedings of the 8th SCS, pp. 37–46. Australian Computer Society Inc. (2003)
17. de Lemos, R., Fiadeiro, J.L.: An architectural support for self-adaptive software for treating faults. In: Proceedings of the 1st WOSS, pp. 39–42. ACM (2002)
18. Leymann, F.: Cloud computing. IT - Inf. Technol. 53(4), 163–164 (2011)
19. Liggesmeyer, P., Rothfelder, M.: Improving system reliability with automatic fault tree generation. In: Proceedings of the 28th FTCS, pp. 90–99. IEEE (1998)
20. Nagatou, N., Watanabe, T.: A model-checking based approach to robustness analysis of procedures under human-made faults. In: Ouyang, C., Jung, J.-Y. (eds.) AP-BPM 2014. LNBIP, vol. 181, pp. 117–131. Springer, Heidelberg (2014)
21. OASIS: Topology and Orchestration Specification for Cloud Applications (2013). http://docs.oasis-open.org/tosca/TOSCA/v1.0/TOSCA-v1.0.pdf
22. Qiang, W., Yan, L., Bliudze, S., Xiaoguang, M.: Automatic fault localization for BIP. In: Li, X., et al. (eds.) SETTA 2015. LNCS, vol. 9409, pp. 277–283. Springer, Heidelberg (2015). doi:10.1007/978-3-319-25942-0_18

Improving Reliability of Cloud-Based Applications

Hong Thai Tran[1(✉)] and George Feuerlicht[1,2,3]

[1] Faculty of Engineering and Information Technology,
University of Technology, Sydney, Sydney, Australia
{hongthai.tran,george.feuerlicht}@uts.edu.au
[2] Unicorn College, V Kapslovně 2767/2, 130 00 Prague 3, Czech Republic
[3] Department of Information Technology, University of Economics, Prague,
W. Churchill Sq. 4, Prague 3, Czech Republic

Abstract. With the increasing availability of various types of cloud services many organizations are becoming reliant on providers of cloud services to maintain the operation of their enterprise applications. Different types of reliability strategies designed to improve the availability of cloud services have been proposed and implemented. In this paper we have estimated the theoretical improvements in service availability that can be achieved using the Retry Fault Tolerance, Recovery Block Fault Tolerance and Dynamic Sequential Fault Tolerance strategies, and we have compared these estimates to experimentally obtained results. The experimental results obtained using our prototype Service Consumer Framework are consistent with the theoretical predictions, and indicate significant improvements in service availability when compared to invoking cloud services directly.

Keywords: Reliability of cloud services · Fault tolerance · RFT · RBFT · DSFT

1 Introduction

With the increasing use of cloud services the reliability of enterprise applications is becoming dependent on the reliability of consumed cloud services. In the public cloud context, service consumers do not have control over externally provided cloud services and therefore cannot guarantee the levels of security and availability that they are typically expected to provide to their users [1]. While most cloud service providers make considerable efforts to ensure the reliability of their services, cloud service consumers cannot assume continuous availability of cloud services, and are ultimately responsible for the reliable operation of their enterprise applications. In response to such concerns, hybrid cloud solutions have become popular [2]; according to Gartner Special Report on the Outlook for Cloud [3] half of large enterprises will adopt and use the hybrid cloud model by the end of 2017. Hybrid cloud solutions involve on-premise enterprise applications that utilize external cloud services, for example Paypal Payment Gateway (www.paypal.com), cloud storage service Amazon S3 (aws.amazon.com/s3), or entire SaaS (Software as a Service) applications. With a hybrid delivery model

© IFIP International Federation for Information Processing 2016
Published by Springer International Publishing Switzerland 2016. All Rights Reserved
M. Aiello et al. (Eds.): ESOCC 2016, LNCS 9846, pp. 235–247, 2016.
DOI: 10.1007/978-3-319-44482-6_15

where enterprise applications are partially hosted on premise and partially in the cloud, enterprises can balance the benefits and drawbacks of both approaches, and decide which applications can be migrated to the cloud and which should be deployed locally to ensure high levels of data security and privacy. However, from the reliability point of view, hybrid cloud introduces a number of significant challenges as IT (Information Technology) infrastructure and enterprise applications become fragmented over multiple environments with different reliability characteristics.

Another reliability challenge concerns service evolution, i.e. changes in functional attributes of services that may impact on existing consumer applications. Services are often the subject of uncontrolled changes as service providers implement functional enhancements and rectify defects with service consumers unable to predict when or how services will change [4]. Consequently, service consumers suffer service disruptions and are forced to upgrade their applications to maintain compatibility with new versions of cloud services, often without any notification. As the complexity of service-oriented applications grows, it is becoming imperative to develop effective methods to manage service evolution and to ensure that service consumers are protected from service changes.

In this paper we describe the reliability features of the Service Consumer Framework (SCF) designed to improve the reliability of cloud-based enterprise applications by managing service outages and service evolution. In the next section (Sect. 2) we review related literature dealing with the reliability of cloud-based solutions. In Sect. 3 we describe three reliability strategies (Retry Fault Tolerance, Recovery Block Fault Tolerance, and Dynamic Sequential Fault Tolerance) and calculate their expected theoretical impact on the probability of failure and response time. In Sect. 4 we discuss how these reliability strategies are implemented using the SCF framework. Section 5 describes our experimental setup and gives a comparison of the theoretical results calculated in Sect. 3 with the experimental measurements of availability and response time. Section 6 contains our conclusions and proposals for future work.

2 Related Work

Traditional approaches to developing reliable, fault tolerant on-premise SOA (Service Oriented Architecture) applications include fault prevention and forecasting. For example, Tsai et al. [5] propose a SOA testing and evaluation framework that implements group testing to enhance test efficiency. This framework uses coverage relationships and recent test results to rank and to eliminate test cases with overlapping coverage. Using redundancy-based fault tolerance strategies, Zibin and Lyu [1] propose a distributed replication strategy evaluation and selection framework for fault tolerant web services. Authors compare various replication strategies and propose a replication strategy selection algorithm. Developing highly reliable cloud-based applications introduces a number of new reliability challenges, as enterprise applications are no longer under the full of control of local developers and administrators. In response to such challenges, Zibin et al. [6] present a FTCloud component ranking framework for building fault-tolerant cloud applications. Using two different ranking algorithms: structure-based component ranking and hybrid component ranking, authors identify the most critical components of cloud applications and then determine an optimal fault-tolerance strategy for these components. Based on this work, Reddy and Nalini [7] propose FT2R2Cloud as a fault tolerant solution using time-out and retransmission of requests for cloud applications. FT2R2Cloud measures the reliability of the software components in terms of the number of responses and the throughput. Authors propose an algorithm to rank software components based on their reliability calculated using a number of service outages and service invocation.

In recent research, Zhengping et al. [2] propose the S5 system accounting framework to maximize reliability of cloud services. The framework consists five different layers: service existence examination, service availability examination, service capability and usability examination, service self-healing layer, and system accounting user interface. Authors also propose a new definition of quality of reliability for cloud services. In another work, Adams, Bearly [8] describe fundamental reliability concepts and a reliability design-time process for organizations. Authors provide a guideline for IT architects to improve the reliability of their services and propose processes that architects can use to design cloud services that mitigate potential failures. More recently, Zheng and Lyu [9] identified major problems when developing fault tolerance strategies and introduced the design of static and dynamic fault tolerance strategies. Authors identify significant components of complex service-oriented systems, and investigate algorithms for optimal fault tolerance strategy selection. A heuristic algorithm is proposed to efficiently solve the problem of selection of a fault tolerance strategy. The authors describe an algorithm for component ranking aiming to provide a practical fault-tolerant framework for improving the reliability of enterprise applications. Zheng et al. [10] describe a Retry Fault Tolerance (RFT) that involves repeated service invocations with a specified delay interval until the service invocation succeeds. This strategy is particularly useful in situations characterized by short-term outages.

Focusing on improving the reliability of cloud computing, Chen et al. [11] present a lightweight software fault-tolerance system called SHelp, which can effectively recover programs from different types of software faults. SHelp extends ASSURE [12] to improve its effectiveness and efficiency in cloud computing environments. Zhang et al. [13] propose a novel approach called Byzantine Fault Tolerant Cloud (BFTCloud) to manage different types of failures in voluntary resource clouds. BFTCloud deploys replication techniques to overcome failures using a broad pool of nodes available in the cloud. Moghtadaeipour and Tavoli [14] propose a new approach to improve load balancing and fault tolerance using work-load distribution and virtual priority.

Another aspect of cloud computing that impacts on reliability involves service evolution. Service evolution has been the subject of recent research interest [4, 15–19], however, the focus of these activities so far has been mainly on developing methodologies that help service providers to manage service versions and deliver reliable services. In the cloud computing environments where services are provided externally by independent organizations (cloud service providers) a consumer-side solution is needed to ensure the reliability of cloud-based service-oriented application [10].

3   Reliability Strategies

In this section we discuss three reliability strategies that are implemented in the SCF framework: Retry Fault Tolerance (RFT), Recovery Block Fault Tolerance (RBFT), and Dynamic Sequential Fault Tolerance (DFST). As noted above in Sect. 2, these strategies have been described in the literature for on-premise systems [6, 7, 10]. We have adapted the RFT, RBFT and DFST reliability strategies for cloud services to address short-term and long-term service outages, and issues arising from service evolution. Short-term outages are situations where services become temporarily inaccessible, for example as a result of the loss of network connectivity; automatic recovery typically restores the service following a short delay. Long-term service outages are typically caused by scheduled and unscheduled maintenance or system crashes that require service provider intervention to recover the service. Service evolution involves changes in functional characteristics of services associated with functionality enhancements and changes aimed at improving service performance. Service evolution may involve changes to service interfaces, service endpoints, security policy, or may involve service retirement. Most cloud service providers maintain multiple versions of services to limit the impact of such changes on service consumers, and attempt to ensure backward compatibility between service versions. However, in practice it is not always possible to avoid *breaking* consumer applications, resulting in a situation where service consumers are forced to modify their applications to ensure compatibility with the new version of the service. Service overload occurs when the number of service requests in a given time period exceeds the provider limit.

3.1   Retry Fault Tolerance

Retry Fault Tolerance (Fig. 1) is a relatively simple strategy commonly used in enterprise application. Using this strategy, cloud services are repeatedly invoked following a delay period until the service invocation succeeds. RFT

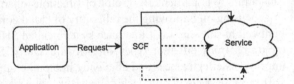

Fig. 1. Retry Fault Tolerance

helps to improve reliability, in particular in situations characterized by short-term outages. The overall probability of failure (PF_{RFT}) can be calculated by:

$$PF_{RFT} = PF^m \tag{1}$$

where PF is the probability of failure of the service and m is a number of retry attempts. While RFT reduces the probability of failure, it may increase the overall response time T_{RFT} due to delays between consecutive service invocations. The total delay can be estimated as:

$$T_{RFT} = \sum_{i=1}^{m} (T_{(i)} + D \times (i - 1)) \times (PF)^{i-1} \qquad (2)$$

where D is the delay between retry attempts and T_i is the response time of ith invocation. The above calculations assume independent modes of failure of subsequent invocations; this assumption only holds in situations where the delay D is much greater than the duration of the outage, i.e. for long duration outages the invocation will fail repeatedly, invalidating the assumption of independence of failures of subsequent invocations.

3.2 Recovery Block Fault Tolerance

Recovery Block Fault Tolerance (Fig. 2) is a widely used strategy that relies on service substitution using alternative services invoked in a specified sequence. It is used to improve the availability of critical applications. The failover configuration includes a *primary* cloud service used as a default (active) service, and *stand-by* services that are deployed in the event of the

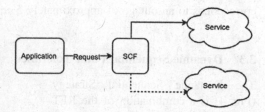

Fig. 2. Recovery Block Fault Tolerance

failure of the primary service, or when the primary service becomes unavailable because of scheduled/unscheduled maintenance. Now assuming independent modes of failure, the overall probability of failure for n services combined can be computed by:

$$PF_{RBFT} = \prod_{i=1}^{n} PF_{(i)}; A_{RBFT} = 1 - PF_{RBFT} \qquad (3)$$

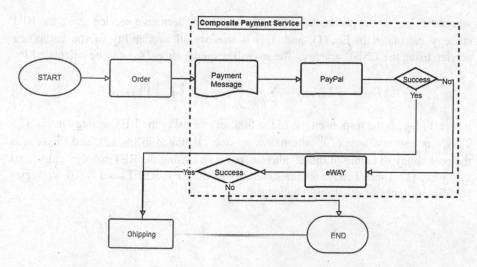

Fig. 3. Online shopping scenario using a composite payment service

where n is the total number of services and PF_i is the probability of failure of the ith alternative service. The overall response time $T(s)$ can be calculated by:

$$T_{RBFT} = T_{(1)} + \sum_{i=2}^{n} \left(T_{(i)} \times \prod_{k=1}^{i-1} PF_{(k)} \right) \tag{4}$$

where T_1 is response time of first service invocation and T_i is response time of ith alternative service invocation. In the online shopping scenario illustrated in Fig. 3, the composite payment service uses eWay payment service as an alternative (stand-by) service for the PayPal (primary) service. Assuming that the availability of both PayPal and eWay services is 99.9 % (corresponding to an outage of approximately 9 h per year), and that the probability of failure $PF = 0.01$ for each service, the overall RBFT probability of failure $PF = 10^{-6}$, and the overall availability $A_{RBFT}s = 99.9999$ % (this corresponds to an outage of approximately 5 min per year).

3.3   Dynamic Sequential Fault Tolerance

The Dynamic Sequential Strategy (Fig. 4) is a combination of the RFT and RBFT strategies. When the primary service fails following RFT retries, the dynamic sequential strategy will deploy an alternative service. The overall probability of failure for the n services combined is given by:

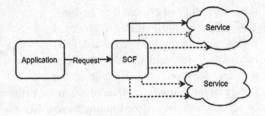

Fig. 4. Dynamic sequential strategy

$$PF_{DSFT} = \prod_{i=1}^{n} PF_{RFT(i)}; A_{DSFT} = 1 - PF_{DSRF} \tag{5}$$

where $PF_{RFT(i)}$ is the probability of failure of the ith alternative service using the RFT strategy calculated in Eq. (1), and $A(s)$ is the overall availability of the composite service using the DSFT strategy. The overall response time $T(s)$ can be calculated by:

$$T_{DSFT} = T_{RFT(1)} + \sum_{i=2}^{n} \left(T_{RFT(i)} \times \prod_{k=1}^{i-1} PF_{RFT(k)} \right) \tag{6}$$

where $T_{RFT(1)}$ is the response time of the first service using the RFT strategy in Eq. (2), $T_{RFT(i)}$ is response time of ith alternative service calculated in Eq. (2), and $PF_{RFT(k)}$ is the probability of failure of the kth alternative service using the RFT strategy calculated using Eq. (1). Table 1 indicates the suitability of the RFT, RBFT, and DSFT strategies to different types of reliability challenges.

Table 1. Suitability of reliability strategies

Method	Short outages	Long outages	Service evolution	Service overload
RFT	Yes	No	No	No
RBFT	Yes	Yes	Yes	Yes
DSFT	Yes	Yes	Yes	Yes

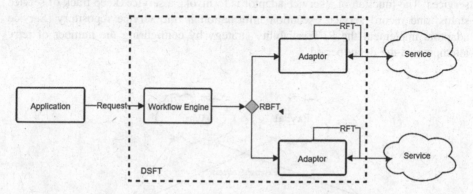

Fig. 5. Service consumer framework reliability features

4   Implementation of Reliability Strategies Using the SCF

The SCF framework is designed to manage hybrid cloud environments and aims to address the main issues that impact on the reliability of enterprise applications. The SCF framework implements RFT, RBFT and DSFT strategies and is briefly described in the following sections. The framework consists of four main components: Service Repository, Workflow Engine, Service Adaptors and a Notification Centre. Detail description of the SCF framework can be found in [19]. Figure 5 illustrates how service adaptors and the workflow engine can be configured to implement the various reliability strategies.

4.1   Service Repository

Service repository maintains information about the available services and adaptors, including metadata that describes functional and non-functional attributes of certified services. The information held in the service repository is used to manage services and to design reliable applications. The functional and non-functional QoS (Quality of Service) attributes held in the service repository enable the selection of suitable services by querying the service repository specifying desired service attributes. Services with identical (or similar) functionality are identified to indicate that these services can be used as alternatives to the primary service to implement the RBFT strategy.

4.2   Service Adaptors

Service adaptors are *connectors* that integrate software services with enterprise applications. Each cloud service recorded in the repository is associated with a corresponding service adaptor. Service adaptors use a native interface to transform service requests to a request that is compatible with the current version of the corresponding cloud service, maintaining compatibility between enterprise applications and external services. The function of a service adaptor is to invoke a service, keep track of service status, and record service execution information in the service repository. Service adaptors implement the RFT reliability strategy by configuring the number of retry attempts and the delay period.

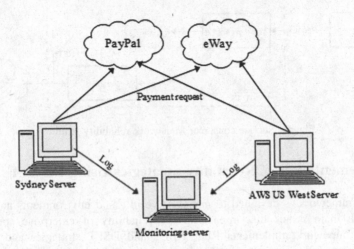

Fig. 6. Experimental configuration

4.3   Workflow Engine

The workflow engine implements service workflows, facilitates service failover and the composition of services. The workflow engine executes workflows and routes requests to corresponding cloud services. Workflows can be configured to implement the RBFT strategy by using a number of alternative services redundantly. Another important function of the workflow engine is load balancing. Service adaptors can be configured as *active* or *stand by*. By default, active service adaptors are used to process the requests and stand by adaptors are deployed in situation when the primary (active) adaptor requests fail or when the primary adaptor becomes overloaded.

4.4   Notification Centre

The SCF framework maintains execution logs and updates service status records in the service repository. When service faults occur, notification centre notifies application administrators so that a recovery action can take place. The administrators are able to rapidly react to service failures and maintain application availability minimizing downtime. In addition, execution logs are used to monitor services and to analyze QoS attributes.

5 Experimental Verification of Reliability Strategies

Figure 6 illustrates the experimental configuration that was used to verify the theoretical calculations in Sect. 3. The experimental setup consists of two servers that host the SCF framework and a separate Monitoring Server. Both SCF servers implement identical payment scenario illustrated in Fig. 3 using PayPal Pilot service (pilot-payflowpro.paypal.com) and eWay Sandbox (https://api.sandbox.ewaypayments. com). The payment requests are randomly generated and sent to the PayPal and eWay payment servers from two different locations. The US West Server uses Amazon Web Services (AWS) cloud-based infrastructure located on the West Coast of the United States and has a high quality server with a reliable network connection. The Sydney server is a local server in Sydney, Australia with a less reliable Internet connection.

5.1 Experimental Setup

We have collected experimental results from both servers for a period of thirty days, storing the data in the logs on the Monitoring Server deployed on AWS. The log data records were analyzed computing the experimental values of availability and response time for the composite payment service using different reliability strategies. Both SCF servers generate payment requests in intervals varying randomly between 5 and 10 s, and use the following four strategies:

Strategy 1: Payment requests are sent directly to the payment service without applying any reliability strategy

Strategy 2: Payment requests are sent to the payment service using RFT strategy with three retry attempts ($R = 3$) and a delay of five seconds ($D = 5$)

Table 2. Consumer service transaction logs

Service	Start time	Response time	Result
eWay	31/03/2016 12:51	3.59 s	Success
PayPal	31/03/2016 12:50	1.48 s	Success
PayPal	31/03/2016 12:50	1.39 s	Success
PayPal	31/03/2016 12:49	1.39 s	Success
eWay	31/03/2016 12:49	2.50 s	Success
PayPal	31/03/2016 12:48	1.44 s	Success
eWay	31/03/2016 12:48	1.51 s	Success
eWay	31/03/2016 12:47	1.72 s	Success
PayPal	31/03/2016 12:47	1.41 s	Success
PayPal	31/03/2016 12:46	1.39 s	Success

(Continued)

Table 2. (*Continued*)

Service	Start time	Response time	Result
eWay	31/03/2016 12:46	2.17 s	Success
PayPal	31/03/2016 12:45	1.39 s	Success
PayPal	31/03/2016 12:45	1.00 s	Error
eWay	31/03/2016 12:44	2.14 s	Success

Strategy 3: Payment requests are sent to a composite payment service using the RBFT strategy

Strategy 4: Payment requests are sent to a composite payment service using the DSFT strategy which is combination of RBFT and RFT with PayPal (R = 3, D = 5) and eWay (R = 3, D = 5)

5.2 Experimental Results

We have collected the payment transaction data independently of the values available from the cloud service providers, storing this information in the log files on the Monitoring Server (Table 2 shows a fragment of the response time measurements). The use of two separate servers in two different locations enables the comparison of availability and response time information collected under different connection conditions.

Table 3. Availability of payment services

Server	PayPal	eWay	PayPal RFT	eWay RFT	PayPal-eWay RBFT	PayPal-eWay DSFT
US West	90.48 %	93.86 %	97.90 %	97.26 %	99.80 %	99.95 %
Sydney	90.18 %	93.53 %	97.28 %	97.03 %	99.29 %	99.82 %

As shown in Table 3, using Strategy 1 (i.e. without deploying any reliability strategy) the availability for PayPal and eWay services on the US West server is 90.4815 % and 93.8654 %, respectively. Deploying the RFT strategy (Strategy 2) the availability increases to 97.9033 % and 97.2607 %, for PayPal and eWay services, respectively. Using the RBFT strategy (Strategy 3), the availability of the composite service (PayPal and eWay) increases to 99.8091 %, and finally using the DSFT strategy (Strategy 4) the availability of the composite service (PayPal + eWay) increases further to 99.9508 %. The theoretical values obtained in Sect. 3 are slightly higher than the experimental values; this can be explained by noting that connection issues may affect both PayPal and eWay services concurrently, invalidating the assumption of independent modes of failure.

Table 4 shows the average response time of PayPal and eWay services using different reliability strategies during the period from March 15th to April 15th 2016. The average response time of the US West Server is considerably lower than the Sydney Server when connecting to the PayPal service in the US. However, for the eWay

Table 4. Response time of payment services in seconds

Server	PayPal	eWay	PayPal RFT	eWay RFT	PayPal-eWay RBFT	PayPal-eWay DSFT
US West	1.35	1.84	2.33	2.66	2.06	2.44
Sydney	3.70	1.75	5.67	3.02	4.98	5.43

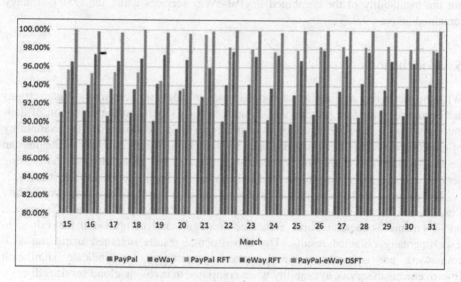

Fig. 7. Availability of reliability strategies from 15th to 31st of March

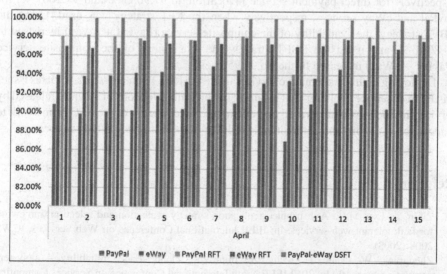

Fig. 8. Availability of reliability strategies from 1st to 15th of April 2016

service (https://www.eway.com.au/), which is located in Australia, the response time of the Sydney Server is slightly better than for the US West server. The bar charts in Figs. 7 and 8 give a comparison of the availability values for various reliability strategies for the period of March 15th to April 15th 2016. As the figures illustrate, the availability of PayPal and eWay services using any of the reliability strategies is significantly higher than without deploying a reliability strategy. During the measurement period the availability of the PayPal service varied between 88 % and 92 %, but the availability of the combined PayPal-eWay services using the DSFT strategy remained above 99.9 %.

6 Conclusions

With the increasing availability of various types of cloud services many organizations are becoming reliant on providers of cloud services to maintain the operation of their enterprise applications. Different types of strategies designed to improve the availability of cloud services have been proposed and implemented. These reliability strategies can be used to improve availability of cloud-based enterprise applications by addressing service outages, service evolution, and failures arising from overloaded services.

In this paper we have estimated the theoretical improvements in service availability that can be achieved using the Retry Fault Tolerance, Recovery Block Fault Tolerance, and Dynamic Sequential Fault Tolerance strategies and compared these values to experimentally obtained results. The experimental results obtained using the SCF framework are consistent with theoretical predictions, and indicate significant improvements in service availability when compared to invoking cloud services directly (i.e. without deploying any reliability strategy). In the specific case of payment services, the availability for PayPal and eWay services increased from 90.4815 % and 93.8654 %, respectively for direct payment service invocation, to 97.9033 % and 97.2607 %, for PayPal and eWay services, respectively when the RFT strategy was used. Using the RBFT strategy, the availability of the composite service (PayPal + eWay) increased to 99.8091 %, and using the DSFT strategy the availability of the composite service (PayPal + eWay) increased further to 99.9508 %.

Deploying multiple alternative services using the RBFT strategy also alleviates issues arising from service evolution that results in incompatible versions of services released by service providers. We are currently extending the functionality of the SFC framework to detect such situations and automatically redirect requests to alternative services.

References

1. Zibin, Z., Lyu, M.R.: A distributed replication strategy evaluation and selection framework for fault tolerant web services. In: IEEE International Conference on Web Services, ICWS 2008 (2008)
2. Zhengping, W., Nailu, C., Peng, S.: Improving cloud service reliability – a system accounting approach. In: 2012 IEEE Ninth International Conference on Services Computing (SCC) (2012)

3. Rivera, J., van der Meulen, R.: Gartner says nearly half of large enterprises will have hybrid cloud deployments by the end of 2017. In: Gartner Special Report Examines the Outlook for Hybrid Cloud (2013)
4. Andrikopoulos, V., Benbernou, S., Papazoglou, M.P.: On the evolution of services. IEEE Trans. Softw. Eng. **38**(3), 609–628 (2012)
5. Tsai, W.T., et al.: On testing and evaluating service-oriented software. Computer **41**(8), 40–46 (2008)
6. Zibin, Z., et al.: Component ranking for fault-tolerant cloud applications. IEEE Trans. Serv. Comput. **5**(4), 540–550 (2012)
7. Reddy, C.M., Nalini, N.: FT2R2Cloud: fault tolerance using time-out and retransmission of requests for cloud applications. In: 2014 International Conference on Advances in Electronics, Computers and Communications (ICAECC) (2014)
8. Adams, M., et al.: An introduction to designing reliable cloud services. Microsoft Trustworthy Computing (2014). https://www.microsoft.com/en-au/download/details.aspx?id=34683
9. Zheng, Z., Lyu, M.R.: Selecting an optimal fault tolerance strategy for reliable service-oriented systems with local and global constraints. IEEE Trans. Comput. **64**(1), 219–232 (2015)
10. Zheng, Z., Lyu, M., Wang, H.: Service fault tolerance for highly reliable service-oriented systems: an overview. Sci. China Inf. Sci. **58**(5), 1–12 (2015)
11. Chen, G., et al.: A lightweight software fault-tolerance system in the cloud environment. Concurrency Comput. Pract. Experience **27**(12), 2982–2998 (2015)
12. Sidiroglou, S., et al.: ASSURE: automatic software self-healing using rescue points. In: Proceedings of the 14th International Conference on Architectural Support for Programming Languages and Operating Systems 2009, Washington, DC, USA, pp. 37–48. ACM (2009)
13. Zhang, Y., Zheng, Z., Lyu, M.R.: BFTCloud: a byzantine fault tolerance framework for voluntary-resource cloud computing. In: 2011 IEEE International Conference on Cloud Computing (CLOUD) (2011)
14. Moghtadaeipour, A., Tavoli, R.: A new approach to improve load balancing for increasing fault tolerance and decreasing energy consumption in cloud computing. In: 2015 2nd International Conference on Knowledge-Based Engineering and Innovation (KBEI) (2015)
15. Eisfeld, A., McMeekin, D.A., Karduck, A.P.: Complex environment evolution: challenges with semantic service infrastructures. In: 6th IEEE International Conference on Digital Ecosystems Technologies DEST-2012 (2012)
16. Romano, D., Pinzger, M.: Analyzing the evolution of web services using fine-grained changes. In: ICWS-2012, IEEE 19th International Conference on Web Services (2012)
17. Zhenmei, Y., Fengming, L.: Small-world based trust evaluation model for web service. In: 2012 International Conference on Computer Science and Service System (CSSS) (2012)
18. Ziyan, X., Haihong, Z., Lin, L.: User's requirements driven services adaptation and evolution. In: Computer Software and Applications Conference Workshops (COMPSACW), 2012 IEEE 36th Annual, pp. 13–19 (2012)
19. Feuerlicht, G., Tran, H.T.: Service consumer framework: managing service evolution from a consumer perspective. In: ICEIS-2014, 16th International Conference on Enterprise Information Systems. Springer, Portugal (2014)

A Short Survey on Using Software Error Localization for Service Compositions

Julia Krämer[(⊠)] and Heike Wehrheim

Department of Computer Science, Paderborn University, Paderborn, Germany
{juliadk,wehrheim}@mail.uni-paderborn.de

Abstract. In modern software development, paradigms like component-based software engineering (CBSE) and service-oriented architectures (SOA) emphasize the construction of large software systems out of existing components or services. Therein, a *service* is a self-contained piece of software, which adheres to a specified *interface*. In a model-based software design, this interface constitutes our sole knowledge of the service at design time, while service implementations are not available. Therefore, correctness checks or detection of potential errors in service compositions has to be carried out without the possibility of *executing* services. This challenges the usage of standard software error localization techniques for service compositions. In this paper, we review state-of-the-art approaches for error localization of software and discuss their applicability to service compositions.

1 Introduction

Debugging, i.e., the *detection, localization* and *correction* of software errors, is one of the most time-intensive tasks in software development. Within this process, error localization is considered the most expensive task [43]. In order to support developers in debugging, a lot of research effort has been spent on the deployment of *automated* error localization methods. Today, existing error localization methods for software are numerous. They can broadly be separated into two categories.

(1) *Approaches based on the inspection of test cases.* In this category, we find error localization methods like *delta debugging* introduced by Zeller [17,49–51] or the approaches underlying the tools *Tarantula* [27], *Pinpoint* [14] or *AMPLE* [19].

(2) *Approaches based on the computation of dependence information between program statements.* Herein, we locate all techniques based on *static program slicing* as originally introduced by Weiser [46] as well as dynamic slicing.

This work was partially supported by the German Research Foundation (DFG) within the Collaborative Research Centre "On-The-Fly Computing" (SFB 901).

M. Aiello et al. (Eds.): ESOCC 2016, LNCS 9846, pp. 248–262, 2016.
DOI: 10.1007/978-3-319-44482-6_16

When it comes to a model-driven design approach of service composition (or to model-driven software development in general), the situation is different. On the one hand, a model typically abstracts from details of the final software, thus facilitating the construction of automatic methods and tools for error detection (like being done in numerous settings, for functional as well as QoS requirements, e.g. [12,21,39,42]). On the other hand, the *localization* of errors, once correctness checks have reported it, lacks automated methods and tool support. So far, to the best of our knowledge, automated, tool-based approaches for localizing faults in models of service compositions do not exist, at least when it comes to *functional correctness*, i.e., the adherence of the model to functional requirements. With respect to performance analysis of systems, feasible approaches to localize components that negatively impact the overall performance of the system, have been devised in the area of *performance blame analysis* [13,18].

Unfortunately, this lack in tool support cannot easily be amended by applying the abundant existing approaches for standard software development to the service composition approach. The reason is rooted in fact that almost all existing approaches in the standard software setting rely more or less on the availability of execution traces, both faulty and correct, or even the possibility to execute the programs under consideration at will. While this requirement is entirely unproblematic in the software setting, for service composition it is a veritable obstacle, as services, which are offered by external providers and possibly charged for their use, may not be available for execution during design time and fault analysis.

Contribution. In this paper, we survey existing error localization techniques for software, analyze their applicability to *models of service compositions* and propose suitable adaptions. Our focus is on *functional* correctness, more specifically, the adherence of the service composition to specified pre- and postconditions. We assume that services are solely specified in terms of their pre- and postconditions (more precisely, their *interface* specification) and that no other information is available about services. In particular, no implementation is given and thus, they cannot be arbitrarily executed. In this setting, error localization can be rephrased as the task of locating the precise service call, which is responsible for the service composition to invalidate the postcondition when started in a state satisfying the precondition.

In comparison to existing surveys, such as [47] and [3], which focus on methods of the first category, we also investigate methods of the second category and thus, include novel methods for error localization, especially formula-based approaches such as [28–30] and [32]. In contrast to [47] and [3], we do not only review existing methods but also examine their applicability to service compositions.

Organization of the Paper. We introduce basic terminology (services and service compositions) in Sect. 2. In Sect. 3, we present the most important error localization methods for software and discuss their usability for service compositions in the context of model-based software design. We conclude the paper with a conclusion and future work in Sect. 4.

2   Services and Service Compositions

Services, i.e. self-contained software components, which can be used platform independent, are at the core of Service-Oriented Architectures (SOA). In this section, we introduce service descriptions, which constitute all information about a service, and service composition as depicted in Fig. 1. We denote service composition in a textual representation inspired by *service effect specifications* (SEFFs) of [11] (making some of the notations closer to programming languages), while we still use standard concepts of workflow modelling like sequential composition, decisions and repetition. Possible alternative representations for service compositions include graphical or structural notations for workflow modelling like WS-BPEL [40]. The following definition specifies our textual representation of services formally.

Definition 1. *Let* Serv *be a set of given services,* Types *be a set of types and* Var *be a set of variables. The set of all* service compositions *SC is given by the following grammar in Backus-Naur-form:*

$$SC \ni \varphi, \psi :: = Skip \mid \varphi; \psi \mid \text{if } B \text{ then } \varphi \text{ else } \psi \mid \text{while } B \text{ do } \varphi \mid T \ x = \mathsf{S}(x_1, \ldots, x_n)$$
$$\mid \text{foreach } x \text{ in } Set \text{ do } \varphi,$$

where $x, x_1, \ldots, x_n \in$ Var *,* $S \in$ Serv*,* $T \in$ Types *and* Set *is a set.* B *is a predicate in propositional logic with the logical constants* true*,* false *and service calls* S *as atomic formulas.*

Please note that we use assignments in Fig. 1, which are not service calls, for example, in Line 1, Line 3 and Line 8. We consider these assignment as very basic service calls usually not offered by an external provider but by the service specification language. Thus, we do not write them down as service call.

The service composition GVRes in Fig. 1 contains the service restaurantIn that retrieves all restaurants near a given location, the service isVegan, that tests whether a given restaurant offers vegan food, the service validate that provides the rating of a restaurant, and finally, the service isGoodRating, which specifies when a rating is considered a *good* rating. The purpose of the service composition GVRes is to compute the set B of all vegan restaurants with a good rating near a specific location L provided by the user. However, it is faulty. While the purpose of the `foreach`-loop is to filter all the restaurants with a good rating, the negation in the second `if`-statement (Line 7) causes only bad restaurants to be in the set B. At the best, fault localization would precisely indicate the condition of the `if`-statement `!(IsGoodRating(y))` as the location of the error.

The semantics of single services is cruel to the correctness of a service composition. We specify the semantics using *service descriptions*, which include input and output variables as well as pre- and postconditions (or effects, all together typically called IOPE, like in WSDL[1]).

---

[1] https://www.w3.org/TR/wsdl.

```
1 Location  L:=input();
2 Set<Restaurant> A:=
       restaurantsIn(L);
3 Set<Restaurant> B:=emptyset;
4 foreach  z  in  A  do
5    if  isVegan(z)  then
6       Rating  y:=validate(z);
7       if  !(isGoodRating(y))  then
8          B:=B  union  {z};
9       else
10          Skip
11    else
12       Skip
13 return  B;
```

Fig. 1. The service composition GVRes

Definition 2. *A service description* SD *is a tuple* SD = (I, O, Pre, Post) *such that*

- I *and* O *are disjoint sets of input and output variables,*
- Pre *and* Post *are first-order logic formulas, which describe the precondition and the effect (postcondition) of the service, respectively.*

All free variables (i.e. all variables not bound by a quantifier) in Pre *are elements of* I *and all free variables in* Post *are elements of* I ∪ O.

The service validate has the input variable z of type Restaurant and the output variable y of type Rating. Its postcondition guarantees that the returned rating is indeed a rating for the given restaurant if the input is indeed a vegan restaurant.

Service compositions are also specified using service description, e.g. the service composition GVRes has the input variable L of type Location, the output variable B of type Set <Restaurant>, the pre- and postcondition

$$Pre_{GVRes} = true$$
$$Post_{GVRes} = \forall b \in B : isVegan(b) \land isGoodRating(validate(b)).$$

In the following, we say that a service composition is *functionally correct* with respect to a precondition Pre and a postcondition Post, if we can prove that for each input to a service composition, which satisfies the precondition, the output satisfies the postcondition. We say, that a service composition *contains an error*, if it is not functionally correct. The service composition in Fig. 1 will thus be functionally correct if it ensures that no bad vegan or non-vegan restaurant is returned (which is not the case). It can be proven that a service composition is or is not functionally correct, for example, using the approach in [44].

3   Survey on Error Localization

So far, error localization in service compositions has been a sparsely researched topic and only few approaches are known. In contrast, many localization methods for standard software (especially for imperative program) are known. Unfortunately, while imperative programs and service compositions are syntactically similar, they differ in their nature. While error location methods for programs can usually safely assume that the whole program can be executed arbitrarily, this is not the case for service compositions. At the time of analysis, the services called in the composition are in general not available for execution. The reason is that services are usually not locally available, but offered by external providers and charged for their usage. Thus, depending on the concrete services, their repeated execution for testing purposes might either not be given at the moment of analysis, or be economically infeasible.

Thus, in order to make use of the rich source of error localization methods for standard software for service composition, we need to investigate how these methods can be adapted – if at all.

Remark 1. The services and service compositions we discuss cannot be compared to *dynamic* web services, in the sense of applications written in PHP or JavaScript involving dynamically generated web pages or client-server-interaction. Therefore, our setting is very different from the setting in [6–9, 38, 45] and thus, these approaches are inapplicable in our setting.

In this section, we first establish a set of criteria to evaluate existing automated error localization methods. Subsequently, we present an overview on existing error localization methods of both categories when applied to service compositions as in Definition 1 instead of to software.

3.1   Criteria for Error Localization Approaches

In [3, 47], criteria to evaluate error localization methods for software are discussed. We use a subset of these criteria, slightly adapted to the special challenges arising in the context of service compositions (Fig 2).

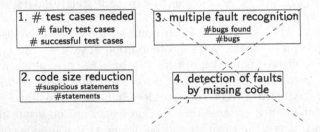

Fig. 2. Criteria for error localization methods and our choice

Number of test cases needed: In model-driven software design, one cannot execute services at *design* time. In the best case, few test cases are available in form of input/output pairs witnessing erroneous behavior, for example resulting from a previous model checking analysis.

Our first evaluation criteria is thus the number of (faulty /correct) test cases a technique needs.

Code size reduction: The second criteria we use is code size reduction, i.e., the percentage of suspicious statements (in which the fault is potentially located) returned by the error localization method with respect to all statements.

Another criterion, which is often used is multiple fault recognition, i.e. the possibility of discovering multiple bugs at once. We do not use it here since service compositions tend to be relatively small, and verification and error localization can thus be executed several times to find several bugs. Detection of faults caused by missing code is not a criterion of primary interest, as the results of existing approaches in general fail w.r.t. multiple bug detection to be specific enough to be of use in a setting where the programs to be analyzed consist of only few lines of code.

3.2   Error Localization Approaches in Service Compositions

In the following, we discuss different error localization methods for standard software. We group approaches, which are similar w.r.t. the number of tests cases they need to be applicable. If necessary, we further distinguish methods by their overall approach, for example, whether it relies on statistics or not.

Neither Relying on Test Cases Nor on Execution. We start our survey with *static slicing*, which also was the first error localization method proposed in 1981 by Weiser [46]. Slicing in general means to cut out statements, which cannot influence a certain variable or a certain property. The "influence" is captured by a number of dependency relations between program statements, e.g., a statement within a branch of a decision depends on the condition of the decision. With respect to error localization this means that the number of statements possibly responsible for the error can be reduced by slicing. Slicing approaches can mainly be divided into *static* and *dynamic* slicing. Whereas the first can be obtained without executing the program and thus, does also not rely on any tests, dynamic slicing gathers information during execution. In [52], it is stated that a static slice definitely contains the bug if it is contained in a Boolean condition or an assignment. Unfortunately, static slices are the largest ones among all slices. Nevertheless, static slicing can easily be modified to be used on service compositions, for example, in [37], static slicing is discussed for software relying on web services.

Application to Service Compositions. For faulty service compositions, we compute slices with respect to the intended postcondition. The static slice with respect to our postcondition $Post_{GVRes}$ of the service composition in Fig. 1 contains all lines except the lines 9 to 12 (which are uninteresting anyway). We see that the gain in this case is close to zero. For finding the error, we still need to inspect the entire service composition. This is an effect, which occurs very often in service compositions because data is passed from one service call to the next, and thus service calls often depend on all prior calls.   □

Relying on One Faulty Input. All of the following error localization methods need at least one faulty input, i.e., one input, which itself satisfies the precondition, but leads to an output, which does not satisfy the postcondition.

Dynamic Slicing. Dynamic slicing was originally introduced in 1988 in [31]. The key idea to dynamic slicing is to collect all relevant information directly during the execution of the program. In the literature, there are mainly three types of dynamic slices: *data*, *full* and *relevant* slices. They differ in the way they take dependencies between program statements into account: data slices just use data dependencies, full slices also control dependencies, and relevant slices in addition partially include static dependencies, i.e., dependencies on program paths, which are not included in the current dynamic execution, but might be if the control-flow is altered. At first, dynamic slicing was considered *not useful* for error localization [4,5]. In 2005, an experimental evaluation in [52] showed that relevant slices are smaller than static slices, but contained all bugs in the experiments performed on the Siemens test suite [25].

   Application to Service Compositions. For service compositions, an *abstract symbolic execution* – i.e., an execution, which does not rely on concrete but on symbolic values for variables – could allow us to use dynamic slicing for error localization. Important questions to be investigated are then whether dynamic slices relying on a symbolic execution are smaller than static slices, and whether all faults are covered. For our example, a symbolic execution would – like for the static slice – return the whole service composition except the lines 9 to 12. We conjecture that this will very often be the case due to the tight dependencies between service calls.   □

Trace Formula Approaches. In this section, we consider all approaches to error localization, which basically rely on a trace formula. The original idea to use trace formulas for *verification* was introduced in [16]. The basic idea therein is to code executions of a program (or even whole programs) as logical formulas, employing either propositional or predicate logic. In [44], this basic principle has been used for the verification of service compositions. We mainly consider the error localization approach presented in [48], where a trace formula is encoded as constraint satisfaction problem. In more detail, in [48], a test defining inputs and expected outputs together with its symbolic execution trace, is transformed into a constraint satisfaction problem and solved using an existing constraint solver. The solution to the constraint satisfaction problem allows to easily extract a set of suspicious statements, which can be returned to the user.

   In [28,29], a similar approach using partial MaxSMT to locate errors in programs has been implemented in the tool BugAssist. MaxSMT is the maximal satisfiability problem, which determines the maximal number of clauses in a logical formula that can be simultaneously made true. MaxSMT instances allow to tag clauses as hard (definitely needs to be true) or soft (candidate for not making it true). With respect to error localization, this allows us to state where the error potential is (or definitely not is) by making this a soft (hard) clause. The test input and the property to be verified (e.g., the postcondition) are encoded as hard clauses, whereas the trace formula representing the program is encoded as soft clause. Using partial MaxSMT, a set of clauses is returned, which can simultaneously be set to true. The complement of this set then serves as set of suspicious statements.

Application to Service Compositions. Although we cannot rely on concrete input and outputs for service compositions, it seems worthwhile to investigate whether the approach can be adapted to work with pre- and postconditions instead of test cases. A verification technique like [44] could for instance be used to generate *abstract inputs* leading to errors. Abstract input means that we do not have concrete values but just names for values. Given that this is possible, we could for instance get an abstract input like *city* for L with the following properties (also given via freely chosen names[2]):

$$\mathsf{restaurantsIn}(city) = \{res\}$$
$$\mathsf{isVegan}(res)$$
$$rat = \mathsf{validate}(res)$$
$$\neg\mathsf{isGoodRating}(rat)$$

Given such a "test case", the trace formula of the given service composition encoded for MaxSMT may look like this:

$$\underline{\mathsf{L} = city} \qquad\qquad\qquad\qquad\qquad\qquad\qquad\qquad \text{input}$$
$$\wedge \underline{A = \{res\}} \wedge B_0 = \emptyset \qquad\qquad\qquad\qquad\qquad \text{before loop}$$
$$\wedge\mathsf{isVegan}(res) \wedge y = rat \wedge \neg\mathsf{isGoodRating}(rat) \wedge B_1 = B_0 \cup \{res\} \quad \text{loop once}$$
$$\wedge \underline{\forall b \in B_1 : \mathsf{isVegan}(b) \wedge \mathsf{isGoodRating}(\mathsf{validate}(b))} \qquad \text{postcond.}$$

In this example, the underlined clauses are hard clauses, all other clauses are soft. This formula encodes a path through the service composition when "run" on the test case plus the desired postcondition at the end. In order to encode the same trace and the same expected outputs as constraint satisfaction problem (similar to the approach in [48]), we introduce a predicate AB_i per statement i, which represents whether the statement i is *abnormal*. Abnormal statements are candidates for the root cause of the error. For instance, the first statement of the service compositions is then encoded as

$$(\neg AB_1) \Rightarrow A = \{res\}.$$

---

[2] The SMT solver underlying the verification technique in [44] treats all service calls and types as undefined function symbols, and thus returns just some randomly chosen identifier for instance of these symbols.

Inputs, the precondition and the postcondition are encoded as so-called observations. The encoding of the statements as well as the observations are then given to a constraint solver, which computes valuations for the predicates AB_i.

Both the MaxSMT and the constraint satisfaction encoding lead to a candidate root cause at line 7, which is exactly where the fault is located.   □

Another formula-based approach are error invariants [22]. Intuitively, an error invariant is a formula φ at a statement st such that the program input and the trace formula constructed from the beginning to st imply φ, and φ and the trace formula from st to the end of the execution does imply false. *Inductive error invariants*, i.e. error invariants, which hold for several consecutive statements, allow to identify irrelevant transitions in error traces. Afterwards, they are used as an approach similar to [28, 29, 32] to compute a set of suspicious statements.

Application to Service Compositions. A first idea for using error invariants for error localization in service compositions is to split abstract symbolic error traces at every service call, use the precondition of the service as assertion to be proven to hold after the split, and the postcondition of the service as additional initial assumption for the next part. This allows to analyze service calls one by one. Nevertheless, a lot of solver calls are necessary to analyze all parts of a service composition this way, and therefore experimental studies need to examine the performance of such an approach.   □

An extension of error invariants in order to make fault localization flow sensitive is done in [15]. *Flow-sensitive* trace formulas are used to compute suspicious statements with the help of a software model checker and an interpolating theorem prover. In [32], a *full flow-sensitive trace formula* is published, which is again analyzed using partial MaxSMT. Clauses of the trace formula, which belong to the control flow are marked as hard and all others are marked as soft. The *push & pop mechanism* of the solver Yices [20] yields an efficient solution, which gives quite the same code size reduction as BugAssist but is faster. As flow-sensitive and standard trace formulas are very similar, we think that these approaches are also applicable to service compositions.

Relying on One Faulty and One Correct Input. Delta debugging [49–51] is a divide-and-conquer algorithm to compute the smallest difference between a working and a failing test. In [49], delta debugging is applied to changes introduced between the last correct version of a program and the current faulty version. Intuitively, the algorithm splits all existing changes (if it is not only one) into two non-empty subsets and tests, which changes lead to a successful and which changes to an unsuccessful run of the program. Subsequently, the algorithm recursively computes the faulty change in the set of changes that lead to the error. In [51], a very similar strategy is applied to turn test cases into minimal ones, in [50], the delta debugging approach is applied to program states in order to compute the minimal difference between a working and a failing program. Since we typically do not have different correct and faulty variants of a service composition available, this technique seems less applicable to service compositions.

Relying on Several Faulty Inputs. In [30], all faulty inputs and the respective execution traces are encoded into an instance of SAT. The results are used to compute new right-hand sides to assignments in order to correct the program. In service compositions, the right-hand side of assignments are usually service calls, which cannot be modified, just completely replaced. In addition, the methods perform better if there are several faulty inputs, which we typically cannot provide in our setting.

Relying on Several Faulty and Correct Inputs. In this section, we discuss existing error localization approaches, which use several faulty ad several correct tests in order to generate a set of suspicious statements. For a detailed overview on these error localization methods, we refer the interested reader to [3].

Spectrum-Based and Statistical Methods. Tarantula [26,27] is a spectrum-based error localization method, which computes the suspiciousness of a statement by comparing the number of successful and failing test cases, in which the statement has been executed. Different methods to compute the suspiciousness of a statement, for example, using the Jaccard or Ochiai distance are discussed in [1,2]. Statistical methods such as [14,19,33–36] also rely on successful and failing test cases, but compute the suspiciousness with statistical methods. For example, Pinpoint [14] uses data mining methods to correlate successes and faults to determine the most likely faulty component. As we neither have tests nor the implementation of services and thus, cannot rely on multiple faulty and correct test inputs, we do not consider those error localization methods as easily applicable to service compositions.

Set-based Methods. Two very simple and common techniques to error localization are introduced in [41] and compared to more effective methods like the cause transition approach in [17] and the Tarantula approach [26,27] in [52]. The *set-union technique* computes a set of suspicious statements by removing all statements, which are executed by all passing tests, from the set of statements, which are contained in at least one failed test case. In contrast, the *set-intersection technique* computes a set of suspicious statements by removing all statements, which are executed in a single failing test case, from all statements, which are executed by every passed test case. As their effectiveness is already very limited on programs, we do not expect them to perform well in service compositions, especially as we do not have successful test cases at hand.

Relying on Model Checking. In [10], correct traces produced by a model checker are used to localize the error in existing error traces, more specifically, to report *one single* error trace per error, and to generate multiple error traces for multiple faults. The core of their method is to find transitions in error traces, which do not occur in any correct execution. With respect to service compositions, it could be worthwhile to examine whether there exists services, which do not occur in a correct execution and then, to add the respective service to the set of suspicious ones.

In [24], a SAT-based approach relying on CBMC [16] to minimize counterexamples of model checkers is published. In [23], the difference (in terms of statements) between a correct and a wrong execution is computed and returned to the user as set of suspicious statements. The approach in [23] only relies on a counterexample and then generates program inputs, which do not violate the specification. Again, we consider it worthwhile to investigate, whether the approach can be adapted to work with service compositions.

Remark 2. In general, one distinguishes between *control-* and *data-flow* errors. A control flow error, is an error, which can be corrected by changing the predicate of a branch or a loop.

As the control-flow of models of service compositions and of standard software do not widely differ and as our example shows, applying standard error localization methods to find control-flow errors in service compositions seems promising.

A data-flow error is an incorrect variable state, which occurs during execution and is caused by wrong assignments. In service compositions, variables are only used to pass data from one service call to another service call. Therefore, the root cause of the data-flow error is likely the service call prior to the failing call. We thus think that the *correction* of data-flow errors is more promising to investigate than simply finding data-flow errors.

	ACSR	test cases	app.	category
MaxSMT Approach	8%	one faulty	✓	2
Constraint Satisfaction Approach	—	one faulty	✓	2
Fully Flow-Sensitive TF	11%	one faulty	✓	2
Static Slicing	≈ 30%	—	✓	2
Error Invariants	—	one faulty	(✓)	2
Dynamic Slicing	≈ 30%	execution	(✓)	2
Set Union	1% yield 10% or less	faulty & correct	f	1
Set Intersection	5.5% yield 10% or less	faulty & correct	f	1
Delta Debugging with Cause Transitions (relevant)	35.66% yield 10% or less	faulty & correct	f	1

Fig. 3. Overview on properties of the presented error localization methods. Column *ACSR* shows the Average Code Size Reduction as stated by the respective authors of the approaches, the column *test cases* states the number and kind of test cases needed, or if even executable code is required. In column *app.*, we summarize the applicability of the approach for service compositions. Column "category" refers to the category, to which the approach belongs with respect to our classification in Sect. 1. Note that early works give the code size reduction in "percentage of programs yielding percentage of code size reduction".

4   Conclusion and Future Work

In this paper, we have shown that error localization methods for standard software do not carry over to service compositions easily. Especially, the unavailability or at least the lack of test cases as well as the impossibility to execute service compositions at will, render most error localization methods inapplicable.

Figure 3 summarizes our findings. It seems that, in general, approaches in the second category (cf. Sect. 1) are easier to adapt to the setting of models of service compositions than approaches in the first category. The MaxSMT approach, the fully flow-sensitive trace formula approach and the constraint satisfaction approach are adaptable to the service setting by enhancing the respective trace formula by additional predicates, which stem from the pre- and postcondition of the single services as well as the overall service composition. Thus, the application of trace formula approaches seems worthwhile to investigate as similar encodings of traces are already in use for verification of service compositions. As service compositions tend to be small, we do not think that the application of error invariants drastically improves the performance of error localization although the method is applicable in general. Dynamic slicing as in [52] gathers information during the execution of programs. As we cannot execute services, but statically compute traces, we suspect dynamic slicing to perform as good as static slicing in our context.

We believe that error localization in service compositions might not only support developers in debugging, but might also be useful to speed up automatic configuration approaches for service compositions. Service compositions tend to be simple. Thus, a systematic approach supporting developers might not be necessary, but when it comes to automatic configuration of service compositions, finding errors will help to only reconfigure erroneous parts and not the overall service composition.

As future work, we plan to examine the proposed modifications to the existing software error localization methods and practically evaluate their effectiveness. Most promising seems to be the use of logical formula-based approaches combined with symbolic executions since the interfaces to services are already given as logical formulas (pre- and postconditions), and the structural aspects of service compositions can easily be encoded by logic.

References

1. Abreu, R., Zoeteweij, P., van Gemund, A.J.C.: An evaluation of similarity coefficients for software fault localization. In: 12th Pacific Rim International Symposium on Dependable Computing, PRDC 2006, pp. 39–46 (2006)
2. Abreu, R., Zoeteweij, P., van Gemund, A.J.C.: On the accuracy of spectrum-based fault localization. In: Testing: Academic and Industrial Conference Practice and Research Techniques - MUTATION, TAICPART-MUTATION 2007, pp. 89–98 (2007)
3. Agarwal, P., Agrawal, A.P.: Fault-localization techniques for software systems: a literature review. SIGSOFT Softw. Eng. Notes **39**(5), 1–8 (2014)

4. Agrawal, H., Demillo, R.A., Spafford, E.H.: Debugging with dynamic slicingand backtracking. Softw. Pract. Exp. **23**, 589–616 (1993)
5. Agrawal, H., Horgan, J.R.: Dynamic program slicing. In: Proceedings of ACM SIG-PLAN 1990 Conference on Programming Language Design and Implementation, PLDI 1990, pp. 246–256. ACM (1990)
6. Artzi, S., Dolby, J., Jensen, S.H., Moller, A., Tip, F.: A framework for automated testing of javascript web applications. In: 2011 33rd International Conference on Software Engineering (ICSE), pp. 571–580 (2011)
7. Artzi, S., Dolby, J., Tip, F., Pistoia, M.: Directed test generation for effective fault localization. In: Proceedings of 19th International Symposium on Software Testing and Analysis, ISSTA 2010, pp. 49–60. ACM (2010)
8. Artzi, S., Dolby, J., Tip, F., Pistoia, M.: Fault localization for dynamic web applications. IEEE Trans. Softw. Eng. **38**(2), 314–335 (2012)
9. Artzi, S., Kiezun, A., Dolby, J., Tip, F., Dig, D., Paradkar, A., Ernst, M.D.: Finding bugs in web applications using dynamic test generation and explicit-state model checking. IEEE Trans. Softw. Eng. **36**(4), 474–494 (2010)
10. Ball, T., Naik, M., Rajamani, S.K.: From symptom to cause: localizing errors in counterexample traces. In: Proceedings of 30th ACM SIGPLAN-SIGACT Symposium on Principles of Programming Languages, POPL 2003, pp. 97–105. ACM (2003)
11. Becker, S., Koziolek, H., Reussner, R.: The palladio component model for model-driven performance prediction. J. Syst. Softw. **82**(1), 3–22 (2009). Special Issue: Software Performance - Modeling and Analysis
12. Becker, S., Grunske, L., Mirandola, R., Overhage, S.: Performance prediction of component-based systems – a survey from an engineering perspective. In: Reussner, R., Stafford, J.A., Ren, X.-M. (eds.) Architecting Systems with Trustworthy Components. LNCS, vol. 3938, pp. 169–192. Springer, Heidelberg (2006)
13. Brüseke, F., Wachsmuth, H., Engels, G., Becker, S.: PBlaman: performance blame analysis based on Palladio contracts. Concurr. Comput. Pract. Exp. **26**(12), 1975–2004 (2014)
14. Chen, M.Y., Kiciman, E., Fratkin, E., Fox, A., Brewer, E.: Pinpoint: problem determination in large, dynamic internet services. In: International Conference on Dependable Systems and Networks, DSN 2002, Proceedings, pp. 595–604 (2002)
15. Christ, J., Ermis, E., Schäf, M., Wies, T.: Flow-sensitive fault localization. In: Giacobazzi, R., Berdine, J., Mastroeni, I. (eds.) VMCAI 2013. LNCS, vol. 7737, pp. 189–208. Springer, Heidelberg (2013)
16. Clarke, E., Kroning, D., Lerda, F.: A tool for checking ANSI-C programs. In: Jensen, K., Podelski, A. (eds.) TACAS 2004. LNCS, vol. 2988, pp. 168–176. Springer, Heidelberg (2004)
17. Cleve, H., Zeller, A.: Locating causes of program failures. In: Proceedings of 27th International Conference on Software Engineering, ICSE 2005, pp. 342–351. ACM (2005)
18. Crnkovic, I., Chaudron, M.R.V., Larsson, S.: Component-based development process and component lifecycle. In: ICSEA, p. 44. IEEE Computer Society (2006)
19. Dallmeier, V., Lindig, C., Zeller, A.: Lightweight defect localization for Java. In: Gao, X.-X. (ed.) ECOOP 2005. LNCS, vol. 3586, pp. 528–550. Springer, Heidelberg (2005)
20. Dutertre, B.: Yices 2.2. In: Biere, A., Bloem, R. (eds.) CAV 2014. LNCS, vol. 8559, pp. 737–744. Springer, Heidelberg (2014)

21. Engels, G., Güldali, B., Soltenborn, C., Wehrheim, H.: Assuring consistency of business process models and web services using visual contracts. In: Schürr, A., Nagl, M., Zündorf, A. (eds.) AGTIVE 2007. LNCS, vol. 5088, pp. 17–31. Springer, Heidelberg (2008)

22. Ermis, E., Schäf, M., Wies, T.: Error invariants. In: Giannakopoulou, D., Méry, D. (eds.) FM 2012. LNCS, vol. 7436, pp. 187–201. Springer, Heidelberg (2012)

23. Groce, A., Chaki, S., Kroening, D., Strichman, O.: Error explanation with distance metrics. Int. J. Softw. Tools Technol. Transf. **8**(3), 229–247 (2006)

24. Groce, A., Kroening, D.: Making the most of BMC counterexamples. Electron. Notes Theor. Comput. Sci. **119**(2), 67–81 (2005)

25. Hutchins, M., Foster, H., Goradia, T., Ostrand, T.: Experiments on the effectiveness of dataflow- and control-flow-based test adequacy criteria. In: 16th International Conference on Software Engineering, Proceedings, ICSE-16, pp. 191–200 (1994)

26. Jones, J.A., Harrold, M.J.: Empirical evaluation of the tarantula automatic fault-localization technique. In: Proceedings of 20th IEEE/ACM International Conference on Automated Software Engineering, ASE 2005, pp. 273–282. ACM (2005)

27. Jones, J.A., Harrold, M.J., Stasko, J.: Visualization of test information to assist fault localization. In: Proceedings of 24th International Conference on Software Engineering, ICSE 2002, pp. 467–477. ACM (2002)

28. Jose, M., Majumdar, R.: Cause clue clauses: error localization using maximum satisfiability. SIGPLAN Not. **46**(6), 437–446 (2011)

29. Jose, M., Majumdar, R.: Cause clue clauses: error localization using maximum satisfiability. In: Proceedings of 32nd ACM SIGPLAN Conference on Programming Language Design and Implementation, PLDI 2011, pp. 437–446. ACM (2011)

30. Könighofer, R., Bloem, R.: Automated error localization and correction for imperative programs. In: Proceedings of International Conference on Formal Methods in Computer-Aided Design, FMCAD 2011, pp. 91–100. FMCAD Inc. (2011)

31. Korel, B., Laski, J.: Dynamic program slicing. Inf. Process. Lett. **29**(3), 155–163 (1988)

32. Lamraoui, S.-M., Nakajima, S.: A formula-based approach for automatic fault localization of imperative programs. In: Merz, S., Pang, J. (eds.) ICFEM 2014. LNCS, vol. 8829, pp. 251–266. Springer, Heidelberg (2014)

33. Liblit, B., Aiken, A., Zheng, A.X., Jordan, M.I.: Bug isolation via remote program sampling. SIGPLAN Not. **38**(5), 141–154 (2003)

34. Liblit, B., Aiken, A., Zheng, A.X., Jordan, M.I.: Bug isolation via remote program sampling. In: Proceedings of ACM SIGPLAN 2003 Conference on Programming Language Design and Implementation, PLDI 2003, pp. 141–154. ACM (2003)

35. Liblit, B., Naik, M., Zheng, A.X., Aiken, A., Jordan, M.I.: Scalable statistical bug isolation. In: Proceedings of 2005 ACM SIGPLAN Conference on Programming Language Design and Implementation, PLDI 2005, pp. 15–26. ACM (2005)

36. Liblit, B., Naik, M., Zheng, A.X., Aiken, A., Jordan, M.I.: Scalable statistical bug isolation. SIGPLAN Not. **40**(6), 15–26 (2005)

37. Mao, C.: Slicing web service-based software. In: 2009 IEEE International Conference on Service-Oriented Computing and Applications (SOCA), pp. 1–8 (2009)

38. Minamide, Y.: Static approximation of dynamically generated web pages. In: Proceedings of 14th International Conference on World Wide Web, WWW 2005, pp. 432–441. ACM (2005)

39. Mirandola, R., Potena, P., Riccobene, E., Scandurra, P.: A reliability model for service component architectures. J. Syst. Softw. **89**, 109–127 (2014)

40. OASIS. Web services business process execution language v2.0. http://docs.oasis-open.org/wsbpel/2.0/OS/wsbpel-v2.0-OS.pdf
41. Renieres, M., Reiss, S.P.: Fault localization with nearest neighbor queries. In: 18th IEEE International Conference on Automated Software Engineering, Proceedings, pp. 30–39 (2003)
42. Schäfer, W., Wehrheim, H.: Model-driven development with MECHATRONIC UML. In: Engels, G., Lewerentz, C., Schäfer, W., Schürr, A., Westfechtel, B. (eds.) Nagl Festschrift. LNCS, vol. 5765, pp. 533–554. Springer, Heidelberg (2010)
43. Vessey, I.: Expertise in debugging computer programs: an analysis of the content of verbal protocols. IEEE Trans. Syst. Man Cybern. 16(5), 621–637 (1986)
44. Walther, S., Wehrheim, H.: Knowledge-based verification of service compositions - an smt approach. In: 2013 18th International Conference Engineering of Complex Computer Systems (ICECCS), pp. 24–32 (2013)
45. Wassermann, G., Yu, D., Chander, A., Dhurjati, D., Inamura, H., Su, Z.: Dynamic test input generation for web applications. In: Proceedings of 2008 International Symposium on Software Testing and Analysis, ISSTA 2008, pp. 249–260. ACM (2008)
46. Weiser, M.: Program slicing. In: Proceedings of 5th International Conference on Software Engineering, ICSE 1981, pp. 439–449. IEEE Press (1981)
47. Wong, W.E., Debroy, V.: A survey of software fault localization. Technical report, The University of Texas at Dallas (2009)
48. Wotawa, F., Nica, M., Moraru, I.: Automated debugging based on a constraint model of the program and a test case. J. Logic Algebraic Program. 81(4), 390–407 (2012). Special Issue: NWPT 2009Special Issue: NWPT 2009
49. Zeller, A.: Yesterday, my program worked. Today, it does not. Why? In: Wang, J., Lemoine, M. (eds.) ESEC 1999 and ESEC-FSE 1999. LNCS, vol. 1687, pp. 253–267. Springer, Heidelberg (1999)
50. Zeller, A.: Isolating cause-effect chains from computer programs. In: Proceedings of 10th ACM SIGSOFT Symposium on Foundations of Software Engineering, SIGSOFT 2002/FSE-10, pp. 1–10. ACM (2002)
51. Zeller, A., Hildebrandt, R.: Simplifying and isolating failure-inducing input. IEEE Trans. Softw. Eng. 28(2), 183–200 (2002)
52. Zhang, X., He, H., Gupta, N., Gupta, R.: Experimental evaluation of using dynamic slices for fault location. In: Proceedings of Sixth International Symposium on Automated Analysis-driven Debugging, AADEBUG 2005, pp. 33–42. ACM (2005)

Author Index

Printed in the United States
By Bookmasters